NATIONAL UNIVERSITY PUBLICATIONS
KENNIKAT PRESS CORP.
90 SOUTH BAYLES AVENUE
PORT WASHINGTON, N. Y. 11050 · (516) 883-0570

We take pleasure in sending you this review copy of

LES AMERICANISTES: NEW FRENCH
CRITICISM ON MODERN AMERICAN FICTION

Edited by Ira D. Johnson and
Christiane Johnson

DATE OF PUBLICATION April 15, 1978

PRICE $12.95

*Direct quotation in reviews is limited to 500 words unless special
permission is given.*

Please send us two copies of your review

Les Américanistes

Kennikat Press

National University Publications

Literary Criticism Series

General Editor
John E. Becker
Fairleigh Dickinson University

Les Américanistes

New French Criticism
on
Modern
American Fiction

Ira D. Johnson and
Christiane Johnson

National University Publications
KENNIKAT PRESS   //   1978
Port Washington, N. Y.   //   London

4/1978
Am. Lit.

Manufactured in the United States of America

Published by
Kennikat Press Corp.
Port Washington, N. Y. / London

Library of Congress Cataloging in Publication Data

Main entry under title:

Les americanistes.

(Literary criticism series) (National university publications)
Includes bibliographical references and index.
1. American fiction—20th century—History and criticism—Addresses, essays, lectures.
2. Criticism—France. I. Johnson, Christiane.
II. Johnson, Ira.
PS379.A56   813'.009'5   76-58512
ISBN 0-8046-9176-2

Ira Johnson died before the publication of this book. May it be a tribute to his desire to bridge two cultures.

CONTENTS

Les Américanistes

Christiane Johnson and Ira D. Johnson

INTRODUCTION

It is not the intention of the editors to offer this volume as a mirror of modern French criticism—for several reasons. Not only would such a task be too ambitious for anything but a collection far larger than this, but our contributors are not typically "French critics" in certain respects. The common denominator is that all of them were born in France, have been educated in French schools and universities, have spent some time in the United States (many of them a year or more), and are specialists in American Literature—*Américanistes*— in French universities. Teaching in English or American departments, they have been constantly aware of the gap between their high expectations for the teaching of literature and what could actually be accomplished with students for whom English was, after all, a foreign language. Yet, as time went on, their critical skills increased, and so did their perceptions of cultural differences as they sought to communicate these in the classroom.

In any case, the avatars of American literature with the French audience are a long story. Writing in the early 1830s, Alexis de Tocqueville found that in the United States there were "the remarkable works of a small number of authors, whose names are, or ought to be, known to all Europeans," but he did not tell us who they were, and he went on to comment that most of them produced works "English in substance and still more so in form." At the time, he concluded, America had, "properly speaking, no literature."[1]

When did the French cultivated reading public begin to hear about American literature through their critics? Although the *Revue des Deux Mondes,* from its inception in 1832, always showed some interest in the subject, by 1887, with the exceptions of Poe and Whitman, American literature had received little comment from critics in France. Poe, of course, remains the unique case in influence and esteem, a critic named Forgues having introduced him in 1846 to the French in the *Revue des Deux Mondes,* Baudelaire translating his tales in 1855, and Mallarmé his poems in 1875. Whitman, whose *Leaves of Grass* was translated for the first time in 1887, set loose passions for and against him (for reasons as political as they were literary). Professor Cyrille Arnavon, in documenting with meticulous care French critical views of American literature to 1917,[2] has emphasized that for a long time those French critics who could read English were guided mainly by British journals, which rarely, and then only with a long glance down their noses, had anything to say about American writers.

When they turned to the United States itself, the French found little to change their preconceptions. American universities, after all, especially the most prestigious, often regarded the literary productions of their native land with little interest and even some disdain all through the nineteenth century and on into the 1920s. The *Atlantic Monthly,* the *North American Review,* and *Harper's* so long ignored anything but the genteel tradition that when William Dean Howells and the realists appeared, the French hardly noticed them. Not only were many of the French commentators careless and confused about literature from America; some of them even invented biographical facts, and their concepts of the nation were often bizarre. Their aristocratic and bourgeois prejudices or their chauvinism tended to obscure an understanding of Whitman, Twain, or Bellamy.

The actual volume of critical comments on American literature was still very small at the turn of the century, and it was not until the inception of the *Revue du Mois* (1906) and the *Revue Germanique* (1909) that any serious attention was forthcoming. The first genuine *Américaniste, Régis Michaud,* wrote in the *Revue Germanique,* although the majority of his work was published after 1920. An Emersonian with a wide cultural background, who had taught in the U. S. A. before 1914, his familiarity with America and his intuition concerning its literature was at that time singular. The New England tradition became somewhat better known by 1920, and there was a certain awareness of those American expatriates residing in England: Bret Harte, Stephen Crane, Harold Frederic, and Francis Marion Crawford. There began to be quite a number of critical articles on Mark Twain from the time of the translations of *Tom Sawyer* (1884) and *The Adventures of Huckleberry Finn* (1886).

After 1900, as with Jack London, Twain's popularity grew with the larger public, for, as Professor Arnavon comments:

> The oversimplified conception of the good-natured humorist (which Michaud's analysis had far from succeeded in dispelling) was added to already accepted ideas of America. A rudimentary view of American literature, the one which makes of Poe a victim, of Emerson a philosophical recluse, and of Cooper a writer of children's books about redskins, which denies that there is any contemporary production worthy of interest, was satisfied with the existence of a buffoon, all the more so because this buffoon spoke of the Far West and gold prospectors. (pp. 79–80)

Although there were individual and disparate replies to the often-discussed question, "Is there a distinct American literature?" the general opinion was that although there had been a New England literature during the Transcendental period, and there existed the atypical cases of Poe and the "admirable" Whitman, no really national literature had grown from American cultural soil by 1890 or 1900.

The answer, then, from two generations of French critics was an overwhelming "No." Even expatriates James and Wharton were obscure figures compared to Lafcadio Hearn, and for many French readers Henry James was a British writer. Before 1917 Lew Wallace, with his *Ben-Hur* (1880), and Mrs. Burnett with *Little Lord Fauntleroy* (1886), got much more attention than Frank Norris, and except for the notoriety that the censorship of *The Genius* received in 1915, nothing at all was written on Dreiser until after World War I. After 1919 the profound changes in international politics and the military, political, and economic influence of the U. S. A. on Europe and its culture is obvious enough, but, as Arnavon points out, the interest and influence of American literature could not possibly have been so great if the American writers of the twenties had not been what they were—very different indeed from their countrymen of twenty years before.

Academic specialists in France then, as in America, were still conservative for the most part, and those Frenchmen who knew there was a literature with a specific American quality at first hesitated to comment on its value; but at least an elite was aware that there was an American culture worthy of the name, and the myth of a barbaric America was disappearing.

If twentieth-century American poetry has had little influence in France, the novel has been another matter, and the 1955 study of Thelma M. Smith and Ward L. Miner, *Transatlantic Migration: The Contemporary American Novel in France,*[3] analyzes in detail "the vogue in France of the contemporary American novel" from the early twenties to the early fifties, and "when, how, and why this vogue grew." (p. 13). In the thirties Jean Simon, looking backward on French confusion about American novelists, remarked in his *Le Roman américain au XXe siècle:*

> We can't ignore these American writers, we said to ourselves, and then read with almost complete lack of critical judgment and discernment. We made best sellers of such books as *Gentlemen Prefer Blondes* and *Show Boat*. We attributed genius to Bromfield, and mixed up Melville, Upton Sinclair, Sinclair Lewis, Tarkington, Hawthorne, London, Hemingway in a frightful "Irish stew."[4]

Transatlantic Migration squints and sniffs at the stew from up close and from afar on through the war period, when reading anything American was considered an act of resistance, into the further proliferation of postwar translations, concentrating finally on those five novelists, *les cinq grands,* who were, and to some extent still are, the most popular: Faulkner, Hemingway, Steinbeck, Dos Passos, and Caldwell. It is startling to notice the absence of F. Scott Fitzgerald, who did not attract widespread critical attention in France until the 1960s.

The translation of *Sanctuary* appeared in 1933 with an enthusiastic preface by André Malraux which was to become famous, particularly for the statement at the end that Faulkner had introduced Greek tragedy into the detective novel.[5] Quoted many times, the remark led to a continued emphasis (well into the fifties) on the elements of Greek tragedy in the Big Five and the American novel in general, and its domination by a vision of impersonal fate controlling man's destiny.

Intellectuals in France never questioned the importance of the new influx of

American novels, even though in the late 1940s American authors were not yet taught at the undergraduate level in university English departments. "There is no contemporary literature which excites my interest more than that of young America," André Gide remarked in 1943.[6] Among so many others, Jean-Paul Sartre is worth quoting:

> The greatest literary development in France between 1929 and 1939 was the discovery of Faulkner, Dos Passos, Hemingway, Steinbeck. . . . To writers of my generation, the publication of *The 42nd Parallel, Light in August, A Farewell to Arms* evoked a revolution similar to the one produced fifteen years earlier in Europe by the *Ulysses* of James Joyce. . . . At once for thousands of young intellectuals, the American novel took its place, together with jazz and the movies, among the best of the importations from the United States. (Smith and Miner, pp. 20-21)

In 1946, Smith and Miner point out, "the director of one of the largest publishing houses in Paris said that seven out of ten French novelists who submitted manuscripts to him had borrowed something from Faulkner or were deliberately imitating him. At the same time Sartre said that two-thirds of the manuscripts he received for *Les Temps Modernes* were written à la Caldwell, à la Hemingway, à la Dos Passos" (p. 61).

From all indications, the public in France was as enthusiastic as the critics and young writers. At the same time there remained a strain of ignorance of America and its literature which took various forms, such as lumping together American novelists into an *école américaine* thought to represent all of American literature. But there were such critics as Albert Guérard, Gilbert Sigaux, and Raymond Las Vergnas, who demanded that one realize that there was more to the American novel than a cult of violence.

The reasons for the tremendous vogue of the postwar novel include the long-growing interest and curiosity about things American that had begun in World War I and which was accelerated at the end of World War II. There was the additional attraction of the American novel as escape literature, as well as, for certain readers, a satisfaction in the portrait of an America far from perfect. Added to this was a reaction against the excessive intellectualism of the French novel of the time and a general dissatisfaction with it as indicated by the French novelists themselves, as well as the welcome the Existentialists accorded to the despair expressed by American novelists as representative of the human condition. Generally there were

> . . . an overwhelming number of writers who in dozens of articles puzzled over the influence of American literature, particularly the novel, in France. . . . the final answer, they wrote, rests in the qualities of the American novel itself. With some amazement the Old World learned that from the other side of the sea a "healthy and strong" literature was establishing itself. The reader found a full, rich content, a dynamism of thought and action. He called the American novel objective, impersonal. He found in it a hidden allegory and a nearness to Greek tragedy. He discovered it working with fresh, new material, which had hardly been exploited. He sensed an atmosphere of freedom, a new method of recognizing and feeling. (Smith and Miner, p. 43)

The qualities of American novelists and their novels that were pointedly remarked on by French commentators, journalistic reviewers, and critics in the late forties and early fifties often emphasized the biographical. There was marked surprise that American novelists were not intellectuals and men of letters, that so few had university educations and consequently were lacking a broad background of past literature; there was amazement at the numerous menial jobs and trades the writers followed before becoming professionally established, and a self-confident belief that journalistic training was the secret of American prose style. Yet, considering the novel as an art, the reviewers' most universal remarks concerned the "poetic" quality and "lyricism" of the works, apparently to them a matter of content as well as form. The interior monologue was much discussed as a characteristic device; to the French the use of colloquial American speech was new and experimental, most of them being unaware that the tradition existed in our literature in the nineteenth century. Narrative technique in American novels, thought many, was nervous and jerky, a *style saccadé*. That the novel owed much of its techniques to the cinema was a popular subject traceable to the careful discussion by Claude Edmonde Magny, whose influential views, new after World War II, were developed in *L'Age du roman américain* (1948). Another important subject was time, with Faulkner especially attracting much discussion; and apparently a great portion of the influence on younger French novelists was marked by the quality of time as rendered by Faulkner and Dos Passos. The remarkable handling of concrete detail, the use of objectivity, sometimes discussed as form but more often as content, plus two qualities felt for the most part as lacking in French novels, were emphasized: a highly developed social sense and a "strong human quality" as "opposed to the so-called diseased, morbid French novel of psychological analysis. . . . The human quality of the Americans represented an art closer to the people and the aesthetic needs of the time" (Smith and Miner, pp. 79, 80). But some critics stressed the lack of intellectuality and the sentimental primitivism they found, which to others was intrinsic to a positive, prevalent "exoticism." The *dépaysement*, or solitariness, of the individual in American novels they saw often as part of an immaturity due to America's lack of strong traditions, but at the same time it was a metaphor for modern man's condition in the world of the cold war and the atom bomb.

American morality, it was generally agreed, is puritan, and sooner or later almost all novelists were so labeled by someone, often with the vaguest definition in mind, but generally taking a cast from French history and experience in which the Protestant tradition was Calvinistic. The frequency of pessimism and the attempt to terrify the reader were sometimes associated with puritanism, but all this was puzzling to critics and difficult to reconcile with America's reputation for rabid optimism. But above all, the greatness of American novels was felt to come from their close affinity to Greek tragedy and its concept of fate, its lyricism, and its poetry.

There arose a genuine debate over the value of American novels generally, much of this involving implied or stated comparison and contrast with the French novel. By the early fifties the American vogue had leveled off enough so that it no longer seemed completely to overwhelm the French market, but there is no doubt that the post–World War II French novel was generally influenced by American novels, although it is difficult to measure such an influence.

Although the tidal wave of the forties and the fifties has calmed, there are always novels by dozens of American writers available in translation; some of the better-known apparently reach the French public within a year of their American publication. There are always the best-selling Frank Yerby and Irving Stone, but Saul Bellow, Norman Mailer, John Updike, Rhilip Roth, James Baldwin, and many others of literary merit seem easy to find. Frequent reviews appear in French newspapers and magazines as well as the literary periodicals, yet the qualities that strike the reviewers and critics are no longer those that were hailed in the forties and fifties. After having stared at the American novel with old European critical eyes, then having been struck by its newness, critics today still regard it with great interest, but with completely new European critical eyes.

Even though our contributors may have studied intensely to pass the long and difficult competitive examination, the *agrégation*, and diligently labored on their doctorates, they have had throughout their student years very little formal training in criticism as such, although most of them admit they were exposed to "good minds" during their graduate studies. In fact, many of them affirm attempting to rid themselves later of the conventional academic critical approaches (for the most part historical, biographical, and sociological) advocated for the competitive examinations. All our critics, then, consider themselves to be self-trained. All have felt the need of a critical method and critical tools, and each has gone about finding these in his own way. As a result, being *Américanistes,* they are aware of much of English and American criticism, but they are even more aware of criticism being written in their own language these days. To a greater or lesser degree then, directly, obliquely, or negatively, recent criticism in France has its bearing on the performance found here.

A sketch of the contemporary critical background that can be assumed for our contributors is difficult to give in a few simple strokes; it is certain that criticism in France at present is in a very fertile and ebullient period. The chart presented here is an attempt to make clear the major forces at work, but it is oversimple, in some ways misleading, for it does not succeed in taking into account the reciprocal influences, the specific changes of direction and explorations of individual critics. It is hoped that at least it does indicate the critical variety which no one in literature, French or foreign, can avoid being aware of these days, whether he finds them amenable or not. The contributors to this volume all affirm being influenced by one or another and, most often, several of these currents. Yet it is doubtful if any one of them can be fitted comfortably into a single category.

In the 1950s what shook the French out of the prevailing academic criticism was the influence of the American New Critics; this was especially the case among those who were interested in American literature or were specializing in it. Although this influence can still be felt, it is for the most part as a stage in the evolution which has led to the present practice.

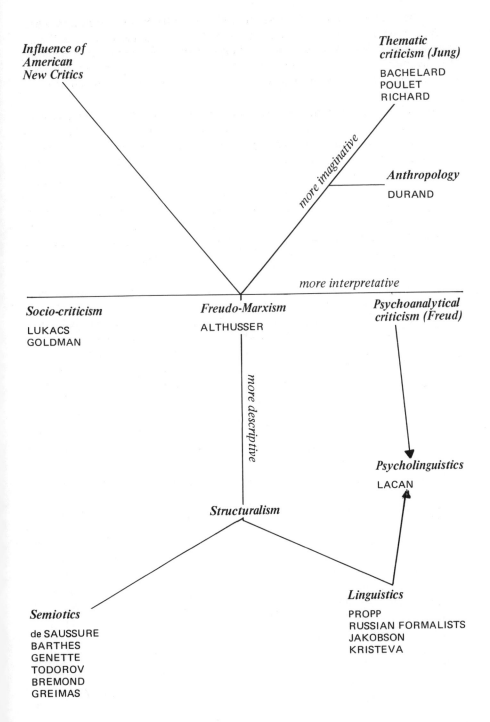

Influence of American New Critics

Thematic criticism (Jung)
BACHELARD
POULET
RICHARD

more imaginative

Anthropology
DURAND

more interpretative

Socio-criticism
LUKACS
GOLDMAN

Freudo-Marxism
ALTHUSSER

Psychoanalytical criticism (Freud)

more descriptive

Psycholinguistics
LACAN

Structuralism

Linguistics
PROPP
RUSSIAN FORMALISTS
JAKOBSON
KRISTEVA

Semiotics
de SAUSSURE
BARTHES
GENETTE
TODOROV
BREMOND
GREIMAS

At the same time the work of Vladimir Propp and the Russian formalists, whose heyday in Russia ended in the early thirties (1915–30), had begun to reach France, and somewhat later America: Propp's *Morphology of the Folktale* was published by the Indiana Research Center of Anthropology, Folklore, and Linguistics in 1958. This was the beginning of what became a wider structuralist approach to literature.

Roland Barthes, surveying the critical landscape in 1963 for the *Times Literary Supplement,* saw French criticism as having developed for the preceding fifteen years inside four main "philosophies"—existentialism, Marxism, psychoanalysis, and structuralism (or formalism). Of these four, the first, which Barthes limited mostly to the works of Jean-Paul Sartre, is now felt by most of our contributors to have lost most of its influence, although the other three movements have continued to develop. Perhaps it is because a philosophy of fragmentation, alienation, and despair is in direct contradiction to a view of the world as real and intelligible, a view that psychoanalysis, Marxism, and structuralism have in common, even though existential Marxism with its belief in historical progress is directly contrary to structuralist tenets.

Out of Marxism came what is now called sociocriticism, George Lukacs being its earliest pioneer, and Lucien Goldman its most brilliant developer in his Marxist-structuralist study of Pascal and Racine in *The Hidden God,* and especially his *Pour une sociologie du roman* (1964), in which the attempt to combine structuralist methodology and a Marxist view of society is by means of "genetic structuralism." Some of the more recent critics feel that they are refining this approach, even going rapidly beyond it, but that, nevertheless, all work done in sociocriticism finds its source in Lukacs and Goldman.

What Roland Barthes a dozen years ago labeled "psychoanalysis," then by far the most influential and pervasive of critical schools, is now generally thought of as belonging to a broader category of thematic criticism *(thématique)* and includes what Paul Ricoeur has called hermeneutics. Ricoeur, in *Freud and Philosophy* (1970), opposes the stricter structuralist view that language derives its meaning not from its references to things but from the inner relationships within the autonomous system of language: for him semiology and semantics in combination are sublimated to the service of the symbolic function. This approach, or intersubjective criticism, opposes the view that the work or the text is an object, and it works toward a subject, "recovering" the meaning of the text by seeking the "spiritual" activity of the artist as he sought to create meaning. Georges Poulet in his earlier criticism examined literary works by abstracting the concepts of time and space which the writer shared with his epoch, using these categorical universals as a means of interpretation. In his *Studies in Human Time* (1956) his attitude is very close to Ricoeur's as he investigates words and especially images to plumb for the moment how the writer's sensibility works toward meaning.

But the critic who has given the strongest impulse to thematics is the philosopher Gaston Bachelard. Owing much of his inspiration to Jung, he began his well-known studies of the elements: *La Psychanalyse du feu, L'Eau et les rêves, L'Air et les songes, La Terre et les rêveries de la volonté,* and *La Terre et les rêveries du repos.* It is the image or images at the threshold between the conscious and unconscious that he explicates, finding here the "originative moment" to which the reader, through the image, responds or "reverberates." An innovator of great intuition, he has stimulated Poulet, Starobinski, and many others, including younger critics such as Jean-Pierre Richard, also a poet, whose major work is a study of *L'Univers imaginaire de Mallarmé.* Both Bachelard and Richard have been definite influences on several of our contributors. G. Durand, an anthropologist with a structuralist approach, has attempted to organize the matter imaginatively exposed by Bachelard in *Les Structures anthropologiques de l'imaginaire:* his brilliant conjoining of thematics and structuralism in turn has been found extremely useful by some of our critics.

What has just been described is *not* what is indicated on our chart as psychoanalytical criticism, for the latter is more orthodox in its use of Freud, and most often combines with sociocriticism into Freudian-Marxism. Robert Silhol, who qualifies his essay included here as "a critique on criticism," is one of a group formed since 1968 that opposes beginning with the text and deducing from it an analytical method, on the grounds that such a method must then vary with each text; instead, they believe that the basis for approaching all literary works must be a body of nonliterary theoretical thought, for in their view the literary object cannot contain a methodology suitable for its own analysis. "Talent" is considered as nontransmissible, and the critic should not build his method on it, but on theory that can be communicated. Such concepts were delineated by P. Macherey in *Pour une théorie de la production littéraire,* and approaches along these lines are being explored by critics at the University of New York at Buffalo.

Important in the regeneration of Freudian criticism are two philosophers who have given "psychoanalytics" a strong impulse in France: Louis Althusser (*For Marx,* Vintage, 1970) and Jacques Lacan. Althusser is often categorized as a structuralist, and his approach to the writings of Marx as a body of scientific material could be called that of a structuralist. Lacan's *The Language of Self: The Function of Language in Psychoanalysis* (Johns Hopkins, 1968) is even more important for psychoanalytics, very influential, and remarkable for the high level of its innovative criticism.

Even though we may be guilty of labeling the aforementioned critics, one must keep in mind that the categories on the accompanying chart are at best fluid, with questionable boundaries (many of our contributors, for example, would place Barthes with others under *thématique*), while taking note of structuralism's pervasiveness and usefulness in giving direction to the unique talents of individual critics. Structuralism continues to have a very complex development; its success came from the continuing, deeply felt need for a methodology, and for tools which would help the advance of criticism. The New Critics had already felt the need for a linguistic tool, but their distrust for science and their belief that it could not contribute to the methods of literary analysis led them to make only a timid use of elementary linguistics. On the contrary, many French critics felt that the categories defined by structuralism and linguistics could aid in approaching literature, not only because they found the traditional methods very unsatisfactory, but also because the sciences stressed the importance of language as a mode of apprehending reality.

It was with the discovery of Vladimir Propp, and after him the other Russian formalists, that structuralist criticism can be said to have begun in France. Propp's study of the simple narrative forms in the specific universe of the Russian folktale revealed the basic narrative structure of these prototypes and was the first major step in the modern structural study of fiction; his formalist attitude is still at the center of the structuralist movement which came after him. The translation into French in 1965 by structuralist Tzvetan Todorov of important formalist criticism *Théorie de la littérature* (an anthology including Propp), was of great importance. However, some acquaintance with formalism was evident in French criticism even ten years earlier with the publication in English by Mouton of Victor Erlich's *Russian Formalism: History-Doctrine.*

The formalists worked so closely together, building on each other's work and refining their tools, that they resembled a scientific team. Their concepts were methods that could be and were picked up and refined by French critics even forty to fifty years later. Boris Thomashevsky's concentration on the motif and its narrative arrangement in relation to literary convention as the core of the artistic structure; the general formalist view of the *sujet,* or plot, as the nonchronological arrangement of events for meaning (theme) and emotional effect as elementary to the art of fiction; Boris Eichenbaum's study of literary history which exposed the fallacy of reducing literature to history or to socioeconomics, while revealing *literary* tradition itself as the only fundamentally exterior conditioning influence; Victor Shklovsky's concern with mimesis, the relation of the art of fiction to life, and his consequent development of the concept of defamiliarization as the process, end, and justification of art, achieved by techniques that themselves become conventional, familiar, and necessitating defamiliarization and parody; his distinction between the short story and the novel, between poetry (as close to vocal performance) and written language (as developing its own techniques); the novel as breaking with narrative (and oral) form and becoming in the nineteenth century syncretic, absorbing other forms; his concern with the degeneration of forms, such as the novel, leading to parody and comedy as the means of finding new possibilities for renewing and recreating the form—these are only some of the more important contributions of the formalists to French literary structuralism and to a poetics of fiction.

The works of three important contemporary critics, A. J. Greimas, Tzvetan Todorov, and Claude Bremond, form a kind of three-way dialogue, especially when they are concerned with the isolation and interaction of the basic units of fictional structure (Propp being their point of departure) in search of a general theory of narration. For Bremond the sequence, represented as a logical triad, moving from logical categories without semantic content, is the basic narrative unit, and the completed narrative is a pattern of these. In *Logique de récit* he divides fictional roles into two types as a means of searching for fundamental narrative action. Greimas attempts to move beyond Propp and the dramatic categories of Souriau in the direction of establishing permanent categories of *actants* divided into three sets of opposed pairs. He works as well in another direction toward a basic list of syntagms, bringing to light three types of syntactic structures in the same Russian folktales Propp had examined: performative, contractual, and disjunctual.

Finally, there is Todorov's *Grammaire du Décaméron* (1969), which is the most fundamental development in pushing further basic narratology since Propp. Todorov continues vigorously to refine and develop his thought; a few lines cannot adequately hint the characteristics of it; one must consider him at the immediate center of the structuralist movement.[7]

The critics in this anthology, being specialists in a foreign language, have all had some form of linguistic training, and their attitudes toward the application of linguistics to literature vary with the individuals. What bearing modern linguistics has on contemporary criticism lies in its intrinsic importance to structuralism in providing the basic conceptual tools for structural analysis, originated by Swiss linguist Ferdinand de Saussure and first appearing in print as *Cours de linguistique générale,* published in 1915. Redefining language *(language, langue,* and *parole)* and redefining the sign *(signifiant* and *signifié),* he called for a science of signs as they work in society, calling it *sémiologie,* and viewing linguistics as only part of the general science of semiology. It is only recently that semiology has begun to be a significant approach, with, as we have indicated, Roland Barthes as the supreme practitioner. Saussure also viewed the sign and all other units of language as essentially narrative—leading linguistics to the study of narration.

His distinguishing between the diachronic and synchronic approaches to language was not only his most influential concept for modern linguistics, but it, like his delineating the difference between syntagmatic and paradigmatic relations among signs, became importantly applicable for the study of literature. To these conceptual tools Roman Jakobson added his significant one, relating the polarity he found in linguistic performance to Saussure's syntagmatic and paradigmatic categories, to traditional rhetoric (metaphor and metonymy), and thus to poetics. As revealed by Jakobson, the thought processes of similarity and continuity are basic, applicable to literary works, to literary style, and to all sign systems; in any symbolic process their dynamics are evident.

Perhaps just as well known is Jakobson's communication theory, which provides a lucid and systematic approach distinguishing the poetic function of language and the relationship of it to the other functions of language. His critical formulations were put into practice in collaboration with Claude Lévi-Strauss in "Charles Baudelaire's 'Les Chats'"—which in turn evoked refutation by structuralist Michael Riffaterre's critical study "Describing Poetic Structures: Two Approaches to Baudelaire's 'Les Chats.'" The controversial interest it evoked indicates a healthy diversity among the defenders of structuralism, and to many critics some of its serious limitations as well.

A younger linguist, Julia Kristeva, is attracting a good deal of attention in defining a new approach to language in *Le Texte du roman* and *La Révolution du langage poetique.* The two contemporary critics who are considered most influential and stimulating by most of our contributors are Roland Barthes and Gérard Genette. Genette's theory, exemplified by his study of Proust, among others, in *Figures 1, Figures 2,* and *Figures 3* (1966, 1969, 1972), accepts as given Jacobson's revelation of the paradigmatic and of the dynamics of metaphor and metonymy; he explores the fundamental nature of Proust's art in total structure and meaning, while building an intricate and nearly inclusive system for exploring the techniques of fiction. Among his original analytical tools are "iterative frequency" and the "pseudo-diegetic voice." Both Barthes and Genette, in contrast to most other structuralists and linguists, place an emphasis on the role of the reader in completing the literary work—the importance of which cannot be overemphasized. Many view this as one of the most promising signs in recent structural development. Barthes, in his own very important ways, like Genette in his, cannot be defined by such a restrictive label as structuralism, even though some of his work is that in the best sense. Barthes, as the supreme developer of semiology, finds evidence of the structures, both in human experience and in literary texts, of systems of signs, or "codes." By means of these he explicates exhaustively aspects of our society, or of individual texts, as he has done in *S/Z* with Balzac's "Sarrasine." This is only one direction of his investigations, however, and the quality of his stimulative influence is indicated by our contributors, who most often describe his work as "imaginative" or "creative."

The distinction made on our chart between linguistics and semiotics (as involving the analysis of words in relation to their referents) is perhaps too arbitrary and artificial. Although Saussure in 1915 defined what would be the science of semiology, and classified linguistics as belonging to the broader field of semiotics, both Barthes and Lévi-Strauss conclude that no other systems of meaning can function without language. Many of the critics here mentioned partake of "linguistics" and "semiotics," and linguistics has forced critics to define and redefine such categories as narrative and *diégèse, discours,* and *énonciation.*

Of prime importance in structuralism and semiology has been the theoretical elaboration accomplished at the Paris École Pratique des Hautes Études, Centre d'Études des Communications de Masse, to which several of the critics mentioned (Barthes and Bremond, among others) belong and where they work together, publishing the results of their research in the series *Communications.* An important structuralist journal is *Poétique: Revue de Théorie et d'Analyse Littéraire,* edited by Todorov, Genette, and another influential critic, Hélène Cixous. More *engagé* is the group *Change,* which publishes a series, *Change,* from time to time and which in 1974 brought out Noam Chomsky's book on Vietnam after it was refused publication in the United States. The group *Tel Quel* (Philippe Sollers, Marcellin Pleynet, and Julia Kristeva), publishers of a journal of research by that name, concerns itself with semiotics and the relationship between literature, linguistics, and ideology, holding that there is no distinction between literature and criticism.

Such is the critical atmosphere which may have its effects in varying degrees on our *Américanistes.* Some of them, fascinated by methods developed in French on French authors, are now attempting to apply them in their examination of American writers.

The arrangement of the contributions in this text is by subject matter. The first five essays deal with authors firmly established in the modern tradition: Bellow, Berger, O'Connor, Percy, and Updike. André Le Vot's piece deals in general terms with postmodern fiction and is followed by articles on three of its practitioners:

Robert Coover, John Hawkes, and Vladimir Nabokov. Jacques Favier then comments on science fiction which is beginning to attract serious attention in France, and Robert Silhol writes on criticism, ignoring national boundaries.

Jean-Pierre Vernier

1. MR. SAMMLER'S LESSON

"Shortly after dawn, or what would have been dawn in a normal sky, Mr. Arthur Sammler with his bushy eye took in the books and papers of his West Side bedroom and suspected strongly that they were the wrong books, the wrong papers."[1] This is our introduction to Mr. Sammler, whom we follow through three days to his final realization that he too knows the "terms of his contract. The terms which in his inmost heart, each man knows" (p. 286). Bellow's novel, following in the wake of *Herzog,* raises a great number of questions often adumbrated in his earlier work, questions which appear more clearly and yet seem at the same time to open up new abysses of darkness. In his critical study of Bellow's work, Robert B. Dutton stated: "The themes of Saul Bellow are hardly original: they include the old established counterclaims of the individual versus society and the individual in self-conflict. What Bellow offers is a clarity of vision concerning these issues that is, above all, honest."[2] It seems to me that, while there is absolutely no reason to question Bellow's honesty, a point which is anyhow hardly relevant, his vision often appears very far from clear, and *Mr. Sammler's Planet* epitomizes some aspects of the basic ambiguity underlying most of his writing.

My purpose here will be to analyze the novel in terms of narrative technique in order to find out the system of values implicit in the text, and then to relate these values to the type of narration used by Bellow. Only through a careful examination of the text, excluding references to nonliterary elements, can one hope to grasp if not *the* meaning of the novel, at least one of its meanings. In his essay "Distractions of a Fiction Writer," Bellow clearly warned the critics against the danger of imposing on his books an intellectual pattern which would claim to exhaust their meanings:

> In a work of art the imagination is the sole source of order. There are critics who assume that you must begin with order if you are to end with it. Not so. A novelist begins with disorder and disharmony, and he goes toward order by an unknown process of the imagination. And anyway the order he achieves is not the order that ideas have. Critics need to be reminded of this, I think.[3]

Since the product of the writer's imagination is the text of the novel, as published, it follows that any interpretation of the work must start from an analysis of this same text. I shall therefore use this procedure: after an examination of the main characteristics of Sammler and of the various episodes of the novel, we shall study the main themes and the way these reveal the values illustrated by the narrative. Finally we shall be led to discuss the type of fictional discourse used in *Mr. Sammler's Planet* and to offer an interpretation of this work, that is, to suggest a possible answer to the following question: "What does Bellow tell us in this particular case?"

The action of the novel is, at first sight, precisely limited in time and space: it covers three days in Sammler's life and takes place in New York and in Gruner's country house in New Rochelle. As with most of Bellow's prior novels, the setting is exclusively urban; what we are shown of New Rochelle is mainly the inside of the house at night, under rather exceptional circumstances. But since most of the action is seen through Sammler's eyes, this basic framework is constantly expanded by means of recollections and reflections which keep crowding in on the old man's brain, modifying the development of the narrative and forcing the reader to see the various incidents in terms of their relationship with the past and the future. Thus, as Sammler's mind moves backward through time, it embraces episodes situated after his arrival in the States, when he was rescued from a displaced persons camp by his now dying uncle; events which occurred during his two journeys to Israel, one to bring back his daughter threatened by her murderously brutal son-in-law Eisen, the other during the Six-Day War; memories of his experiences during World War II, of his years spent in London as a journalist when he moved in intellectual circles lorded over by H. G. Wells; and finally recollections of his childhood days in Cracow.

For most of the characters we are similarly given a fragmentary account of their past. In addition, we are given to understand that Sammler's experience has practically always been interpreted in terms of books (see initial quotation), and the first problem Sammler is confronted with is whether this type of interpretation can lead him to the discovery of meaning in life. The whole book is centered on Sammler's consciousness; like most of Bellow's heroes, Sammler is a "dangling man," but one who has reached a stage in life when the past is abundant enough to color the present and possibly explain it. However, this "Remembrance of Things Past" is not the result of a conscious effort of the will, but rather a haphazard accumulation of details stored up in the memory and recreated by the imagination working along lines which remain mysterious. Even the incidents which take place during the three days covered by the narrative remain largely unconnected according to superficial logic: they point to the existence of a symbolical meaning.

It should be pointed out at the beginning that the confusion between narrator and main protagonist creates an ambiguity that is not entirely due to the density of the character created, but to a deliberate confusion of the narrator's persona with the traits attributed to the main character. As K. M. Opdahl remarked:

> His protagonist's inability to break out of himself parallels the most criticized fault in his work, the fact that the mind of the protagonist is that of the novel. Bellow creates one of the most fully realized physical worlds in fiction, and his use of irony implies a standard outside of the work, but the vision of the novel is ultimately that of the central character.[4]

Although the story is told in the third person, from the point of view of an unidentified narrator, Bellow constantly shifts from commentary to narration of the events as seen by his character. The frequent use of free indirect style and a deliberate lack of precision in the use of personal pronouns create the blurred outlines of a vision not unlike the flat perception of a one-eyed man. Which is of course Sammler's case.[5] To take only one example of the way Bellow manages to achieve this effect, in chapter 1 a paragraph begins thus: "With the pickpocket we were in an adjoining region of recklessness. He knew the man was working the Riverside bus" (p. 10). Whom does this "we" refer to? Is it the communion formed by the narrator taking the reader into his confidence? Is it an inside view of Mr. Sammler's mind reflecting upon the incident? Or an impersonal comment made by the narrator? The answer is that we do not know and are given no means of knowing. Like Mr. Sammler himself, we are made to witness a number of incidents which are apparently unrelated; and if any order is to emerge at the end, we must find it by ourselves.

Sammler's fictional personality colors the whole novel, and all the action revolves around him. He is the first central character in Bellow's fiction who is an old man: he has reached an age when he can look back on his life, knowing that what years he has left are necessarily few. Since, as we have seen, he is one-eyed, that is, endowed with a sight that lacks depth, there is no perspective in his vision: thus, we are given only the raw materials of experience.

As with Moses Herzog, Sammler's name exemplifies his function in the novel. Bellow in fact resorts to the time-honored device of allegory to indicate what his character stands for, but the names he selects, instead of referring the reader to a precise abstract quality, only increase the ambiguity. Thus, Sammler is a collector, a gatherer of heterogeneous elements which he puts together, a particularly fitting name for a journalist; but this name, through its etymology—the Anglo-Saxon root "sem"—also implies the reverse notion: similarity or simplicity. We may thus surmise that Sammler's function is to reconcile opposite notions. Sammler has indeed, throughout his past life, been a collector of experience at two different levels: through what has happened to him and through the books he has read.

This second aspect, already very important in *Herzog*, is here developed at great length. Sammler is an intellectual, his mind has been trained to think along logical lines, but when he is first presented to us, we know that this process of rational analysis has proved unsatisfactory: "Intellectual man had become an explaining creature. . . . The soul wanted what it wanted. It had its own natural knowledge. It sat unhappily on superstructures of explanation, poor bird, not knowing which way to fly" (p. 3). Finding a way to assuage the longings of the soul will be the aim of his quest. We are also told (p. 37) that he has reached a point when the only books he reads are Meister Eckhart and the Bible. However, his previous reading has apparently been extremely varied, ranging from Aristotle's *Metaphysics* to Norman O. Brown, through Mario Praz, Krafft-Ebing, and hundreds of others, including H. G. Wells, whose role deserves a more detailed scrutiny. The narrative is interspersed with literally hundreds of names of writers, thinkers, politicians, historical figures, giving the impression that Sammler's mind is cluttered with the thought of most of the men who have been instrumental in shaping modern civilization. Part of Sammler's consciousness is actually molded by other writers' consciousness of what concrete experience is and by their attempts to find meaning in the world. In this field he appears as a collector of the consciousness of mankind; he plays a purely passive role since he has apparently become a simple repository of past culture but has produced nothing himself. The memoir on H. G. Wells remains an abortive project, and we are made to understand that it will never be written.

However, this familiarity with the intellectual past of mankind, or, more precisely, of Western man, explains why each incident in Sammler's life and about him evokes references to or comparisons with those great names of our intellectual past. Not that these can provide him with a satisfactory explanation: when the action described in the book begins, Sammler has practiclaly lost whatever faith he might have had in the powers of the intellect to account for the evolution of our civilization. His niece Margotte symbolizes this reliance on intellectual explanation and ponderous argumentation, but Sammler is no longer taken in by this kind of activity, for he knows that all explanations are fragmentary and will be superseded by others:

> Arguments! Explanations! thought Sammler. All will explain everything to all, until the next, the new common version is ready. This version, a residue of what people for a century or so say to one another, will be, like the old, a fiction. More elements of reality perhaps will be incorporated in the new version. But the important consideration was that life should recover its plenitude, its normal contented turgidity. All the old fusty stuff had to be blown away, of course, so we might be nearer to nature. (p. 21)

The sexual vocabulary used to describe the reality of future life should be noticed, since it is closely connected with one of the main themes of the book.

A failure as an intellectual, an observer of the world about him, Sammler is also, like almost all of Bellow's heroes, deeply alienated. This alienation is due to several factors: his Jewishness, his social position, which largely depends upon his past, and the nature of his concerns about the world in which he finds himself. Jewishness as a source of alienation leading to a privileged ironic vision is of course one of the main themes of the modern American novel, but Sammler's case is somewhat peculiar. Arnold Gruner, his daughter Angela, Feffer, and a good many other characters appear fairly well adapted to the society they live in; even Wallace, the perpetual misfit, does not find it particularly difficult to survive in the American society of the seventies; only Sammler is different because he embodies a number of traits characteristic of Jewishness, among which the main one is probably a sense of *belonging,* of being willy-nilly a representative of the Jews and a witness to their fate. Hence his attitude during the Six-Day War, his inability to stay in New York while the fighting was going on: "No Zionist, Mr. Sammler, and for many years little interested in Jewish affairs. Yet, from the start of the crisis, he could not sit in New York reading the world press" (p. 131). This awareness of his Jewishness also explains his particular status among his relatives: he is for them the only link with the Old World, the symbol of a wisdom that is inseparable from a world now extinct. Hence the part of a patriarch which is almost forced upon him by his family: thanks to Sammler, Arnold Gruner, the successful and dying physician, becomes Elya Gruner, the descendant of somewhat mythical Jewish ancestors in the old country; and Sammler is also the one Angela and Walter Bruch turn to when the weight of their sexual experimentation becomes too much for them to bear alone. Out of tune with practical everyday life, he stands as a kind of father figure that keeps the family together.

But Sammler's origin and past probably account not only for the part he plays in his family but also for his particular kind of alienation. Large fragments of his past life remain unknown; Bellow's careful selection of episodes relating to this period makes them all the more significant. Sammler is a victim—one is tempted to write *The Victim:* captured by the Nazis, he has been forced to dig his own grave with his wife and dozens of other Jews; he, and he only, miraculously managed to survive this mass extermination and to crawl out of the grave after pushing aside the corpses that lay over him; after several episodes, including months spent hiding in a tomb, Sammler finally found himself in the displaced persons camp in Salzburg, from which he was rescued by Gruner who brought him to New York. Strictly speaking, Sammler remains, in the true meaning of the phrase, a displaced person, a new embodiment of the Wandering Jew, but what should be stressed is the amount of arbitrariness involved in his past life: we are told that in 1939 Sammler, who then lived in London, went back to Poland in order to settle business matters, a move which, when seen in perspective, was almost like a surrender to a suicidal impulse; his escape from the grave was also something of a miracle, just like his rescue from the camp in 1947. He is the man *things happen to,* and in this his Jewishness is particularly apparent. As Bellow puts it somewhere else, "The Jews of the Ghetto found themselves involved in an immense joke. They were divinely designated to be great and yet they were like mice. History was something that *happened* to them; they did not make it."[6] Sammler is precisely a man to whom history happened and who, because of his culture and intellectual training, was apparently very well equipped to understand its workings. But understanding how things work does not mean that one is, as H. G. Wells believed, able to change the course of events.

The circumstances in which Sammler finds himself in New York also contribute to his isolation. His economic situation, entirely dependent on Gruner's charity and good will, compels him to merge with a world in which his own identity is constantly threatened with dissolution: "It was always Mr. Sammler's problem that he didn't know his proper age, didn't appreciate his situation, unprotected here by position, by privileges of remoteness made possible by an income of fifty thousand dollars in New York" (p. 9). His alienation comes in fact less from his Jewishness than from his belonging to another age, from being aware of the past of our civilization through his reading, and from his consciousness of his own past when the years spent in London, in the shadow of H. G. Wells, were but a prelude to the most terrible trial. In New York Sammler is literally nobody. The comic scene in which he reports to the police the Negro pickpocket he has seen on the bus makes the point very clearly: not only is Sammler unable to be taken seriously, he does not even succeed in establishing his own identity. In the same way the interrupted Columbia lecture also emphasizes his isolation, his inability to understand the modern world and to reconcile its trends with the lessons of the past:

> He was not sorry to have met the facts, however, saddening, regrettable the facts. But the effect was that Mr. Sammler did feel somewhat separated from the rest of his species, if not in some fashion severed—severed not so much by age as by preoccupations too different and remote, disproportionate on the side of the spiritual, Platonic, Augustinian, thirteenth-century. (p. 43)

His search for spiritual values in a world apparently given over to materialistic pursuits is indeed the main cause of his isolation and, by putting Mr. Sammler in this privileged position, Bellow is able to comment upon modern civilization and ask the reader to see it in perspective, through comparisons with the past as reflected in Sammler's actual experience and encyclopedic knowledge, and with the future as imagined by Dr. Lal. Sammler thus finds himself at the crossroads of past, present, and future (but of a past lived through the consciousness of others and of a future expressed largely by comparisons between Lal's thories concerning the moon and H. G. Wells's utopian vision), and of the three different worlds of the Holy Land, Europe, and modern America.

But this wide-ranging vision is actually encompassed within three days in Sammler's life. The incidents which occur during this short span of time are apparently imperfectly articulated, and their significance can only be appreciated at the level of a symbolical structure. Besides the recurrence of events belonging to Sammler's past and coloring the present, these incidents are relatively few in number, and most of them are imposed upon him by circumstances. In very few cases does he play an active part, and when he does, the outcome of his action is usually even greater isolation for him, as his telephone call to the police station shows. His Columbia lecture, the result of acceptance if not of choice, also ends in disaster and violent rejection. In both cases his manhood is questioned, first through the silent self-exposure of the pickpocket in the lobby of Sammler's building, second by the exhibitionistic interruption of a professional troublemaker. Sammler's power of acting is thus equated with sexual potency—a major theme in the book—and the divorce between intention and action is made particularly obvious. But, for the main part, Sammler's function is passive; it is basically that of a witness providing an easy outlet for the overburdened souls of others. Almost every part of his life during this short span is governed by exterior elements.

Another remarkable fact is that the various incidents occurring in the present fulfill very different functions. The episode of the Negro pickpocket runs through the book as a sort of leitmotif. It introduces the exposure scene, which remains unexplained at the factual level, then leads to Feffer's scheme for making money out of the incident, and to the fight between the pickpocket, Feffer, and Eisen. Thematically it is related to the concepts of money, sex, and violence, but it directly affects Sammler only insofar as he is made to witness the Negro's genitals. Its further significance largely depends on coincidence: Sammler, on his way to Gruner's deathbed, happens to be passing the spot where the fight is taking place.

Thieving is also illustrated by Shula's appropriation of Lal's manuscript on the future of the moon, which is, in its turn, related to Sammler's concern with H. G. Wells's view of the future of mankind or, to be more precise, with the problem of knowledge twice removed from reality—knowledge seen through Wells's eyes, at a period that was to prove a crucial moment in Sammler's experience. Thieving is, of course, directly connected with the theme of money that provides one of the mainsprings of the action: it accounts for the relative positions of Sammler and Gruner, whose wealth, we are made to understand, was largely acquired through performing illegal operations for the Mafia and evading taxes, but it is also the motive behind Feffer's and Wallace's schemes, the bait that draws Eisen to New York. Through the exposure scene the pickpocket also introduces the theme of sex that recurs throughout the book with an almost obsessive force. Angela, Feffer, Bruch in particular, illustrate the importance of this theme, which prevents Sammler from ignoring the part played by this urge in his past life. It is also a link between what could be called the axiological aspect of the book and its ontological inquiry on man. The interaction of these two levels of inquiry is indeed one of the main reasons for the complexity of the novel: *Mr. Sammler's Planet* is concerned with the behavior of one character during a short period in 1970 New York, but also and simultaneously with the nature of man at a certain stage in his historical development. The question which ends chapter 2: "What *is* One?" (p. 96) sums up Sammler's and Bellow's main line of inquiry.

This query about the difficulty of defining man's essence and of establishing his identity is directly connected with Sammler's consciousness of his own approaching death and with his familiarity with death. Death is indeed at the very center of the work, probably because this cardinal, inescapable fact is what gives life a meaning. As I shall try to show, Bellow's patterns of thematic development depend on a consideration of opposite elements and a reconciliation of apparently contradictory notions.

Sammler's concern with death illustrates the ambiguity of Bellow's attitude: not only does death strike arbitrarily, so that no significant pattern emerges from the circumstances in which it occurs, it is also one of man's characteristics insofar as inflicting death, reducing other beings to nothingness, is a privilege inseparable from our condition. From the start Sammler is surrounded with death and memories of the dead: "Wherever you looked, or tried to look, there were the late. It took some getting used to" (p. 12). His niece Margotte is a widow whose husband was killed in a plane crash three years before the story begins; his own wife was the victim of a mass murder in Poland; Dr. Gruner, himself a widower, is slowly dying in a hospital, and, finally, Sammler himself has literally escaped from among the dead, first when he had to crawl out from under the bodies of people shot by the Germans, and then when, a second time, he escaped death at the hands of the Poles.

But the New World where he seems to have found a refuge is also threatened by death, just like the rest of humanity. It is the ultimate reality, bent on defeating all human endeavor, and the cardinal fact man has to live with: "Humankind could not endure futurelessness. As of now, death was the sole visible future. A family, a circle of friends, a team of the living got things going, and then death appeared and no one was prepared to acknowledge death" (p. 71). No one, except a few individuals who, like Sammler, had been conditioned by their past to accept its presence as part of their daily lives. Genocide, mass executions, atomic slaughters, have imposed a new weight on human consciousness; although modern man is as prone to accidental death as his forebears, he cannot escape the fact that doom is constantly lurking around the corner, and doom no longer means the individual's possible translation to a Kingdom Come, or a long wait for the Last Trump, it has become synonymous with complete annihilation.

Mr. Sammler's Planet is not a book about a certain form of civilization embodied in modern New York; it deals with the eternal problem of death only made more apparent because of the historical evolution of the past few decades. Mr. Sammler possesses, above the other heroes of Bellow's novels, the advantages of age, experience, and the consciousness inseparable from his alienated position in society. Because he has had firsthand experience of death, he possesses a clarity of vision which most of the other characters, safely ensconced in their little worlds of make-believe and mundane pursuits, lack in various degrees. He is able to contemplate the inevitable end of people and things with an equanimity which often appears as a form of fatalism. As the narrator puts it, "The luxury of nonintimidation by doom—that might describe his state" (p. 124). In times characterized by what Sammler calls "a peculiar longing for nonbeing," no other individual reaction is apparently possible.

However, the complexity of man's attitude toward death is made clear, at the thematic level, in two different ways: first, by Sammler's awareness of the pleasure found in inflicting death; second, in the linking of this theme with that of life, both being in fact complementary aspects of the same phenomenon. Sammler's wartime experience provides a symbolical embodiment of the theme: after his escape from the hole in which he was buried under the bodies of other Jews, Sammler found refuge in a cemetery. This tomb proved to be the instrument of his rebirth but also the place where, for the first time, he acquired the habit of considering the world as a system of meaningful signs: "It was in Poland, in wartime, particularly during three or four months when Sammler was hidden in a mausoleum, that he first began to turn to the external world for curious ciphers and portents" (p. 84). This indication is important because it not only shows the connection between the tomb and life and significance, but also clearly tells the reader that all the memories that keep crowding through Sammler's mind have a symbolical value. The crowning moment of Sammler's rebirth took place when the hunted became the hunter, and he himself killed a German in cold blood. His memory of the event makes its value particularly clear: taking life meant appropriating life, as if its flickering flame could be transferred, through the act of killing, from one man to another: "Was it only pleasure? It was more. It was joy. You would call it a dark action? On the contrary, it was also a bright one, It was mainly bright. When he fired his gun, Sammler, himself nearly a corpse, burst into life" (p. 129). Killing is one of the privileges of man, and Sammler is seen meditating on a view of history considered as the transference of the right to kill from one social class to another (p. 133).

The same symbolical experience characterizes Eisen: his intervention during the fight between Feffer and the pickpocket brings home to Sammler the terrible logic of violence and murder. Through his desire to bring violence to an end, Sammler almost has the Negro killed before his eyes and Eisen's flawless reasoning makes him realize that, in spite of all principles and ethical values, any man can be both a victim and a murderer: "You can't hit a man like this just once. When you hit him you must really hit him. Otherwise he'll kill you. You know. We both fought in the war. You were a Partisan. You had a gun. So don't you know?" (p. 266).

Eisen, the victim of drunken Russian soldiers, nearly becomes the murderer of a Negro, just as Sammler, the victim of Nazi genocide, had pitilessly killed a defenseless German. There are no fixed values left, nor is there any single system on which one might base one's faith, and, as a result, all values are ambivalent. The desire to kill is inherent in man: as such, it is not related to any particular ethics and has no bearing on the fundamental qualities of an individual. Dr. Gruner finally appears as a physician who made a fortune through performing illegal abortions, yet Sammler's final judgment emphasized the positive qualities of the man: "At his best this man was much kinder than at my very best I have ever been or could ever be" (p. 285).

At a more general level, the same ironic confusion pervades all human actions: history is but a record of cruelty, slaughters, barbarism in all conceivable shapes. History in the making is Sammler watching the telltale marks of napalm in the Sinai desert, listening to the technical explanations about warfare provided by a Jesuit father clad in full battle dress. Nor can man even call upon his ignorance as an explanation for his crimes: "Everybody (except certain bluestockings) knows what murder is. That is very old human knowledge. The best and purest human knowledge. The best and purest human beings, from the beginning of time, have understood that life is sacred" (p. 21).

The best illustration of the theme may be found in the parable of the gaucho Sammler meets on his way from Nazareth to Galilee: the man breeds nutrias for their furs and, on being asked whether he ever feels tenderness for the little animals he slaughters after breeding them, he denies the possibility of such a reaction: "He said the nutrias were very stupid" (p. 27). The implications of the short dialogue between the two men are pointed out by the narrator's remark: "Neither spoke Hebrew. Nor the language of Jesus" (p. 26). In the land of Jesus the language of love is no longer understood.

In this second half of the twentieth century, when the world is precariously balanced on the brink of the abyss, the individual has broken free from the rules imposed upon him by the values connected with the respectability of the previous century. What Sammler discovers in modern New York is the commonplace fact that the main drive behind people is provided by the twin urge to get more and more money and to achieve sexual gratification at whatever cost.

Money is nothing new in Bellow's world: it played a prominent part in the previous novels and its pervades the whole texture of *Mr. Sammler's Planet*. Absence of it is, of course, one of the main reasons why Sammler can remain an observer, and this fact delineates his particular role in the novel. But practically all the other characters revolving about Sammler are concerned with it and, there again, it appears as an element endowed with an ambivalent value. It is the source of Gruner's benevolence, and it is what enables him to create a world of his own, sheltered from all the influences of the outside world, a sort of universe symbolized by the Rolls Royce driven by a shady Mafia character, but it is mainly something to be appropriated by any means. From the petty stealing of the Negro pickpocket to Wallace's numerous designs to get rich quick through Feffer's schemes to buy a locomotive, a rich gamut of devices for making the "fast buck" is unfolded before Sammler's eyes. And money, like death, has a way of turning up in the most unexpected places: it appears that Sammler has been sleeping on it throughout the night he spent at New Rochelle, and Wallace eventually makes the news, with all the publicity value added to it, only when he has to make a crash landing in some rich property. No sense is apparently attached to the acquisition or possession of money; it is merely an aim pursued because of the material advantages attached to it. It is not the reward of a life of toil; it does not entail any particular curse; it does not even seem to have any influence on people other than to enable them to indulge their whims, whatever these may be.

Foremost among these stand sexual pursuits. The theme of sex, already more fully developed in *Herzog* than in the other novels, is here of paramount importance. It is, in fact, one of the mainsprings of comedy in the book, but it is probably more than just that. In his role of father confessor Sammler is made to listen to various tales of sexual vagaries characteristic of the times. One feels that some characters were created precisely to fulfill this function and for no other reason: Angela—evidently a fallen angel with "fucked-out eyes," to borrow Gruner's phrase—has only one part to play in the book: she exists to acquaint Sammler with the various complexities born of her many-sided love affairs; Walter Bruch, in the single scene in which he appears, is made to give Sammler a verbatim account of his obsession with female arms. The whole world is literally wallowing in sex, people like Feffer, for example, apparently rising from one bed to burst into frantic activity around some commercial pursuit before getting back to another bed, while others desperately try to get their kicks through various forms of sexual experimentation. "The thing evidently, as Mr. Sammler was beginning to grasp, consisted in obtaining the privileges, and the free ways of barbarism, under the protection of civilized order, property rights, refined technological organization, and so on" (pp. 10–11).

However, Sammler himself is not presented as a prude; he is aware of the existence of powerful sexual drives in man: H. G. Wells had apparently confided in him, long before Angela did, and the way most of the female characters are seen through his consciousness makes it clear that he is aware of their sexual qualities. Even his memories of his days in London, when his wife was alive, bring back to his mind sexual connotations: "If a little social-climbing made her handsomer (plumper between the legs—the thought rushed in and Sammler had stopped trying to repel these mental rushes), it had its feminine justifications" (p. 29). But, in spite of Sammler's moral judgments on the consequences of sexual freedom, an important distinction is made in this field. Sammler clearly realizes the permanence of sexual feelings in man, he does not blind himself to the fact that these are, for any individual, the source of experiences that are a fundamental element in his life; but the tendency to link sex with excrement, to consider it as a form of refusal of all intellectual pursuits, is what escapes his understanding. Man as a sexual animal he can conceive, man as a highly sexed beast he considers with uncomprehending surprise. This is best expressed by his reaction after the interruption of his Columbia lecture by a student whose obscene abuses drive him off the rostrum: "What a passion to be *real*. But *real* was also brutal. And the acceptance of excrement as a standard? How extraordinary! Youth? Together with the idea of sexual potency? All this confused sex-excrement-militancy, explosiveness, abusiveness, tooth-showing, Barbary ape howling" (p. 43). What strikes him most is the deliberate self-abasement of these young people, their bias against anything that could give them a certain amount of personal dignity:

> The worst of it, from the point of view of the young people themselves, was that they acted without dignity. They had no view of the nobility of being intellectuals and judges of the social order. What a pity! old Sammler thought. A human being, valuing himself for the right reasons, has and restores order, authority. When the internal parts are in order. But what was it to be arrested in the stage of toilet-training! (p. 45)

In other words, sex has become either an aimless promiscuous activity, the source of innumerable and often inconsequential difficulties, or a weapon used by the younger generation in the war it wages against the adult world and what it stands for. In all cases it is inseparable from the violence that runs rife in the city, just as it permeates the whole world. Society has reached a hopeless stage, and Sammler has too great an experience of the past, both through his own life and through his historical knowledge acquired from books, not to realize that all attempts at social changes by means of revolution made in the name of lofty principles only lead to more violence and eventually worse anarchy.

In these circumstances is there any hope left for man? Is Mr. Sammler's vision utterly pessimistic? These are difficult questions to answer in this particular context, all the more so as the complexity due to Bellow's presentation of characters and events eliminates all notions of causality. No episode happens as a logical consequence of a preceding move made by the characters; it is not even clear whether the events affecting Sammler during the three days covered by the narrative lead to any change in him. Things just happen, bringing back memories, suggesting reflections, in a sort of endless stream. The consequence of this narrative method is that the possible meanings of the book have to be reconstructed by the reader from the elements he is given.

As we have seen, a study of the main themes only stresses the existence of duality at all levels: all events are ambiguous and fraught with irony, and no value system is made apparent. However, I have purposely understressed two important elements which seem to have a different function in the novel: the character of the Negro pickpocket, and the memoir Sammler is supposed to write on H. G. Wells. They have in common the fact that they recur throughout the book and that they are connected with several themes at the same time, money, sex, and violence.

The Negro pickpocket is probably the most mysterious character in the novel. He is seen stealing money in the bus, exhibiting his genitals to Mr. Sammler in the lobby of his apartment building, and then bleeding on the pavement after Eisen has knocked him down at the end of the fight with Feffer. Apart from that, he never speaks a word, no explanation is given of his motivation; his character is defined simply through his appearance and his behavior as seen by an outside observer. R. B. Dutton considers him as a sort of symbol of the jungle, and it is true that the man is compared to a wild beast ("He [Sammler] was never to hear the black man's voice. He no more spoke than a puma would" [p. 48]), but Dutton's description of the pickpocket as a type reflecting the lessons of Nietzsche and Freud hardly accounts for his function in the narrative: "He possesses all the silent assurance, strength, super power, barbaric law-unto-himself of Nietzsche's great criminal. Finally, when he exposes himself to Sammler, he is asserting Freud's thesis on the primacy of sexual power."[7] In fact, his function is mainly symbolical, and this symbolism is expressed at several complementary levels. Reduced to its basic elements, the exposure scene shows us a Negro forcing an old Jew to look at his penis—the narrator stresses the fact that the Negro is uncircumcised—and it may be taken as an ironical exploitation of the biblical myth of genesis. Far from spying upon his sleeping father's nakedness, this son of Ham exposes himself to the father, denying the latter's supremacy. Sammler is now the outcast. In addition, this "servant of servants" is also an ironic echo of the Thief in the Night.[8] Mythical imagery is reversed just as values are reversed. I am not suggesting that Bellow deliberately wants us to interpret the scene in this precise way, but there are a number of elements suggesting a rhetorical comparison between Sammler and Noah. Sammler has miraculously escaped the universal deluge of World War II, but he is unable to stop the flood released by Wallace during his search for the money hidden in Gruner's house.

At another level the pickpocket is the perfect foil to Sammler: his main characteristics are those of a beast of prey, endowed with all-powerful instinct and an absence of formalized language. As Sammler recognizes, communication with him is based on elementary signs which strike one directly, bypassing the intellect. His gaudy clothes fulfill this function, as shown by Sammler's remark when he notices, during the fight, that the Negro's belt matches his tie: "A crimson belt! How consciousness was lashed by such a fact" (p. 263).

Thus, his exposing himself is the equivalent of a statement of fact; he simply draws Sammler's attention to what *is,* regardless of all explanations; his attitude is the epitome of the moronic cult of a return to nature, accompanied by a refusal of all intellectual activity, which is the basic creed of Sammler's young readers. This Sammler understands clearly when he reflects on the Negro's sexual organ: "It was a symbol of superlegitimacy or sovereignty. It was a mystery. It was unanswerable. The whole explanation. This is the wherefore, the why. See? Oh, the transcending, ultimate, and silencing proof" (p. 54). But, in spite of this manifestation of phallic primitivism, in spite of all his animal characteristics, the Negro possesses a quality that lifts him above the rest of humanity: he has dignity. He may be the exact opposite of Sammler, yet he shares with him an innate sense of the worth of man. Serene, unquestioning, powerful, whereas Sammler is anxious, weak, and unsure of himself, he gives an impression of essential immovability in a precariously balanced world: "The man's expression was not directly menacing but oddly, serenely masterful. The thing was shown with mystifying certitude. Lordliness. Then it was returned to the trousers. *Quod erat demonstrandum*" (p. 49). It is precisely this lordliness which accounts for Sammler's sympathy for him when he gets beaten up: "The black man was a megalomaniac. But there was a certain—a certain princeliness. The clothing, the shades, the sumptuous colors, the barbarous-magestical manner. He was probably a mad spirit. But mad with an idea of *noblesse*" (p. 268). Logically enough, in a mad world, this prince of darkness, this outcast, brings by his very presence a light of hope; this mad thief embodies greater sanity than most other characters. He represents the mystery of being, the sheer will of man to survive through adaptation to a world of violence. In fact, he is a rather convincing illustration of the primitive man Wells saw lurking behind his utopias toward the end of his life.

Which brings us to Sammler's particular interest in Wells. This is a recurrent motif in the book: Wells is part of Sammler's memory of his London days before the war; he frequently appears in his thoughts, and this interest is a major spring of the action since it leads to the theft of Lal's manuscript and the subsequent trip to New Rochelle. In typical Bellow fashion, Sammler keeps thinking about the memoir, or is reminded of it by his daughter, but does not write it. To him Wells is both a landmark in his past and one of the best modern exponents of utopia. Furthermore, his personality connects him with the theme of sex, and his lifelong concern with the future of mankind is a natural introduction to Lal's manuscript on *The Future of the Moon*. One could even say that Lal's subject, although rooted in the present—Bellow obviously capitalizes on the first moon landing—is typically Wellsian, a fact emphasized by the manuscript being written in Edwardian colonial English. Sammler's knowledge of Wells and his writing is presented convincingly on the whole, except for one detail which is significant: Wells is associated, in Sammler's memory, with two years spent in Woburn Square from 1937 to 1939. Now, the connection between Wells and Bloomsbury is evidently a deliberate twist of historical reality: Wells's relationship with Bloomsbury circles was extremely tenuous, to say the least, and he spent most of these two years between the Savile Club and his elegant house in Hanover Terrace, rummaging through the frustrations accumulated during his past years and sallying forth only to further the cause of Universal Education or to meet important people connected with political circles.

It may be conjectured that the picture left in Sammler's mind is meant to emphasize both the Sammlers' snobbery at being intimate with "the cultural best of England" (p. 29), certainly not an accurate description of Wells, and a type of utopian vision that proved incapable of influencing the course of events. In other words, the projected memoir would deal with an interpretation of the future of a mankind that had gone wrong. The Bloomsbury connection ironically stresses the almost parochial isolation of Sammler at a time when history was rapidly catching up with him. Through Wells's writings Sammler's consciousness perceives the plight of humanity as seen through another consciousness leading in direct line to Lal's manuscript. Whereas the pickpocket's attitude to life was all action and no thought, Wells's and Lal's is all thought and no action. Now Sammler, his mind overloaded with wide-ranging interpretations of the past, all containing probably a grain of truth, but all incapable of altering things, is caught between the two contrary positions and unable to find in the world a satisfactory answer to the question: "What *is* One?"

If the world cannot provide an answer, man can only find one in himself, that is in looking for loneliness and isolation amidst crowds. This is probably the core of Sammler's predicament: his situation is privileged in that he was practically reborn from among the dead and thus made to start a new life in which only essential concerns mattered. His alienation is not only a consequence of this particular situation, it is also something he profoundly desires, the means of achieving an identity that owes nothing to exterior circumstances. In order to exist, the Negro pickpocket has to show himself, to be seen by others; Wells had to believe he could influence others; all the main characters assert their existence through possessing things or people, through abiding by or rebelling against standards defined by the world at large. Only Sammler, the observer, remains an outsider, by his own choice as much as because of circumstances. His alienation is deliberate and leads to a refusal of action. We know that he will never write the memoir on Wells, not only because he is no longer interested in the man, but mainly because such attempts are meaningless in the modern world. He has reached the same stage in his evolution as Herzog, who has given up research after writing his Ph.D. and is left with some eight hundred useless pages stacked in a cupboard. Sammler is aware of the futility of writing: "The answer of private folly to public folly (in an age of overkill) was more distinction, more high accomplishments, more dazzling brilliants strewn before mankind. Pearls before swine?" (p. 106).

Even writing a book would mean joining the universal ratrace and jeopardizing one's chances of being a man. The natural consequence of this self-imposed isolation is that it would be pointless to hope for happiness, insofar as being happy in this world of ours means being fully integrated in one's time—that is, accepting things as they are without asking questions:

> Accept and grant that happiness is to do what most other people do. Then you must incarnate what others incarnate. If prejudices, prejudice. If rage, then rage. If sex, then sex. But don't contradict your time. Just don't contradict it, that's all. Unless you happened to be a Sammler and felt that the place of honor was outside. (p. 69)

But refusing to follow the herd instinct does not lead to revolutionary action or even to attempts at accelerating evolution. All hopes of changing the world, any striving toward a new social order, preferably along radical lines, lead only to more and more cruelty and violence: madness superseding a different form of madness. There remains love as a supreme value, but how does one define it in a world given over to all forms of sexual variations? And, more important still, how does one translate it into meaningful action? Sammler's views on the subject point to the same direction: the concentration of one's attention on the self. This is what he tells Lal:

> Though I feel sometimes quite disembodied, I have little rancor and quite a lot of sympathy. Often I wish to do something, but it is a dangerous illusion to think one can do much for more than a very few.
> What is one supposed to do? said Lal.
> Perhaps the best is to have some order within oneself. Better than what many call love. Perhaps it *is* love. (p. 208)

The emphasis is deliberately put on the self, the disembodied self, the essential, not the existential man. But how elusive this essential man is, if he exists at all! It looks as though the individual could come into his own only by denouncing the absurdity of human behavior through dying, like Rumkovski, the Jewish king of Lodz, whose fate obsesses Sammler. The paradoxical aspect of this attitude is that one can really become human at the price of a complete dehumanization. And things have an ironical way of thwarting the deepest metaphysical reasonings, as when, for example, Sammler finds his long disquisition on the condition of man brought to an abrupt end by Wallace's experiments with the water pipes in the New Rochelle house. He had, a short time before, tried to define his position for the benefit of Lal: "The best I have found, is to be disinterested. Not as misanthropes dissociate themselves by judging, but by not judging. By willing as God wills" (p. 215). But such a position, it must be admitted, is hardly tenable when one is confronted with a flood of water rushing down the stairs.

However, in spite of the various tricks reality plays on the individual, Sammler's pursuit is basically metaphysical and relies on a form of mysticism. When we meet him, he has already given up reading everything except the Bible and Meister Eckhart. These form the basis of his intellectual diet. They are the last possible source of comfort in a meaningless world, or rather, the only voices capable of providing a reasonable ground for faith in mankind. Belief in God as pure spirit, unintelligible to man and yet ever present as an object of love—such is apparently the ultimate solution or, at least, the one Sammler yearns for. But this is not a panacea, and he realizes that, while one part of himself longs for the status of disembodied spirit, completely divorced from life, the rest is solidly anchored in concrete reality. After all, a man who boils water, grinds his own coffee, and urinates in his washbasin, even though he may meditate on Aristotle at the same time (p. 17), can hardly hope to escape from the preposterous implications inherent in the human condition. In accordance with Jewish faith, Sammler has no hope of another world beyond death; if there is to be a better world, it can only exist on the earth and be brought about by man's striving after a life more and more in keeping with God's will. But all history and all the aspects of modern civilization run contrary to this expectation. Therefore, man has only one door left open: to make a separate peace with himself through loving God, although He may be unconcerned with mankind, and to trust and revere Him. The only trouble is that the individual is essentially unable to ignore the rest of the species. Sammler realizes this very lucidly:

> He wanted, with God, to be free from bondage of the ordinary and the finite. A soul released from Nature, from impressions, and from everyday life. For this to happen God Himself must be waiting surely. And a man who has been killed and buried should have no other interest. He should be perfectly disinterested. Eckhart said in so many words that God loved disinterested purity and unity. God himself was drawn toward the disinterested soul. What besides the spirit should a man care for who has come back from the grave? However and mysteriously enough, it happened, as Sammler observed, that one was always, and so powerfully, so persuasively drawn back to human conditions. . . . It was a second encounter of the disinterested spirit with fated biological necessities, a return match with the persistent creature. (p. 109)

The soul may hanker after God; the creature may try to find in self-imposed alienation the way that leads away from mankind and toward the Creator, but this must necessarily remain an aimless pursuit. Eckhart may provide Sammler with the comforting strength he needs to go on living and to maintain a certain amount of faith in man, but he cannot do much more. Sammler quotes Eckhart, whom he reads alone, without the help of his young readers—the point is worth mentioning— and the narrator makes this significant comment: "Mr. Sammler could not say that he literally believed what he was reading. He could, however, say that he cared to read nothing but this" (p. 231). The point is clear: Eckhart's writings—and we may presume the Bible fulfills a similar function—play a prominent part in Sammler's outlook not because they provide him with a rule of life, a model to be followed, but simply, and more basically, because they suggest a way of looking at the world which, although it may be proved impracticable by all the entanglements in which we are caught, appeals to the imagination. I would suggest that this explains Sammler's final address to God, when he prays over Elya Gruner's body, emphasizing the fact that Elya, whatever the moral reprobation attached to some of his actions, always did what was expected of him:

> He was aware that he must meet, and he did meet—through all the confusion and degraded clowning of this life through which we are speeding—he did meet the terms of his contract. The terms which, in his inmost heart, each man knows. As I know mine. As all know. For that is the truth of it—that we all know, God, that we know, that we know, we know, we know. (pp. 285–86)

Of course, we are told neither *what* we know, nor *how* we know. But, if we realize that the lines given Sammler at the end of the novel clearly belie the lesson which seems to be implied by all the rest of the book, that is, the fact that we know nothing and can know nothing, we see that, through irony, Bellow is asserting the rights of the human imagination. What he tells us is that we are human because we can imagine things: we can imagine that, in spite of the all-embracing chaos, there is purpose, a divine will at work in the universe. Wells's Mind of the Race was an attempt at defining a purpose justifying human actions, but one that was presented as grounded on an objective observation of concrete reality; Bellow has gone beyond the concept of "Human Evolution with God as Intelligence" (p. 182), and back to the romantic notion of the imagination as the manifestation of the godhead in man. However, there is no reason to believe that the acting imagination duplicates God's creation. One may as well think, as Lal puts it, that "the imagination is innately a biological power seeking to overcome impossible conditions" (p. 100). What matters is that it exists as a cardinal element in man. In the end, Sammler's prayer and assertion of knowledge may be pure products of the imagination, but this does not make them any less real. What matters is not the creation of a clear-cut system but the achievement of a vision. Its coherence is irrelevant; in fact, life, as it is presented in the novel, is incoherent, but since it exists, it demands our attention. Torn between the attraction of a disembodied life in which the individual would find his true fulfillment through strict obedience to God's wishes, and the impossibility of achieving this aim because concrete reality forces itself upon each man's consciousness, Sammler can never reach harmony. One may even wonder whether there is or can be any evolution in him. But the main fact is that, even though he strives to refrain from passing judgment on his contemporaries, even though he carefully preserves his position as an outsider, he never for a moment stops caring for man. Collecting facts and visions, finding out that these make no intelligible pattern, do not lead him to the conclusion that the universe is absurd. We may be unable to understand its meaning, but this is no reason why we should stop caring for it.

Although it would be preposterous to assume that Sammler is a mouthpiece for Bellow's views, one must admit that this attitude is somewhat similar to Bellow's statements on novel writing. Discussing the motives that lead a man to write, he said:

> It is possible—all too possible—to say when we have read one more modern novel: "So what? What do I care? You yourself, the writer, didn't really care." It is all too often like that. But this caring or believing or love alone matters. All the rest, obsolescence, historical views, manners, agreed views of the Universe is simply nonsense and trash.[9]

Sammler, like Herzog, has reached the stage when *he* can no longer write, but his life, for what it is worth, represents an attempt at accepting things as they are, at transcending the desire to judge others through what is probably a form of loving kindness. A chance remark on the projected memoir on H. G. Wells casts an interesting light on Sammler's outlook: "The book would take the form of dialogues like those with A. N. Whitehead which Sammler admired so much" (p. 31). One might suggest that this admiration was based on a certain community of views rather than on the use of a form which is certainly not original and evokes the

Wellsian "discussion-novels," which were themselves conceived as imitations of Platonic dialogues. To the interviewer who asked him whether modern writers knew enough, Whitehead replied: "It is true that most great writers did know quite a lot. But it is possible to know too much. What is wanted is our immense *feeling* for things."[10] This is precisely what Sammler experiences: the enormous knowledge accumulated during his past years has been of very little use to him, but his old age is gradually teaching him to feel more and more. The part God plays in our world was defined by Whitehead in these terms:

> God is *in* the world, or nowhere, creating continually in us and around us. This creative principle is everywhere, in animate and so-called inanimate matter, in the ether, water, earth, human hearts. But this creation is a continuous process, and "the process is itself the actuality," since no sooner do you arrive than you start on a fresh journey. In so far as man partakes of this creative process does he partake of the divine, of God, and that participation is his immortality, reducing the question of whether his individuality survives death of the body to the estate of an irrelevancy. His true destiny as co-creator in the universe is his dignity and his grandeur.[11]

There is a rather striking parallelism between this view of God's function and Sammler's final assertion that we *know.* Knowledge does not have to be ordered by the intellect; feeling for things and people without attempting to judge them is a form of knowledge, since it expresses the consciousness of the creative process at work on our planet. It is true that Sammler has chosen a passive stance rather than a creative one, but who knows whether observing things, feeling for them, may not be part of the creative process?

Obviously, Mr. Sammler's lesson is far from clear: dangling between a chaotic world in which most traditional values have disappeared but which however cannot be ignored, and the temptation of an impossible self-imposed isolation, Sammler can only in the end assert his faith in the possibility of communication between the godhead and the inner self of man—but not between man and man. All the same, much of the ambiguity of Sammler's character may be due to Bellow's own attitude toward his creatures. Admittedly, Mr. Sammler's planet is the image of our planet recreated by the imagination of Sammler, just as *Mr. Sammler's Planet* is a child of Bellow's imagination. But the laws of the imagination are not those that govern the outside world and, although Bellow's concern is mainly with the human condition and our basic instinctive curiosity about ourselves, the fact remains that Sammler is primarily a fictional character moving in a fictional world. Here lies the source of Bellow's main ambiguity: Mr. Sammler's planet exists only through the consciousness of the main protagonist, and yet the image thus created tends to give the reader the illusion that he is looking at our own contemporary world; Sammler's experience obeys the laws of fiction, but its ultimate reference is to the condition of modern man and the problem of his identity. These are questions which are in the foreground of modern consciousness, and several critics have remarked on the fact that Bellow, refusing to echo the many contemporary pronouncements on the absurdity of human existence, and to find in a barren formalism the be-all and end-all of novel writing, has deliberately turned his attention to the old theme of the quest of the self. He has even asserted his faith in the didactic function of the novel, but with the important qualification that acceptable ideas do not necessarily make an acceptable novel. When considering the future of the novel, he wrote:

> The novel, to recover and to flourish, requires new ideas about humankind. These ideas in turn cannot live in themselves. Merely asserted, they show nothing but the good will of the author. They must therefore be discovered and not invented. We must see them in flesh and blood. There would be no point in continuing at all if many writers did not feel the existence of these unrecognized qualities. They are present and they demand release and expression.[12]

True enough, except for the fact that fictional characters can never be made of flesh and blood and that the illusion of life is achieved through language. This is a point which no writer can afford to ignore, and Bellow's elaborate craftsmanship shows he is quite aware of it; but, in bypassing the world of fiction—that is, the world of illusion created by means of words—and referring to man as though the process which gives rise to this illusion were taken for granted, he achieves an ambiguity that owes little to the density of the text and much to the writer's attitude.

Basically, *Mr. Sammler's Planet* might be taken as a traditional novel of character, everything in it being centered on the main protagonist's experience. This character is revealed through a dramatization of consciousness, sometimes reminiscent of James's method. But, significantly, Sammler, as we have seen, has stopped writing when the novel beings; caught between two poles of reference, on the one hand Lal's lecture on the moon and Wells's utopian vision of the world state— that is, the part of Wells's work furthest from any literary purpose—and, on the other, the Bible and the writings of the German mystics—that is, works written primarily in order to convey a truth—he is completely divorced from the world of literary representation. Language exists for him only to convey a message or a lesson. He could not be further from the concerns of a novelist.

A great deal of the ambiguity surrounding Bellow's work, and *Mr. Sammler's Planet* in particular, derives from his constant reference to the nonliterary world, that is from an apparent refusal to face the issues of novel writing. And yet the technique used to convey Sammler's experience is particularly significant. It is based on the juxtaposition of linear and nonlinear developments. The three days covered by the narrative represent the linear aspect of the story, but with important qualifications. There is hardly any causal relationship at the level of events: these occur independently of Sammler's reactions, and no motivation is ever made clear. What is more, these three days seem to represent a time selected at random: we start and end *in medias res.* The only element that matters is Sammler's gradually expanding consciousness. Sammler is different at the end only insofar as he has reached a different level of consciousness. And this evolution is conditioned by the influence of two elements presented in a nonlinear way and organically connected with each other. First, the historical past, seen through the writings and thought of various philosophers, novelists, or public figures—in other words, the raw material of history already interpreted and given different significances. Second, Sammler's individual past—that is, a number of localized elements meaningful only because they keep recurring to his mind. What gives them importance is their being recalled by Sammler's consciousness and incorporated in the pictures created by his imagination.

In the end Sammler is left with a consciousness which tends to blur out the exterior world, to dematerialize reality, and to assert the primacy of thoughts and signs over so-called facts. He can claim knowledge but is unable to communicate it, because the only knowledge he can reach is pure essence—that is, something which, not unlike Eckhart's *Gottheit,* has no beginning and no end, cannot be named or apprehended through words. One could argue that the boundary between this uncommunicable knowledge and nothingness is very difficult to define, but to Sammler faith in the ultimate resource of man's consciousness is the only alternative to chaos. To Sammler the world has literally become unspeakable, but even this does not prevent him from probing into the fundamental mystery of mankind. Wells could write "novels of ideas" in which characters talked and talked and talked endlessly; in the seventies Sammler can only rely on pure idea directly shaped by consciousness and, as such, unnamable. The main irony is, of course, that matter cannot be reduced to a semiotic system and that things have a way of imposing themselves on man's body, but, in spite of this fact which Sammler is unable to ignore completely, his final reliance on consciousness represents an act of faith in man. What Bellow refuses is the conclusion reached by many contemporary novelists, that human life is absurd and that literature cannot *say* anything. Bellow is aware of the fact that the forces shaping the self are extremely mysterious and cannot be accounted for by elementary causality, but his characters—and Sammler is conceived as a character, not merely as a "function" in a narrative system—achieve dignity through this quest of the self. In the end, Sammler can hardly communicate more than the Negro pickpocket, but both characters are given a human status by their awareness and acceptance of their condition.

In 1963 Bellow wrote:

> We have so completely debunked the old idea of the Self that we can hardly continue in the same way. Perhaps some power within us will tell us what we are, now that old misconceptions have been laid low. Undeniably the human being is not what he commonly thought a century ago. The question nevertheless remains. He is something. What is he? And this question, it seems to me, modern writers have answered poorly. They have told us, indignantly or nihilistically or comically, how great our error is but for the rest they have offered us thin fare. The fact is that modern writers sin when they suppose that they *know,* as they conceive that physics *knows* or that history *knows.* The subject of the novelist is not knowable in any such way. The mystery increases, it does not grow less as types of literature wear out.[13]

Mr. Sammler's Planet is an attempt at putting this question in fictional terms, and what constitutes Bellow's originality and, at the same time, increases the ambiguity of his work, is this constant reference to the condition of man. His fictional technique, extremely sophisticated and "modern," implies a questioning of the capacity of literature to convey truth and stresses the autonomous quality of the world of the imagination; but on the other hand, Bellow apparently refuses to be concerned with the various problems connected with the creation of artistic illusion by means of writing. Thus, his ontological quest constantly bypasses the level of fictional representation in order to refer directly to a metaphysical question. However, fiction cannot be dismissed so easily, and its requirements create a sort of feedback effect on the extraliterary level, just as linear and nonlinear developments coexist in the novel as opposing elements reconciled by Sammler's unifying consciousness. This does not mean that Bellow is unaware of or uninterested in the problems raised by his medium, but simply that, for him, no novel can find in itself sufficient justification and *raison d'être*. In other words, I believe that *Mr. Sammler's Planet* is basically a didactic work, one that is intended to teach the reader a lesson, not through statements uttered by characters, but through the representation of a fictional world inseparable from Sammler's consciousness. What this lesson is, the reader must decide for himself; Bellow's ideological position is far from clear, but this is hardly to be taken as an artistic weakness. The experience collected by Sammler is presented in religious and philosophical terms: Bellow does not claim he has reached a knowledge that can be communicated to others; he simply asserts that, although the mystery of man cannot be solved, the individual possesses the faculty of reaching a personal intimate knowledge of his own self.

In a dehumanized world balanced on the verge of absurdity, old Sammler asserts the reality of the human condition and his faith in its fundamental value. His planet revolves around him, filling his consciousness with the certainty that there is a meaning, although perhaps not clearly comprehensible, in life and that this life is worth living. The world of the seventies has become a "Country of the Blind" which Sammler's single-eyed sight can perceive only superficially, but this imperfect vision suffices to warrant Bellow's interest and faith in man. This attitude is apparently neither fashionable nor widespread among contemporary American novelists, but it certainly accounts for Bellow's success. Going back to traditional themes while remaining aware of the need for a new form of fictional discourse, is after all an original attitude in these days, and *Mr. Sammler's Planet*, with its depth of vision, its irony which does not lead to self-destruction, and its concern with moral and religious issues, illustrates the validity of a very ancient pronouncement: "I am that I am."

Daniel Royot

2. ASPECTS OF THE AMERICAN PICARESQUE IN "LITTLE BIG MAN"

The French public now considers the American West as part and parcel of its own cultural background. Our critics have thus appropriated the Western and tried hard to make it fit into their Cartesian categories. *Touchez pas à la femme blanche,* a movie on Custer's Last Stand, was made recently in the huge hole dug out after the removal of the Paris "Halles," but its title suggested the Concert Mayol rather than Little Big Horn. After Sergio Leone's baroque operas there is still room for a Nouveau Roman de l'Ouest à la Robbe-Grillet. Such mimesis makes it clear that the American panorama tends to become the metaphor of contemporary European obsessions. French romantic intellectuals confusedly yearn for radical changes of behavior, and American self-conscious attitudes provide vicarious gratifications of such desires. Our age-old addiction to philosophizing is no longer seriously upheld by a sustained artistic vision. As long as American fiction supplies profuse imagery, French critics will be well provided with elaborate methods to change it into sets of symbols. In fact, America currently appears as France's anticipated or dreaded future, thus allowing either expert ratiocination on psychedelic phantasms, gloomy prognosis, or utopian wishful thinking. Any objective appraisal of *Little Big Man* should thus avoid the main pitfall of transcultural criticism, which too often consists of ascribing prophetic value to any postmodernist material trademarked in the United States.

It is true that Thomas Berger's novel appears as a mock-epic depiction of the West. Yet was not American history too compressed ever to evolve a genuine epic genre? Etiological tales have an impact on peoples whose mythopoetic imagination still draws on a lore of superstitions and folk beliefs. But such creeds had already been shattered by the Age of Reason on the eve of independence. In the Middle Ages *La Chanson de Roland* could not afford to stage Charlemagne's nephew slicing twenty Saracens in a row with his magic sword Durandal. On the contrary, American folklore was early in a position to make fun of culture heroes and convert historical giants into comic demigods through tall tales. To a certain extent I agree with Leslie Fiedler that *Little Big Man* is "a compulsive antimythical burlesque,"[1] a parody of the Western formula. Listing all the characters and situations involved in such debunking would certainly constitute a rewarding task. However, the book evinces a certain degree of equivocation which blurs its final impact. Besides, it is generally admitted that the frontier material in *Little Big Man*—whether epic or comic—assumes a literary value. Since Thomas Berger initially judged his work as "a Western to end all Westerns,"[2] its amplitude and comprehensiveness cannot be seriously challenged. Moreover, the novel grows more seriously emblematic in the final sections, thus undergoing an unmistakable tonal change from black humor and irreverence to unqualified horror and solemnity. For instance, the hilarious slaughter of the pioneers on the wagon train in the opening chapters hardly compares with the last vision of gutted corpses and Custer's crucifixion on the battlefield of Little Big Horn. Similarly, Old Lodge Skins, the Cheyenne chief who initiates Jack Crabb into the mysteries of life, is introduced as a type figure of slapstick comedy, but his mythical death eventually transfigures him into a tragic New World bard. The coexistence of satire and drama thus induces a candid foreign reader to analyze *Little Big Man* in the light of the picaresque tradition. Series of converging elements might be gathered under three headings. First, the point of view of the actor-narrator, i. e., Jack Crabb, as central intelligence, social archetype, and American folk hero; second, the basic conflict as revealed through Berger's persona, which entails a clash of mythologies. The picaro's vagrancy amounts to a journey through myths, and the narrative perspective mirrors both the significance and the absurdity of Crabb's straggling itinerary. The third and final point of this study will bear upon the aesthetic implications of the mythological issue. *Little Big Man* not only cuts through social appearances according to the picaresque pattern of successive disclosures but also offers a burlesque treatment of western romance. A willful distortion of genteel fiction and soap operas as a whole, parallels the caricature of approved history. Hopefully, this method might bring out the novelty of the book, especially the manner in which it departs from a genre that dates back to the sixteenth century but first attained American shores with *Moby Dick* and *Huckleberry Finn*.

The earliest evidence of Berger's deliberate use of the picaresque in *Little Big Man* is the name of the man of letters who drags the rogue out of obscurity. Ralph Fielding Snell is the archetype of the meditative writer who collects the memories of the retired tramp. The allusion to the eighteenth-century English novelist obviously foreshadows a mock-heroic picture of the sentimentalized West by means of a mammoth episodic structure, a diversity of settings, ample parallel actions, and an enormous fictional population. However, Snell's credibility remains highly questionable. Not only has he just recovered from a mental collapse, but high-pressure scholarship has also damaged his intellect in the recent past. The fretful, fumbling editor and collector of Americana disqualifies Crabb's account because Crazy Horse does not wear a war bonnet in the old-timer's record. But the question is not whether Snell or Little Big Man should be trusted to evaluate the truth of the story. Throughout the preface and epilogue the reader is implicitly invited to derive no meaning from the novel, a warning which echoes Mark Twain's prefatory note to *Huckleberry Finn*. Perhaps Thomas Berger humorously discredits criticisms which would sprinkle allegorical pepper on a book already seasoned with the zest for life.

Anyway, it is not my intention to find a moral in *Little Big Man* but rather to show how Crabb's unique experience withstands efforts toward generalization. The protagonist asserts his independence as sole operator by establishing a distance between Snell and himself, just as a novelist holds back critics. His system of references is more biological than ideological. In Freudian terms, he thus embodies a principle of reality, whereas Custer stands for the principle of pleasure. His character should not be conceived as a sum of determinations but, on the contrary, as a compendium of indeterminations. In short, Crabb helps reveal the interplay of reality and fiction at work in genteel literary forms; hence the recurrent counterpointing of real events with the juxtaposed parody of them. This has been precisely the function of the picaresque element since *Lazarillo de Tórmes* and *Guzmán de Alfarache*. Initially the genre consists of a series of moral paradigms which reflect an intricate process toward salvation. As an image of the universe, it is both destructive and constructive since the picaro recites comic events conducive to his conversion.

Apparently, Crabb conforms to the archetype as he confesses himself to an honorable listener. However, the twentieth-century would-be convert, perfectly acquainted with the star system, demands an exorbitant financial compensation. The inflationary autobiographical notes of the 111-year old sole survivor of Little Big Horn should thus explain how the West was won and lost. Anyhow, *Little Big Man* substitutes the derisive stylization of daily experience for the idealized picture of a dreamlike Far West and persistently tarnishes the gloss of sham cultural values. Myths become inverted, mankind depreciated but entertaining. In short, the picaro alters inherited visions by disclosing negative signs. Indeed, his own condition makes it easy for him to change our focus on a period of history. Being a loser and an outcast, he can see individuals from below and outside. Meanwhile the rogue's experiences, though breeding disillusion and scepticism, also pave the way to superior self-knowledge. Because of his lower rank Crabb may be more available than anyone else to rediscover purity. Anyhow, throughout his adventures Little Big Man is torn between two selves, as indicated by his patronymic discordance. Similarly, Alemán's picaro in *Guzmán de Alfarache*[3] epitomizes antihonor; he is condemned to abjection by society but compelled to adopt its prejudices for self-preservation. Jack Crabb also remains faced with himself, at the center of irreconcilable principles, ever bound to be his own antagonist. As his vision encompasses two races and mirrors both attraction and repulsion, he divulges the relativity of the notion of honor. Whether in the Cheyenne camps or in western mushroom cities, he is endowed with a double mental equipment, and his personality is built up through subtle dialectics that constantly annihilate former attitudes.

Crabb's depiction of lifestyles reflects his divided allegiance and emphasizes the sheer incompatibility between Palefaces and Redskins, close to one another in space but standing in the same relation as history to prehistory. Therefore, by confusedly though earnestly trying to bridge the gap between the Cheyenne and the whites, Little Big Man expresses spontaneous, irrational empathy. Accordingly, the chameleon style of his freewheeling commentaries bears witness to his protean gifts. To wit, this portrait of Wild Bill Hickok:

> "Hoss," Hickok says, "you are the trickiest little devil I have ever run across. You know there are a couple of hundred men who would give all they owned to get a clear shot at Wild Bill Hickok, and you throw it away." He was laughing, but I reckon somewhere deep he was actually offended, such was his idea of himself. He would rather I had killed him than take pains to show I was basically indifferent to the fact of his existence. (p. 323)[4]

The humorous blending of colloquial and speculative terms delineates a dual point of view. Crabb is the instinctive mid-nineteenth-century frontiersman but also the self-conscious intellectual who successively or simultaneously takes a detached view of his brash actions. The same voluntary incongruity can be detected in the florid use of understatement, hyperbole, Yankee indirection, and absurd skits. When he suggests that some westerners would "screw a snake" (p. 41) if someone held its head, his art of stretching facts in a deadpan manner smacks of Mike Fink's and the ringtailed roarers' acrobatic pranks.

Crabb's metamorphic nature combines the innocent pose with the swashbuckler's swagger while he winks at the audience. The range of his experiences thus permits him to discuss man's temporal and spiritual value with unwavering stoicism and naive though acute perceptiveness. He has outlived the frontier long enough to turn dispassionate and allow comic resilience to parry terror. At any rate, the narrator brings out a social archetype in conformity with our traditional image of the picaro. First, Little Big Man's adventures span twenty-four years while he tears around the West. Apparently, there should be little resemblance between the stratified, rigid Spanish society that gave birth to the literature of roguery and the fluid, inchoate social structures of the western frontier. Yet both were ages of transition when hierarchies no longer seemed to receive the pragmatic sanction of popular consensus. In the sixteenth century Europe suffered from an acute economic crisis which threw underfed crowds around cities while aristocrats desperately clutched their privileges. Meanwhile the rising class of merchants replaced lineage with money as the new criterion for high society membership. Both hidalgos —the lower upper class—and rogues were penniless, but none of them could resolve to work, the former because nobility banned labor, the latter because money could be more easily gained by emulating the trickery of shopkeepers. In *Little Big Man* WASP culture heroes actualize the concept of honor while "white trash" embodies antihonor.

In keeping with the picaresque tradition, Crabb's roguery is atavistic. His erratic father, a phony jack-of-all-trades, turns barber, minister-trickster, Mormon convert, polygamist in the abstract, and worst of all, a good mixer with Indians. Born in a family of lunatics, Little Big Man ends his life in a mental hospital, like his sister Caroline, an oversexed, sadomasochistic alter ego of Calamity Jane. If he thus moves about in a halo of insanity, there should be nothing in his adventures but a self-defeating process. Yet the picaro willingly accepts the law of destiny foreshadowed by his heredity. Captured by the Cheyenne on the Oregon Trail when he was ten years old, he lives five years with the band of Old Lodge Skins, a Redskin Oedipus estranged from the mainstream of Indian society for killing a kinsman. After fleeing from his captors, Crabb, then a western Huck Finn, cannot bear to be "sivilized"[5] by Mr. Pendrake, his puritanical adopted father. While periodically returning to Old Lodge Skins for spiritual regeneration, he earns a living as gambler, bounder, gunslinger, speculator, and buffalo hunter before being selected by history to become the sole survivor of Custer's Last Stand. Though largely partaking of the western mercenary spirit—he ignores ecology when slaughtering herds of buffalo—he assumes his social roles out of necessity but ignores cupidity. Aware that money alone can confer an identity, Crabb readily accepts the most disgraceful functions.

But roguery remains fundamentally irrelevant to financial stability. Fated to live on a shoestring, he appears as a sophisticated bum in search of the good life. Whether idle or busy, the frontier dropout is a delinquent hedonist. In a world of pretense he pays lipservice to accepted ethics and determines to choose an empirical code of behavior. Hence the prevailing struggle within himself between laws which have preordained his existence and his will to transgress them. Thus instinct fights prejudice and psychology conflicts with behavior in his own mind. Crabb cannot afford to remember a former allegiance in a Darwinian universe. For instance, he yells, "God bless George Washington" (p. 114), to attract the soldiers' attention when the Cheyenne are attacked by the U. S. Cavalry at Solomon's Fork. Another time he treacherously stabs a friendly but potentially dangerous Crow. Honor is obviously incompatible with commonality. But vile blood does not preclude humanity. In fact, generosity specifically belongs to the underworld, as shown by Crabb's efforts to save his niece Amelia from the gutter. "What is moral is what you feel good after," he could say like Hemingway when, quite expectedly, Amelia repays him with ingratitude and scorn. A spiritual heir to Huck Finn, he dutifully preserves a sound heart in a deformed conscience. Therefore Little Big Man always manages to avoid complete degradation. "Morally low at sixteen" (p. 164), when he takes up with a Mexican woman in Santa Fe, he nevertheless rises up from his successive self-defeats. His instinct always impels him to change a well-worn identity, even his ethnological commitments, when his personality is threatened with physical and mental annihilation. Within narrow limits Crabb can momentarily alter the course of events, but nothing deflects him from his lifelong companionship with misery. Aware of such dramatic necessity, he deplores the frequency with which circumstances seem to disintegrate upon him shortly after he has got settled in them. The picaro notices that most of his troubles come "from having standards" (p. 164). But his habits of self-accusation do not prevent him from ascribing his immorality to the world's little ironies when he wants to release his guilt complex. His confused moral attitude evinces a dialectic pattern of trials and errors, a constant strife between the promptings of an instinctive moral sense and an uncontrolled lust for life.

Little Big Man is thus torn between the necessity to play roles and his preoccupation with personal integrity. He realizes that society is enslaved to the image it gives itself of human perfection, founded on race and rank. His metamorphic nature enables him to assume varied masks but never to the point of dissolving his character. Anyhow, he retains sufficient sensibility for intense emotional response when harassed by misfortunes. It is the loss of female companions which especially distresses him. Mrs. Pendrake, his puppy love, turns out to be a bitch; Olga, his Swedish wife, held captive by the Cheyenne, finally loses her mind; Sunshine, his squaw, does not survive the Washita massacre. Such events leave him a clownish or prostrate drunkard. But whatever impact the blows of fate may have on him, he soon forgets about former hardships. Like Ishmael in *Moby Dick,* he seems endowed with a sense of invulnerability: Old Lodge Skins has taken over from Queequeg to protect the pagan white happy few. Crabb's natural resilience makes him recognize that he is "mean but not rotten" (p. 95) after so many ordeals. Forgetfullness thus becomes a saving grace. Similarly, it is when he feels utterly despicable that he becomes "a conscious dandy" (p. 155) and chooses flashy clothes to conceal his disgrace to himself.

At this juncture it is useful to compare the American picaro with some of his most significant predecessors. It seems at first that Crabb's ethnological schizophrenia further estranges him from Christian ethics. Moll Flanders, Defoe's antiheroine, identifies her recurrent frustrations as the normal punishment for her guilt, in a typically puritan manner. Gil Blas, Lesage's picaro,[6] ultimately rediscovers bourgeois values. Guzmán de Alfarache's experiences constitute the parable of a moral sermon. Alemán's protagonist also constantly faces a negative image of himself along his back-and-forth movements. Through an inverted process he is always confronted with a reversed unattractive reflection of his personality, wherever he may go. It remains for him to understand belatedly that his roguery is in fact his allotted path to salvation. Antihonor frees man from his baneful chimera and teaches him that social structures are ephemeral and meaningless.

Naturally, Thomas Berger does not suggest such possibilities of atonement, for Jack Crabb never transcends his discordance to adhere to Christian ethics. First of all, he cannot attain a coherent vision of society. Harshly critical of western towns, he comments:

> All you had to do to make an enemy in Dodge was to be seen by another human being: he immediately loathed your guts. . . . I would only have been interested could I have got enough dynamite to blow the whole place sky high. For I was no exception to the rule: I hated everyone there. (p. 347)

But elsewhere he praises the dynamism of Denver and sets the whites' spirit of enterprise against Cheyenne nomadism:

> Indians loved their land, but the peculiarity was that the most miserable cabin of a white man had a relation to the earth that no nomadic Redskin could claim. One way of looking at it was that in any true connection, each thing being joined makes a mark on the other: a tree, say, is fastened to the earth and vice versa. In Denver, they was erecting buildings now with foundations; not only on the ground but in it; so that if one day the whites left that place again, it would still bear their brand for a long time. I never heard of a natural force that would tear cellar walls from the earth. (p. 182)

Crabb's impressions sometimes suggest the naturalistic lyricism of Frank Norris. The West both fascinates and repels him as he emphasizes the grandeur of elemental forces and the squalor of mining camps. Thus, the identity of Berger's picaro cannot be merely found in an archetype emerging from a dialectic conflict between good and evil. Instead of merely narrating the ups and downs of moral life, Crabb reports on the way Little Big Man devours space and time. In fact, his to and fro motions in the West reduce distance and duration. Through such motions he also deflates the western myths, since through him immensities become graspable. As ubiquitous as Moby Dick, Crabb offers a condensed view of anthropological ventures. Perhaps Lévi-Strauss would have contrived a similar story if he had been requested to write a Western dime-novel overnight. As ethnological material becomes the fabric of the picaresque tale, the persona has to be grounded in folklore, were it only to denounce it from inside.

In fact, Jack Crabb is the ebullient, self-assertive, preternaturally clever yarn spinner whose candid pose tones down a narrative otherwise horrifying. In a way, his homespun commentary constitutes an understatement of American heroic self-projections. He reveals how absurdly normal people can behave under the pressure of a strange environment. His recording often sounds like a hoax, but the West was actually outrageous, unbelievable, hilarious, and terrifying. The reduction of horror to comedy could thus be worked through the pseudonaive commentator. Making fun of appalling dangers strengthened the pioneer's courage. The tall tale belittled forces formerly judged ominous or indomitable. While Jack Crabb kids the West, Little Big Man straddles the Pacific slope and sways imaginations. He is both heroic and homely, subhuman as picaro and superman as frontier comic demigod, a Davy Crockett of the Platte. Mystifying and mystified, he masquerades through the American past revived by comics.

But he is also a more elaborate figure: his dichotomy suggests Thurber's little man and the mighty midget of cartoons. A paleface David versus prairie Goliaths but cringing before buxom white females, he has Priapus' erectile stamina with his three Indian sisters-in-law on the eve of the Washita massacre. As a matter of fact, Little Big Man achieves unity as a trickster, whereas Leatherstocking, Cooper's splendid "moral hermaphrodite" as Balzac tagged him, was a romantic symbol of racial reconciliation. At any rate, the trickster belongs to both white and Indian cultures. Confronted with restrictive laws, he determines to give egotistical freedom to personal action. By turns a wise fool, a buffoon, or a shrewd ignoramus, he never acts in full consciousness. He clouds the reader's vision with suggestions of lawless, anarchistic disorder. Actuated by no spirit of rebellion, he prefers to get around taboos instead of waging losing battles. Little Big Man thus represents the compensatory myth of the small creature that overpowers larger enemies, a welcome change from the narcissistic, hieratic he-men who occupied the scene before postmodernist criticisms extirpated those dinosaurs. His mock showdown with Bill Hickok and his various single-handed fights with Redskins illustrate this function. Thrown among strangers, he relies on his mental and physical pliability. His vagrancy should make him a permanent misfit, but the outsider readily turns into an interloper. He thus gains such versatility as allows him to point to the lack of common sense in his new surroundings. Too innocuous a lawbreaker to threaten order, Little Big Man dangles between value systems. He only mildly subverts legality by cheating at poker or swindling a jeweler. As picaro and trickster, he refuses to be recruited to specific moral views. Confronted with absurd situations, he remains a western Sisyphus in permanent exile, with memories of lost homes but with no hope for a promised land. His emotional instability reflects his mental uncertainties. At times he despises the Cheyenne or hates them, but later, when back with the whites, he misses their smell. In the same ironic manner he is celebrated by the Indian tribe: they ascribe to him supernatural powers after he kills the Crow who initially spared his life. However, he does not quite experience the qualms of Henry Fleming in the *Red Badge of Courage,* though the situation is identical. Later he wants to take revenge on Custer who had his Cheyenne family murdered at Washita, but sympathizes with him when looking at his pathetically receding "yellow" hair.

The West has gone topsy-turvy—or rather, the real West takes over from the mythical—making it hard for Little Big Man to disentangle himself from a web of absurdities. In the cruel game of hide-and-seek with the Indians, the Seventh Cavalry retaliates on innocents. Conversely, the Redskin warriors slaughter peaceful ranchers. However, Little Big Man does not surrender to nihilism. On the contrary, he often fights back with a cheerful heart. In the midst of the battle of Washita, he saves Old Lodge Skins, who was blinded four years earlier at Sand Creek. But first the aging chief had told him to sit down beside him and smoke. Such a fatalistic, suicidal point of view, unexpected with a determined leader, is challenged by his white adopted son who draws him out of the tepee. Immediately after, Old Lodge Skins shoots a soldier with renewed gusto. Such scenes clearly epitomize the impossibility of inferring coherent judgments from individual behavior. Therefore, the American picaro is left without his bearings in a meaningless universe, like Sisyphus pushing his rock.

Picaresque antihonor can only be defined in contrast with the aristocrat's concept of honor. According to Leslie Fiedler, it would seem that such duality never quite applied to the American literary scene. He states:

> What is involved in the mythology of class is the projection by adherents to the Code of honor of all which that Code forbids them on to certain members of their society—different not ethnically, but in training, garb, diet, speech, habits of love making, etc. Such a mythology leads to the creation of characters like Sancho Panza and Leperello, privileged cowards and boors who have no precise counterpart in our literature. Similarly, the comradeship of gentleman and manservant is unheard of in classic American books. . . . [7]

In the picaresque tradition the love-hate relationships between nobles and rogues suggest the Custer–Little Big Man diptych as reflected in the Little Big Horn–Little Big Man anticlimactic conjugation. The European picaro questions the moral standards of hidalgos and merchants while seeking dignity amidst harships which he persistently deems transitory. A sense of transcendence underlies his apparent carelessness and cynicism when he sees the human condition as a prey to tragic ironies.

On the contrary, Berger's persona more easily transcends social antagonisms. Yet Crabb's connection with Custer cannot fail to recall the contrasting and complementary attitudes of Don Quixote and Sancho Panza. American aristocracy as seen through *Little Big Man* is also based on lineage and military expertise. Custer emerges as a replica of the hidalgo who defends his ideal of chivalry against primitive, occult powers. He is even more averse to the white renegades who betray their race than to his Cheyenne opponents, the WASP general's favorite sparring partners until Little Big Horn. Whereas the fundamental opposition between honor and anti-honor does not affect western philistines, the Seventh Cavalry and the Cheyenne tribe are synecdoches of a vanishing frontier spirit which, anachronistically, Custer tries to maintain. But the Knight with the Sorrowful Countenance tilted only at windmills. Custer's attitude, just as irresponsible, entails a good deal of violence reminiscent of Goya's *Disasters of War*. The other frontier demigod, Bill Hickok, stands halfway between the American hidalgo and the "fishbellywhite" (p. 85) underdog.[8] In fact, he perfectly fits the image of the Spanish "squire." Both figureheads are burlesqued by Crabb, who, unabashed, enters the rarefied world of WASP obsolete chivalry.

George Armstrong Custer offers a contrasting image to the picaro. At first he looks like an archangel of the prairie, riding a prancing mare, an insecure narcissistic adolescent who conscientiously plays the part of the heroic general in a soap opera. "Everything he done said to all other living creatures: I win and you lose" (p. 274). The public's great favorite, he is hated for his courage but everyone acknowledges his inborn authority. Custer thus embodies brutal aggressiveness disguised as military gusto. Self-centered, arrogant, he is also compassionate, odious, inaccessible. Such is Crabb's impression of him before Little Big Horn: "Well I expect Custer was crazy enough to believe he would win, being the type of man who carries the whole world within his own head and thus when his passion is aroused and floods his mind, reality is utterly drowned" (p. 404). His single-mindedness gives him a sense of invulnerability, but basically he is inadequate. He belongs to a caste of easterners who "come West for adventure in them days, like the frontier was some type of exhibit put on for their education and entertainment, rather than the often mortal matter it was for us who lived there permanent" (p. 402). Custer replicates a Tom Sawyer who would have gone west, still encumbered with the Walter Scott paraphernalia. In the picaresque tradition the hidalgo also devotes his efforts to showing off and thus compensating for his subjection to those who actually hold power. With similar grudging haughtiness Custer rails at General Grant and his corrupt politicians.

Custer's tragic flaw is his incapacity to reach maturity and learn from experience. Losing his hair too soon, he has to give up his "usual natty habits" (p. 377). Therefore, the young old man becomes a powerless Samson, since in his world appearance seems to condition reality. Hence his inability to confront the Sioux at Little Big Horn when, for the first time, they do not see themselves in a hunting game: "Our adversary was 100 per cent red. It was simply that they no longer fought for fun but was out to kill us the most effective manner with the least damage to themselves" (p. 413). Custer cannot acknowledge the reality of defeat when he sees his army dwindling around him. In an ultimate address he abuses the enemy, accusing them of having shattered his dreams.

Hickok is as insecure as Custer in his impersonation of the fastest draw of the West. Though he cannot claim charisma, he takes pains to conform to his myth. Like the "squire" who does not quite belong, Wild Bill appears shadowy, unpredictable, vain, though never hateful. With him Berger splits up the image of the westerner, opposing his innate skill to his mental defectiveness and physical fragility. Hickok reminds Crabb of a "real tall girl" (p. 323) with small hands, long, blond, curly locks, and "a fleeting glance from sky-blue eyes." Meanwhile he can shoot ten bullets into the O of a saloon sign at a hundred yards. Neither mad nor cowardly, he seeks new means by which to risk his life, but he loathes killing. He constantly seeks to offer new tokens of his honor and, according to Crabb, would be the ideal sheriff type rather than the outlaw. Obsessed with personal promotion but rejected by the upper caste, the "squire" desperately tries to conform to the ideal image of the hidalgo. With Little Big Man, Hickok trains a perfect adversary to add to his glory, but the picaro tricks the master at the final showdown by dazzling him with a mirror placed in his ring. This betrayal ruins a man who cherishes reputation more than life. An egotistical meliorist, Wild Bill keeps staking his life in the unending process of self-improvement as Crabb's comment reveals: "In fact I don't think Hickok enjoyed anything. Life to him consisted of doing what was necessary, endlessly measuring his performance against the single perfect shot for each occasion. He was what you call an idealist" (p. 318). Further on Crabb adds: "That was the trouble with them long haired darlings like him and Custer: people talked about them too much" (p. 323).

Intent on gaining historical recognition, both Custer and Hickok lose touch with the real while building up their own myths. They eventually prove unable to hold their ranks but still conceal the ridiculous distress of men who sacrifice themselves to a chimera. Like Don Quixote they desperately try to abide by obsolete values and thus become ideological misfits. More pathetic than farcical, their attitude is in keeping with what George Lukacs calls "abstract idealism."[9] They both forget about the distance between the self and the ideal. When reality is not equal to their dreams, they ascribe their disillusion to weird powers. True mythic heroes would eventually triumph because they could measure up their forces against the universe. On the contrary, Berger's burlesque demigods only seize a perverted image of the world. They are obsessed with an ideal which they consider as the sole reality. The intensity of their sublime vision also enhances the grotesque contradiction between the vagaries of their imagination and solid facts. In short, they can no longer bridge the gap between spirit and action as their idealistic ravings are conducive to erratic behavior. Impervious to either doubt or despair about the necessity of their ludicrous task, they wage losing battles. Their fatal inadequacy urges them to choose violence to confirm their identities. Accordingly, they hasten to take action, for the world which they face seems pregnant with heroic potentialities. However, they bypass the essential. Furthermore, their lofty ideal gradually changes them into inveterate monomaniacs. Custer does not even hear when Crabb calls him a bastard; later he blames the Indians for their lack of fair play. Hickok also attributes his madness to the insignificance of the world around him. Berger's knights errant inextricably combine grandeur and paranoia. Conversely, Crabb's down-to-earth commentary evokes the American Don Quixote's incongruous quest in terms which always suggest that no class has a monopoly of truth. Yet the thematic conflict which opposes honor to antihonor largely overlaps social issues in *Little Big Man.* Perhaps Berger's original contribution to a renewal of the picaresque could be found in his introduction of a newfangled notion of honor through the picaro's spiritual odyssey among the Cheyenne.

From his privileged standpoint Little Big Man beholds two contiguous cultures in his lifetime. Any contact between white and Indian societies is bound to start a process of elimination. Few like Lavender, the Negro who marries a squaw, work hard toward racial integration. Crabb thus demonstrates the impossibility of acculturation for those who, unlike him, have no magic power. Berger castigates the white vision of a static, inalterable Indian society but also the Cheyenne willful ignorance of whatever exists beyond their experience. Each race judges the other barbarous, accusing the so-called barbarians of belonging to wildlife because they have different norms of behavior. The Cheyenne thus limit the notion of mankind to their own tribe, the Human Beings. Strangers are assimilated to ghosts. When Old Lodge Skins first met Jack and Caroline, "he at last decided we was demons and only waiting for dark to steal the wits from his head; and while riding along he muttered prayers and incantations to bring us bad medicine" (p. 46). Elsewhere, in a Cheyenne etiological tale, it is recalled that the Redskins took the Wasichu, or whites, for grizzly bears. Therefore, both races negate what clashes with their emotions or ideas. Naturally, Berger seasons such anthropological developments with humor, suggesting kinky physiological reasons for their ethnocentrism. For instance, he asserts that an Indian sneezes when he encounters a white woman. Only Crabb and Old Lodge Skins ignore primitive racial discrimination and prove capable of judging men in their own image. However, Little Big Man is never possessed of the Cheyenne warrior's equanimity. Too often emotional commitments obscure his rational views. Intolerant, self-opinionated, unduly abusive toward the natives, he may thus misunderstand the Cheyenne system of values and detect absurd prejudices in their attitudes. The fact that they did not invent the wheel nor take it after the white man he ascribes to their dislike of regular, monotonous movement. It is difficult to see how far Berger is kidding Crabb or Margaret Mead, racial discrimination or anthropological extrapolations. However, it is not simply an apt substitute for the WASP code of honor which is to be derived from the Cheyenne outlook on life but a deep-seated conception of man's dignity. Whereas Custer lapses from grandeur to absurdity, Old Lodge Skins insensibly grows from farce to tragic myth. Sometimes the reader's appreciation of him may be ambiguous. When he magnanimously forgives the whites for having let them rape the pioneers' wives and cause havoc in the wagon train, Old Lodge Skins, while offering material compensation only alleges that whiskey has a boomerang value, and thus politely resents white pollution. His leniency indirectly ridicules the westerner's sense of superiority.

The Cheyenne philosophy of life is based on a network of sense impressions which intimately connect man with the universe. Yet, whereas a Cooper Indian ceremoniously displays outstanding flair in those solemn Leatherstocking tales which Mark Twain tagged the "Broken Twig Series,"[10] Berger uses quips to suggest the underlying seriousness of the Cheyenne syncretic vision. For instance, a jackrabbit owes a grudge to Old Lodge Skins because he had exhorted a prairie fire to burn the hares' homes; elsewhere a frog calls a Cheyenne an insulting name. Leo Oliva has shown that Crabb's picture of Cheyenne cosmogony and rituals is accurate when compared with scholarly studies.[11] At any rate, despite its mock-heroic tone, *Little Big Man* vindicates the Redskin's primitive ethics. Cheyenne life is framed by customs which have become laws. The tribesmen's social obligations correspond to the needs of daily experience. Hence, the sense of honor originates in a coherent pragmatic approach to reality. Killing another Cheyenne is the worst crime because it endangers the life of the community. Otherwise, giving death partakes of a natural process, all creatures—whether vegetal, mineral, or animal—being linked together in the life and death cycle in accordance with a cosmic circular movement. Such phenomena do not merely suggest the concrete world but a multifaceted universe of which the former is the visible face. The Cheyenne thus trust their instinct and memorize their sensations for ulterior experiences. Such intuitive monism enables them to maintain ethnocentric pride but also induces them to keep their vision to themselves: sacredness precludes proselytization. On the contrary, WASP honor incites to moral imperialism and impels the whites to conquer the minds of the vanquished. Moreover, the westerner seems in metaphysical trouble, since he apparently strays around, looking hopelessly for the center of the world like a forlorn crusader. When Old Lodge Skins sees death approaching, he understands that the Cheyenne will be ultimately wiped out from the face of the earth. But he also senses that their power may be instilled in those inferior white beings who, so far, have brought spiritual death in their train.

The Indian's sportive love of risks and unwavering self-reliance are thus utterly incompatible with the muddled, abstract code of the whites. Similarly, Crabb opposes the sense of freedom prevailing among the Cheyenne to the absolutism of repressive Christianity as shown in the following comment:

> "The works of the flesh," answers the Reverend. "And 'the works of the flesh are manifest, which are these: adultery, fornication, uncleanness, lasciviousness, idolatry, witchcraft, hatred, variance, emulation, wrath, strife, seditions, heresies, envyings, murders, drunkenness, revellings and such like.'" It was a funny thing the most important years of my rearing so far had been handled by my second father, who was Old Lodge Skins. Now you take away "envying" from that list—for he did not covet much, owing to his belief he had everything of importance already—and you had a perfect description of that Indian's character. Yet he was as big a success among the Cheyenne as a man could be. (p. 140)

By watching the Cheyenne from inside, Crabb substitutes admiration, tolerance, and amusement for repulsion or fascination as aroused by traditional Westerns. It is true that, in the fifties Delmer Daves's *Broken Arrow* and Samuel Fuller's

Run of the Arrow had already replaced the symbolic Indian with a more realistic figure. However, Berger's image is even more forceful as it combines mythic, comic, and tragic elements, which add depth to his characterization. Introducing Negroes or Indians too good to be true, American writers overreached themselves in the past. If only Jim had had a streak of bad faith in *Huckleberry Finn,* Twain would be completely exonerated: but the self-conscious southerner could not go that far.

Little Big Man gives mock serious though convincing utterance to the American thematic conflicts between European and native cultures, mind and instinct, individual and society, Christianity and paganism. As W. Pilkington stresses, "Like Faulkner's humor, while it often depends for its effect on the absurd or the grotesque, it sheds revealing light, not only on regional attitudes and myths but on the human condition as well."[12] Should we thus regard Berger's book as a successful blend of western history and myth, "an extended cultural parable"[13] on the dilemma of civilization versus barbarity, as Turner puts it? Tentative definitions abound. For Elliott, the tale buckles under excess baggage—"epic, mock epic, anthropology, historical research, popular lore, TV westerns, Wild West pulp magazines."[14] Walker contends: "It is a Cowboys and Indians version of *Tom Jones,* Pecos picaresque, to coin a genre," but "the book ends up not working, its force dissipated, the fantastic unreality of the plot undercuts the reality of the narrative style and vividness of incidents."[15]

Leaving aside the controversy, it might be inferred from those multiple views that *Little Big Man* is first and foremost a spoof of the "true narrative" literary type. Originally the picaresque also denounces dominant aristocratic ideology through a parody of its idealizing fiction. Romantic genteel fiction gradually crumbled because its undermined literary forms were frequently put to a quizzical use. In France, Voltaire's *Candide*[16] combined the fantastic unreality of the tale with a picaresque debunking of the genre in its depiction of wars. Though censorship did now allow an overt reinterpretation of history in the eighteenth century, Voltaire nevertheless established that history was linked with individual destinies in accordance with the picaresque wheel of fortune. Similarly, *Little Big Man* constitutes an apocalyptic climax which closes the cycle of the Western Saga, floundering in grim absurdity. But the tragic inevitability of the plot is paralleled with seemingly haphazard episodes. Characters circulate in an open world, appear and disappear, apparently free from causality but actually dependent on the whims of unpredictable historical elements. Picaresque fiction is apocopate, elliptic, thus distorting the glamorous coherence of romance. The genteel tale is unpreoccupied with explicit social criticism while unraveling fanciful sequences of incidents; the accumulation of adventures seems to challenge the possibilities of life; individuals have distinctive features harmoniously combining physical with mental delineations; fiction is thus exhibited as such, unconcealed by artifice as in a novel. The teller of tales does not seek verisimilitude, whereas the novelist manages to have his story ring true with characters and events that look like reality. Moreover, Time and Space are mythical in a tale. Therefore, the sudden intrusion of realistic elements subverts its pattern and distorts the expected *données.*

Little Big Man is, in this respect, instinct with romantic elements. Coups de théâtre, recognition scenes, fortuitous meetings, reversals of situations, and coincidences seem to liken the story to some Walter Scott material. But the subplots, though intertwined with the principal action, reveal the superficiality of fiction compared to the tragic necessity of history. What surrounds the battle of Little Big Horn in the book is a fresco of mental stereotypes accumulated in age-old western Americana. The coexistence of pathos and parody abolishes the unity of the romantic approach by disintegrating the fictional process.

Another picaresque distortion of romance is to be found in Berger's manipulation of the marvelous. The Cheyenne's lifestyle suggests the usefulness and the limits of utopian fantasies. Crabb's back and forth movements both initiate the reader into a daydream universe and point to the absurdity of transcultural experiences in nineteenth-century America. Hence the dual treatment of Indian animism. Old Lodge Skins uncannily combines sense perceptions and intuitions, a privilege which the Cheyenne consider as a divine gift. He visualizes the elephants which adorn the soda fountain when Crabb is staying with the Pendrakes at Leavenworth; during a hunt his eyes focus miles away in order to catch an antelope. In the death scene he summons the rain from a cloudless sky before forming with his spiritual son a community of saints, reminiscent of Huck and Jim on the Mississippi. The Cheyenne believe in "sympathetic magic," which implies permanent union between objects or beings formerly in contact with each other, and throughout their nomadic lives use their outlandish power to overcome adversity. But the marvelous of Indian supernaturalism is tragically inoperative with the whites. At the Battle of Solomon Fork, Crabb notices first:

> We was still holding back our power, bottling it up while working the charm, paralyzing the whites by our magic as we walked in the sacred way. (p. 113)

But a moment later, he observes:

> Now we was the paralyzed, and froze to our ground until the oncoming ranks was within one hundred yards, then seventy five and then we burst into fragments and fled uttermost rout. The magic, you see, had been good against bullets, not the long knives. (p. 114)

The structural disjunction achieved by the intrusion of the realistic element in a tale is also conspicuous in the disparity between physical features and mental attitudes, especially reversing the genteel norms of female fragile beauty and male cool virility. Therefore, a character's countenance generally contrasts with his psychology. Old Lodge Skins, the handsome, stately Cheyenne, is at first foolish and savage; Mr. Pendrake, the forbidding minister, proves a gluttonous cuckold; Allardyce T. Meriweather appears as a smart, benevolent crook; Amelia, the dainty, priggish teenager, rises from whoredom to wealthy respectability:

> Now I know that with the normal dirtiness of mind in which a person picks up someone else's reminiscences, you are expecting to find sooner or later that Amelia went back to her earlier ways. People just hate to see others reform.

I just have to disappoint you. There wasn't no force on earth that could have kept Amelia from becoming a fine lady now she had got a taste of it. (p. 334)

Mrs. Pendrake, the refined, immaculate minister's wife, is a nymphomaniac. Such devices help expose the basic nonsensicality of romantic characterization by giving verisimilitude to perverted behavior, wickedness being a return to normalcy. It is in fact this discordance with creates the specific value of *Little Big Man.*

In picaresque fiction reading thus amounts to deciphering. Characters are seen in profile with a camera eye until they slacken their pace. Then the writer changes our focus on them so that they acquire transparency. Innumerable signifiers correspond in fact to a few formalized meanings. Therefore, the reader naturally converts clues into signs as plots crop up. Meanwhile neither do we watch characters developing in a unique time sequence but, on the contrary, observe them at separate stages of their lives, once they have attained fixity. Throughout her adventures Caroline is shown as a frustrated female, forever humiliated at not having been raped by the Cheyenne. In whatever circumstances she may be, it is this aspect of her character that delineates her caricature. Moreover, all her abortive love affairs give an impression of redundance in spite of their multiplicity. For instance, she is a luckless rival of Calamity Jane, then of a homosexual male nurse during the Civil War, among many other mishaps:

> The point was that while Caroline survived them romantic disasters in her earlier years, she wasn't getting any younger. Indeed, she was forty four if she was a day, and hadn't so far as I knowed ever got married yet, which she had been trying to do as far back as '52 when the drunken Cheyenne massacred our menfolk.
> But you couldn't have told it from her appearance. She had looked much the same for twenty years except, as I mentioned, her front teeth was knocked out and her ear was some chawed up, etc. (p. 357)

Similarly, Little Big Man seems arrested in his physical development early in life. In fact, he has ceased to grow for the whites but, conversely, has found a coherent physical aspect with the Cheyenne. However, after Little Big Horn, removed from his familiar Indian surroundings, he returns to destitution and accomplishes the Cheyenne prophecy by becoming a black bird, "a large turkey buzzard" (p. 17). His experiences have wrung out the incoherence and disorder of life in "a tale full of sound and fury told by an idiot." Retrospectively historical reality looks like a hoax because the American past appears as a sustained tall tale. Ultimately Little Big Man's picaresque adventures teach that reality is at best seen as someone's make-believe. A French reader might be tempted to regard *Little Big Man* as a sarcastic, slightly masochistic condemnation of the way the West was won, assimilating the civilization of the New World to "antinature" on behalf of current hip values. Yet, though Thomas Berger lampoons the western saga by ironically inverting its mythical values, he nevertheless recaptures the Herculean ebullience of pioneer life with nostalgia. Jack Crabb dramatically shifts from one civilization to the other but fails in his effort to save both. Perhaps the movie was more trendy than the book since Old Lodge Skins was first unable to achieve a proper mythical death. Altogether, Berger's novel fits into a secular American tradition which describes a quest and an initiation organized in a masquerade. By dint of the picaresque approach Berger derides individual disintegration, mental diseases, cultural taboos, reason, and logic, but his satire is progressively diluted in black humor. It is perhaps the kind of attitude that some French readers would misinterpret since they trust American fads too much and do not realize that humor may be conservative rather than subversive. They believe in the lethal power of words, whereas American social criticism most often transmutes itself into either madcap fantasies or provocative exhibitionism. Jack Crabb is no radical dropout keeping *Without Marx or Jesus* in his pocket, but an American picaro teasing his reader out of conformity and confirming once more America's saving grace which is to laugh at herself.

André Bleikasten

3. THE HERESY OF FLANNERY O'CONNOR

L'écriture est pour l'écrivain, même s'il n'est pas athée, mais s'il est écrivain, une navigation première et sans grâce.

Jacques Derrida

A devout Roman Catholic, Flannery O'Connor was not reluctant to acknowledge her Christian position as a novelist. A hazardous position for a writer to adopt: literature and orthodoxy—religious or otherwise—make uneasy bedfellows. He who knows, or thinks he knows, the answers even before the questions have been asked, may be sincere as a person but compromises his honesty as a writer. Literature has its own truths, elusive and modest; truths it generates in close cooperation with each individual reader outside the massive certainties and ready-made patterns of fixed beliefs. This does not mean, of course, that religious faith—especially one so pregnant with mystery and so rich in paradox as the Christian faith—cannot find its way into literary texts, but that it can only do so at the cost of temporary suspension. What has prevented Bernanos, Mauriac, T. S. Eliot, and other so-called "Christian writers" from becoming trapped in apologetics is the fact that in their best work the demands of writing clearly prevailed over their private preconceptions, impelling them, whatever their avowed goals, to use language in such ways as to make it an instrument of questioning rather than of affirmation, and to produce texts whose plural significance no amount of exegesis is likely ever to exhaust.

Flannery O'Connor's work is no exception to this rule of the literary game, although the validity of the rule has seldom been fully recognized by her critics. Admittedly, no reader can fail to discern the permanence and seriousness of her religious concerns. Fall and redemption, nature and grace, sin and innocence—every one of her stories and novels revolves around these traditional Christian themes. It is hardly surprising that O'Connor should have acknowledged close affinities with Hawthorne. Her fiction is of a coarser fabric than his, less delicately shaded in its artistry and far less muted in its effects, but it belongs without any doubt to the same tradition of American romance: characters and plots matter less than "the power of darkness" one senses behind them; symbol, allegory, and parable are never far away, and with O'Connor as with Hawthorne, the accumulated mass of allusions and connotations derives in a very large measure from the rich mythology of Christian culture. The temptation is therefore great to decipher works like theirs through the cultural and hermeneutic codes which the Christian tradition provides, and in O'Connor's case it is all the more irresistible since we have the author's blessing. Yet between intended meanings and completed work there is necessarily a gap, whatever the writer's efforts to close it. In the creative process the author's shaping mind is not alone at play, and language uses him as much as he uses language. Literature always says something more—or something else—than what it was meant to say. Its order is that of multivalence and reversibility. Ambiguity is its very life.

Not that we should feel free to discount the writer's intentions, and to discard the conscious assumptions on which his work was built as irrelevant to critical inquiry. But we can dispense with his approving nods over our shoulders while we read his books. O'Connor's public pronouncements on her art—on which most of her commentators have pounced so eagerly—are by no means the best guide to her fiction. As an interpreter, she was just as fallible as anybody else, and in point of fact there is much of what she has said or written about her work that is highly questionable. The relationship between what an author thinks, or thinks he thinks, and what he writes, is certainly worth consideration. For the critic, however, what matters most is not the extent to which O'Connor's tales and novels reflect or express her Christian faith, but rather the problematical relation between her professed ideological stance and the textual evidence of her fiction.

SEEDY SATAN

Ideologically O'Connor was an eccentric. Her commitments were definitely off-center: antisecular, antiliberal, antiindividualistic, and she had as little patience with the cozy assumptions of conventional humanism as with the bland pieties and anemic virtues of its fashionable Christian variants. What counted for O'Connor was not so much man as his soul, and perhaps not so much his soul as the uncanny forces that prey on it. Hers is a world haunted by the sacred—a sacred with two faces now distinct and opposed, now enigmatically confused: the divine and the demonic. Hence, we find in most of her characters the double postulation noted by Baudelaire: one toward God, the other toward Satan.

In accordance with this dual vision, the human scene becomes in her fables the battleground where these two antagonistic powers confront each other and fight for possession of each man's soul. To judge from O'Connor's hellish chronicle, however, the chances hardly seem to be equal. To all appearances, Evil wins the day. Or rather: Satan triumphs. For in her world Evil is not just an ethical concept; it is an active force, and it has a name, personal, individual. In the middle of the twentieth century O'Connor, like Bernanos, was rash enough to believe not only in God but also in the Devil. And, like the French novelist, she had the nerve to incorporate him into her fiction. In *The Violent Bear It Away* we first hear his voice—the voice of the friendly "stranger" who accompanies young Tarwater during his tribulations; then we see him in the guise of a homosexual sporting a black suit, a lavender shirt, and a broad-rimmed panama hat. For the reader he may be little more than a *diabolus ex machina;* for the author, however, he was not just a handy device: "I want to be certain that the devil gets identified as the devil and not simply taken for this or that psychological tendency."[1]

But the Devil does not have to strut about the stage to persuade us of his existence and power. Reflected in the implacable mirror O'Connor holds up to it, the whole world becomes transfixed in a fiendish grimace: mankind has apparently nothing to offer but the grotesque spectacle of its cruel antics. At first glance, it almost looks as if all souls had already been harvested by the Demon. For, despite O'Connor's firm belief in the existence of immortal souls, her world strikes us most often as utterly soulless. There is indeed little to suggest the "depths" and "secrets" of inner life which are the usual fare of religious fiction. The ordinary condition of most of her heroes is one of extreme emotional exhaustion and spiritual numbness, and from that catatonic torpor they only emerge to succumb to the destructive forces of violence or insanity. Moreover, in their deathlike apathy as well as in their sudden convulsions, O'Connor's characters are ruthlessly stripped of any pretense to dignity. People, in her fiction, suffer and die, but pettily, just as they are pettily evil. Wrenching from the Devil the dark, handsome mask afforded him by romantic satanism, O'Connor exposes his essential banality and restores him to his favorite hunting ground: the everyday world. The color of evil, in her work, is gray rather than black—a grim grayness set off by lurid splashes of red. Its face is difficult to distinguish from that of mediocrity, and its most characteristic expression is meanness. The banality of evil is what brings it within range of mockery: insofar as it thrives on human folly and wretchedness, it becomes laughable.

Yet with O'Connor laughter is never harmless, and her savage humor seldom provides comic release. It is not an elegant way of defusing horror. Far from dissolving evil in farce, it emphasizes its demonic character, and calls attention to its terrifying power of perversion and distortion. Woven into the fabric of everydayness, evil becomes trivial, but at the same time the world of common experience is defamiliarized and made disquieting through its contagion by evil. Under Satan's sun the earth spawns monsters. O'Connor's tales drag us into a teratological nightmare, a ludicrous Inferno partaking at once of a hospital ward, a lunatic asylum, a menagerie, and a medieval *Cour des Miracles.* Like a Brueghel painting or a Buñuel film, the stories of *A Good Man Is Hard to Find* invite us to a sinister procession of freaks and invalids: a 104-year-old general, doddering and impotent ("A Late Encounter with the Enemy"), a retarded deaf-mute, a one-armed tramp ("The Life You Save May Be Your Own"), a hermaphrodite ("A Temple of the Holy Ghost"), and a thirtyish bluestocking with a weak heart and a wooden leg ("Good Country People"). Elsewhere the same obsession with infirmity is attested by the presence of a hideous clubfoot (Rufus in "The Lame Shall Enter First"), or reverberates through the theme of blindness (Hazel Motes in *Wise Blood*) or deafness (Rayber in *The Violent Bear It Away*). And just as evil deforms, corrupts, and maims the body, it distills its poisons into the mind. There are almost as many cases of mental debility in O'Connor as in Faulkner, and there is hardly a character in her fiction whom a psychiatrist would not identify as, at least, neurotic. Most of her stories deal with sick individuals entrapped in sick families: they oppose domineering father figures (grandfathers and great-uncles more often than fathers) and possessive, ghoulish mothers to rebellious and helpless children, and they end almost invariably in explosions of violence, if not in death.[2]

O'Connor's penchant for freaks, idiots, and cripples, her fascination with the morbid, macabre, and monstrous, are traits she shares with many southern writers. The same gothic vein can be found to varying degrees in Erskine Caldwell, Eudora Welty, Carson McCullers, William Goyen, and Truman Capote, as well as in William Faulkner. Like them, she belongs to the manifold progeny of Poe. Yet the primal function assumed in her art by the grotesque cannot be explained away by fashion or tradition. Nor can one ascribe it merely to the gratuitous play of a perverse imagination. O'Connor used the grotesque very deliberately, and if it became one of her privileged modes, it was because she thought it fittest to express her vision of reality. As she herself stated, its meaning in her fiction is closely linked to her religious concerns; in her eyes, the grotesque can no more be dissociated from the supernatural than evil can be separated from the mysteries of faith.[3] The grotesque has the power of revelation; it manifests the irruption of the demonic in man and brings to light the terrifying face of a world literally *dis-figured* by evil. The derangement of minds and deformity of bodies point to a deeper sickness, invisible but more irremediably tragic, the sickness of the soul. Gracelessness in all its forms indicates the absence of grace in the theological sense of the term.

This, at least, is how O'Connor vindicated her heavy reliance on grotesque effects and how she expected her readers to respond to them. Yet her vigorous denunciation of spiritual sickness is not devoid of ambiguity, and its ambiguity partly proceeds from the very rage with which she fustigates man's sins and follies. Christian novelists have often been taken to task for their self-indulgence in describing evil, and in reading them the suspicion grows indeed time and again that they feel secretly attracted by what they pretend to censure. In Mauriac's novels, for example, one often senses a half-hidden complicity between the writer and his criminal heroines. This is surely not the kind of complacency and duplicity O'Connor could be accused of. Between her and her characters (with a few notable exceptions) lies all the distance of contempt, disgust, and derision, and it is the very harshness of the satire that arouses suspicion. By dint of hunting evil, O'Connor—like most evil hunters—descries its hideous leer at every turn. Nothing finds grace in her eyes, nothing is spared her avenging fury. Wherever she looks, she discovers nothing but meanness and ugliness, horror and corruption. Or is it not rather her inquisitorial stare that distorts and diminishes, defaces and defiles all she sees? With O'Connor, character creation is a process comparable to the baptismal drownings described in her fiction: the very gesture that calls her creatures into life, stills them in the stark contours and absurd postures of caricature. When she describes a face, she transforms it into a cabbage,[4] gives it the expression of "a grinning mandrill,"[5] or likens it to "a big florid vegetable" ("A Stroke of Good Fortune," p. 95).

Characters, in her hands, become mere puppets, and she does not even care to hide the strings: "Haze got up and hung there a few seconds. He looked as if he were held by a rope caught in the middle of his back and attached to the train ceiling" (*WB,* p. 12). With methodic thoroughness and almost sadistic glee, O'Connor exploits all the resources of her talent to reduce the human to the nonhuman, and all her similes and metaphors have seemingly no other purpose than to degrade it to the inanimate, the bestial, or the mechanical. Like Gogol and Dickens, she possesses a weird gift for deadening people into things while quickening things into objects with a life of their own (Hazel's rat-colored Essex in *Wise Blood,* the giant steam shovel in "A View of the Woods").

Hence a world both frozen and frantic, both ludicrous and threatening. O'Connor's landscapes—her fierce, fiery suns, her blank or blood-drenched skies, her ominous woods—are landscapes of nightmare. But at the same time nature shrinks to laughable proportions: clouds come to look like turnips ("The Life You Save May Be Your Own," p. 156), and raindrops like "tin-can tops" (ibid.). True, there are also fleeting glimpses of natural beauty. Yet, even though O'Connor defended her use of the grotesque as a necessary strategy of her art, one if left with the impression that in her work it eventually became the means of a savage revilement of the whole of creation.

Questions then arise on the orthodoxy of her Catholicism. For Barbey d'Aurevilly, Catholicism was, in his own phrase, an old wrought-iron balcony ideally suited for spitting upon the crowd. It would be unfair, certainly, to suggest that O'Connor used it for similar purposes. Yet one may wonder whether her Catholicism was not, to some extent, an alibi for misanthropy. And one may also wonder whether so much black derision is compatible with Christian faith, and ask what distinguishes the extreme bleakness of her vision from plain nihilism. Péguy and Bernanos were just as hostile to the secular spirit of modern times and no less vehement in their strictures, but after all Péguy also celebrated the theological virtue of hope, and Bernanos was also the novelist of Easter joy. In O'Connor, on the other hand, the most arresting feature, as in Swift, Kafka, or Beckett, is a compulsive emphasis on man's utter wretchedness, and what gives her voice its unique quality is a sustained note of dry and bitter fury.

If we are to believe the Christian moralists, one of the Devil's supreme wiles is to leave us with the shattering discovery of our nothingness and so to tempt us into the capital sin of despair. From what one knows of O'Connor's life, it seems safe to assume that this was the temptation she found most difficult to resist, and it might be argued that her writing was in many ways a rite of exorcism, a way of keeping despair at a distance by projecting it into fiction. Small wonder then that in her work the demon of literary creation, as John Hawkes so judiciously noted,[6] is inseparable from the Demon himself. When, as in *The Violent Bear It Away,* O'Connor makes the Devil speak, his sarcastic voice sounds startlingly like the author's. That her voice and vision so often verge on the diabolical should not surprise us: what better vantage point is there to observe and describe hell than Satan's, and who could know it better than he?

BY GOD POSSESSED?

Yet it is not enough to say that O'Connor was of the Devil's party. Many ironies and paradoxes interact in her work, and exegetes of Christian persuasion would probably contend that in its very abjection O'Connor's world testifies to the presence of the divine, the fall from grace being the proof *a contrario* of man's supernatural destination. O'Connor's heroes live mostly in extreme isolation, yet they are never truly alone. However entrenched in their smugness or embattled in their revolt, they find no safe shelter in their puny egos, and sooner or later, by degrees or—more often—abruptly, some invisible force breaks into their lives to hurl them far beyond themselves. They are *called*—called by whom? By what? How can anyone tell if the calling voice is God's or the Devil's?

A major theme in O'Connor's fiction, the enigma of *vocation,* is nowhere more fully explored than in her two novels. As most critics have pointed out, *Wise Blood* and *The Violent Bear It Away* offer very similar narrative and thematic patterns. Their heroes, Hazel Motes and Francis Marion Tarwater, are likewise obsessed by their vocation as preachers and prophets, and in both of them the obsession is significantly embodied in the figure of a despotic old man, the more formidable since he is dead: a fanatical grandfather, "with Jesus hidden in his head like a stinger" (*WB,* p. 20) for Hazel; a great-uncle no less single-minded and intolerant for young Tarwater. Both of them start by resenting the prophetic mission laid upon them as a cumbersome legacy and an intolerable violation of their free will. Hazel and Tarwater rebel alike: the former by leading a life of deliberate sin and crime, and by preaching the anti-Gospel of "the Holy Church Without Christ"; the latter by fleeing from the old prophet's wilderness to the godless city. Yet, do what they will, they equally fail in their frantic attempts to escape, and ultimately submit to their destinies as prophets.

Prophets or false prophets? The question is not easy to answer. Many of O'Connor's backwoods preachers are simply frauds, and for a sincere Christian there is perhaps nothing more scandalous than religious imposture. As J. M. G. LeClézio remarks, "The illusion-monger, the sorcerer, tries to capitalize on something infinitely serious. He degrades. He dishonors."[7] Satirizing southern evangelism, however, was obviously not O'Connor's main concern. Her preachers and prophets are by no means all vulgar charlatans. Nor are we supposed to regard them as lunatics. The reader is of course free to dismiss characters such as Hazel Motes or the two Tarwaters as insane, and to interpret their extravagant stories as cases of religious mania, but it is clear that this is not how the author intended them to be read. As a Roman Catholic, O'Connor must have had her reservations about the fanatic intolerance and apocalyptic theology of primitive fundamentalism. Yet, as she herself admitted on several occasions, its integrity and fervor appealed to her, for she found them congenial to the burning intransigence of her own faith.[8] Her fascination with the southern evangelist—whom she came to envision as a crypto-Catholic—is not unlike the attraction Bernanos and Graham Greene felt for the priest figure. No matter how crazy and criminal they are, Hazel Motes and Tarwater are for her witnesses to the Spirit, and their madness is God's madness.[9]

Violent men, prone to every excess, they sin with a vengeance, but strenuous sinners are precisely the stuff saints are made of. As O'Connor reminds us in the title and scriptural epigraph of her second novel, "The kingdom of heaven suffereth violence, and the violent bear it away."

In O'Connor violence rules man's relation to the sacred, just as it rules his relation to other men. Nothing here that suggests "spirituality": the word is too smooth, too polished, too blandly civilized to apply to the compulsions and convulsions of these savage souls. For Motes and Tarwater as well as for the "Misfit" of "A Good Man Is Hard to Find," God is above all an idée fixe, and the divine is primarily experienced as an intolerable invasion of privacy, a dispossession—or possession—of the self. What torments O'Connor's heroes, at least at first glance, is not their being deprived of God but rather the fact that their obsession with Him cannot be escaped. Religious experience, as it is rendered dramatically in her fiction, comes pretty close to Freud's definition: a variant of obsessional neurosis.

God is the Intruder. Therefore the first move of O'Connor's "prophet freaks" (as she herself called them) is to resist or to flee. Hazel Motes tries his utmost to get rid of God. Even as a child he imagines he can avoid Jesus by avoiding sin; later, on the other hand, he blasphemes, fornicates, and even murders to prove to himself that sin does not exist. What is more, he sets out to preach a new church, "the church of truth without Jesus Christ Crucified" (*WB*, p. 55), publicly denies the Fall and the Redemption, and calls Jesus a liar. Each one of his words and actions becomes an open defiance to the revealed God. With young Tarwater, the mutinous impulse is just as radical. Hardly has his great-uncle died when he listens to the voice of the Tempter: "Jesus this and Jesus that. Ain't you in all your fourteen years of supporting his foolishness fed up and sick to the roof of your mouth with Jesus?"[10] In a sense, the old man's death is for Tarwater the equivalent of the (provisional) death of God, and if God is dead, everything is permissible: "Now I can do anything I want to. . . . Could kill off all those chickens if I had a mind to" (*TVBIA*, p. 25). Intoxicated with a sudden sense of absolute freedom, Tarwater —a lamentable latterday Ivan Karamazov whose field of action has shrunk to a chickencoop—resolves to flout his great-uncle's last wishes. Instead of burying him decently, he gets drunk and sets fire to his house so as to destroy both the cumbrous corpse and all the past it symbolizes. He then goes to the city, not to baptize his uncle's dim-witted child, as the old man had ordered him, but intent on renouncing once and for all his prophetic mission. Yet these two gestures of denial are plainly not sufficient to rid him of Christ: "You can't just say NO . . . You got to do NO. You got to show it. You got to show you mean it by doing it. You got to show you're not going to do one thing by doing another. You got to make an end of it. One way or another" (*TVBIA*, p. 157). The break with God requires consummation by an act beyond atonement: to demonstrate his freedom, Tarwater consequently murders the child he should have baptized.

Rebellious children, O'Connor's heroes assert themselves only by willful transgression of the divine order, as if only the certainty of flouting God's will and of doing evil could give them an identity of their own. Their revolt springs essentially from a refusal to submit, to alienate their freedom and have their fate coerced into some preestablished pattern. In their stubborn striving for autonomy, they commit what Christian tradition has always considered to be the satanic sin par excellence: the sin of pride.

Yet pride is not the only obstacle to the fulfillment of their spiritual destinies. Soiled from birth by the sin of their origins, how could these fallen souls hoist themselves up to God's light? They do not know God; they experience only his burning absence. For the theologian and the philosopher God is a matter of speculation; for the mystic he may become the living object of inner experience. For O'Connor's Christomaniacs he becomes "the bleeding stinking mad shadow of Jesus" (*TVBIA*, p. 91). Their God is above all a haunting specter, a power felt and feared in its uncanny emptiness, and this ominous power they can only apprehend anthropomorphically through the incongruous phantasmagoria of their guilt-ridden imaginations. There is apprehension, but no comprehension. Their notion of the godly is not exempted from the distortions of the corrupt world in which they live, and therefore the divine gets so often confused with the demonic. In its extreme form, this rampant perversion comes to manifest itself as radical inversion. Everything, then, is turned upside down, and the religious impulse is subverted into its very opposite: desire for God is transformed into God-hatred, prayer into blasphemy, and the quest for salvation turns into a mystique of perdition.

Nothing exemplifies this inversion better than the *imitatio Christi* in reverse which O'Connor presents us in *Wise Blood*. After turning himself into the prophet of the Church Without Christ (the negative of the Church of God, the very image of the "body of sin" referred to by St. Paul), Hazel Motes ironically becomes a Christ without a church, an anonymous, solitary pseudo-Christ or anti-Christ. His disciples are morons and mountebanks, his preaching meets only with indifference, and his calvary at the close of the novel ends in a seemingly pointless death. Worn out by self-inflicted pain and privation, he is clubbed to death by two fat policemen. Motes dies like a dog, and his atrocious end reminds one strongly of the last pages of *The Trial*, when two men appear and lead Joseph K. to the outskirts of the town to kill him. The life and death of O'Connor's hero appear likewise as an absurd Passion. Or are we to assume that Motes is eventually saved? At the very end of the novel, the imagery of light and darkness, sight and blindness is manipulated in such a way as to suggest a less sinister meaning to Motes's martyrdom and death: staring into his burned-out eye sockets, Mrs. Flood, his landlady, sees him "moving farther and farther away, farther and farther into the darkness until he was the pin point of light" (*WB*, p. 232). Earlier this pinpoint of light had been identified as the star over Bethlehem (see *WB*, p. 219), and it might be taken as a hint that this "Christian *malgré lui*" (as the author called him in her note to the second edition) has been redeemed after all. The oblique reference to the birth of the Savior, however, is a little too pat, and the ultimate flicker of light, instead of lessening the horror of what precedes, simply adds a final twist to the novel's baffling ambiguity.

Christian references and Christian parallels abound in O'Connor's fiction, and more often than not they strike us as ironic. In *Wise Blood*, especially, parodic overtones are so frequent that the whole novel might almost be read as sheer burlesque. A "new jesus" appears in the guise of a shrunken museum mummy; a slop-jar cabinet becomes the tabernacle to receive him, and Sabbath Lily Hawks, a perverse little slut, cradles the mummy in her arms as if she were the Madonna. O'Connor's penchant for travesty is likewise reflected in the eccentric ritualism of many of her characters: baptismal drownings (in "The River" and *The Violent Bear It Away*), rites of exorcism (Tarwater setting fire to his great-uncle's house), purification rites (Tarwater firing the bushes where the rape occurred), initiation rites (Enoch Emery's shedding of clothes in *Wise Blood* and Tarwater's in *The Violent Bear It Away*), sacrificial rites (Motes's self-blinding), etc. In their appalling extravagance, these ritual actions are likely to shock any reader, whether Christian or not. But here again, if we are prepared to accept the premises of the author, we shall avoid mistaking them for mere fits of madness, for to her, in a desacralized world like ours, these savage and sacrilegious rites paradoxically assert the presence of the sacred through the very excess of its distortion or denial.

Yet what would we make of all these outrageous scenes had we not been told to read them in terms of Christian paradox? There are as many scenes of religious travesty in the films of Buñuel (the best-known being probably the Last Supper scene in *Viridiana*). Buñuel, however, has never made bones about his contempt for Christianity, and he has been as explicit about his atheism as O'Connor was about her Catholicism. This has not deterred well-meaning Christian critics from re-claiming him (after Baudelaire, Rimbaud, Kafka, Joyce, Camus, Beckett, and many others) as an errant son of the church. Why then, one might perversely ask, could not unbelievers pay them back in their own coin and, O'Connor's professions of faith notwithstanding, assert equal rights upon her work?

This is not to insinuate that O'Connor was an atheist *malgré elle*, but rather to suggest again the possibility of more than one reading of her fiction. O'Connor's satiric stance, her penchant for parody, her reliance on the grotesque, and her massive use of violence—the features of her art we have examined so far all con-tribute to the subtle interplay of tensions and ambiguities through which it comes alive, and they resist alike reduction to a single interpretative pattern. The same irreducible ambiguity also attaches to another significant trait of her fictional world: the enormous amount of suffering and humiliation which is inflicted on most of her characters, and the inevitability of their defeat and/or death. Hazel Motes's destiny probably offers the most telling example of this process: after an active career in sin and crime, all his aggressiveness is eventually turned against himself, driving him to a positive frenzy of masochism and self-destruction. He blinds himself with quicklime, exposes himself to cold and illness, walks in shoes "lined with gravel and broken glass and pieces of small stone" (*WB,* p. 221), wraps three strands of barbed wire round his chest, and when his baffled landlady protests at so much self-torture, Motes replies imperturbably: "I'm not clean," or again "I'm paying" (see *WB,* pp. 222, 224). The same compulsive concern with purity/impurity and the same need for penitential suffering bred from a deep-seated sense of guilt are also found, although to a lesser extent, in *The Violent Bear It Away.* With Tarwater, however, they rather take the symbolic form of fire rituals. After having been drugged and raped, he burns all the bushes around and is not content until every last bit of soil has been burned clean by the flames. Similarly, after the "friend's" last temptation, Tarwater sets fire to the forked tree from which the voice seems to emanate. Erecting a wall of fire between himself and "the grinning presence" (*TVBIA*, p. 238), he exorcises once and for all his demonic double. The hour of expiation has arrived. Tarwater atones for his rebellion by accepting at last his prophetic mission. Purified by fire, he turns, in the book's last sentence, "toward the dark city, where the children of God lay sleeping" (*TVBIA*, p. 243).

According to the prototypal Christian pattern, the hero's journey leads in both novels from sinful rebellion to the recognition of sin and to penance. O'Connor would have us believe that her protagonists are responsible for their fates, that they possess freedom of choice, and are at liberty to refuse or accept their vocation: "Tarwater is certainly free and meant to be; if he appears to have a compulsion to be a prophet, I can only insist that in this compulsion there is the mystery of God's will for him, and that it is not a compulsion in the clinical sense" (*MM*, p. 116). But her readers, even those who sympathize with her Christian assumptions and are willing to make allowances for the mysterious working of grace, will hesitate to take her at her word. For in the text of the novel there is indeed little to indicate that Motes or Tarwater could have made a different choice and that events might have followed another course. Her heroes are not allowed to shape their destinies; they only *recognize* fate when it pounces upon them. Consider, for example, Tarwater's reaction at his first meeting with Rayber's child:

> Tarwater clenched his fists. He stood like one condemned, waiting at the spot of execution. Then the revelation came, silent, implacable, direct as a bullet. He did not look into the eyes of any fiery beast or see a burning bush. He only knew, with a certainty sunk in despair, that he was expected to baptize the child he saw and begin the life his great-uncle had prepared for him. (*TVBIA*, p. 91)

True, O'Connor tells us that Tarwater was "expected" to obey his great-uncle's command, not that he had to. But his attitude, in its mixture of impotent revolt and bitter resignation, as well as the similes which the author uses to describe it, point to the contrary. In the same scene, in one of those duplications which indicate her heroes' self-estrangement, Tarwater's eyes reflect "depth on depth his own stricken image of himself, trudging into the distance in the bleeding stinking mad shadow of Jesus" (*TVBIA*, p. 91). Tarwater suddenly realizes that he is forever in bondage to that shadow. He tries "to shout, 'NO!' but it [is] like trying to shout in his sleep" (*TVBIA*, p. 92). O'Connor's heroes are indeed like sleepers: they traverse life in a driven dreamlike state, and with the sense of impotence and anxiety one experiences in nightmares. They go through the motions of revolt, but their violent gestures toward independence are all doomed to dissolve into unreality. They are nothing more than the starts and bounds of a hooked fish. Tarwater and Motes both act out scenarios written beforehand by someone else.

As Josephine Hendin has aptly noted, O'Connor's novels are about "the impossibility of growing up."[11] On the face of it, they develop in accordance with the three major phases of the *rite de passage:* separation, transition, and reincorporation, but they give no sense of moving forward in time and no evidence of psychological development. Instead of inner growth, there is a backward circling which takes O'Connor's heroes inexorably back to where they started. *Wise Blood* and *The Violent Bear It Away* both follow the same circular and regressive pattern, made conspicuous by the close similarities between opening and final scenes. In *Wise Blood* Mrs. Hitchcock's fascination with Hazel's eyes in the initial train scene anticipates Mrs. Flood's perplexed watching of his burnt-out eye sockets at the close of the novel. In much the same way the punishment he inflicts upon himself at ten—walking through the woods, his shoes filled with pebbles—prefigures the penitential rites preceding his near-suicidal death. In *The Violent Bear It Away,* on the other hand, the parallelism is emphasized by the use of the same setting: the novel starts with Tarwater's departure from Powderhead and closes with his return to it. "I guess you're going home" (*WB,* p. 10), Mrs. Hitchcock says to Hazel Motes on the train; in symbolic terms, his journey is indeed a journey home, and Tarwater's is quite literally a homecoming. These repetitions, to be true, are repetitions with a difference, and one could say that the movement is spiral-like rather than circular: there are intimations that through his harrowing ordeals Motes has moved toward a state of saintliness, and his physical blindness may be taken for an index to the spiritual insight he has at last achieved. It is obvious too that in *The Violent Bear It Away* the fire symbolism of the closing scenes reverses the meaning it was given in the first chapter. And it might be argued finally that recurring situations, settings, and imagery are part of the author's elaborate technique of foreshadowing.

But this is perhaps precisely where the shoe pinches: O'Connor's foreshadowing is so dense as to become constrictive; the signs and signals of destiny clutter so thickly around the protagonists of her novels that no breathing space is left to them. The author plays God to her creatures, and foreshadowing becomes the fictional equivalent of predestination. Everything propels her heroes toward submission to their predetermined fates and, at the same time, pushes them back to their childhood allegiances. Not only does their rebellion fail, it also ends each time in unconditional surrender to the parental powers from which they had attempted to escape.

In *Wise Blood* the prophetic mission is anticipated in the haunting figure of the grandfather, but Hazel's backward journey is essentially a return to the mother. The return motif is already adumbrated in the remembered episode of his visit to Eastrod after his release from the army. The only familiar object Hazel then found in his parents' deserted house was his mother's walnut chifforobe, and before leaving he put warning notes in every drawer: "This shiffer-robe belongs to Hazel Motes. Do not steal it or you will be hunted down and killed" (*WB,* p. 26). In the claustrophobic dream touched off by this reminiscence, the chifforobe is metamorphosed into his mother's coffin, while the coffin itself is fused with the berth in the train where Hazel is sleeping. What is more, Hazel, in his dream, identifies with his dead mother (see *WB,* pp. 26-27). This dream is significantly related to another one, in which Motes dreams that he is buried alive and exposed through an oval window to the curiosity of various onlookers, one of whom is a woman who would apparently like to "climb in and keep him company for a while" (*WB,* p. 160). Furthermore, these two coffin dreams relate back to the traumatic childhood scene of Motes's initiation into evil: the disturbing sight of a nude blonde in a black casket, exhibited in the carnival tent where the ten-year-old boy had secretly followed his father. At his return from the country fair, his mother (whose image he superimposed mentally on that of the woman in the casket) knows, after one look at him, that he has sinned, and it is her accusing look that induces his first penitential rite. In the visual symbolism of the novel, the urge to see and the fear of being seen are recurrent motifs, and in this scene as in several others they both point to sin and guilt.[12] What also appears through the interrelated imagery of these oneiric and actual scenes is the close conjunction of sex and death. But the most remarkable feature is that the themes of sin and guilt, sex and death, all coalesce around the mother figure and its surrogates.[13] Motes's mother, while being deviously linked to his sordid sexual experiences, is at the same time a haunting reminder of the demands of religion: when he goes into the army, the only things he takes with him are "a black Bible and a pair of silver-trimmed spectacles that had belonged to his mother" (*WB,* p. 23). It is through her glasses that he reads the Bible, and later, when he puts them on again and looks at his face in a mirror, he sees "his mother's face in his" (*WB,* p. 187). It is no surprise then that Motes's erratic quest should end in oedipal self-blinding and self-destruction. His tragic end completes identification with the dead mother: it is both fulfillment and expiation of the same desire.

In *Wise Blood* Motes is finally reabsorbed into his mother. In *The Violent Bear It Away* Tarwater is likewise reabsorbed into his great-uncle. Raising the orphan boy to be a prophet like himself, the tyrannical old man has molded him in his own image and conditioned him for a destiny similar to his. When he dies, young Tarwater does his utmost to assert his own separate self through repeated acts of defiance, but what the novel seems to demonstrate is that there can be no escape from the self-ordained prophet's posthumous grip. In the concluding scene the repentant boy submits to what he so fiercely rejected, and his act of submission reminds one of the etymological origin of "humility" (humus = soil): prostrate on old Tarwater's grave, smearing his forehead with earth from his burial place, he acknowledges at last the absolute power of the past over the present, of the dead over the living or, to put it in terms of kinship, of the father over the son. The story comes full circle: otherness is resolved into sameness, difference into repetition. Having forever renounced his desire for autonomous selfhood, young Tarwater is now willing to become a faithful replica of old Tarwater, and in all likelihood his ulterior fate will be nothing more than a reenactment of the dead prophet's.

For neither protagonist of O'Connor's novels, then, is true separateness possible. Nor can they ever achieve true relatedness. Theirs is a demented mirror world of doubles, where the self is always experienced as other, and the other apprehended as a reflection of self. The schizophrenic dilemma they are both confronted with is either the madness of extreme isolation or the deadness of total engulfment.[14] In both cases, the failure to define a viable identity leads ultimately to complete self-cancelation; in both cases, the inability to grow up provokes helpless surrender to an omnipotent and all-devouring parent figure.

Such a reading is of course likely to be dismissed as reductive psychologizing by those of O'Connor's critics who insist on interpreting her on her own terms. Old Tarwater, they would object, was intended metaphorically as a representative of God, and the boy's final submission to the old man's will as a symbol of his surrender to the power of Christ. But it is at this very point that ambiguity and reversibility intervene. While the Christian reader quite naturally takes his cue from the author and translates the psychological conflict into religious drama, the non-Christian reader is tempted just as naturally to discuss the religious allegory in psychological terms. The former will see in old Tarwater an analogon of the heavenly Father; the latter will reverse the metaphor and regard O'Connor's God as a magnified fantasy-projection of her overpowering parent figures. To ask which of the two approaches is the more relevant is probably an irrelevant question. Both may be considered valid insofar as they provide operational procedures of analysis which are not contradicted by the evidence of the work under consideration. And both may also become reductive to the extent that they pretend to have the monopoly of a "correct" understanding.

By whom are O'Connor's driven souls possessed? By God or by the Devil? By supernatural powers or by unconscious fantasies? Her work raises the questions; it does not give the answers. Neither is it the critic's task to provide them. He reverberates her questioning in his own language and tries to do justice to its complexities, and this is about all he can do without exceeding his prerogatives.

THE COUP DE GRÂCE

For almost all of O'Connor's characters there is a time for denial and a time for submission, a time for sin and a time for atonement. The passage from one to the other is what she has attempted to describe in her two novels, but as we have seen, she shows relatively little interest in the continuities and intricacies of inner growth. Her heroes do not change gradually; they progress—or regress—in fits and starts, through a series of switches and turnabouts rather than through a slow process of maturation. What engages most deeply O'Connor's imagination—and this, incidentally, may account for her feeling more at home in the short story than in the novel—is not so much time as the sudden encounter of time with the timeless: the decisive moments in a man's existence she would have called moments of grace. "My subject in fiction," O'Connor wrote, "is the action of grace in territory held largely by the devil" (*MM*, p. 118). Grace plays indeed a major part in her novels as in most of her stories, especially the later ones, and as a religious concept it forms the very core of her implicit theology. Left to his own devices, man, as he appears in her fiction, is totally incapable of ensuring his salvation. Whether it degrades itself in grotesque parody or exhausts itself in mad convulsions, his quest for the holy is doomed to derision and failure from the very start. Grace alone saves, and even that is perhaps going too far: reading O'Connor's tales, one rather feels that grace simply makes salvation possible. As for fallen man, he collaborates in his redemption only by default. Instead of grace coming to complete and crown nature—as the mainstream Catholic tradition would have it—it breaks in on it. Bursting like a storm, it strikes with the unpredictable suddenness of a thunderbolt. And paradoxically it is more often than not at the very last moment, at the climax of violence or at the point of death that grace manifests itself, as though these boundary situations were God's supreme snare and the sinner's ultimate chance. It is when Tarwater yields to the temptation of murder and drowns Rayber's son that the hand of God falls upon him, forcing him to baptize the child against his will, and so converting the moment of sin and death into one of rebirth for both murderer and victim. In most of the stories of *Everything That Rises Must Converge,* the flash of grace occurs in similar circumstances, and spiritual conversion is accomplished likewise through a staggering if not annihilating shock. For Mrs. May, the self-righteous widow of "Greenleaf," it is achieved through the fatal encounter with a wild bull; for others it is effected through a son's suicide ("The Lame Shall Enter First") or a mother's death ("Everything That Rises Must Converge"). In the story significantly entitled "Revelation," on the other hand, a seemingly trivial incident is enough to spark off the deep inner commotion that, in O'Connor's fiction, inevitably precedes the moment of supernatural vision: a respectable lady is abused and assaulted by a girl in a doctor's waiting room, and, with her monumental smugness forever shattered, she is eventually granted a vision of heaven in her pig parlor.

Grace takes men by surprise. It catches them unawares, stabs them in the back. Nothing heralds the passage from darkness to light. And the light of grace is so sudden and so bright that it burns and blinds before it illuminates. Consider Mrs. May on the verge of death: ". . . she had the look of a person whose light had been suddenly restored but who finds the light unbearable" ("Greenleaf," p. 333). The impact of grace, as evoked by O'Connor, is that of a painful dazzle; it does not flood the soul with joy; her characters experience it as an instantaneous deflagration, a rending and bursting of the whole fabric of their being. For the revelation it brings is first and foremost self-revelation, the terrified recognition of one's nothingness and guilt. As each character is brutally stripped of his delusions, he sees and knows himself at last for what he is: "Asbury blanched and the last film of illusion was torn as if by a whirlwind from his eyes" ("The Enduring Chill," p. 382). Not until the soul has reached that ultimate point of searing self-knowledge does salvation become a possibility. Then begins for those who survive the fire of grace, the "enduring" death-in-life of purgatorial suffering: "[Asbury] saw that for the rest of his days, frail, racked, but enduring, he would live in the face of a purifying terror. A feeble cry, a last impossible protest escaped him. But the Holy Ghost, emblazoned in ice instead of fire, continued, implacable, to descend" ("The Enduring Chill," p. 382). For Asbury as well as for Julian, grace means "entry into the world of guilt and sorrow" ("Everything That Rises Must Converge," p. 420). For others, on the contrary, like Mrs. May or the grandmother of "A Good Man Is Hard to Find," the beginning is quite literally the end, and the price paid for spiritual rebirth is an immediate death.

In O'Connor, grace is not effusion but aggression. It is God's violence responding to Satan's violence, divine counterterror fighting the mutiny of evil. The operations of the divine and of the demonic are so disturbingly alike that the concept of God suggested by her work is in the last resort hardly more reassuring than her Devil. In fairness, one should no doubt allow for the distortions of satire, and be careful to distinguish the God of O'Connor's faith from the God-image of her characters. Her handling of point of view, however, implies no effacement on the part of the narrator, and her dramatic rendering of spiritual issues as well as the imagery she uses to evoke the actions of grace, provide enough clues to what God meant in her imaginative experience.

O'Connor's imagination is preeminently visual and visionary. Like Conrad's, her art attempts in its own way "to render the highest kind of justice to the visible universe,"[15] and far from clouding her perception, her sense of mystery rather adds to its startling clarity and sharpness. It is worth noting too how much of the action of her stories and novels is reflected in the continuous interplay of peeping or peering, prying or spying eyes, and how much importance is accorded throughout to the sheer act of seeing—or not seeing. *Wise Blood* is a prime example: a great deal of its symbolism springs from the dialectic of vision and blindness, and a similar dialectic is also at work in *The Violent Bear It Away* and in many of her stories. For O'Connor seeing is a measure of being: while the sinner gropes in utter darkness, the prophet—in O'Connor's phrase, "a realist of distances"[16]—is above all a seer. In God the faculty of vision is carried to an infinite power of penetration: God is the All-seeing, the absolute Eye, encompassing the whole universe in its eternal gaze.

The cosmic metaphor for the divine eye is the sun. Through one of those reversals of the imagination analyzed by Gaston Bachelard, the sun, in O'Connor's fiction, is not simply the primal source of light that makes all things visible, it is itself capable of vision, it is an eye. In *The Violent Bear It Away* there are few scenes to which the sun is not a benevolent or, more often, malevolent witness. After the old man's death, while Tarwater is reluctantly digging his grave, the sun moves slowly across the sky "circled by a haze of yellow" (*TVBIA*, p. 24), then becomes "a furious white blister" (p. 25) as he starts listening to the seductive voice of the "stranger." And when he resolves to deny Christian burial to his great-uncle, the sun appears "a furious white, edging its way secretly behind the tops of trees that rose over the hiding place" (p. 44). The sun is likewise a symbol of God's watchful, but this time approving presence in the two parallel scenes (see pp. 145-46, 164-65) where Bishop, the innocent child—rehearsing, as it were, the baptismal rite—jumps into the fountain of a city park:

> The sun, which had been tacking from cloud to cloud, emerged above the fountain. A blinding brightness fell on the lion's tangled marble head and gilded the stream of water rushing from his mouth. Then the light, falling more gently, rested like a hand on the child's white head. His face might have been a mirror where the sun had stopped to watch its reflection. (p. 164)

Almost obtrusive at times in its symbolic emphasis, sun imagery runs throughout the novel. Tarwater's attempted escape from Christ is a flight from God's sun/son, and the failure of the attempt is metaphorically equated with the sun's triumph: on the morning after his baptismal drowning of Bishop, the "defeated boy" watches the sun rise "majestically with a long red wingspread" (p. 217), and at the close of the novel the victory of its burning light is again proclaimed through Tarwater's "scorched eyes," which look as if "they would never be used for ordinary sights again" (p. 233).

O'Connor's sun is both cosmic eye and heavenly fire. It thus condenses two of her most pregnant symbol patterns in a single image. For fire imagery is indeed as essential in her symbolic language as eye and sight imagery: incandescent suns, flaming skies, burning houses, woods, trees, and bushes—hers is an apocalyptic world forever ablaze. Fire is the visible manifestation of the principle of violence governing the universe, and the ordeal by fire is the *rite de passage* all of O'Connor's heroes are subjected to. A symbol of destruction and death, and a reminder of hell, it is also the favorite instrument of divine wrath and, as the old prophet taught young Tarwater, "even the mercy of the Lord burns" (*TVBIA*, p. 20). Associated with purification and regeneration as well as evil, fire is the ambiguous sign of the elect and the damned, and its voracity is God's as much as Satan's.

That eye, sun, and fire are all emblems of the sacred is confirmed by another symbolic figure which both unites and multiplies them in animal form: the peacock. In "The Displaced Person," instead of being associated with human pride and ostentatiousness, the peacock becomes a symbol of the Second Coming, evoking the unearthly splendor of Christ at the Last Judgment. His tail, in O'Connor's description, expands into a cosmic wonder: ". . . his tail hung in front of her, full of fierce planets with *eyes* that were each ringed in green and set against a *sun* that was gold in one second's light and salmon-colored in the next" ("The Displaced Person," p. 200; italics added). Later in the same story the peacock reappears, with his ocellated tail gorgeously fanned out against the vastness of the sky: ". . . a gigantic figure stood facing her. It was the color of the *sun* in the early afternoon. It was of no definite shape but there were *fiery* wheels with fierce dark *eyes* in them, spinning rapidly all around it" ("The Displaced Person," p. 210; italics added).

Immensity, brilliance, splendor, a dizzying profusion of eyes and suns, such are the features O'Connor chooses to celebrate God's power and glory. And one can hardly refrain from the suspicion that power and glory are in her imagination if not in her belief the essential attributes of divinity. In cosmic terms, her God is sun and fire. If one examines her bestiary, one finds birds of prey, cocks, and bulls—animal metaphors which all suggest phallic potency and male aggressiveness. O'Connor's God is Christ the Tiger rather than Christ the Lamb, a God infinitely distant who confronts us with the agonizing mystery of absolute otherness and whose abrupt transcendence is manifested in sudden deflagrations of power. He is the Most High and the Wholly Other. Man's relation to Him is one of vertical tension precluding any form of reciprocity. Small wonder then that the spiritual errancy of O'Connor's heroes turns into a paranoid nightmare: aware of being watched and scrutinized by the relentless eye of the almighty Judge, they are unable ever to see their remote and silent persecutor. Not until grace descends to seize and possess their tormented souls is the infinite distance separating them abolished. Now the celestial Watcher, now a God of prey; first hovering, motionless, above his victim, then swooping with terrible speed to devour it.

One might have expected so fervent a Catholic as O'Connor to focus her fiction on the figure of Christ. In a sense, to be true, she does: whether in prayer or profanity, his name is obsessively referred to, and the question of whether Jesus suffered and died for our sins is indeed of vital concern to many of her characters. Yet her work is not so much Christ-centered as Christ-haunted. Unlike T. S. Eliot's later poetry, it is by no means a reaffirmation of the Christian mystery of the Incarnation. O'Connor's divisive vision perpetuates the idealistic cleavage between spirit and body, eternity and time, God and man, and Christ is likewise split into two irreconcilable halves. His image in her work constantly oscillates between the extremes of radical humanity and radical divinity. Now he is the mythical paradigm of human suffering, as Christ crucified and recrucified,[17] now he appears in the plenitude of his majesty as Christ the King, most startlingly represented in the image of the Byzantine Pantocrator tattooed on Parker's back. Or, to put it otherwise, he is alternately the impotent victimized Son and the omnipotent Father. These are images quite common in Christian literature and iconography. The point is that in O'Connor they never meet and merge in the dual unity of Christ, the God become man, the Word become flesh. The mediating function associated with Jesus by the Christian and particularly the Catholic tradition is hardly acknowledged, and what characterizes O'Connor's fictional world is precisely the absence of all mediation, of all intercession. On the one hand, there is the utter darkness of evil, on the other, the white radiance of divine transcendence. Between the two: man, battered and blinded, the victim of Satan or the prey of God, doomed to be defeated and dispossessed whatever the outcome of the dubious battle fought over his wretched soul.

O'Connor identified her vision as a fiction writer with the vision of her faith: "I see from the standpoint of Christian orthodoxy. This means that for me the meaning of life is centered in our Redemption by Christ and that what I see in the world I see in its relation to that" (MM, p. 32). It is a far cry, however, from the reassuring bluntness of her public statements to the puzzling evidence of her tales. O'Connor envisioned the writer's relation to his work on the same pattern as God's relation to his creation, as if art were simply the fulfillment of preexisting intentions, the embodiment of a fixed vision prior to the writing process. In defining herself as a writer, she failed to acknowledge the insight so admirably dramatized in her fiction: that the self is not even master in its own house. For the writing self is certainly not exempted from the common lot: its imaginative constructs escape its mastery both in their deeper motivations and in their ultimate effects.

The truth of O'Connor's work is the truth of her art, not that of her church. Her fiction does refer to an implicit theology, but if we rely, as we should, on its testimony rather than on the author's comments, we shall have to admit that the Catholic orthodoxy of her work is at least debatable. O'Connor is definitely on the darker fringe of Christianity, and to find antecedents one has to go back to the paradoxical theology of early church fathers like Tertullian, or to the negative theology of stern mystics like St. John of the Cross. Pitting the supernatural against the natural in fierce antagonism, her theology holds nothing but scorn for everything human, and it is significant that in her work satanic evildoers (the "Misfit," Rufus Johnson) are far less harshly dealt with than humanistic do-gooders (Rayber, Sheppard). What is more, of the two mysteries—or myths—which are central to Christianity, the Fall and the Redemption, only the first seems to have engaged her imagination as a creative writer. Gnawed by old Calvinistic ferments and at the same time corroded by a very modern sense of the absurd, O'Connor's version of Christianity is emphatically and exclusively her own. Her fallen world, it is true, is visited by grace, but is grace, as she evokes it in her last stories, anything other than the vertigo of the *nada* and the encounter with death? And who is this God whose very mercy is terror?

It may be argued of course that these are the paradoxes of faith, or that O'Connor's rhetoric of violence was the shock therapy which her benumbed audience needed. There is little doubt that there will be many further exercises in exegetical ingenuity to establish her orthodoxy. Yet her work is not content with illustrating Christian paradoxes. It stretches them to breaking point, leaving us with Christian truths gone mad, the still incandescent fragments of a shattered system of belief.

Flannery O'Connor was a Catholic. She was not a Catholic novelist. She was a writer, and as a writer she belongs to no other parish than literature.

Simone Vauthier

4. NARRATIVE TRIANGLE AND TRIPLE ALLIANCE: A LOOK AT "THE MOVIEGOER"

In several interviews and essays Walker Percy has asserted that art is just as cognitive as science. "The novel," he once said, "[is] a perfectly valid way to deal with man's behavior."[1] Nor has he made any bones about his philosophical premises:

> ...the philosophy I was interested in was what was called existential philosophy. Of course, the word no longer means much. It still means a concrete view of man, man in situation, man in a predicament, man's anxiety, and so on. And I believe that this view of man could be handled very well in a novel.[2]

Yet, while he has freely acknowledged his debt to the major exponents of existential philosophy, he thinks that "nothing is worse than a novel that seeks to edify the reader."[3] *The Moviegoer,* his first novel, "begin[s]" (and one may add, ends) "with a *man* who finds himself in a *world,* . . . in a very concrete place and time."[4] It reports one Mardi Gras week in the life of a young New Orleans stockbroker, John Bickerson Bolling, also called Jack or Binx, with hardly any explicit reference to philosophical underpinnings. No wonder then that the growing body of criticism on *The Moviegoer* has been predominantly concerned with the characterization of this man, attempting to "translate Binx's entirely subjective discourse into a language of wider currency," and/or engaged in a search for and discussion of the themes and ideas bodied forth in the novel.[5] But no proper evaluation of Walker Percy's real achievement can be made until his novelistic technique—i. e., his way of exploring reality—has been systematically studied. In reversal of Binx's evolution from the aesthetic to the ethical (or is it religious?) stage, it is time to turn from the quest for the philosophical and moral meaning of *The Moviegoer* and investigate its aesthetics. The horizontal exploration of the here-and-now of the text, however, cannot be undertaken within the limited scope of this essay. In congruence with Binx's diffidence, I shall address myself to the concrete problem of the narrative situation and shall examine the relations within the narrative triangle between narrator, narratee, and narration.

That Binx the (anti)hero narrates his experience, or rather that the pronoun "I" establishes the identity of narrator and protagonist, needs no belaboring. Percy's election of the first-person narration deserves comment but is irrelevant to this inquiry. Significant here, however, is the discrepancy between the title and the narrative stance. Were the book entitled *A Moviegoer,* we could perceive it as a condensation of "I am (was) a moviegoer," the kind of sentence that ushers conventional "confession stories": "I am an alcoholic," "I was a drug addict." The syntagm definite-article-plus-general-noun with a human designation is rarely used to introduce an "I" narration, because it creates a discontinuity between the *object* of the titular inscription and the *subject* of the enunciation which yet have the same referent. The title asserts the authority of the novelist at the expense of the "I" narrator. An egregious use of this device was made by Camus, whose *L' Étranger* starts with: "Aujourd'hui, maman est morte. Ou peut-être hier, je ne sais pas." Both works open on the same dissonance which later reverberates into a full-scale questioning of the self and of self-knowledge, and which adumbrates, from the start, the *doubleness* of the narration: writing act of the novelist and fictitious act of enunciation of a fictive "I" that is fleshed out in the process.[6] Since the illusory enunciation which is the subject of this paper purports to be the narration, I shall so call it. But we must keep in mind the writing act and the triangular relationship it generates between author, story, and reader.

To begin with, if the virtual reader is the ultimate receiver of the novel, he is not to be confused with Binx's partner in the structure of discourse. As a matter of fact, this narratee is a fluid persona. It is not even certain at the beginning that Binx is directing his narration toward an audience: he seems to be addressing himself, first thinking over the day's event—his getting a note from his aunt—and its probable significance, then recalling for the present self an important moment in his past relationship with this aunt. In the first paragraph perhaps only the phrase "I confess" implies an exterior allocutor. Later, since there is little, if any, distance between experiencing self and narrating self,[7] the narrator-hero asks questions of himself: "But I am uneasy over the meagerness of her resources. Where will her dialectic carry her now? After Uncle Jules what? Not back to her stepmother, I fear, but into some kind of dead-end where she must become aware of the dialectic" (p. 46).[8] To be sure, the numerous interior dialogues briefly scattered through the text seem to be carried less between an "I" narrator and an "I" narratee than within the experiencing self, here split into observing and wondering selves: "But these fellows: so friendly and—? what, dejected? I can't be sure" (p. 205, see also pp. 46, 54, 214-15). The rather frequent inner conversations thus dramatize one essential feature of Binx's insertion in a world where he is "solitary and in wonder." His search for "clues," his refusal to live "from cliché to cliché without explanation or expectation,"[9] demand a constant silent questioning of the events and faces with which every day confronts him, or eventually, of himself: "Am I irritable because, now that she mentions it, I do for a fact sound like Bobo and her god-damn iron deer?" (p. 82). Contrasting with this lonely questioning there stands the complacent, cliché-ridden report by Nell Lovell of how she and her husband have just "re-examined [their] values" and "found them pretty darn enduring" (pp. 101-2)—an inauthentic sharing of consciousness if there ever was one. Speaking to himself, Binx is less alienated than Cousin Nell talking to her husband. Moreover, Jack's inner debates reflect his diffidence when it comes to interpreting reality:

> [The Negro's] forehead is an ambiguous sienna color and pied; it is impossible to be sure that he received ashes. When he gets in his Mercury, he does not leave immediately but sits looking down at something on the seat beside him. A sample case? An insurance manual? I watch him closely in the rear-view mirror. It is impossible to say why he is here. Is it part and parcel of the complex business of coming up in the world? Or is it because he believes that God himself is present here at the corner of Elysian Fields and Bons Enfants? Or is he here for both reasons: through some dazzling trick of grace, coming for the one and receiving the other as God's own importunate bonus?
> It is impossible to say. (pp. 234–35)

The mystery can be puzzled over, but no pat answer will ever solve it.

If the inner dialogues—while throwing light on the nature of the narrating act—blur the distinction between narrator and hero, on other occasions Binx, clearly performing as narrator, yet addresses a narratee who is none other than himself. Thus, the narration can become a memorandum to himself: "A line for my notebook: Explore connection between romanticism and scientific subjectivity . . ." (p. 88). This is meant for a narratee who in the permutations that role playing involves (and fiction stages) is about to turn narrator. More ambiguous is the often-quoted passage:

> I am a model tenant and a model citizen and take pleasure in doing all that is expected of me. My wallet is full of identity cards, library cards, credit cards. . . . It is a pleasure to carry out the duties of a citizen and to receive in return a receipt or neat styrene card with *one's* name on it certifying, so to speak, *one's* right to exist. What satisfaction I take in appearing the first day to get my auto tag and brake sticker! I subscribe to *Consumer Reports* and as consequence I own a first-class television set, an all but silent air conditioner and a very long lasting deodorant. My armpits never stink. I pay attention to all spot announcements on the radio about mental health, the seven signs of cancer, and safe-driving, though, *as I say,* I usually prefer to ride the bus. (p. 6–7; emphasis added)

Binx is not drawing an authentic self-portrait but is fondly describing a role. Assuredly a role is something for the Other. But who is the Other here? Does he not include the self as narratee? Part of the irony—and fun—of this auto-portrait comes from the rehearsing of a good part.[10] In the mirror of the narration the self splits into multiple, inverted images in which the narratee is also the "I," while the experiencing "I" is in effect turned into the indefinite "one." The narrator himself seems to catch his own reflection. So a piece of information which is really redundant is offered not with the expected "as I said," which would imply that the narrator *remembers* his act of narration, but with "as I say," which simply shows awareness of a narrative act being performed in some timeless present.

The combination of a narrative stance in which narrating "I" and experiencing "I" seem to coincide, and of occasional addresses to a self-narratee, dramatizes the nature of consciousness and the cleavage on which it depends. The discourse of the self *to* the self, whether immediate or delayed, is a paradigm of self-awareness, a discourse of the self *on* the self.

The narration, however, is not always as narcissistic: in many passages Binx's utterance is clearly oriented toward an exterior allocutor, whether reader or listener. The posited addressee has many faces, sometimes even a name, as when Binx invokes diegetic[11] characters. While Sam is talking to him about the absent Kate, Binx meditates: "Aye, Sweet Kate, and I know too. I know your old upside-down trick: when all is lost, when they despair of you, then it is, at this darkest hour, that you emerge as the gorgeous one" (p. 172). A brief imaginary dialogue suddenly relates the narrator to one of the significant others in his life. Characteristically, though, even this rapprochement must be somewhat distanced by the archaic note, the rhetorical tone, and the casting of Kate as a Shakespearean heroine. On another occasion Jack addresses his aunt in an aside: "But they do not fit, I think *for the hundredth time:* your student prince and the ironic young dude on the mantel" (p. 50, italics added). There the narrator tells what the hero has never actually told the aunt. Such occurrences are rare. Their very scarcity is in a sense a measure of Binx's estrangement. He does not really care whether others really understand him. It is simpler to let his aunt project on him the various roles she assigns to him, no matter how unreal. And with the only person who counts, Kate, he can achieve moments of communication, verbal or nonverbal, which obviate the necessity of explaining himself.

More frequent—and altogether more remarkable—are Binx's apostrophes to extradiegetic characters that do indeed play an important role in his imaginative life—movie actors. They start with the quiet remark addressed to William Holden, "Ah, William Holden, we already need you again" (p. 18), and culminate in the disquisitions on modern man and sin addressed to Rory Calhoun. One of the most characteristic is a triple invocation: "O Tony. O Rory. You never had it so good with direction. Nor even you Bill Holden, my noble Will. O ye morning stars together. Farewell forever, malaise . . ." (p. 127). These raptures are brought on by the happiness which Jack feels when a car accident alters his hitherto businesslike relationship to his secretary Sharon into something more tender. Reality turns out to be stranger than Hollywood fiction, precisely because it is apprehended in terms of a screenplay. And whereas a Shreve McCannon was content with stating that "it is better than the movies," Binx has to call upon movie stars (and surely there is an intended pun in that mock poetic exclamation) in order to evaluate his luck, and "certify" it. It is ironical that he should depend not on real persons but on images of the screen projections of parts—which incidentally reach the reader at the fourth remove—for confirmation of his reality. Because his enjoyment of the occasion has to be mediated through the movie actors, Binx is in fact screening himself off from experience. At the same time the lofty tone of the invocation undermines the heightening of reality which Jack is seeking and betrays the narrator's ironical detachment. The mediation through Rory, Tony, and others appears as highly equivocal.

Similarly, although the diegetic situation is reversed and "real life" does not come up to the expectations aroused by the stereotyped world of the movies, the other important addresses to Rory Calhoun function as ambiguously. The use of Rory as a narratee enables the narrator to make a confession of his double failure and a profession of faith:

> I'll have to tell you the truth, Rory, painful though it is. Nothing would please me more than to say that I had done one of two things. Either that I did what you do: tuck Debbie in your bed and, with a show of virtue so victorious as to be ferocious, grab pillow and blanket and take to the living room sofa, there to lie in the dark. . . . Or—do what a hero in a novel would do . . . give her as merry a time as she could possibly wish for. . . .
>
> No, Rory, I did neither. We did neither. We did very badly and almost did not do at all. Flesh poor flesh failed us. (pp. 119–200)

Binx then goes on to explain why poor flesh, "rendered null by the cold and fishy eye of the malaise" when it is "summoned all at once to be all and everything" should quail and fail:

> I never worked so hard in my life, Rory. I had no choice: the alternative was unspeakable. Christians talk about the horror of sin, but they have overlooked something. They keep talking as if everyone were a great sinner, when the truth is that nowadays one is hardly up to it. There is very little sin in the depths of the malaise. (p. 200)

The choice of a blandly wholesome cinematic persona to be the recipient of a discourse on the abysses of the malaise and later on the sickness of "this latter-day post-Christian sex" (p. 207) is singularly inappropriate and/or deeply ironic. What with Binx's doubleness of vision and tongue-in-cheek way of speaking, it is difficult to decide whether he is *fully* aware of the irony. In any case, this is an I-It relationship masquerading as an I-Thou one, since Binx is relating to an "iconographic image rather than [to] the human actor."[12] In fact, he is accomplishing his usual feat of being both truthful and cunning. In the process he demonstrates that everything indeed is "upside down" for him. A detached philosopher, he plays it cool, reporting on modern man's predicament: "The highest moment of a malaisian's life can be that moment when he manages to sin like a proper human. (Look at us, Binx—my vagabond friends as good as cried out to me—we're sinning! We're succeeding! We're human after all!)" (pp. 200-1). But all the time he is implicitly saying: Rory (Tony, Bill, You, whoever you are, whatever you are), look at me! I'm sinning/not sinning! I am *not* succeeding! I'm human after all! Only here, his *ostensibly* telling Rory and not a diegetic character, or a posited reader, or even himself, makes him a little less human after all, a little less authentic. (Needless to say, since Binx is a function of the text and not a real speaker, all these ambiguities, so economically wrought in, testify to Walker Percy's control of a novel that is as rich and many-layered as a *mille-feuilles*.) In short, his choosing movie stars as narratees exposes Binx as a voyeur[13] who yearns to be seen, seen especially by those who are cynosures themselves; and it reveals the "felt meagerness" of his relational life.

Aside from these unconventional allocutors, Binx directs his narration toward a more traditional narratee. Although anonymous, the addressee is described through a number of signs, direct and indirect, which can only be cursorily examined here. The amount of information he has to be provided with indicates that he does not know the Bollings, or New Orleans for that matter. When Binx defines what a krewe is (p. 17), qualifies Mrs. Schexnaydre's fear of Negroes by saying that "one seldom sees Negroes in this part of Gentilly" (p. 76), explains that "'the other' is a way we found of getting through it before" (p. 61), he is endeavoring to depict his world as clearly as possible for an outsider. Frequently, as the allocutor is tendered Binx's observations on "the case of the world" or on his experience, the assumption is that he will understand. He is likely to make something out of such statements as

It is the dry litigious way of speaking in closely knit families in times of trouble. (p. 110)

Places get used up by rotatory and repetitive use. (p. 145)

Businessmen are our only metaphysicians, but the trouble is, they are one-track metaphysicians. (p. 217)

When the generalizations are clichés, he is probably expected to take them *cum grano salis:* thus with "Love is invincible" (p. 125), an assertion which stands on its own merits at the very beginning of a paragraph and which the following sentences barely qualify. Likewise, many analogies are evidence that Binx trusts that his narratee shares in his cultural background. He must be able to make something out of the allusions to Arthur and Modred, Rupert Brooke and Kierkegaard, Cato, the Black Prince and Beauregard, comic book characters and Shakespearean heroes, the wine-dark sea and TV commercials. He must have some knowledge of anatomy to understand such words as "apex," "pleura," "empyema," "iliac crest," "portal bein," "triceps," "areolas," "fossa," "mucous glands," "dormant vascular nexus," "renal calculi," and the rest.[14] Above all, he must be familiar with a good number of movies and movie stars, from old-timers like Clark Gable to contemporary newcomers like Paul Newman and Marlon Brando. Without this cinematographic background, he would miss much of the vividness of Binx's sketches of people which rely on comparisons with actors for quick iconic (and ironic) efficiency.[15] He would for instance fail fully to appreciate the self-derision in Binx's description of his own intonation: "Old confederate Marlon Brando—a reedy insinuating voice . . ." (p. 230)—the Louisianan taking on "a voice from old Virginia" as spoken by Omaha-born Actor's Studio Brando. Although, as Scott Byrd has remarked, Binx "knows that most of the movies he sees offer him no more communion or alliance than do the murder mysteries read by his father and by Kate,"[16] at least he uses them as a basis for his alliance with the narratee, thus transforming a potential medium of alienation into a means of intersubjectivity, the sharing of common symbols.[17] At the same time as the narratee is assumed to be a moviegoer, so is, by association, the reader. Therefore *our* alienation is both affirmed and aesthetically reversed.

Binx, however, does not imagine his narratee to be an altogether passive recipient of his narration. Questions are the most evident clues to the narratee's supposed activity:

A successful repetition.

What is a repetition? A repetition is the re-enactment of past experience toward the end of isolating the time segment which has lapsed. . . . (p. 79–80)

An odd thing. Ever since Wednesday I have become acutely aware of Jews. There is a clue there, but of what I cannot say. How do I know? Because whenever I approach a Jew, the Geiger counter in my head starts rattling away like a machine gun. . . . (p. 88)

Unidentified as their source remains, such questions can only emanate from the narratee. They may even be implicit rather than explicit: "A good rotation. A rotation I define as the experiencing of the new beyond the expectation of the experiencing of the new" (p. 144). Occasionally, however, the questioner is grammatically represented in the text, and an exchange of some length between him and the narrator may ensue:

What is the nature of the search? you ask.

Really it is very simple, at least for a fellow like me; so simple that it is easily overlooked.

. . . .

What do you seek—God? you ask with a smile.

I hesitate to answer, since all other Americans have settled the matter for themselves and to give such an answer would amount to setting myself a goal which everyone else has reached. (p. 13)

Such conversations deal with precisely those subjects which Binx cannot talk about to the people around him. They define the malaise, the different kinds of search, vertical and horizontal, and what Walker Percy has elsewhere called the existential modes: alienation, repetition, and rotation.[18] On the thematic level, therefore, the device allows the author to bring in important philosophical material, while it contributes much to the characterization of the narrator. In an effort to overcome his isolation, Binx projects a narratee who is more curious than his associates, thereby granting himself the opportunity to formulate existential positions and clarify his views. Yet the relationship between narrator and narratee is sophisticated. In the conversation mentioned above the narratee is politely but unmistakenly derisive; in the following, his interest at first cannot be taken for granted:

Yet how, you might wonder, can even a minor accident be considered good luck?
Because it provides a means of winning out over the malaise, if one has the sense to take advantage of it.
What is the malaise? you ask. The malaise is the pain of loss. The world is

lost to you, the world and the people in it, and there remains only you and the world and you no more able to be in the world than Banquo's ghost.

You say it is a simple thing surely, all gain and no loss, to pick up a good-looking woman and head for the beach on the first fine day of the year. So say the newspaper poets. Well it is not such a simple thing and if you have ever done it, you know it isn't—unless, of course, the woman happens to be your wife or some other everyday creature so familiar to you that she is as invisible as yourself. Where there is chance of gain, there is also chance of loss. . . . (pp. 120–21)

In the clause that introduces the exchange, the modalization of the verb "you might wonder" is further underlined by the use of the conditional instead of the present. Moreover, the narratee raises objections: "You say it is a simple thing surely. . . ." Yet the narrator had tried to involve him in his own experience of the malaise by using in his illustration the indefinite "you." In "What is the malaise? *you* ask," the pronoun is exclusive, referring only to the allocutor, but in "The world is lost to *you*," the "you" is inclusive and indefinite, embracing locutor and allocutor in the commonalty of a basic human experience. Unconvinced, the narratee does not accept the narrator's vision of things, for which he will then be gently rallied. The narrator not only reverses his allocutor's assertion (". . . it is not such a simple thing"), he teases him for repeating pseudoromantic clichés ("So say the *newspaper poets*"), finally advising him to face reality: ". . . if you have ever done it, *you know* it isn't." Once Binx, starting with the hypothesis that he and the narratee occupy the same locus in regard to some imaginary act of interlocution, is led to use an inclusive "you" only to switch to an exclusive "you" in the next breath as he realizes the possibility of being misunderstood: "When it dawns at last on a man that *you* really want to hear about his business the look that comes over his face is something to see. *Do not misunderstand me.* I am no do-gooding José Ferrer going around with a little whistle to make people happy" (pp. 74–75, emphasis added). So the narrator is basically uncertain of his narratee, and for all his presence in the text the "you" allocutor is in reality at a greater distance than the grammatically unrepresented narratee implied in the many similes and analogies. Binx cannot trust that his act of consciousness will be shared. And even his attempt at sharing it is, in a sense, or rather at times, only half-hearted.

The moments of identification between narrator and narratee that do occur are therefore all the more significant. Describing his walk with Sharon to the beach, Binx instead of using "we" throughout the paragraph suddenly resorts to an unexpected "you":

Over the hillock lies the open sea. The difference is very great: first, this sleazy backwater, then the great blue ocean. The beach is clean and a big surf is rolling in; the water in the middle distance is green and lathered. You come over the hillock and your heart lifts up; your old sad music comes into the major. (p. 130)

The commutation of pronouns is of course highly equivocal. We can interpret the "you" as disjunctive, referring in fact to the "I" narratee, i. e., to a facet of the self for the benefit of which the experience is verbalized. The identification would then be narcissistic and would depend on a preliminary splitting of the self. The transformation, the coming into major of the old sad music, only affects the speaking "I" by contiguity. Or we can read the "you" as an inclusive "you." (Given the context, I think this is the more likely interpretation, but the hesitation between the two readings is also an effect of the writing.) As the narration names the experience of the open sea's bursting upon sight, it establishes its redemptory value for every and any participant in the interlocutory act. It "illimitates," so to speak, the experience just as, together with the unmarked simple present, it renders it repeatable, provisional though it be, and endows it with permanence. One more example will show how the pronominal shift can emphasize the meaning:

> Today he seems particularly glad to see me. Uncle Jules has a nice way of making you feel at home. Although he has a big office . . . and although he is a busy man, he makes you feel as if you and he had come upon this place in your wanderings; he is no more at home than you. He sits everywhere but in his own chair and does business everywhere but at his own desk. (p. 97)

The generalizing "you" displaces the "me" in syntactical mimesis of the diegetic action, since Uncle Jules, refusing the conventional sitting arrangements between boss and employee, changes places: there opens a possibility that narrator and narratee can also exchange places in the action.

The possibility indeed is once actualized: the narrator puts himself in the position of the narratee to the extent that the "you" becomes the seeing agent. What he sees is the acting self turned into a discursive third person. Describing his office building, Binx concludes:

> A little bit of New England with a Creole flavor. The Parthenon facade cost twelve thousand dollars but commissions have doubled. The young man you see inside is clearly the soul of integrity; he asks no more than to be allowed to plan your future. This is true. This is all I ask. (p. 72)

The passage gives us an insight into part of the unconscious motivation that impels Binx to his act of narration; the desire to be seen, suggested in the utterances oriented toward actors, is here made visible in a figure of speech. Whether this is simply the existentialist onlooker's wish to be looked at in his turn, "the sense of being at last what I am but a distance from myself, for another who is over here,"[19] or whether it is related to some deeper psychic need is not for us to say. In any case, the narrator-hero is reduced to being "the young man," "he," the third person who for Benveniste is a nonperson, being excluded from the *corrélation de subjectivité*.[20] Of course, the narrator reasserts his identity in the next sentence with the deictic "this" and in the explanation "This is all I ask." But how dubious the affirmation! It may be true that Jack as the young man at the counter asks for nothing more, but Jack as the experiencing self is engaged in quite another quest, which the narrator is conveniently ignoring, and Binx as the narrating self is in fact asking something entirely different from the "you" narratee. What with the momentary permutation which transforms the "I" into a "he" and the fragmenting of the self, the other meaning of the word "integrity"—the state or quality of being complete, undivided, unbroken—is superimposed on the contextual denotation of honesty in ironical transparence.

In conclusion, the many faces and roles of the narratee, the constantly altering distance between him and the narrator, dramatize Binx's estrangement, his conscious (and unconscious) role playing, his doubts regarding the communicability of his alienation. They become indirectly emblematic of the unformulability of the self, its noncoincidence with itself. Yet they also dramatize the possibility of not getting altogether entrapped in impersonations, the ever-renewed attempts at enlarging self-knowledge and establishing intersubjectivity. Moreover, insofar as the addressees serve as relays between narrator and reader, their mediation may be efficient, as when the allocutor asks our questions, ("What is a repetition?"), or conversely, may work against our too facile acceptance of the story. According to Genette, the more discreet the evocation of the narratee, the more irresistible the identification of the reader to the virtual narratee.[21] The obtrusiveness and "reality" of some of the allocutors would alone tend to distance us from the narration. Then the shifting of narratees contributes to the same effect.[22] Unable to settle comfortably on one locus from which to view the teller and the tale, we experience a mild sense of dislocation; we are made aware of our outsider status.

Faced with the changeable narratee, we may look to the narrative *act* for a stabilizing point of reference. But what is the nature of this act? From what space-time is the narrator addressing the narratee? On close analysis, the same trembling effect that shivered the narratee into fragmented allocutors ripples through the narration.

True, at first everything seems clear-cut and the novel begins conventionally enough: "This morning I got a note from my aunt asking me to come for lunch. I know what this means. . . ." The first sentences convey information on the two registers of time meshing into the novel. Both the diegetic action and the narrative act take place on the same day. Since the narrator still ponders on the significance of his aunt's invitation, narrational time may be pinpointed as before noon. With one exception, all the data supplied in the next pages are reported in the tenses that normally relate the narrated events to the time of the narration: I remember when my older brother Scott died. . . . It reminds me of a movie I saw. . . . For the four past years now I have been living uneventfully in Gentilly. . . . In the evenings I usually watch television. . . . Last night I saw a TV play. . . . Although the reader's attention may be arrested by the transformation between "*I have been living* in Gentilly" and "*We live,* Mrs. Schexnaydre and I, in Elysian Fields," both sentences are perfectly grammatical and congruent with the prevailing time scheme. The one departure from it is not even perceived as such by the reader, since, when he reads about Linda and her feelings about Jack ("She actually loves me at these times" p. 5), he has no way of knowing the affair is over. Only the narrator catches himself up: "But all this is history. Linda and I have parted company." At this point we may suppose that he lapsed into the present because the memory is still vivid for him.

This familiar pattern having been firmly set up in the first ten pages, we are ready, when confronted with the sentence "The idea of a search comes to me again as I am on my way to my aunt's house. . . ." (p. 11), to accept it as the utterance of a locutor telling about what he experiences as he is experiencing it. The narrating self seems to merge with the acting self; the slight distance between narrating time and narrated time has now been reduced to almost nothing. This illusion is maintained—at least for the unwary reader seduced by the apparent simplicity of the novel and its linear development—since the story, except for some reminiscences appropriately reported in the past tense, is throughout told in the present. If experiencing self and narrating self occupy the same space-time, then unlike Roquentin, the narrator cannot be writing. The hypothesis of a diary is further excluded by three tantalizing allusions to a notebook which Binx keeps and in which he will later jot down thoughts to which the narration makes us privy (pp. 88, 146). Binx can therefore be immediately "thinking" or mediately "speaking." If the latter, the diverse narratees cannot be accounted for realistically and neither can the lack of distance. So we tend to assume that he is "thinking," or monologuing. Although dimly bothered, for instance, by the obtrusiveness of the act of enunciation and the insistent "to tell the truth," we accept on the whole that "Walker Percy's fiction," in the words of Jim Van Cleave,[23] is that his narrator "records his consciousness moment by moment" during one week of his life. Certainly, we seem to be made the witnesses of an ongoing present.

Under the circumstances, to any reader the epilogue must be something of a jolt: "So ended my thirtieth year to heaven, as the poet called it. In June Kate and I were married . . ." (p. 236). The time locus of the narration has drastically changed and the narrator is now looking back, in the more conventional first-person narrative posture, at a past period of his life which started with that last day of the narrated week, and which he now proceeds to summarize. The break of the narrative convention shatters retroactively the illusion of reality created in the body of the novel.

Now, one might regard this as a flaw in the book, and consider that the author, presumably anxious to set Binx's week of self-awakening against the larger background of his life, before and after, chose a swift but clumsy method of presenting the existential consequences of the hero's search. Some critics' dissatisfaction with the conclusion, though expressed in thematic terms, may partly arise from a reaction of this kind to the handling of the epilogue.[24]

In fact, the sudden rupture in the time scheme functions as a signal, denouncing the fictionality of the scheme. This is already suggested by the wording of the opening sentence, which contains minor but nonetheless significant departures from normal usage. The "it," in "as the poet called it," which can only refer to the hero's thirtieth year, is absurd, and the absurdity is further strengthened by the preterit "called." One would have expected a comparison pronominally and perhaps temporally unattached to the main statement, something like "as the poet says" (or "said"). If the complex thematic function of the allusion to Dylan Thomas's "Poem in October," a celebration of the world of the senses and the world of memory, and of poetic self-identity, cannot be studied here,[25] the literariness of the sentence, undercut by the familiar tag, is itself a cue. "Thus ended my thirtieth year to heaven," though or because parodistic, invites us to read what precedes not only as the "document" Binx claims it is but also as a poetical statement, a statement therefore in which time does not quite play the part it plays in ordinary utterances or fiction.

This impression is almost immediately verified: after summing up the main events of the last fifteen months or more,[26] Binx, coming *back* to "the day before Lonnie died," tells about it in a mixture of past and present tenses. "*The day before Lonnie died,* Kate *took* a notion to pay him a visit. Ordinarily I pick her up at Merle's office, drop her off at her stepmother's and drive downtown. . . . But *today* we *have* only to walk across the street from Merle's office to Touro Infirmary" (p. 238; emphasis added). He then resorts to the past to describe Kate, only to shift back once more to the present for the rest of the narration. Obviously, the use of the present here (or of the deictic "today") does *not* signify the coincidence of narrating and narrated times. Nor is it a temporal present. The contrast between past and present tenses in the passage affords us a clue as to their functioning which is thematic, not chronological. The past is used to evoke Kate's "womanish whim" and her reaction to Lonnie's approaching death, which, however well-meant, is nevertheless conventional, "dead." The present, on the contrary, appears with Binx: characteristically, his response to his brother's death is free from sentimentality, and he tries to establish with his other sisters and brothers a more authentic relation than his aunt established with him on the similar occasion of Scott's death, when she asked him to "act like a soldier." Furthermore, the present signals a climactic moment which is otherwise told with so much restraint that its thematic importance might go unnoticed. In an interview, Percy has stressed that when Binx tells the children that the crippled Lonnie is going to rise up on the Last Day, "like Alyosha he tells the truth."[27] Now, since the simple present is the "tense of the truth,"[28] Binx, by using it here, throws on the episode a new light: he unlocates it, so to speak, freezing it in an eternal present, setting it up in a timeless, meaningful dimension. To this extent, the present is epiphanic—a metaphor for the baptism which occurs in the story whether readers see it or not.[29]

The effect of the epilogue is, in consequence, to shake us into a new awareness of what has been taking place in the narration. What if the present was not a temporal mark but a convention? Reinterpreting his experience, the enlightened reader becomes aware that the simple present in *The Moviegoer* was never that simple.

For one thing, it becomes clear that in many occurrences the present is no present at all. While they are on the bus bound for New Orleans, Kate, we read, "*is* well. The summons from her stepmother has left her neither glum nor fearful. She *speaks* at length to her stepmother and . . . *gets* her talking about cancelling reservations and return tickets, *wins* her way, *decides* we'll stay, then changes her mind and *insists* on coming home to ease their minds" (p. 213; emphasis added). All the presents italicized have no temporal value, as is frequently the case in *The Moviegoer*.[30] Or else the present may have more than a hint of futurity: "My duty in life is simple. I go to medical school. I live a long useful life serving my fellowman"

(p. 54). Interrupting the relation of his encounter in the present with Mr. Sarta-lamaccia, the narrator comments: "Later, Sharon *tells* me I was smart to trick him into revealing the true value of my duck club. But she *is* mistaken" (p. 94).

Again revealing that the tense does not necessarily convey a chronological rela-tion between the events reported, or between the events narrated and the time locus of the narrator, are the frequent instances of time shifts within the same narrative sequence.

> Tonight, Thursday night, I carry out a successful experiment in repetition.
>
> Fourteen years ago, when I was a sophomore, I saw a western at a movie house on Freret Street. . . . Yesterday evening I noticed in the *Picayune* that another western was playing at the same theater. So up I went by car to my aunt's house, then up St. Charles in a streetcar with Kate so we can walk through the campus.
>
> Nothing had changed. There we sat, I in the same seat I think. . . . A suc-cessful repetition.
>
> *
>
> "Where to now?" asks Kate. She stands at my shoulder under the marquee. . . . (p. 79)

For a more extended example than can be quoted here, see the account of Aunt Emily's telling off Binx (pp. 219-21).

On closer reading, then, we perceive that within the larger linear frame in which day is followed by day, morning by afternoon, the pattern of the narrative units often disrupts with lesser or greater amplitude the basic chronological succession. A favorite device is the synoptic introduction which summarizes the whole action and its effect beforehand. "The mystery deepens. For ten minutes I stand talking to Eddie Lovell and at the end of it, when we shake hands and part, it seems to me that I cannot answer the simplest question about what has taken place" (p. 18). Though the end of conversation is proleptically[31] announced, there follow three pages of exchange with Eddie in the present. Or take "We meet Mr. Sartalamaccia *and a queer thing happens*" (p. 90), or "It *turns out* that my misgivings about Chicago were justified . . ." (p. 201); each of these synoptic introductions consti-tutes a minor disruption of the parallelism between narrating time and narrated time. Such disruptions are sometimes quite complex, obfuscated though they are by the use of the present. "Early afternoon finds us spinning along the Gulf Coast. Things have not gone too badly. As luck would have it, no sooner do we cross Bay St. Louis and reach the beach drive than we are involved in an acci-dent . . ." (p. 120). Crossing Bay St. Louis preceded spinning along the Gulf Coast: it is therefore an explanation of the summary statement "Things have not gone too badly." Then, instead of a description of the accident, we are treated to a discus-sion of the malaise in general, the role of certain cars as "real incubators of malaise," the immunity of the MG as tested in the past, the happiness Binx used to experience with Marcia in the said MG, before we come back to what is inscribed in the text as the present, to Sharon and the narrator as they *"pass* through the burning swamps of Chef Menteur." But the moment is in reality still anterior to that which saw them spinning along the Gulf Coast. Next a flashback takes us to the even earlier hour when they left Sharon's house—an episode also told in the present.[32] Then we seem to go forward to the climax of the accident, which is in fact situated in the past in relation to the introductory paragraph. The predominant use of the present throughout such sequences—together with an occasional but by no means consistent use of the preterit for a few flashbacks—blurs the time levels and effaces the prolepses and analepses, which may well be ignored by the casual reader. Yet now and then the narration may subtly draw attention to them, as in what is probably the first prolepsis of the novel. "This morning," Binx had the unfamiliar experience of suddenly "seeing" the little pile of his belongings on the bureau. "Once I saw it, however, the search became possible" (p. 10). Though put in the past tense, the remark is a judgment of the narrating self and we accept it as such. Then we read, "The idea of a search comes to me again as I am on my way to my aunt's house." Do we believe that he is entertaining the thought as he is telling about it? We are wrong: this is another intrusion of the narrating self who pro-leptically tells what is going to happen later: "*Then it is* that the idea of the search occurs to me" (p. 13). Here the *repetition* (modulated by "Then it is"), while keeping in our minds the theme of the quest, underlines that the two presents which recount a single event cannot have the same temporal value and that the first, in reality, refers to a diegetic future.

Thus, numerous signs indicate that the tense system of *The Moviegoer* is a convention employed by the narrator for his own purposes. Our impression that there is little distance between narrating self and experiencing self is an illusion created (and denounced) by the text. The distance is in reality variable and cannot be assessed with any certainty. The inner organization of the narrative units implies that they are not the fictively simultaneous reproduction of moments of consciousness but the a posteriori production of acts of narration which purport to record the struggle into consciousness. But what they pretend to do they also symbolize. They are emblematic of the very nature of consciousness which is struggle into language and the structure of linguistic temporalization.

When the illusion of immediacy is shown up as illusion, our part as readers changes: no longer merely invited to look on the spectacle of an emerging awareness, we must, more importantly, enjoy and participate in the performance that verbalization constitutes. The difficulty we had to label the narration, whether in terms of inner monologue, diary, or shared consciousness, is explained away. Assuredly, *The Moviegoer* is a story "about a young man in a certain situation," "put down into the world under certain circumstances"[33] which are defined in reference to a real place, New Orleans, to a job typical of twentieth-century economic society, and so on. But the novel is not, for all that, "a document," as Binx with the guile of many a fictional narrator calls his story. It is a creative statement building with words a fictive consciousness engaged in the unlocated and unlocatable—virtual—task of apprehending itself through the matrix of language.

To observe that the use of the present designates the first-person discourse as an artifice does not of course entirely account for its use in *The Moviegoer*. Two lines of inquiry remain open. What other effects on the narration originate from its use? And more particularly, what does it contribute to the creation of the narrator-hero? To be sure, the distinction is somewhat arbitrary since one or another of the points to be considered next might be studied under either heading. But to bypass the problem of Binx would be to discount the fact that the story comes through him alone, and to ascribe all the narrative effects to him would be to make him into a conscious artist—in short, to confuse him with the author.

In the words of Roy Pascal, the present "establishes a character for whom the present is all."[34] To some extent this is true of Binx, a "sensualist-thinker," immersed in the moment which brings him its unique bundle of sensations, perceptions, and food for thought. This existential attitude is probably part of Binx's reaction against the family tradition that looks at today's life from the standpoint of the once significant southern past and against the aunt who "wanted to pass on to [him] the one heritage of the men of [the] family, a certain quality of spirit, a gaiety, a sense of duty, a nobility worn lightly, a sweetness, a gentleness with women—the only good things the South ever had" (p. 224). Aunt Emily's insistence on tradition reminds one of a remark which William Alexander Percy passed on the blacks:

> This failure on their part, to hold and to pass their own history, is due, I think, not so much to their failure to master any written form of communication as to their genius for living in the present . . . [The Negro] neither remembers nor plans. The white man does little else; *to him the present is the one great unreality.*[35]

It is as though Binx wanted to assert himself against his aunt by making the present the one reality. Moreover, if the preterit accentuates the alterability and alterity of the self, conversely the present is the tense of self-confirmation ensuring the identity of the speaking "I" if only for the time of the utterance. Thus, throughout his conscious role playing and notwithstanding his intermittent awareness of being an "exile," Binx keeps reassuring himself as to his self-identity. Indirect proof is found in the past tense part of the epilogue: then Binx, though still saying "I," can afford to become another, a character whose life can be summarized in terms of the society page. But rather than a man for whom the present is all, the narrator-hero appears as a man who would like the present to be all. He is less interested in recording the emerging instant, the immediacy of any given event, the particular process, than he is in suspending time. Hence his preference for the simple present over the progressive form, which he employs sparingly, although in many cases it would be more idiomatic.[36] The predominance of the simple present reveals Binx's unconscious fear of change, process—death. The simple present insulates the moment, restores to time some of its "purity" by being in essence timeless. Its frequency also gives evidence of Binx's interest in events not so much in themselves but as "particularizations of truths." The simple present is part and parcel of the search for meaning—being. These aspects we shall deal with again. It suffices here to observe that the present (as distinguished from both the progressive form and the past perfect) also enables Binx to cocoon himself in discrete time units and thereby to preserve his attitude of indifference, his self-protecting estrangement from the world around him.

As readers we easily relate the present to the locutor, yet we are also aware that the choice of the tense is the novelist's and that it affects us as participants in the act of communication. For one thing, the use of the present blots out one salient characteristic of first-person narration, whose "essence," as A. A. Mendilow has pointed out, is to be "retrospective."[37] In *The Moviegoer* the illusion is that the story is told "forward from the past" and not "backward from the present." To this extent, the reader's stance is akin to what it is when he reads a third-person novel; yet, in another respect, *The Moviegoer* places the fictive reader in a different time locus. However much the past-tense novel "presentifies" the action, and even though we should translate its past into a present, it nevertheless secures the reader in his position since, whatever the problems raised, they have been either resolved, no matter how dramatically or inconclusively, or at any rate put aside. In the novel written in the present tense, everything—including the narration—is still problematic,[38] or as problematic as anything in a work of fiction. We only know that the novel has a certain length, which the thickness of the book, the kind of type, and so on, enable us to evaluate. We do not know but that Walker Percy may have Binx die on us, for instance, and another narrator take over to explain how and why. The further we read, of course, the more remote this possibility becomes, but the possibility of such a surprise is never precluded, and indeed a surprise awaits us in the epilogue. If the novel written in the past tense is, as Charles Grivel insists, *répétition*,[39] the first-person novel in the present tense, insofar as it gives us the impression of building up a world and creating signification as it goes along, is, to adapt Binx's (and Walker Percy's) language, a "rotation": it is a metaphoric zone-crossing enabling the reader imaginatively to "explore the It while retaining his option of non-commitment,"[40] offering him a temporary mode of deliverance from alienation without an aesthetic reversal.

On the whole, the predominant use of the simple present may be said to work in two ways which, albeit not absolutely contradictory, establish a tension that energizes the novel. The use of the present is *a device of alienation,* inasmuch as it paradoxically keeps the reader from identifying too closely with the hero. Certainly, one cannot agree with A. A. Mendilow that "a narrative in the first person and written throughout in the present tense would, if it were possible at all, appear so artificial as to make any identification impossible. It would obviously be limited to sensations and thoughts and exclude all action."[41] Yet one must observe that the present makes the hero more remote and the narrator more obtrusive. In this regard, it achieves here, with a different modus operandi, something of what the *passé composé* did to Meursault's narration in *The Stranger.* Not that the simple present is a conversational tense, as is the *passé composé* in French; it is, on the contrary, "unspeechlike" (Wright's word). However difficult it is to pinpoint individual instances of this (e.g., "I speak with my aunt several times on the telephone"), the cumulative effect of the simple present when one would rather expect perfects, or progressive presents—in the description of physical events and of attitudes, for instance—confers on Binx's utterance some quality of elusive strangeness. This something ever so slightly foreign that hangs about the narrator's speech arouses in *us* a faint feeling of estrangement.

In addition, all actions tend to be seen in isolation—an effect which is often increased by the short sentences and the lack of connectives.

> We wander along the dark paths of the campus and stop off at my weedy stoop behind the laboratory. I sit on the concrete step and think of nothing. Kate presses her bleeding thumb to her mouth. "What is this place?" she asks. A lamp above the path makes a golden sphere among the tree-high shrubs. (p. 81)

This at times gives the narration a choppy tempo that prevents us from slipping easily and unconsciously into the world it creates. (In the description of Eddie Lovell (p. 18), the effect works counter to the impression which the narrator wants to impose upon us—but does not quite believe in—of a man with an identity and a purpose, and rather shows us a scattered man in a fragmented world.)

Another conspicuous effect of the simple present is the leveling out of the difference between the "autobiography" and the synopsis of some movie or other:

> On the way home I stop off at the Tivoli. It is a Jane Powell picture and I have no intention of seeing it. However, Mr. Kinsella the manager sees me and actually pulls me in by the coat sleeve for a sample look. . . . There go Jane and some fellow walking arm in arm down the street in a high wide and handsome style and doing a wake up and sing number. The doorman, the cop on the corner, the taxi driver, each sunk in his own private misery, smile and begin to tap their feet. I am hardly ever depressed by a movie and Jane Powell is a very nice-looking girl, but the despair of it is enough to leave you gone in the stomach. I look around the theater. Mr. Kinsella has his troubles too. There are only a few solitary moviegoers scattered through the gloom, the afternoon sort and the most ghostly of all, each sunk in his own misery, Jane or no Jane. On the way out I stop at the ticket window and speak to Mrs. de Marco. . . . (pp. 73–74)

If the present is the appropriate tense for critical summaries because it is "unemphatic" and "toneless,"[42] one may wonder whether this tonelessness does not contaminate somewhat the account of "actual" events. More clearly, since cinematographic reality and autobiographic reality merge so smoothly, since the hero's life seems to have the same degree of reality/unreality as that of the movie hero, we feel distanced from both. One may add that the occasional breaking of the general tense system is also instrumental in keeping us aware of the unusual pattern of tenses to which otherwise we would become accustomed. Thus, variability is a factor of detachment.

At the same time and divergently, the simple present is used to establish a lyrical mode.[43] Granted all the differences between poetry and prose, the fine analysis which George T. Wright makes of the "lyric present" seems to me to be germane to our study of *The Moviegoer*. To give but a few brief examples, Wright shows how verbs describing a physical action "perhaps repeatable but taking place only once as far as we can judge," when used in the lyric present, acquire "a portentousness, a freedom from singleness"; the action is definitely there "not only in the sense that it can be returned to again and again but in the sense that it remains, it abides."[44] Such portentousness is easily perceived, for instance, in the description of the "downtown swing of Neptune" (pp. 61-62). Every action of the participants and onlookers is magnified and suspended in a timeless dimension through the use of the simple present. The whole parade takes on a hallucinatory quality until a very simple and harmless fact comes to be apprehended as fraught with meaning and perhaps threat.

> Negro boys run along behind the crowd to keep
> up with the parade and catch the trinkets that
> sail too high.
> The krewe captain and a duke come toward
> us on horseback.
> I ask Kate whether she wants to see Walter. (p. 62)

Albeit undescribed, the captain and duke "acquire a strangely monumental character," as Wright would say. The effect is, of course, enhanced by the isolation of the sentence in a paragraph of its own and by the diction: though we are conversant with the meaning of "krewe captain" or "duke" in the context of Mardi Gras, the words still radiate a vague historical aura. In the William Holden sequence (pp. 15-16) the simple present confers on Holden's action a special significance and permanence in contrast with those of the crowd, which are temporally subordinated, reduced to mere process: "Holden *crosses* Royal and *turns* toward Canal. As yet he is unnoticed. The tourists *are* either *browsing* along antique shops or *snapping* pictures of balconies . . ." (p. 15; emphasis added). The very minor event of the honeymooners' encounter with Holden turns into a sort of ritual exchange and dubbing whereby Holden bestows some of his own "resplendent reality" on the initiate.

> The boy holds out a light, nods briefly to Holden's thanks, then passes on without a flicker of recognition. Holden walks along between them for a second; he and the boy talk briefly, look up at the sky, shake their heads. Holden gives them a pat on the shoulder and moves on ahead.
> The boy has done it! He has won title to his own existence, as plenary an existence now as Holden's, by refusing to be stampeded like the ladies from Hattiesburg. (p. 16)

The present here is felt as what Wright calls a "ceremonious present." Each gesture is singled out and encapsulated, its theatricality announced. Since, with the exception of "resplendent," "precarious," and "plenary," the diction throughout the passage is quite plain, the illusion of solemnity is projected mostly through the tense system and the sentence structure. And the transformation of the boy is evidenced by a shift in forms. "Why he must *be thinking*, . . . we might as well *be rubbernecking* in Hollywood." "All at once the world is open to him. Nobody threatens from patio and alley. . . ." Moreover, through the sequence the ceremonious present modulates into the sportscaster present, which also signals a public event, stressing the uniqueness and urgency of each act as well as its validity and congruence with the pattern of the ceremonial action. At the end Binx as the announcer comments on the boy's performance in the exclamatory style of such statements. "The boy has done it! He has won his title. . . ." The sequence admirably illustrates how the narration, to picture the "heightened reality" of movie actors, weaves its own verbal heightening of reality.

Similar effects in the descriptions of the outside world impress us with its solidity and permanence even when the scene is full of movement:

> The sky is a deep bright ocean full of light and life. . . . High above the Lake a broken vee of ibises points for the marshes; they go suddenly white as they fly into the tilting salient of sunlight. Swifts find a windy reach of sky and come twittering down so fast I think at first gnats have crossed my eyelids. In the last sector of apple green a Lockheed Connie lowers from Mobile, her running lights blinking in the dusk. (p. 73)

Even fluidity and evanescense are arrested; emergence is no longer a process but a sudden coming into being:

> A deformed live oak emerges from the whiteness, stands up in the air like a tree in a Chinese print. Minutes pass. An egret lets down on his light stiff wings and cocks one eye at the water (p. 148)

Lo! the tree *is* there, frozen into the timelessness of art, as the simile suggests. However uncertain the self, the outside world, for all the meteorological changes, abides as if under a spell. It is ever an enchanted world, of which mystery is an observable albeit changeable dimension: "The mystery *deepens*" (p. 18). Revelation, we are made to feel, is around the corner. Thus, we are estranged too, but our estrangement brings us closer to Binx, "solitary and in wonder." Forgetful of his mediation, we see each scene in a visionary light that makes everything at once transparent and numinous. Endowed with new sight—which gift is the essence of the lyrical mode—we grow confident that it all means something.

Yet Binx is a lyricist *malgré lui.* "A regular young Rupert Brooke was I," says he, deriding his past self (and the present one, as well). Although the lyrical mode is related to his sense of wonder, to his sensuous apprehension of the world through smells, sounds, and tactile impressions, and to the intensity that underlies his flippancy, it functions, as it were, independently from him, again exhibiting the presence of the novelist. What with the inclusion of short poems in prose, the use of cinema techniques, and a language which not only creates but circumvents the narrator-hero, Percy expands the narrator's perceptions into a separate world of images. The establishment of interacting perspectives—together with the plasticity granted the narrator—enables the author to "alter Binx's tone," in the words of Mary Thale, "from mysticism to clichés to plainest prose without producing any incongruity."[45] His dominant tone, however—all the more effective for not being unique—is *irony,* an irony of speech "paralleled by the irony of his life."[46] Mary Thale has too well caught the many inflections of Binx's irony for me to do more than refer to her article. What needs stressing here is that this irony is at times so involuted that the mental calisthenics it requires from the reader, while most enjoyable, prohibit unself-conscious identification with the narrator-hero. Sometimes, too, one cannot help wondering whether he may not, out of the depth of his despair, be trapping himself in one of his ironic poses. Then the double vision is the reader's—reverberating Binx's—in the ever-renewed disengagement which is a requisite for true engagement.

Sincere and lucid as he undoubtedly is, the narrator is not above a little play-acting. Nor is he quite as open as he at first appears or even wishes to be: his frequent "to tell the truth," "to tell the absolute truth," are suspicious. As Bruce Morrissette has pointed out, one of "the technical features in the I-narration that serve to undermine [the] establishment of intimacy or sympathy in the reader's response" is ellipsis.[47] Together with a conventional use of this narrative figure, we find in *The Moviegoer* a subtle variety of ellipsis which Gérard Genette calls *paralipse*.[48] Paralipsis is not the omission of a time segment but the suppression of a *donnée* (a fictional fact) and as such less obtrusive, since it will only appear if and when the information is later provided. Thus, the statement "I have been living uneventfully in Gentilly" (p. 6) is taken up and musically developed for five pages. Then wham! a dissonance: "But things have suddenly changed. This morning, for the first time in years, there occurred to me the possibility of a search" (p. 10). The parallel to the opening sentence of the novel alerts us to the legerdemain that has been practiced on us. The narrator chose to install us in the comfortable intimacy of a life that may have been somewhat humdrum but over which there only hung the slight threat of the aunt's "serious talk." In fact, he knew all the while that this "peaceful existence" was jeopardized from the moment when he had the unusual experience of "seeing" the little pile on his bureau. The narrator has been playing the storyteller's trick of withholding information to spring it on his audience all in his good time, and he has also postponed introducing the metaphor that gives us a key to his life (and possible salvation): "Everything is upside down for me" (p. 10). The narrator makes a habit of deferred communication. In mid-story we read that "for some time the impression has been growing upon me that everyone is dead" (p. 99), yet the feeling, we now learn, came upon him during the early conversation with Eddie which we hitherto believed had been reported in all significant detail. First boasting of his interest in health and hygiene—"My armpits never stink" (p. 7)—Binx later admits that he "do[es] not try to sleep" and could not tell when his bowels last moved (p. 86).[49]

True, such paralipses do not necessarily imply conscious misrepresentation. But whatever the reason for the narrator's evasion, once perceived, they impair his credibility. Conversely, as evidence of the narrator's control over a narration which seemed an act of shared consciousness—and in any case molded by its time-container—they strengthen our confidence in his power to shape experience and our desire to see through his selecting and editing.

And so we come around to the question of the *function* of the narration for the narrator. Apart from any unconscious motivation, which we can only guess at (and which I have alluded to), Binx evidently assigns diverse functions to his recital, stressing now one, now the other. Curiously enough, since he eschews abstractions and generalizations, he makes his story the vehicle of his theories on the malaise, and with a neatness that provisionally turns the speaking "I" into the self-assured and empty "I" of philosophic (and academic) discourse, he defines his many strategies to cope with everydayness. These brief pedagogic outbursts, while they serve the novelist's ideological purpose, also add to the complexity of Binx's personality and exemplify the contradictions inherent to the search. Starting with the meaninglessness of everyday life, the failure of the humanistic discourse to deal with the dissolving of the fabric, the search also involves the need—and use—of symbols that can articulate private experience and express the generality of the malaise—in short, *found* meaning. Furthermore, Binx, certain only of his ability "to recognize merde," feels compelled to record the points of view of other people, especially Aunt Emily's. Her conversations with Binx are reported at length and commented on ("For her too the fabric is dissolving, but for her even the dissolving makes sense," p. 54), so that readers have mistaken her for the author's mouthpiece.[50] The reporting of other worldviews does not initiate a dialogue within the story,[51] just as the talks with Aunt Emily in the diegesis are not real exchanges, Binx's contributions consisting mostly of "yes ma'am" and "no'm" or silence. But it projects the conflict of ideologies that may partly impel Binx's narrative effort. Alienated from both his aunt's humanist stoicism and his mother's Catholicism, Binx is in an existentialist predicament which he "solves" in two ways: experientially by confirming his "vocation" as a listener, "There is only one thing I can do: listen to people, see how they stick themselves into the world, hand them along a ways in their dark journeys and be handed along for good and selfish reasons" (p. 233); and symbolically by verbalizing it and trying to make people listen to him.

Verbalization, naturally, is not confined to bouts of wry didacticism. Usually Binx takes on the role of keen-eyed witness, thereby making his relation a *testimony* to his and the world's sickness. For while he owns that "everything is upside down" for him, he also exposes one or "another thing about the world which is upside down." In this mood he offers not statements, but sketches of himself or of modern man as moviegoer, businessman, romantic, *Reader's Digest* reader, and so forth. In all the kaleidoscopic images that flicker on the screen of his narration, there shimmers a void, the lack of something. (People are "dead" or "ghostly." "I muse along as quietly as a ghost," p. 86.) Or else there trembles an elusive presence. (The world is "haunted"; you can be "bewitched by the presence of a building.") On one hand, a city may look "never-tenanted," on the other, cemeteries "look like cities." The narration testifies both to the impoverishment of reality and to its pregnance. Proclaiming absence/presence, it becomes a paradigm of reversibility.

At other times Binx simply wants to *name* things, thus assuming the role of a poet. Whereas his aunt's words conceal reality under her culture-encrusted private symbols, and have a tendency to make Binx sleepy—an index to their deadness—his words—in his best moments—"discover being," and he becomes "a cocelebrant of what is."[52] One parallel underlines the difference: when Aunt Emily calls Uncle Jules a Cato, she denies his true nature; when Binx suddenly can see Kate plain, "see plain for the first time since [he] lay wounded in a ditch . . ," he names her: she is "a tough little city Celt, no, more of a Rachel, really, a dark little Rachel bound home to Brooklyn on the IRT" (p. 206). Since Binx, aware of "being more Jewish than the Jews," recognizes her as a fellow exile, her existence too is a clue ("Jews are my first real clue," p. 89), and a clue to being. "He is celebrating with someone else a common phenomenon, and this for Percy is the constituent act of consciousness."[53] As a litmus test, Binx is next able to detect in Kate "a touch of the true Creole," whereas Aunt Emily refuses to see Uncle Jules as the "canny Cajun" he is. Whatever his purposes in telling his story, it seems that Binx stops when, concluding that "it is impossible to say," to tell what the truth is, he discovers that it is still possible to do, i.e., to care and to connect.

All in all, Binx's storytelling is a leap in the dark, a religious reaching out to make some kind of connection, an act of faith akin to Pascal's *pari*, which reflects the nature of his search and is reflected in a pattern which is *poetic* and not, appearances to the contrary notwithstanding, mimetic. If all literature is, in the words of Suzanne K. Langer, "virtual memory," the strategy of *The Moviegoer* is to compound that virtuality by virtualizing virtual experience and basically leaving the text unattached to reality. In this view, Binx's act of narration is *not* "an affirmation of being through shared consciousness";[54] the sharing of consciousness that does occur unites Kate and Jack *in the diegesis* and, hopefully, the novelist and the reader in the writing/reading experience. Nor can the narration be said to be the means for the narrator to reverse his alienation: insofar as this can be surmounted, it is transcended by a diegetic breakthrough from the Kierkegaardian aesthetic stage to the religious, not by "aesthetic reversion" as has been implied. In his interview with Walker Percy, Zoltán Abádi-Nagy suggested that "by communicating their alienation [Binx and Barrett] get rid of it."[55] Although Percy seems to agree ("There is something there. In the case of Binx it is left open. The ending is ambiguous"), I cannot concur in what is an oversimplification of the case. (Notice too that the novelist later denies the ambiguity of the ending when he states that Binx "regained his mother's religion"). If one could eliminate the malaise by speaking it, then psychoanalysis, the talking cure, would be the panacea.

In his remarks on the "literature of alienation [which] is in reality the triumphant reversal of alienation *through its representing*,"[56] Percy emphasizes the *mediation* of the writer, although he does not employ the word. When the novelist "writes about one thing and reverses it through communication," then can "the reading commuter rejoice in the speakability of his alienation and in the new triple alliance of himself, the alienated character, and the author."[57] In the triple alliance which *The Moviegoer* so brilliantly establishes, Binx assuredly plays two parts, as "alienated character" and as narrator attempting an "exercise in intersubjectivity." But the latter role originates in a splitting off of the former, to which it must therefore be related. So that the cast of the dynamic triangle consists of Walker Percy, John Bickerson Bolling, and you (or me). Binx's position is made clear through a number of signals which betoken in particular the fictitious character of his narration, whereas in *Nausea* Roquentin's pseudodiary is on the contrary self-dated and certified by the "editor"'s note. Undoubtedly, Binx may relieve some of his malaise by speaking it. But neither content with himself as an audience, nor absolutely confident of reaching anyone else, unwilling moreover to talk about the ulterior stage of his search, the narrator is only free to bring his narration to an end. The time is indeed late, and communication is at best but an uneasy business.

Since the transmuting of everydayness is the achievement of the dissimulated novelist, it is all the more necessary to catch him at his alchemist's trade: analyses of the structure of the story, which though without a conventional plot is not without a design, of the use of space, of the images, are therefore needed. Even in this inquiry centered on Binx's narration, two major strategies have constantly revealed the hidden writer. Alienation devices open up gaps between the figures of the narrative game—between the narrator's vivid fluency and the character's inarticulateness in diegetic conversations, between the protagonist and personae with whom certain readers are likely to sympathize, like Aunt Emily, or, more directly, between the narrator-hero and the fictive reader. Such gaps, mirroring the object/subject split and/or the isolation of the modern castaway, prevent us from thoughtlessly empathizing with the hero as the victim of consumer society; separating us from him, they allow us to apprehend his existential predicament and to experience the shock of recognition.

In the two novels of alienation which Percy acknowledges as models, *Nausea* and *The Stranger*,[58] the protagonist, a self-confessed outsider, is even more radically detached from us, although Camus insidiously reconciles us to Meursault in the last chapters. Indeed, Percy boldly reversed the procedure of *The Stranger* by making identification to Binx easier, if not greater, at the beginning. Using a "middle class dream"[59] hero in order to expose the middle class nightmare, the novelist ran great risks. His tactics are to keep the signals that tell us how to respond to the characters, i.e., how to read the novel, ambiguous and shifting from the first. The impact of *The Moviegoer* partly results from the crisscrossing of our ever-changing responses to Binx as narrator and as hero: now the tricks of the narrator may alienate us from the suffering, disintegrating hero, now his liberating irony and verbal agility may illuminate the abyss of his despair, spotlighting *our* anxiety. On the other hand, the devices of lyricism as they shed new light on Binx's experience paradoxically estrange it from the world as we may know it, only to make it more familiar to our deeper imagination. Thus, the tensions of *The Moviegoer* keep us balancing from identification with to rejection of the narrator-hero, until we must needs accept the total image of the novel in jubilant affirmation: "Yes, yes, that is how it is." Reader and writer have become cocelebrants in the rites of symbolic communication.

Yves Le Pellec

5. RABBIT UNDERGROUND

In a recent interview[1] Jean-Paul Sartre, going over his hybrid activity as novelist and philosopher, makes an interesting distinction between style and expression. Style, the language of fiction and poetry, differs from philosophical or scientific communication—in which "each sentence must have but one meaning"—by the fact that

> . . . it is first and foremost a way of saying three or four things in one. There is the simple sentence, with its surface meaning, and then, underneath, various meanings taking an order in depth. If one isn't capable of making language yield up a plurality of meanings there's no point in writing.

What is true of the sentence holds good for the novel as well. And in this perspective one must admit that Sartre's estimation is rather embarrassing for the critic who, in his desire to clarify a book, is often tempted to give a privileged position to one meaning and to raise it to the status of objective truth. Pierre Macherey, in his challenging *Pour une théorie de la production littéraire,*[2] denounces this attitude as "interpretive illusion" and enumerates its inconveniences. Radical interpretation presupposes that one has accepted the concept of the unity of a literary work, as if all the phenomena of a text served a unique purpose planned beforehand by the author. Or contrarywise, if the meaning is not obvious at first reading, the text comes to be considered as a treacherous excrescence concealing a "message" that the critic has to set free. This leads him to neglect, warp, or simply erase the elements which do not fit his own construction. Finally, however stimulating his conclusion may be, he has destroyed the diversity of the original and replaced it with an inert replica. The book has not been explained, it has been reduced, sometimes to one sentence summing up the writer's "vision of the world." Though it seems hardly possible to avoid the snares of interpretation, one cannot but agree with Macherey when he declares that the function of criticism is to apprehend a text in its dynamics and complexity: by studying its semantic conflicts.

The interest of Updike as a moral fabulist is that his judgments are never univocal. By his own avowal, he has too much tenderness for his characters to condemn their follies. On the other hand, his sense of humor and his ethics do not permit him to let their foibles go unnoticed. He himself acknowledges this duality when he affirms that all his work says "Yes, but."[3] We find the same ambivalence in the definition he gives of the people he considers as spiritually alive: "I feel that to be a person is to be in a situation of tension, is to be in a dialectical situation."[4] Most of the charm of Updike's protagonists in general, and of Harry Angstrom in particular, is that, close to them as we may feel, we can never really anticipate the inconclusive ending to which their contradictions will lead them. We do not even know where Rabbit is heading at the end of *Rabbit, Run*. Perhaps it is because of this ultimate ambiguity that his existence leaves such a lasting impression on our inner sensibilities . . .

Ten years later, bringing him back to life in *Rabbit Redux*, Updike poses the critic another problem: must he consider this book as a continuation or just as another step in the novelist's itinerary? In recent years, as a reaction against the excesses of critical biography and literary history, there has developed a tendency to regard a novel as a self-contained unit producing its own logic, its own reference system. And indeed *Rabbit Redux* can be pleasurable and exciting even if one has not read the first book, Updike providing enough data to enable us to have a fair understanding of the factual links between the two works. Yet it is obvious that there exist shades of meaning perceptible only to those who are already familiar with *Rabbit, Run*. Elements of the decor such as the iceplant, the park, the quarry, images like those of the web, the net, the hole, carry latent connotations that the newcomer cannot grasp. He can neither fully enjoy the comical zest of the inversion of roles—epitomized by Harry's complaint: "Everybody now is like the way I used to be"[5]—nor be aware of the similarities between the two novels, similarities in structure[6] but also in tone since Updike returns here to the present tense he had almost completely abandoned after *Rabbit, Run*. Besides, through a series of echoes, reminders, and private jokes, he establishes with the initiated reader a complicity which greatly contributes to his pleasure. Mirroring scenes and motifs from the first book, even going to the length of repeating complete sentences,[7] the author plays on an intertextual shuttle which modifies the separate meaning of each book. Following his example, one can imagine that it may be instructive to juxtapose or superpose fragments of his prose and either other passages of his books or the production of another writer used as external reference. The purpose of this article is to work out a number of variations on the character of Rabbit, concentrating primarily on his apprehension of "the poetry of space" (*RRe*, p. 77) and on the metaphors which express it.[8]

At the time Updike was writing *Rabbit, Run*, much of the attention of the American literary public was still focused on the breakthrough of the "beat" writers. Though John Clellon Holmes's *Go* came out in 1952, and Burroughs's *Junkie* in 1953, it was not until the *Howl* trial and the publication of *On the Road* in 1957 that the "new barbarians" became a subject of heated discussion in the commercial media and the *Partisan Review*. The excitement began to die down toward the close of the 1950s, many observers concluding that, after all, they had been mistaken in assuming that a new "generation" had just emerged. The youth movement and the counterculture of the next decade were to prove them wrong. It seems obvious today, in the light of the recent reconsideration of the fifties proposed for instance by such films as *The Last Picture Show* or *American Graffiti,* that the beats did give literary shape and significance to the vague expectations and as yet unformulated longings of the young people, who, like John Updike, were eighteen in 1950. And indeed most constituents of the beat mystique appear in the sensibility of Harry Angstrom: his sentimental involvement with the popular culture of his time; his bitter dissatisfaction with the standards of the era of conformity; his instinctive revolt against the forces of depersonalization; his somewhat inarticulate, though insistently asserted, belief in "something else"; his desire, unconsidered but persistent, to get away from it all and go back to nature; all this makes of him an archetypal figure now, that of the pioneer on the trail of modern disaffiliation. It may seem preposterous, or at least far-fetched, to mention Updike in connection with the beats, considering the gulf which separates a "*New Yorker* writer" from a contributor to the now defunct *Beatitude,* or the clash in style, craft, and vision between, say, *The Centaur* and *Doctor Sax*. Though the two books are based on memories of adolescence, Kerouac acknowledges that his writing is an "endless contemplation" of—and a sort of love song to—his life, whereas Updike has stated that, contrary to what one would expect, there is no "essential connection between [his] life and whatever [he] write[s]."[9]

Yet, if the two authors diverge in the treatment of experience, there is no denying some rather striking similarities in the emotions that went into the making of their personalities. Their works give evidence of an uncommon devotion to the memory of their parents, in both cases: a tolerant, humorous, good-hearted father, and an exacting mother of exceptional stature who expects her son to prove equal to the image and ideal she has set for him. The Christian education they received as children was determinant for both authors: it permeates their books not only with a diffuse spirituality which may manifest itself as a quest for what is called in *Rabbit, Run* as well as in *On the Road* the "It," but also with a concern for the more orthodox religious aspect of established churches, an area of experience which has not been explored by many modern American writers. Another trait that sets them apart from their contemporaries, in the age of the big city novel, is their passion for the small town in which they grew up. Shillington and Lowell, their stores, vacant lots, and public libraries, become for the reader a familiar utopia on which he projects his own mythic topography, so that no matter how flimsy the plot may be, he identifies himself with the central character and sympathizes with his problems. Among these the essential one is the riddle of existence suggested to Jackie Duluoz by the snow of Massachussets on winter nights in the French Canadian district of Lowell, and to Harry Angstrom by the blank faces of familiar red-brick houses in Potter Avenue:

> Why does any one live here? Why was he set down here, why is this town, a dull suburb of a third-rate city, for him the center and index of a universe that contains immense prairies, mountains, deserts, forests, cities, seas? This childish mystery—the mystery of "any place," prelude to the ultimate, "Why am I me?"—ignites panic in his heart. (*RRu,* p. 229)

Whether this panic leads to the obsession of flight which takes hold of Harry in the first book or to the kind of stolid despair to which he has resigned himself in *Rabbit Redux,* no solution will be provided to the central enigma. Updike seems to have known this from the start. Kerouac exhausted himself looking for an answer in exile and eventually lost his life in the search, after reaching the disillusioned conclusion that "all is vanity."[10]

Yet the former writer's sense of place in no way cancels out the tension in his works resulting from the juxtaposition of a sedentary existence and interstate travel. In the markedly autobiographical story "The Happiest I Have Been," the narrator drives past his parents' farm on his way to Chicago after an all-night party in Olinger and is thrilled by the thought of them asleep, dreaming he is in Indiana, when he is just setting out on his trip. Then he yields to the pleasure of the road:

> There were many reasons for my feeling so happy. We were on our way. I had seen a dawn. This far, Neil could appreciate, I had brought us safely. Ahead, a girl waited who, if I asked, would marry me, but first there was a vast trip: many hours and towns intervened between me and that encounter.[11]

The journey need not be long or eventful for Updike's heroes to relish the elation of going away. Bech, the world-weary, self-distrustful Jewish writer, gets more of a kick out of a mere hop from Manhattan to rural Virginia than from any of his visits to the communist countries of eastern Europe, thus echoing the loving messages his creator sends to his country when abroad:

AMERICA
you are the only land.[12]

Interestingly, Updike chose to call Bech's first novel, a best seller of the 1950s successful on campuses as "the post-Golding pre-Tolkien fad of college graduates,"[13] *Travel Light.* This book, which describes "the adoration for space and speed"[14] of young people roaming the American continent on motorcycles, is more reminiscent of some *Easy Rider* version of *On the Road* than of anything Updike himself or for that matter any member of the so-called New York Jewish school has, to my knowledge, ever written.[15] In fact, *Travel Light* appears as the picaresque novel *Rabbit, Run* would have been, had his author decided to let Harry be lured into the pursuit of the "mermaids" with orange hair and the exotic "barefoot women" that beckon him away from Brewer (*RRu,* pp. 29, 22). Yet, though he only half-responds to their enticements, he never really turns a deaf ear to the call of faraway places, remembering in *Rabbit Redux* the fascination they exerted upon him as a child:

He imagined then he would travel to every country in the world and send Mom a postcard from every one, with these stamps. He was in love with the idea of travelling, with running, with geography, with Parcheesi and Safari and all board games where you roll the dice and move; the sense of a railroad car was so vivid he could almost see his sallow overhead light, tulip-shaped, tremble and sway with the motion. (p. 323)

Any reader of Updike will unmistakably recognize in this passage a receptiveness to the idea of motion shared by many of his characters and instilled in him by— among other things ranging from a predilection for Whitman's verse to the intensely felt pleasure of the daily ride to Shillington in his father's car—the influence of his mother, who disliked living in Shillington and turned her son's eyes toward the open road. On the top of Slade Hill, the "child's mountain" overlooking Olinger, Allen Dow hears from his mother's lips the thrilling prediction: "You are going to fly," and immediately recognizes it as "the clue [he] ha[s] been waiting all [his] childhood for."[16] Just like Mrs. Dow, who cannot accept her son's "wish to be ordinary," Mrs. Angstrom, though in her declining years, musters enough of her former uncompromising "force" to encourage Rabbit to "run. Leave Brewer" (*RRe*, p. 172). Of course, he is by now too helplessly drowned in humdrum mediocrity to respond to her urging. But even in his reckless twenties he could never face the prospect of deserting his familiar environment, despite all he thought to the contrary. In this he resembles Allen Dow, who intends to "exploit both the privileges of being extraordinary and the pleasures of being ordinary."[17] Being ordinary means for Harry watching a clever TV program, working as a gardener for Mrs. Smith, feeling deliciously guilty when going to bed with a prostitute, standing by one's wife at the moment of birth, and being forgiven by one's parents-in-law after an affair with another woman. But it means in particular belonging in Mt. Judge. Rabbit, except for a stay in Texas as a soldier, has hardly ever gone beyond the boundaries of his town. He has avoided the important stage in the process of alienation city life is made to represent in most renderings of modern exile. On his abortive trip south he is careful to keep out of reach of Baltimore and Washington, which he sees as a "two-headed guard" on the road to adventure (*RRu*, p. 27). But he cannot escape the air waves of their radio stations. Nor can he avoid noticing the billboards by the dispiriting highways or receiving reproaches from the farmer who sells him gas: "The only way to get somewhere, you know, is to figure out where you're going before you go there" (*RRu*, p. 25).[18]

On the other hand, it is typical of Harry's inconsistency that, while fancying himself an enemy of conformity, he panics at the slightest suggestion of the wilderness he is supposed to be returning to. The Amish passengers of a buggy past which he drives frighten him as "devils" and "fanatics" (*RRu*, pp. 25–26); a narrow, twisting "snake of a road" (p. 29) strikes his high-strung senses as ominous; and he dreads to think that some ghost or beast might suddenly appear in the headlights of the car. Unnerved by the irruption of the unexpected, apprehensive of the unknown, Updike's hero cuts a sorry figure indeed as a would-be partner to the protagonists of *On the Road* whose stamina and natural gusto turn every incident between New York and San Francisco into an ecstatic experience.

Surrendering in turn to instinct and reason without ever making up his mind as to which he should follow, Rabbit gets lost, narrowly misses having an accident, finally tears up his map, and drives back to Brewer. Of course, "The trip home is easier" (p. 32), symbolically made so by the assistance of numerous road signs that he had not noticed on the journey outward. They take him right to the door of the Sunshine Athletic Association, an emotional center in the ex-basketball champion's map of the town. Like a tame rabbit that had taken to the fields, been chased by hounds, and had scampered back to domesticity, "he now lies secure in his locked hollow hutch" (p. 35).

The inglorious outcome of Harry's escapade is not only a sample of Updike's irony toward the thoughtlessness of his hero. It is also a warning against the solutions advocated by the beats to dodge the angst of modern life. This is not to say that *Rabbit, Run* was conceived as an anti-beat novel, even though Updike himself expressed in an interview his belief that a style of life based on cross-continental travel could not provide an adequate remedy to the suffering of the characters of *Rabbit, Run,* caught as they are in the meshes of small town life.[19] Unlike Kerouac in *On the Road* he is not content with following the zigzag of his hero's quest but devotes important sections to the other side, to the grief, or rancor, of those who are left behind. Besides, flight appears at best as a form of illusory escapism. Rabbit has not driven twenty miles before he realizes that the road is "a part of the same trap" (*RRu,* p. 23), of the same net now enlarged to the intricacy of the highway system, so that he has no choice left but to turn around and head back to "the center of the net, where alone there seems a chance to rest" (p. 80). Later, when Eccles asks him why he returned, he answers, "It seemed safer to be in a place I know" (p. 87), meaning that being far from Mt. Judge deprived him of his original strength and determination. During his one-night trip southwards he comforts himself, for fear of losing his identity in motion, with memories of "the flowerpot city." What dominates his thoughts then is the feeling of estrangement that creeps over him, paradoxically, at the precise moment when he has decided to "light out for the Territory." He may well picture himself romantically penetrating "right into the broad soft belly of the land" (p. 28), but cannot throw off the persistent impression of being an alien in his own country. Only the stubborn density of Mt. Judge can give substance to his life.[20]

In Updike's fiction departure from one's home town somehow amounts to a betrayal of the self. For Shillington-Olinger-Mt. Judge is not only a compound of maples, telephone poles, neighbors, and brick houses: it is essentially "a state of mind."[21] Hence the uneasy sense of guilt experienced by the characters of *Of the Farm,* "Home," or "A Traded Car" at the moment of return. Nowhere is this guilt more keenly felt than in *Rabbit Redux,* in which the very notion of travel is infected by the remorse Harry nurses over the death of his daughter. "He used to daydream about going South, Florida or Alabama, to see the cotton fields and the alligators, but that was a boy's dream and died with the baby" (*RRe,* p. 64). Notwithstanding the fact that this association is not strictly true to the actual events— Rebecca had not yet been born at the time of Harry's trip, and he ran away again after her death—it is nevertheless consistent with the moral lesson of *Rabbit, Run,* as epitomized in Updike's poem "Minority Report": "Br'er Rabbit demonstrated: freedom is made of brambles."[22] In the sequel novel the demonstration is again ominously convincing. Jill runs away from home only to fall into confusion, go back to drugs, and eventually die. Rabbit is haunted by the memory of his domestic tragedy, often brought back to his mind by the sight of his son's tense face on which he reads a vulnerable sensitivity dating back, he thinks, to the time when Nelson "was three and flight and death were rustling above him" (*RRe*, p. 78). Even Janice connects her lover's heart failure with her adulterous presence in his bed and decides to put an end to an affair that might prove fatal to him. *Rabbit Redux* turns on lack of hope, not only because it stresses the dangers and disillusionment awaiting those who boldly step from the middle of the road, but, more depressingly, because it instills from the first pages the feeling that escape is absolutely meaningless.

Rabbit is thus suspended in a vacuum of the soul, halfway between his dissatisfaction with his life in Brewer and the rooted conviction that no change of scenery could improve his existence. Only in dreams does he allow himself to follow Mim to the West or to head north on a superhighway toward a white city symbolically named The Rise.[23] Otherwise, "He never goes anywhere" (p. 64) because "it isn't Mt. Judge: that is, it is nowhere" (p. 246). In a curious way, stasis has given way to paralysis: remote cities have become "unattainable" (p. 273), guilt is now colored with panic. Harry views his being settled in Brewer as an atonement for his past errors, the price he has to pay for his former mobility, but it strikes the reader as a dangerous form of inertia, a neurotic refusal to face the outside world. Harry turns away from it out of sheer cowardice, as he turns away from the road signs, "awesome insignia of vastness and motion" (p. 101), which remind him of the vagrant he used to be and of the hopes he once cherished. In the last analysis, his dogged allegiance to his home town essentially proceeds from a fear of being confronted with his former self. Feeling that he has already "lived twice" (p. 93), the antihero of *Rabbit Redux* tries hard not to resurrect the questing hero of *Rabbit, Run* and the illusions he entertained about space and flight. Though ten years' time has almost entirely silenced the romantic voice of "the great Harry Angstrom," he still has to be checked when he unexpectedly reappears on some familiar street-corner. Rabbit, cautious as he may be, is occasionally tempted by some mirage of the past, as for instance when he drives up the street where Ruth used to live:

> At the end of Summer Street he thinks there will be a brook, and then a dirt road and open pastures; but instead the city street broadens into a highway lined with hamburger diners, and drive-in sub shops, and a miniature golf course with big plaster dinosaurs, and food-stamp stores and motels and gas stations that are changing their names, Humble to Getty, Atlantic to Arco. He has been here before. (*RRe*, p. 340)

In this passage Updike brings together, as it were, two different characters. The first part of the sentence echoes the words and feelings of the last scene of *Rabbit, Run* in which Harry substituted for an urban decor the landscape of his desires. So great was his urge "to travel to the next patch of snow" in the midst of a suffocating summer that he was able to turn asphalt into grass and streets into rivers (*RRu,* p. 249). This pathetic fallacy has rightly been analyzed by most commentators as the main cause of his ultimate failure.[24] Rabbit's dream of returning to nature was certainly more a headlong, instinctive rush for shelter than the logical outcome of mature reflection. Besides, being based on an ideal which has been degraded by industrial civilization, it could only lead, in the present-day context, to disappointment and destruction. And yet, on the other hand, Harry's desperate faith in the regenerating power of nature was in a way his saving grace. It placed him on the side of spring as opposed to the dead season in which were sunk those he fled. He was all sap and buds, making Ruth "bloom" and keeping Mrs. Smith alive through another year (*RRu,* pp. 89, 181). The old lady's blessing excused, to a certain extent, the damage he wrought in his urban environment: he was a noble savage in the Emersonian tradition of rustic idealism.

Though Harry's adherence to the pastoral myth was largely anachronistic, even in *Rabbit, Run,* there remained a number of elements in the setting to justify his ambition to search for God in the woods. Central to the novel—both symbolically and typographically—was, of course, Mrs. Smith's garden, which, albeit an artificial Eden with its power mower and rhododendron plantation, looked primeval enough for Harry to reflect that "it was sort of like Heaven" (*RRu,* p. 180). There was also the forest above the cemetery in the thickets of which he could stray, or the "pagan groves" (p. 106) of the golf course. Concrete stairs now went up the slope of Mt. Judge, but he could still hope to chance upon a pioneer's cabin like the one he had found in his childhood. And even the pavement seemed at times "a buried assertion, an unexpected echo, of the land that had been here before the city" (p. 60). All such traces of an idyllic past have disappeared in *Rabbit Redux.* Now, when remains from bygone days happen to be uncovered in the course of the demolition and reconstruction which modern Brewer is constantly undergoing, they are presented as historical curiosities in the headlines of the *Vat:* "Local Excavations Unearth Antiquities" (*RRe,* p. 161). The building contractors have stolen the land of the pioneers, covered it with house foundations and "city trees that never knew an American forest" (p. 100), and confined the faun of the glades within the narrow space of suburbia:

> He lives on Vista Crescent, third house from the end. Once there may have been a vista, a softly sloped valley of red barns and fieldstone farmhouses, but more Penn Villas had been added and now the view from any window is as into a fragmented mirror, of houses like this, telephone wires and television aerials showing where the glass cracked. (p. 19)

Updike witnesses the degradation of his favorite locale with an acuteness of vision unparalleled in any of his previous books. Wherever he goes, Rabbit is confronted with the artificiality and cheap commercialism that have invested Brewer and its surroundings. Weiser, the shopping street, with its modern stores selling useless items and its dazzling Burger Bliss in which vanilla milkshakes taste of chemicals, is a typical example of the way the original settlement has been betrayed, especially as Updike reminds us through a *Vat* article that it used to be a lane of a few log cabins and inns in which George Washington once stopped for the night on his way west. Now it is all too clear that the pastoral world has been irremediably defiled and the inhabitants definitely severed from their past. The prairie beasts have petrified into plaster dinosaurs. The Amish, by now just another tourist trap, only appear in the book as giant signs advertising sham country cooking. Harry himself no longer pictures the woods as his natural element. During the single rural scene of *Rabbit Redux*—which covers only 2 pages out of 340 otherwise entirely set in town—he and the other occupants of Jill's Porsche seem oddly out of place among the green hills of Pennsylvania. They gaze at nature like awkward visitors in the hush of a museum, bite suspiciously into worm-eaten fallen apples in an unconscious parody of Eden, then, somewhat disconcerted, rush back to Brewer. "And they cram back into the little car, and again there are the trucks, and the gas stations, and the "Dutch" restaurants with neon hex signs, and the wind and the speed of the car drowning out all smells and sounds and thoughts of a possible other world" (*RRe*, p. 230).

But this other world belongs to an age that has gone forever. By excluding it from the scope of the novel, Updike manages to convey that it is irretrievably lost in time. Not only buried in the past but irrelevant to the present. America has "fallen from grace,"[25] and the pioneer's ethics can no longer provide the bewildered contemporaries of the Nixon era with a meaningful standard of reference. *Rabbit, Run* ignores political affairs to concentrate solely on an egotist trying to sustain his rebellion on the last debris of a vanishing national myth. *Couples* deals with the collapse of domestic values in a country suddenly bereft of a president considered by a large section of the public as the man who had tried to revive the spirit of the frontier. *Rabbit Redux,* with postmythic lucidity, shows a concern with contemporary history which is all the more striking as Updike's involvement with America had been hitherto of a sentimental rather than a political nature. Against a background of ghetto riots, student protest, New Left militancy, Moratorium Day demonstrations, and war in Vietnam, the book pronounces, beyond any doubt, the death of the American Dream.

> Rabbit had come in on the end of it, as the world shrank like an apple going bad and America was no longer the wisest hick town within a boat ride of Europe. . . . (*RRe*, p. 110)
>
> American Dream. When he first heard the phrase as a kid he pictured God lying sleeping, the quilt-colored map of the U. S. coming out of his head like a cloud. (*RRe*, p. 102)

Rabbit's interpretation of a national ideal in geographical terms throws another light on the meaning of his present immobility. For all his old-fashioned chauvinism and "silent majority" cliché thinking, he is secretly persuaded that, the dream being over, the land in which it developed has lost its significance. This is why he pays no attention to Pajasek's advice to go and look for work in another town, or to the motel clerk who urges him at the end of the book to travel to Santa Fe. When Jill mockingly remarks, "Everybody in America has a car except you" (p.

142), his patriotic pride is not hurt because for him there is no primal territory left to drive to. With the disruption of the myth, all space has been cut off. In this respect, *Rabbit Redux* overtly states what *Rabbit, Run* sketched in outline. In the earlier novel, to take a typical example, the frontier myth already takes a knock, if only because Harry is more receptive to the lures of advertisements than to the call of history when he decides to flee to Florida, paradise of middle class vacationists, instead of following the tradition of westward migration. We learn in *Rabbit Redux* that his sister Mim, in every way pluckier than he ever was, did go west: to become a prostitute. She now tells Harry that the West is a "desert" of heartlessness where people "live underground" (p. 308). Ironically, the West is now gradually extending its tar and concrete eastward.

A similar kind of inversion of the myth appears in the first pages of the book when Updike describes in minute detail a TV skit showing the Lone Ranger cuckolded by his faithful Tonto. This irreverent vision of a pair who were the most constant heroes of Harry's childhood is an apt metaphor both for the marital mishaps of the central protagonist—he has to share his girls with a Greek and a black—and for the growing disrespect of racial minorities toward the white establishment. But it is also meaningful as a token of spreading political awareness in a country which can no longer take its mythos seriously. In 1969, as Updike sees it, Wild West heroes have been relegated to vaudeville shows, and it is the Pentagon that is "playing cowboys and Indians all over the globe" (*RRe*, p. 43). The conquest of space has lost its glamour. In this book it is either exposed as imperialism or perceived as technological feat.

Alice and Kenneth Hamilton have pointed out the frequent recurrence in *Rabbit, Run* of the adjective "orange," with its exotic, erotic connotations of warmth and passion.[26] Ten years later—is it that Harry's perception of his surroundings has grown blunt with the waning of his appetite or that Updike views the sixties as a lackluster anticlimax after his gaudy fifties?—colors in *Rabbit Redux* have bleached down to more insipid shades. Harry is constantly visualized as "a pale tall man going fat . . . a ghost, white, soft" (p. 54), "a large white man a knife would slice like lard" (p. 35), a "Paleface" (p. 48) with "milk-white blood" in his veins (p. 202), an eternal white shirt on his back, and white fears in his heart. Of course, this is meant to contrast him with the black characters who surround him. But essentially the insistence on pallid lighting, from the colorless sky of the Pennsylvania summer to the ashen flicker of the television set in most indoor scenes, emphasizes the dullness and vacuity of his life: a monotonous succession of days which he sees as "pale slices between nights" (p. 91). In keeping with a technique he has always favored, Updike plays off the inner perplexity of his protagonist against a cosmic backcloth. *Couples* takes place during the "summer of the solar eclipse" (*C*, p. 249), *Rabbit Redux* during "the summer of the moon" (*RRe*, p. 175).

Remembering the predilection for the galaxies manifested—either out of some vague desire of transcendence or just out of curiosity—by many characters in Updike's novels, one is not surprised that he used the first landing on the moon to give astral dimensions to Harry's plight. The craftsman in him could obviously not resist the pleasure of interspersing the book with lunar references: he mentions at least three times the "mauve moons" on Rabbit's nails; the film shown in the marquee on Weiser is *Space Odyssey;* Rabbit eats hamburgers called Lunar Specials and listens to "moonmood" music on the jukebox.... Each of the four parts of the narrative is preceded by an epigraph reproducing an excerpt from the tapes of the Soyuz 5 and Apollo 11 flights, the astronauts' words being used as a commentary on Harry's developing mood. As for the successive stages of the July 1969 flight, they provide an ironical counterpoint to Harry's vicissitudes. The spaceship is launched as he hears of his wife's betrayal, and the Eagle module reaches the moon after she has left home. Sitting on his mother's bed trying to make out what is night, what is moon, and what is man in the blurred image on the TV screen, Rabbit admits, as Armstrong steps on the new planet: "I don't know, Mom, I know it's happened, but I don't feel anything yet" (p. 90). The numbness of his feelings toward his wife's departure is paralleled by his almost total lack of interest in the national exploit which is rendered in the book as an unreal, almost grotesque enterprise. When Nelson tells his father that the astronauts have left the earth's orbit, the only response he receives is a noncommittal "Good for them" (p. 19). Similarly, Mrs. Angstrom, hearing her husband exclaim that "Uncle Sam is on the moon," contemptuously replies in her faltering voice: "That's just the place for him" (p. 84). Ironically, Nelson and Mr. Angstrom, the only ones who evinced any excitement on the subject, are asleep by the time the first man walks on the moon.

Rabbit's lack of enthusiasm is hard to account for, especially as we learn from Janice that, like Richard Maple who "adores the moon"[27] and keeps watching photographs of it, Harry was up to now "always worrying about how wide the world was, caring about things like how far stars are and the moon shot ..." (p. 327). In fact, it seems that there is a certain amount of frustration in his indifference. In the first scene of the book, as the rocket blasts off for the twentieth time that day on the TV screen, Rabbit reflects about the workers drinking in a bar inappropriately called the Phoenix, that "they have not been lifted, they are left there" (p. 12). Baffling all hopes of identification, the astronaut holds up to the average man the image of his own inadequacy. In terms of heroism, the pioneer of the interplanetary age meets in Harry's mind the basketball star he used to be. This is never explicitly stated but casually intimated, as for instance when Rabbit, driving through the suburbs of Brewer, pictures the kids who have replaced those of *Rabbit, Run*'s first scene as "the next generation of athletes and astronauts" (p. 101). Also, the fact that he associates the moon with Texas is arresting, Texas representing by his present standards the place where he came closer to being some kind of adventurer: a soldier away from home who frequented prostitutes. But it is Janice who best expresses the wretchedness of her husband in his decline, when she perceives him as "her flying athlete, grounded, cuckolded" (p. 35).

Rabbit himself occasionally blurts out his sarcastic awareness of himself as a has-been: "Nobody tells me how good I am" (p. 70), or "Nobody ever calls me Rabbit" (p. 64). Even though he has taken to smoking grass, he cannot shatter the image of the heavy, dispirited, aimless man he has become. Unlike Jill, who can "blow herself to the moon" (p. 201), he is rooted in reality by self-imposed weights which drag him down, and when they make love, she is "moonchild," he "earthman" (p. 176). Incidentally, it is worth noting that in his somewhat childish imagination ascension to the celestial sphere is linked with both sex and religion.[28] But the days are gone when "he could get himself up for anything" (p. 130). His erotic ardor fails him, as does his religious zeal, and he finds it more and more difficult to reach the upper regions occupied by God and woman. Now he only prays on buses to kill time or forget the young Negroes he fears, and never takes the initiative of love. Though capable of successful sexual intercourse, he rarely surrenders to coital bliss, being too preoccupied with the necessity of maintaining an unflagging stiffness and too much aware of the presence of his partner to let himself go. Orgasm by masturbation, "a space flight" when he was a boy (p. 325), can now only be attained through acrobatics of imagination and inventiveness which, by the end of the book, have become ineffectual. "Nothing brings him up" (p. 345), and in the motel room he does not try to celebrate his wife's return with amorous pyrotechnics, but, more safely, cuddles against her back and goes to sleep.

To a large extent, Updike presents Rabbit's spiritual exhaustion and intermittent impotence as a consequence of the asceticism of excess that governed his life in *Rabbit, Run*. At the time, his mystical quest was undissociable from his activity as a womanizer, and Eccles had good reason to remark: "It's the strange thing about you mystics, how often your little ecstasies wear a skirt" (*RRu*, p. 105). Considering the disasters entailed by his search for "first rate" perfection, Rabbit has since almost convinced himself that only a life of caution and conformity can shelter him from evil and keep him from spreading havoc in his surroundings. Since his past ambition to "give people faith" (*RRu*, p. 117) only won him the title of "Mr. Death" (*RRu*, p. 245), he has come to the conclusion that man should not look for salvation. There is still a God for him, but "God . . . isn't people" (*RRe*, p. 98), and all human attempts to identify the self with Him—derided by Kruppenbach in *Rabbit, Run* as "finagling" and "busyness" (p. 138)—are doomed to fail, and to hurt.

The absurd inherent in the mystical enterprise is illustrated in *Rabbit Redux* by the ambiguity of the character of Skeeter, "the black Jesus," a self-styled savior who has replaced Rabbit as the flag bearer of saintliness. Both victim and victimizer, clownish, pathetic, irritating, and frightening by turns, this satanic messiah dreams of postrevolutionary "space" (p. 213) and raves about the coming of chaos followed by a new Dark Age. He encourages Jill to see God's face but destroys her with heroin in the process, and when the house burns he only thinks of saving his own skin. Scared by his apocalyptic raptures, Nelson sensibly resists illumination, screaming, "I don't want God to come," preferring to grow up like his father, "average and ordinary" (p. 226). The latter is more fascinated than his son by the sadomasochistic ritual which goes on every night in his living room, but he nonetheless remains an observer. Even when Jill and Skeeter take off their clothes, he declines the invitation to a threesome, not for moral reasons, but because he is scared: he prefers the security of voyeurism to the risks of participation.

Harry's sexual timidity originates in the same trauma that prevents him from joining in Skeeter's Beatitudes: the drowning of Becky, and, to a lesser degree, the mystery surrounding Ruth's pregnancy. What is certain is that Rabbit always opposed Janice's desire to have another child: "It had all seemed like a pit to him then, her womb and the grave, sex and death, he had fled her cunt as a tiger's mouth" (*RRe*, p. 29). Now he dreads any woman's womb, a threat to himself as a physical entity. They all have "fire in their crotch" (p. 93), and Rabbit has to fight his repulsion against penetrating them: "He cannot overcome his fear of using [Jill's] body as a woman's. Her cunt *stings*, is part of it; he never forces his way into her without remembering thoze razor blades" (*RRe*, p. 138).[29] In *Rabbit, Run* Harry obliges Ruth to take out her diaphragm before love. But he is prompted by a desire to abolish, by the contact of two absolute nudities, the consciousness that they are separate in the flesh and that, being a woman, she belongs to "a different race" (*RRu*, p. 76). Now his phantasms show the predominance of Thanatos over Eros. If Harry fears copulation, it is because "he ha[s] retreated into deadness" (p. 326) and shields himself from the intensity of too much life, for he knows that "life wants death. To be alive is to kill" (p. 268).

Having "nothing to rise by" (p. 245), Rabbit finds that there is nothing to rise to. This is why it would be erroneous to believe that the moon and its pioneers are for him only an object of regret and bitter envy. In a way, as is the case with Ruth's neighborhood revisited, he has already been there. There was a time when, carried away by his metaphysical elation, he was able to soar in imagination into the blank sky, but it has procured him neither self-knowledge nor self-fulfillment. He was merely flirting with emptiness out of a suicidal, destructive impulse. Toward the end of *Rabbit, Run* Updike describes a nightmare in which Harry dreams he is going to found a new religion after having a vision of death under the form of an eclipse of the sun by the moon. In *Rabbit Redux* the moon is just "a big round nothing" (p. 25) repeatedly qualified by the adjective "cold." It symbolizes death, no longer the "lovely death" (*RRu*, p. 228) Rabbit the mystic was courting in the first novel, but death as a negation of consciousness, a fall into abysmal absence. For Harry has come to the dismal conclusion that, like the uncontrolled yearning for a higher spirituality, "Space kills" (*RRe*, p. 84).

This is why he does not run any longer, except, twice in the novel, out of fright. This amounts to saying that he has condemned himself to silence, since running, besides being the small town equivalent of extensive traveling, appears in *Rabbit, Run* as the innate language of the "natural." Rather inarticulate when it comes to philosophizing, fundamentally unable to reflect on his essence, more interested in existence than in knowledge, Harry can find no better means of self-expression than the scissoring of his legs through the spring air. It is the moment of pure ecstasy when the *outside* seems tuned in to the urgent voices of the *inside*. The requirements of morals and society are then forgotten; there only matters the beauty of a life almost exclusively based on aesthetics. In the final scene of the book Harry, abandoning all sense of responsibility and all emotional problems, surrenders to the exhilaration of sheer instinct and plunges into "pure blank space" (*RRu*, p. 248). Rhythmically, exultantly, "he runs. Ah: runs. Runs."

The feeling of magnificent ease and breathless perfection our memory retains from those last words sharply contrasts with the apathetic tone of the opening lines of *Rabbit Redux* describing Harry and his fellow workers leaving Verity Press: "Men energe pale from the little printing plant at four sharp, ghosts for an instant, blinking, until the outdoor light overcomes the look of constant indoor light clinging to them." It is implicit in this first sentence that Updike is going to use again the inside-outside polarity that spatially structures *Rabbit, Run* and supplies its dramatic tension. Except that this time the poles are reversed. In the former novel Rabbit jeopardizes his freedom every time he approaches the precincts occupied by women and relatives who wish to trap the claustrophobic vagrant and tie him down with promises of sex or forgiveness. All the significant episodes of his solipsistic odyssey happen outdoors: on the playground with the kids, on the top of Mt. Judge with Ruth, or on the golf course that Eccles sees from the window of Kruppenbach's smelly den as the setting of a quest "renewed at each tee, in a fresh flood of green" (*RRu*, p. 136). Ten years later Harry is so rarely in the open that his wife exclaims, on seeing him in their garden: "Harry, you're outdoors! How funny of you" (p. 57); which the one-time gardener confirms in another of their conversations: "Only morons work outdoors any more" (p. 340).

About one third of *Rabbit, Run* takes place out of doors; hardly one fifth of *Rabbit Redux*. The dynamics of *Rabbit, Run* proceeds from Harry's repeated departures, whereas the suspense of the other book grows in proportion as more and more people trespass upon the privacy of his household. Building up to the time when the house is burnt down, successively Stavros, Jill, Skeeter, Showalter and Brumbach who want the Negro out of the neighborhood, and children who pry through Rabbit's windows, derange the neat, fixed patterns with which Harry has barricaded his life. Already afraid of burglars and black delinquents at the beginning of the story, he becomes increasingly obsessed with images of poison and rape as the peril of invasion looms larger. He reduces to a minimum his contacts with the outside world: irregular visits to his parents, an occasional evening with Peggy, work at the printing plant from which he hurries home, fearing the worst; foreseeing the catastrophic denouement, he ends up hardly leaving his house, which becomes a kind of fortress where four strange beings crouch in an underground atmosphere.

Harry views himself as the safeguard of the other three. "Always worrying about who needs [him]" (*RRe*, p. 125), he considers it his moral obligation to cater to the "cripples" who live under his roof, and in his moments of self-complacency he prides himself on being a "nursemaid" (p. 309). But Harry is grotesquely inefficient as a good Samaritan, having neither the capacity nor the true vocation to be one. In fact, Updike suggests that Rabbit's seclusion is more pathological than charitable or rational. Since "the world is quicksand" (p. 33) and "freedom means murder" (p. 172), he has confined himself within four walls symbolizing the rules on which he has grounded his life for the last ten years. Now, his wife having deserted him, there is no further object in maintaining those rules. Still, Rabbit regularly comes back home because there is nowhere else to go: he has lost the ability to break the rules and invent new ones, or just, as he does in *Rabbit, Run*, "to play it by ear" (*RRu*, p. 85). No longer in touch with exterior reality—which he perceives only in its duplicated form as newspaper headlines, TV news, and tags from Skeeter's books—he has limited his inner space to the surface of his house. He only ventures out of it for short, furtive, wary excursions, refusing himself any expansion of consciousness though he is sometimes tempted to open up, as for instance when he hears Babe play the blues.

> His inside space expands to include beyond Jimbo's the whole world with its arrowing wars and polychrome races, its continents shaped like ceiling stains, its strings of gravitational attraction attaching it to every star, its glory in space as of a blue marble swirled with clouds; everything is warm, wet, still coming to birth but himself and his home, which remains a strange dry place, dry and cold and emptily spinning in the void of Penn Villas like a cast-off space capsule. He does not want to go there but he must. He must. "I must go," he says, rising. (*RRe*, p. 117)

Rabbit deceives himself into believing that his home is a shelter for meaningful values when it is only a prison of self-centeredness. Another example of his delusion is his position on the Vietnam War, a much debated issue in *Rabbit Redux*. A self-declared "hawk"—he has stuck a flag decal on the back window of his Falcon—Harry argues that his support of the American military presence in Southeast Asia is motivated by patriotism. It turns out, however, that his pro-Vietnam war position is a reflex of self-defense rather than the conclusion of a real political analysis. When Mim squarely reminds him that he was once happy to wriggle out of the Korean War, he answers that one has to fight sometimes, "to keep your options, to keep a little space around you" (p. 306). Similarly, Harry's mistrust of communism derives from a personal phantasm: the fear of being smothered in "a big black bag" (p. 306). So that all his pretensions to positive thinking betray in fact a negative, paranoid apprehension of "the other guy" (p. 306).[30]

But, as Harry himself acknowledges in one of his most discerning statements, "what we most protect is where we want to be invaded" (p. 98). At bottom he hates his house, which, with its "Martian" furniture and "tacky" aspect, reminds him of his own cheapness. Updike gives us ground to think that, just as Rabbit's fear of being raped or murdered by Skeeter goes with an undeniable sexual attraction—or at least curiosity—toward the young black, his obstinate protection of his property conceals an unconscious desire to see it destroyed. After the fire, as if awaking from a dream, Harry realizes there is hardly anything he would salvage from the wreckage. The main impression is not one of regret but of relief: "His house slips from him. He is free" (p. 285). After this turning point in the novel Updike makes it definitely clear that the changes that seemed to have occurred in Rabbit were not as deep as one might have thought from his character's assertions. As Harry disentangles himself from the trammels of routine, he reveals a growing kinship with the Rabbit of the first book. He thus corroborates the analysis Jill makes of him earlier in the narrative, when she describes his personality in terms strongly recalling the reproaches addressed to him in *Rabbit, Run*: "Your life has no reflective content; it's all instinct, and when your instincts let you down, you have nothing to trust" (*RRe*, p. 198). The fact is that there is much expectancy in Rabbit's cynicism, but also a certain amount of cowardice, for he never really takes any step toward self-liberation, waiting, as Stavros puts it, for "any disaster that might spring [him] free" (p. 314). Mim, another good judge of man's frailties, makes about the same comment: "You just do what you feel like and then when it blows up or runs down you sit there and pout" (p. 317). Harry claims that he did "what felt right" (p. 307), indirectly admitting that he never stopped to wonder what *was* right. Because of his self-indulgence, he has proved completely inadequate as a good angel: he has not tried to spare his wife a fruitless experience, he has let Jill "drown," has bruised Nelson again. Besides, unlike what has been suggested throughout the book, he has not learnt anything during his underground conversations with Skeeter and Jill: he tells the police he has only been "entertained" by Skeeter (p. 281), and he still believes at the end, though he is now unemployed, that America is a perfect country. His job lost, his house destroyed, his wife away, Rabbit enjoys a sudden freedom of which, of course, he takes no advantage. On the contrary, he falls back into his old blunders, enters "the same door" (p. 300) to settle with his parents and fall in love with Mim again, and tries his hand at basketball to recover "the touch." With a mixture of compassion and irony toward his character, Updike toys in the last pages of the book with the idea that Harry might revive in himself the Rabbit of the first novel. But the echo sounded in the sentence "Globes of ether, pure nervousness, slide down his chest," is only nostalgic. The impetus is gone, Harry will not run any more. He sinks into unconsciousness against his wife's body, withdraws in his "burrow," in "a space of silence" (pp. 345-46). "The space they are in, the motel room long and secret as a burrow, becomes all interior space" (p. 348). The *outside* merges with the *inside:* another illusion, or peace at last? But Rabbit no longer asks himself any question, he "sleeps. He. She. Sleeps. O. K.?" Updike probably will not wake him up again, for a third Rabbit might be a Rabbit Redundant.

André Le Vot

6. NEW MODES OF STORY-TELLING IN RECENT AMERICAN WRITINGS: THE DISMANTLING OF CONTEMPORARY FICTION

In this study of fictional forms in the last fifteen years, I shall concentrate on what, in the American field, seems to be the more significant, the more puzzling also for the reader accustomed to the established models of storytelling. For this appears to be an age of profound mutation, an age in which the modernist fictional traditions are thoroughly questioned and no longer render adequately the new sense of reality already expressed in other forms of art.

Such an approach necessarily sets aside what is already familiar and more or less belongs to that tradition: the greater part of the Jewish novel as exemplified by Bellow or Malamud, even the earlier pieces of Philip Roth; the black novel, which, with the major exception of Ishmael Reed, does not appear to have made the breakthrough worked out in the theater by Leroi Jones or Ed Bullins; and last but not least the southern novel, which, in spite of its vitality and variety, and again with a few exceptions including Flannery O'Connor and Walker Percy, does not seem to be primarily concerned with the necessity of a radical reconsideration of narrative modes.

This may be due to the fact that in these three cases—and it is also true of other novelists such as John Updike and Joyce Carol Oates—the themes, still focused on social, racial, psychological problems, still deeply anchored in historical reality, do not demand a fundamental renewal of novelistic approaches. Their cultural context can still be competently handled by the techniques elaborated and brought to a point of thorough efficacy by the modernists, from James and Flaubert on.

The opposite attitude is to be found among many members of the new generation, a generation which might be called, for reasons that will become more evident as we proceed, the Wasteland generation. Let us be clear from the outset that the word "generation" does not necessarily apply here to novelists born within a span of years, as was the case with the Lost Generation, but rather to writers linked by a community of refusals and options. It may include those born just before the first world war, like Burroughs or Percy, or a few years later, like Hawkes or Purdy or

O'Connor, as well as those born during the thirties. It may also exclude some of the more traditional modernists mentioned earlier.

What those Wastelanders have in common is an attitude toward fiction which reflects a deep cultural crisis, more specifically, this is the refusal, or incapacity, to deal with the themes inherent in modernism, the impossibility to go on writing quest novels, fiction dealing with identity, destiny, success or failure, moral achievement or deterioration—that is, works resulting from the conflicts opposing the individual, recognized as such, to society, well-defined in its structures. Much has been written, since the twenties and Ortega y Gasset, on the dehumanization of the arts, on the loss of man's certainties concerning the coherence of his universe and his personality. But until recently the mainstream of American fiction seemed unaffected by those questions, uninfluenced by the early responses of Dada and surrealism. *The Waste Land* was certainly influential, but only so far as the themes of sterility, alienation, hopelessness were concerned. No new forms of art emerged until the Wastelanders, having completely assimilated the message, no longer reacting to it through hope or nostalgia, immersed in its daily reality, realized how inadequate the tools and concepts of modernism could be. Absolutely pointless to them were the strategies of viewpoint or narrative distance, the manipulation of time and space, the various ways to make a character come alive, how to endow him with depth, the pertinent use of ambiguity, irony, or epiphany, the inbuilding of symbols, myths, and archetypes. All the tactics that the great moderns devised and that some of them—James, Forster, and Virginia Woolf among others—codified in their theoretical writings. All the time-honored and somewhat moth-eaten panoply which now belongs more to academic critics than to creative writers, an impressing preelectronic machinery that can still solve the most complicated fictional problems but is hardly capable of meeting the needs of postmodern fabulators. Old answers, but not new questions.

Not that the tradition should be systematically rejected by this generation. On the contrary, one can perceive a certain nostalgia for the security it used to provide, for the certainties afforded by a mimetic and figurative type of art, for the dynamic and pleasurable effects provided by the various fallacies which tended to make fiction more exciting, more relevant, more orderly than "life." Listen to the requisites that John Barth makes one of his would-be characters express in *Lost in the Funhouse:*

> If I'm going to be a fictional character, I want to be in a rousing good yarn, not some piece of avant-garde preciousness. I want passion and bravura action in my plot, heroes I can admire, heroines I can love, memorable speeches, colorful accessory characters, poetical language. It doesn't matter how naively linear the anecdote is. Never mind modernity![1]

On the distinction established by Roland Barthes between the *lisible* and the *scriptible* (the "readable" as opposed to the "writable") are here superimposed the antagonistic tensions within the contemporary creator. On the one hand, he would prefer to write like his predecessors, to compete with life and its prolific diversity, to go on building beautiful, well-oiled machines fulfilling the expectations of the reader-as-consumer. But on the other hand he must admit that what can be read with pleasure and profit in the classics and the moderns can no longer be written by the contemporaries. It would be hopelessly outdated, out of keeping with the context of the time. This type of fiction has now been preempted and vulgarized by the popular movie and the TV show. There you have naturalness and immediacy, the social and the psychological, all the sophistication, now taken for granted, of narrative inventiveness. Reality plus "art," without the painful and time-consuming labor of plowing one's way through printed matter. Why now compete with art forms which were brought to a level of excellence by writers who did believe in what they were doing, who worked with the knowledge of a mission to be fulfilled, of new fields to be explored, of an oeuvre to be erected?

Such is the dilemma exposed in *Lost in the Funhouse:* John Barth attempts to write a quest novel dealing with the education of a personage. He presents three fragments of this sentimental biography and gives up: "Is there anything more tiresome, in fiction, than the problems of sentimental adolescents?"[2] Of course, so many people, from Dickens to Joyce, from Turgenev to Fitzgerald, had been there before . . . And the rest of the book is spent deploring his lack of imagination, wondering what possibilities are still open, trying to find replacement solutions, including precisely what he is just doing: "You say you lack a ground situation. Has it occurred to you that that circumstance may be your ground situation?"[3] In this book Barth is, as the author-narrator, the active participant of the situation he described one year earlier in his essay entitled "The Literature of Exhaustion."[4] There he asserts, following Borges, that "literary history . . . has pretty well exhausted the possibilities of novelty," that the situation is made hopeless by "the used-upness of certain forms, or exhaustion of certain possibilities," that "for one to attempt to add overtly to the sum of 'original' literature . . . would be too presumptuous, too naive; literature has been done long since." There we have, so far as literature is concerned, the equivalent of Frederick Jackson Turner's famous historical essay on the end of the frontier. All the virgin lands have been occupied, all the territories exploited. All the rooms in the House of Fiction have now a tenant. No vacancies.

It is the same situation that Robert Coover analyzes in a central piece of *Pricksongs and Descants* intended as a prologue to "seven exemplary fictions." The contemporary writer, he asserts, is in the same predicament as Miguel de Cervantes, who created the classical novel through his boredom with and opposition to the prevalent fictional form of the day, the romance of chivalry:

> Like you, we, too, seem to be standing at the end of one age and on the threshold of another. We, too, have been brought to a blind alley by the critics and analysts: we, too, suffer from "a literature of exhaustion," though ironically our nonheroes are no longer tireless and tiresome Amadises, but hopelessly defeated and bed-ridden Quixotes. We seem to have moved from an open-ended, anthropomorphic, humanistic, naturalistic, even—to the extent that man may be thought of as making his own universe—optimistic starting point, to one that is closed, cosmic, eternal, supernatural (in its soberest sense), and pessimistic.[5]

Hence the necessity, he states, "the need for new modes of perception and fictional forms to encompass them." Those new modes of perception have already found their way, and new fictional forms able to encompass them have been experimented with in the last fifteen years. Those I should like now to analyze in detail.

Two directions may be traced in the new fiction which endeavors to break from the tradition of modernism, in the will to secede and innovate that various American critics have labeled as metafiction, or postmodernism, or even, as Ishmael Reed calls his own work, patarealism. An hypothesis I should like to advance is that the origin, the fountainhead, of these two streams is to be found in the exemplary achievements of two outsiders of the thirties, Djuna Barnes and Nathanael West. Nothing apparently more different than their works, although they were both influenced by the Dada and surrealist experiments of the twenties in Paris. West died in 1940 after having written four short novels within six years, and Djuna Barnes did not publish any other fiction after her extraordinary *Nightwood* (1936). With West we discover a new mood and a new style, the systematic subversion of American myths, the parody of the canonic genres, the pitiless satire, the ruthless burlesquing of all pretenses. With Barnes, on the contrary, the fire and the passion, the irrepressible exuberance of a baroque style, the dark and morbid fascination of night and death. An antithetic opposition between the diurnal and the nocturnal, between the principles of constriction and expansion, between the substantial antinomy of the brittle mineral and the proliferating vegetal. Two temperaments, two stylistic landscapes, two types of representation which may provide us with the archetypal models from which to start in order to situate and define the two main contemporary tendencies that I shall call, for lack of a more adequate terminology, the disjunctive mode and the conjunctive mode.

THE DISJUNCTIVE MODE

Let us first examine briefly the work of Nathanael West, the American prophet of the disjunctive mode. The subtitle of *A Cool Million,* "The Dismantling of Lemuel Pitkin," gives a fair approximation of what West did to traditional fiction. Those who are familiar with *Miss Lonelyhearts* and *The Day of the Locust* have certainly been struck by the stereotyped quality of the characters. No evolution, no depth, no psychological complexity. Motivations and the roundness resulting from the evolution of time are conspicuously absent, or reduced to a minimum: the personages are, with a vengeance, what Forster calls flat characters. Everything is played on surfaces, as in the early "flicks." No background; what happens seems to take place against the backdrop of a pathetic vaudeville stage. Human gestures and feelings are reduced and stylized into mechanical acts and responses:

> Homer was astonished when he bowed again, did several quick jig steps, then let his derby hat roll down his arm. It fell to the floor. He stooped to retrieve it, straightening up with a jerk as though he had been kicked, then rubbed the

seat of his trousers ruefully. Homer understood that this was to amuse, so he laughed.[6]

That is the kind of scene one constantly comes upon in Pynchon's *Gravity's Rainbow,* for instance, where characters are seen to break from their fictional roles into rhythmic attitudes and songs which belong to the music hall platform. Besides, the cutting of the story into short sequences deprives the narrative of its habitual smoothness and continuity. West's first idea was to give *Miss Lonelyhearts* a subtitle, "A Novel in the Form of a Comic Strip": "I abandoned this idea, but retained some of the comic strip technique: Each chapter instead of going forward in time, also goes backward, forward, up and down in space like a picture."[7] Or, if the narrative line is not discontinuous, as happens in *A Cool Million,* we are immediately aware of parody: the myth of success is ridiculed together with its favorite vehicle, the cautionary tale. Those remarks could as well apply to the writings of fictionalists as different as Flannery O'Connor, John Hawkes and James Purdy in their first novels, Richard Brautigan, Donald Barthelme, Richard Coover, and many others. They illustrate what Hawkes defined in an interview as "the terrifying similarity between the unconscious desires of a solitary man and the disruptive needs of the visible world."[8] They will serve as an introduction to a more detailed analysis of the disjunctive mode which will examine what those writings have in common on the three levels of representation, narration, and diction.

Representation: schizoid structures. Considering the way forms are represented in space, one is struck by the disappearance of the third dimension: no depth, no perspective. It is a flat, bidimensional world where objects and characters seem to be cut out from their background, projected into the foreground, allowed a few motions, and spirited away. One example from Brautigan's last novel, *The Hawkline Monster: A Gothic Western,* when a hanged man is seen from the windows of a stagecoach: "Just outside of Gompville a man was hanging from the bridge across the river. There was a look of disbelief on his face as if he couldn't believe he was dead. . . . His body swayed gently in the early winds of morning."[9] The situation of the body, the expression on its face, are briefly sketched as in a child's drawing. No explanation, no comment. Another vignette follows, as sketchy and impersonal. The description may be more elaborate, but everything seems to happen on the same plane, and each detail, magnified as it were, forms an autonomous unit which occupies the whole field of vision. The absence of colors is conspicuous and contributes to the general effect of flatness which excludes all attempt at modeling. Or if colors are introduced—one may think of Barthelme—they are crude and partitioned, without any shade or variation, and contribute to the general effect, that obtained in what West called "the comic strip technique."

The privileged form is the outline, the silhouette, and virtually the shadow, which obliterates all details within the outer line. Those are inscribed against a geometrical plane, framed by a doorway or a window. The windowframe in fact appears to be the favorite device used by the narrator to isolate and circumscribe his vision, also to establish the distance necessary to the dehumanizing process which takes place in those narratives. Even when it is not mentioned, we are constantly aware of a pane of glass, a protective and insulating, cold, transparent sheet interposed between the watcher and the object or person he is looking at. It is a purely spectatorial, highly detached form of art which disconnects outer action and inner feelings.

"The Act Act" of Robert Coover summarizes this technique: the point of view is the spectator's, and the character is represented against the back curtain of a stage. "A man enters, dressed as a magician with black cape and black silk hat. Doffs hat in wide sweep to audience, bows elegantly."[10] In this instance the actor is reduced to the stereotyped gestures expected of a conjurer in his traditional black and white apparel. But the smoothness of the elegant flourish is only there to serve as contrast to the more and more convulsive and breathless actions that will follow. As in Nathanael West, the jerky motion, the disconnected gestures, the broken rhythm of a puppet show seem to be the essence of that fiction, the highlight of the performance, the mock epiphany for which all the rest prepares the reader. We recognize here the features that Gilbert Durand[11] classifies as schizoid in his study on the anthropological forms of the imagination, the prevalence of the broken line and the contour, the predominance of bidimensional geometrical patterns, the contrasting use of white and black, the disconnected quality of the movements. A last example, drawn from the opening pages of John Hawkes's *The Cannibal*, will illustrate this typological obsession, associated here with the typical spectatorial distance:

> The Signalman, his mouth clamped shut, sitting behind the postered windows of the station, saw the boy dashing over the torn rail and saw the man with the cane come behind, his shadow lengthening in the station's candlelight. . . . The shadows about the child seemed like beasts of the circus, groaning out of empty doorways with nothing to mangle in their jaws.[12]

Let us keep in mind, temporarily, this comment by John Barth which might apply to this type of representation: "One manifestation of schizophrenia, as everyone knows, is the movement from reality toward fantasy, a progress which not infrequently takes the form of distorted and fragmented representation, abstract formalism, an increasing preoccupation, even obsession, with patterns and designs for their own sake."[13]

Narration: nonlinear, fragmented fictions. If we consider now the modalities of the narration, we observe the tendency for the narrative to become fragmented into practically autonomous units, the equivalent of the "framing technique" on the level of representation. The fictions of Barthelme and Brautigan are quite significant in that respect. They are composed of a series of very short pieces, two pages as an average, which can in no way be compared to the chapters of a more traditional narrative. The last novel of Hawkes, *Death, Sleep and the Traveler*, is made up of 115 sections whose lengths extend from one or two lines to a maximum of twelve pages. To borrow again from West's description of his own usage, we may notice that "each chapter instead of going forward in time, also goes backward, forward, up and down in space," with the consequence that the very notion of chapter does not apply here. The sections are not connected by the leads of causality or temporality: no chronological sequence, no cause and effect relationship between two neighboring units.

With the very notion of chapter, the idea of the novel also tends to vanish. One can observe here at work a dynamic principle which is the opposite of that which gives coherence and unity to some collections of short stories published before the war, *Winesburg, Ohio, In Our Time, Go Down, Moses,* for instance. In those books the short stories, written and published separately first, aggregate around a polarizing factor, constitute themselves into an homogeneous whole, an organic entity, a "novel" in which each independent story, converted into a chapter, plays a functional role, develops as a stage in the evolution of the hero or the theme. This type of progression, this "becoming," is conspicuously absent in the new fiction. An opposite force, centrifugal in character, tends to shatter and disperse what might have gathered, knotted into a coherent whole. No relationship, it is needless to point out, between this dissemination of facts and episodes and the chronological permutations, the use of flashbacks (structurally justified) with which the fiction of a Faulkner had made us familiar.

Which explains that the alibi of the novel, of the extended fictional form, is in its turn abandoned. Or, which comes to the same, is perverted to the uses of parody, as is the case with *The Sot-Weed Factor.* With Barthelme, Brautigan, Coover, Michaels, Reed, the significant form (we might call it a genre) is the short text, even if a collection of such texts is presented under a collective title as in *Trout Fishing in America:* the analogy then would be more with a collection of poems than with a genuine fictional whole. And those self-sufficient texts are seen to bifurcate, branch off, ramify in their turn into more or less independent segments. Such is the case of Coover's "stories" in *Pricksongs and Descants* which, whenever they reach a certain length, subdivide into new cells, occasionally numbered, as in "The Gingerbread House" and "The Elevator." And it must again be pointed out that this is by no means intended as a convenience for the reader, contrived to separate distinct episodes, to mark the stages in the development of the narrative, which might be the case with the subdivisions of a short story. The function of these microunits is, on the contrary, emphatically to underline the intransitiveness of this type of fiction, to deny it any continuum, to do away with the two fundamental imperatives of traditional fiction, the double necessity, underlined by Aristotle, of having a beginning and an end. Those two are disposed of. Only middles, without either antecedent or conclusion, subsist. In his preface to a discarded fragment of *The Origin of the Brunists,* Coover attempts to give an explanation for this phenomenon: "All narratives, like the universe, are explosive. Man's weak vision is not suited for these infinite explosions. To avoid going blind, he attempts to focus on this and that vector, spark trajectory."[14]

In some border cases—I have in mind "The Glass Mountain" in Barthelme's *City Life*—the fundamental unit is the sentence, whose autonomy is pointed out by numbers preceding each of them. Even, in two cases, isolated nouns. The six pages of the text are in that way distributed into 100 sections, each one containing one or two independent clauses. With again two exceptions: section 71, which is a quotation from the *Dictionary of Literary Terms,* and section 80 which, is a quotation from a story in the *Yellow Fairy Book.* Those exceptions, mere intrusions of the traditional discourse, are there of course to confirm the rule, to attract the reader's attention to the terseness of the rest by contrast with the florid diction of the fairytale, for example. Also to provide the writer with an opportunity to illustrate his method, to show the reader what becomes of the most banal and innocuous story in his hands. Section 80 begins in a significant way: "The Conventional means of attaining the castle are as follows"[15] and indeed follows a short fairytale telling how a youth manages to reach the balcony in a castle where the beautiful princess is waiting for him. Then some of the following sections, 83, 89, 91, 93–96, use section 80 as a kind of storehouse which they pillage, dismantle, scatter, and intersperse with other elements (some belonging to section 71) to create an entirely new text, with a mad logic of its own.

I am now reaching an important point which is not so much concerned with the forms of the narrative as with its nature, the fragmented character of the form being only the manifestation of its essence. What those writers are about is simply the subversion and the destruction of the narrative form itself. If we may borrow for a moment the terminology of the structuralist critics who apply the categories of linguistics to the analysis of fiction, posing for instance the analogy of the syntagmatic axis (subject, verb, complements) with the unfolding of a narrative line, we realize that some of the strategies we have examined so far have a common purpose: to do away with the syntagmatic line, to break the sequential quality which has been associated since the origins with the telling of a story. Our Wastelanders want to make their readers aware of the futility and even impossibility of plodding along the main road of a plot whose issue, whatever the ingenuity of the storyteller, is all too predictable. Those means of communication, they imply, have outlived their usefulness and their credibility. Writers who try to use them again can only, as Barth shows, get stuck in the deep ruts which bear witness to the heavy traffic of the past. Other ways and means, other forms, must be found, oblique, cyclic, spiraloid, anything, provided one can dispense with "the mirror traveling along the highway" in which Stendhal saw the very principle of fiction.

John Barth is clear about it. Nowadays "the plot doesn't rise by meaningful steps but winds upon itself, digresses, retreats, hesitates, sighs, collapses, expires."[16] *Lost in the Funhouse,* we have seen, is a fiction about the impossibility of writing fiction. Playfully, because it makes good fiction and good reading. Other strategies have been devised to get out of this dead end. It is impossible to be exhaustive, but here are, briefly suggested, some of the alternatives prompted by the impatience, the impotence, the scruples, of the new fictionalists.

With Barth, the syntagmatic axis "winds upon itself," to borrow his own expression, forms a circle, abolishing all trace of anteriority: his fiction unrolls itself, without beginning or end (the end is in the beginning) in the same way as the Moebius strip which symbolically is used as a "frame-tale" in the first page of *Lost in the Funhouse.* With satellite rings within rings within rings reproducing varieties of the initial fiction, *regressus in infinitum . . .*

A variant is Henry Mathews's *Tlooth:* the narrative is not cyclical, but proves to be useless. The apparent motivations are only decoys destined to lure the reader into an adventure which turns out to be that of the writing itself. The fictional world collapses under our feet, the episodes evaporate. The text alone, with its linguistic codes (concealing for instance the sex of the characters by a careful juggling with personal pronouns) constitutes the "plot," a plot which involves. the reader in a hide-and-seek game with the writer.

In a more facile but quite efficient way, Kurt Vonnegut uses what he calls the "Tralfamadorian vision" to justify the disruption of linear time in his fiction, more particularly in *Slaughterhouse-Five,* where the narrator's simultaneity of vision makes for an atemporal fragmented story line where chronological order has no sense. The plot here accounts for the technique, and not the other way round. Vonnegut tries in that way to reach the beauty he ascribes to the cosmic literature of the Tralfamadorians:

> There isn't any particular relationship between all the messages, except that the author has chosen them carefully, so that, when seen all at once, they produce an image of life that is beautiful and surprising and deep. There is no beginning, no middle, no end, no suspense, no moral, no causes, no effects.[17]

No fictional journey either with Brautigan, in spite of the picaresque appearance of his stories. No lead to be followed safely to a conclusion. In place of a narrative line a patchwork of unrelated episodes, a series of playing fields which are arbitrarily juxtaposed. It is up to the reader to jump over the hedges. The syntagmatic, or metonymic, flow and smoothness of the conventional tale is as condemned as Trout Fishing in America: trout creeks are sold by the yard in the Cleveland wrecking yards, the romantic cascades to be found in the plumbing department. This seems to be the fate of the stories and the novels in the wrecking yards of the New Fiction.

With Coover it is the sense of the multiplicity of virtualities within a single situation which blocks the narrative. His technique is reminiscent of the methods of the generative grammar: there are no privileged, normative structures, only an extensive body of potential solutions. This transformational model allows him, starting from any given situation, to develop the multifaceted paradigm of its possible developments. The very problematic character of each microunit automatically destroys any relationship based on causality or temporality which might link it to the preceding or the following one. They all have an equal status; all are situated, arbitrarily, on a vertical axis without precedence or priority. Texts out of *Pricksongs and Descants* like "The Magic Poker," "The Elevator," "Quenby and Ola, Swede and Carl," and particularly the extraordinary "Baby Sitter" illustrate the surprising effects triggered by that method.

With Barthelme the syntagmatic unfolding stumbles against the independent clause and even the noun. If we go back to "The Glass Mountain," we notice that section 12 is composed of a single noun, "asshole." Normally, if we refer to Roman Jakobson,[18] this noun should act as a shifter, that is, produce a verb, a complement

—in short, a message. Which, in terms of narration, should produce a fiction, however microscopic. This noun is of course here exclamatory, expletive, and it is significant that it should stand alone in its pigeonhole, safely tucked away under number 12. As if it were standing, superbly indifferent, in its substantivity and intransitivity. In the same way, as soon as a sentence, however modest, is framed, it obeys the same headstrong important principle of self-containment, numbered, pinned down, radically indifferent to what is going on around. Here is the beginning of the text:

1) I was trying to climb the glass mountain.
2) The glass mountain stands at the corner of Thirteenth Street and Eighth Avenue.
3) I had attained the lower slope.[19]

Immense blanks stand between the sentences, as if many possibilities had been envisaged and rejected in the meanwhile, compelling the narrator to come back to his starting point, making no more progress than the climber of the mountain.

Another device that we often meet in such fiction fulfills this function, enumeration. A good example is provided by section 63: "The following-named knights had failed to climb the mountain and were groaning in the heap: Sir Giles Guilford, Sir Henry Lovell, Sir Albert Denny. . . ." Fifteen other senseless names follow in that way, and the catalog ends on the suggestion "and many others."[20] Plethora follows drought, but no more positive action ensues. Individually or collectively the noun resists the solicitations of a virtual verb, refuses to progress, to shift into another position, to constellate, to disseminate—in short, to give the narrative a chance to spread and fumble forward. The shifter does not transmit the orders, the gears grind motionlessly. There only remains a series of sideways motions, a jumping from noun to noun. Passive resistance prevails. No movement, except the tautological naming of names. Headstrong word or intransitive clause remains enclosed in its solipsist cell. Period.

I have deliberately chosen borderline examples in which we catch the author self-consciously asserting his right to experimentation and mystification. Barthelme is quite aware of the reader's reaction in such cases and plays with his feelings of frustration. In one of his particularly indigestible fictions, aggressively entitled "Kierkegaard Unfair to Schlegel," he seems at one moment conscious that some relief is needed: "Well, let me tell you a story."[21] Feeling of elation! But all he does is to enumerate the numberless items of play equipment encumbering a house he once rented in Colorado, passive objects bereft of their function of animation, nouns divorced from their expectant verbs. Nothing else. The poignancy of those unused, useless items is never emphasized. A period separates the perception from the emotion. The emotion itself is never named, only suggested, reduced to the small black dot. Which is not the case with Nathanael West: "He found himself in the window of a pawnshop full of fur coats, diamond rings, watches, shotguns, fishing tackle, mandolins. All these things were the paraphernalia of suffering."[22] The nonomission of the last sentence is all that distinguishes West from his descendants. In the case of Barthelme, only this ironical comment after his enumeration:

> Now, suppose I had been of an ironical turn of mind and wanted to make a joke about it all, some sort of joke that would convey that I had noticed the striking degree of boredom implied by the presence of all this impedimenta and one which would also serve to comment upon the particular way of struggling with boredom these people had chosen. I might have said, for instance, that the remedy was worse than the disease. Or quoted Nietzsche to the effect that the thought of suicide is a great consolation and had helped him through many a bad night.[23]

After the desiccation of fiction, after its regression to the most elementary stages —the section, the paragraph, the sentence, the clause, the noun—only silence and death appear as the last stage, the suicide of language toward which many of those fictions, like Beckett's, seem to tend. And, as an alternative to silence, its opposite, the mindless unfolding of verbiage as exemplified in the monstrous unfinished nine-page sentence of the piece appropriately entitled "Sentence" in *City Life,* the only possible catharsis to the unbreakable self-sufficient noun: "Or a long sentence at a certain pace down the page aiming for the bottom—if not the bottom of this page then of some other page. . . ."[24]

Diction: the paratactic style. This brings us to the third aspect of the disjunctive mode, diction, where, as we have already seen, the obsessive concern for the fragment finds its most efficient field of application. The few foregoing examples have emphasized the importance of the period, of the short factual clause, and also occasionally, in the mood of parody, of its opposite, the long, rambling, abstract commentary which ironically reintroduces the languages of tradition, perversely multiplying in a never-ending cascade the self-generating subordinate clauses.

What is relevant is not so much the length of the sentences as the fact that they are composed of independent clauses. Those may be juxtaposed to form a long sentence without constituting an organic whole: as often as not they will be loosely linked by a series of prepositions whose role of coordination is so slight that they might be replaced by periods without any loss of meaning. Or, if they form a sort of confederation encompassing a precise message, the series, of limited amplitude, is founded upon the principle of repetition. Then we witness nouns, tickled out of inertia, playing for a while the game of reproduction. Just one example out of *Trout Fishing* where we can realize how a flurry of movement activates a group of sentences for a short while, and then passes on to another equally limited group. There are three shifters in this unit, the binary phrases *Mooresville, Indiana, John Dillinger,* and *capital of America:*

> *Mooresville, Indiana,* is the town that *John Dillinger* came from, and the town has a Dillinger museum. You can go in and look around. Some towns are known as the peach *capital of America* or the cherry *capital of America,* and there's always a festival and the photograph of a pretty girl in a bathing suit. *Mooresville, Indiana,* is the *John Dillinger capital of America.*[25] (Italics added)

This pseudoparagraph is in fact one single sentence groping tentatively for the right words, borrowing from its neighbors its missing elements ("capital of America") and, after some whimsical digressions, leaving the scene for the following one to repeat the same process. The genuine period occurs between the completion of one series and the beginning of the next, here activated by another triad, *man, rats, basement:* "Recently a man moved there with his wife, and he discovered hundreds of rats in his basement," etc.

The rule is then, if we discard accessory accretions which may hide its real nature, the succession of independent clauses of the most elementary sort—subject, verb, complements—a loose tissue with ragged holes between its various elements. A characteristic instance can be found in its purity in the following passage from *City Life:* "He will go into the room with Elsa and shut the door. I will be sitting outside reading the business news. Britain Weighs Economic Curbs. Bond Rate Surge Looms. Time will pass. Then they will emerge. Acting as if nothing had happened. Elsa will make coffee. . . ."[26] What is puzzling here is to recognize, used with different effects, the type of diction we associate with the early Hemingway. The same allergy to the profuseness of the interconnected, subordinating linguistic patterns, the same insistent use of short, concrete, independent clauses or words. In both cases, it is a kind of farewell to the arms of rhetoric, a break with the ideology embedded in its romantic curlicues and flourishes, the refusal to explain, to demonstrate or justify. And also the dismissal of history, of psychological or philosophical motivations and commentaries. Accordingly, the same distance preserved between the uninvolved spectator and what he objectively reports, the *hic* and the *nunc.* But when Hemingway uses this style as a mask to assert a tough stoicism, using the blanks to reinsert implicitly a philosophy of despair and fortitude, always aware of a traumatic wound separating the before from the after, the Wastelanders use it as a natural medium to describe their natural habitat and time. It is no longer with them an attitude, a pose maintained with difficulty, always threatened by a suppressed romanticism, by the axiomatic mode of expression of a zeitgeist in which fragmentation and inconsequence are accepted as the rule. The illusions of memory are obliterated, causes and effects considered as reversible, logic and temporality toyed with as period pieces. The world is taken as found, without hope or nostalgia for a better one. And the paratactic style, once exploited by Hemingway as a shield against his weltschmerz, now finds an authentic function in the writings of the Wastelanders, and through them appears as the symptomatic cultural index that Eric Auerbach recognized in his *Mimesis.* As never before in American fiction, we now find a whole group of significant writers who recognize it as their natural and necessary mode of expression and use it to communicate quietly and devastatingly their utter disbelief in the possibility of communication. It is the diction of a walled-in consciousness, peering from behind its insulating pane of glass at an incomprehensible and unexplainable universe, recording its essence without surprise, or expectation, or indignation.

THE CONJUNCTIVE MODE

Needless to point out that the disjunctive mode is neither unique nor exclusive in contemporary writing. It can be opposed to the conjunctive mode mentioned at the beginning of this essay. Or at least be considered as the concave face of a common matrix whose convex fullness can be read in the conjunctive. This second type of fiction can be defined by most of the traits which characterize Djuna Barnes's *Nightwood*. These can be apprehended in terms opposite to the disjunctive features, globality being contrasted with fragmentation, polarization with dispersion, abundance with bareness, hyperbole with litotes. Which does not imply that the conjunctive mode, governed by centripetal forces, ruled by correlating and homogenizing compulsions, should be the expression of a well-balanced adjustment to reality, the medium of a celebratory acceptance of the universe, as one might oppose Walt Whitman's powerful affirmation of a cosmic optimism to Emily Dickinson's agonizingly splintered expression of her alienation. Its unbalance is as far-reaching as in the other case, only outer-directed when the other is inner-directed. In fact, these two major modes can be read as the two faces of the same Janus-like psychic reality.

To begin with, the starting point is very similar. The conjunctive also starts with the realization of a fragmented and meaningless world, and keeps on being aware of a radical split between the individual and his surrounding milieu. With the essential difference, however, that the pane of glass is broken at one point and the individual becomes involved in spite of himself, forcibly wrenched out of his isolation, swept away by the whirlwinds of an uncontrollable power. The description of the common rooms of a big house at the beginning of *Nightwood*, "a house that, large, dark and imposing, became the fantastic museum of their encounters," will help us to understand how the schizoid representation can persist within another mode of perception, but at the same time suffer some rich and strange "sea-change":

> The long rococo halls, giddy with plush and whorled designs in gold, were peopled with Roman fragments, white and dissociated; a runner's leg, the chilly half-turned head of a matron stricken at the bosom, the blind bold sockets of the eyes given a pupil by every shifting shadow so that what they looked upon was an act of the sun. The great salon was of walnut.[27]

There we recognize the now familiar stance of the disjunctive, the enumeration of discrete motionless objects whose dead fragmented nature is explicitly pointed out: "fragments," "dissociated," "chilly," "stricken." All that is summed up by the mention of the first object, whose aspect is emphatically disjointed from its function: a runner's leg, which suggests life and swiftness, but is just a lifeless marble reproduction, amputated from its body. Not unlike the play equipment in Barthelme's story. But at the end of the paragraph the dead eyes are given a new life by the shifting "act of the sun," and the white inanimate fragments are aroused from their inertia by the dynamic framework in which they are placed. They become part of the color and giddy movement of purple plush and golden whorls, if only in the way they bring out the rococo, sinuous nimbleness through their very sturdy repose. Enshrined in the big, womblike, palpitating hollow of walnut and curtains, they are animated with a kind of supernatural resurrection as evinced by the movements of "the blind sockets of the eyes" in the stricken bust. There indeed we are made the witnesses of the "fantastic encounters" and interaction of the disjunctive and conjunctive modes.

Our analysis of schizoid forms was concluded by a quotation from *Lost in the Funhouse* in which Barth was detecting the symptoms of schizophrenia in the manifestations of the disjunctive mode. In a similar way Thomas Pynchon reads those of paranoia in the conjunctive, analogous, he says, to those obtained under the effects of drugs: "About the paranoia often noted under the drug, there is nothing remarkable. Like other sorts of paranoia, it is nothing less than the onset, the leading edge, of the discovery that *everything is connected,* everything in the Creation. . . ."[28] He is quite aware of the sufferings it entails—his novels may be read as a roll call of their varieties—but, if he could choose, he would accept it rather than its opposite, which shuts away the individual in a total alienation: "If there is something comforting—religious if you wish—about paranoia, there is still anti-paranoia, where nothing is connected, a condition not many of us can bear for long."[29] Hence the idea, expressed by one of the characters in *Gravity's Rainbow,* that paranoia may be used as a strategy, a way to answer the pressures and menaces around us: "Yes, well, that can be useful . . . especially in combat . . . to pretend something like that. Jolly useful. Call it 'operational paranoia' or something."[30]

In a similar way it looks as if the writer, pragmatically, exploits the possibilities inherent in literary paranoia (his own brand) to structure his work, using the plots against them discovered by his main characters as the plots of his novels. In other words, he uses his paranoiacs's compulsive need to piece out the elements of a mysterious power threatening his characters as a way to give shape and cohesion to his material. In the same empirical vein, I should like to consider those two categories, schizophrenia and paranoia, as working hypotheses—I am a critic and not a clinician—and not as indices symptomatic of mental diseases. Let us be quite clear that they must not be regarded as diagnoses, but simply as taxonomic helps.

Diction: the hypotactic style. The paranoid, or conjunctive, mode is often characterized, so far as diction is concerned, by the structure of the sentence, in inverse ratio to the disjunctive sentence. Here what is prominent is the elaborate fashion in which the phrase is built, its ramified syntax, the prevalence of subordinate clauses expressing relations of causal, circumstantial, temporal dependence, fussily at work disentangling a jungle of apparently unrelated data. Nothing more alien to the sparseness of the disjunctive independent clause than the organic complexity of those linguistic arborescences. The very length of such sentences makes it difficult to quote any of them. But it will be easy enough to find a prize one by opening any of Pynchon's books to a descriptive or a didactic passage. On the very first page of *Gravity's Rainbow,* for instance, we find the description of people moving away from destruction during the London blitz. In *The Cannibal* this occurrence would have called forth paratactic structures—short, halting, broken sentences—but here the antithetic mode is to be found, which may be called, still following Auerbach's terminology, the hypotactic style:

> No, this is not a disentanglement from, but a progressive *knotting into*—they go under archways, secret entrances of rotted cement that only looked like the loops of an underpass . . . certain trestles of blackened wood have moved slowly by overhead, and the smell begun of coal from days far to the past, smells of naphtha winters, of Sundays when no traffic came through, or the coral-like and mysterious vital growth. . . .[31]

This does not sound so much like the description of a collective body of people making its way into the tortuous depths of space and memory as the mimetic self-reflection of the very sentence's winding and groping into the unknown, through a glass darkly unfolding itself into a "coral-like and mysterious vital growth." The explicit italicized comment *"knotting into"* clearly points at Pynchon's syntactic usage. Danger and terror are not perceived as centrifugal factors of dispersal and discontinuity. The organic coherence of the sentence bears evidence to the polarizing power of a latent catastrophe. We noticed above the apparent similarities between the paratactic style in Hemingway and the Wastelanders' version of it. The same type of remark can be made concerning the hypotactic style, which is indeed prevalent in the writings of William Faulkner, for instance, although paratactic brevity is by no means absent in his work: we have just to think of *As I Lay Dying* to be aware that the two styles are complementary rather than mutually exclusive in the conjunctive stylistic structures.

Those syntactic structures reflect the recognition of the strong link binding man and history, man and his natural surroundings, the interdependence between the past and the present, our acts and their consequences. The difference between Faulkner's sentences and Pynchon's, however important they may be (in the latter, a blurring effect produced by disjointed juxtapositons, the overburdening of the treeline by unexpected growths, the skidding of anacoluths which rupture the syntax), is more a difference in degree than in nature, the difference between organic proliferation and the same running wild as if some powerful radiation or mutating agent were at work upon it.

I have focused these remarks on Pynchon's style for the sake of clarity, but a close scrutiny would evince similar features in other writers, the piling up of detail upon detail, the accumulation of interpolated clauses, the juxtaposition of present and past tenses, the metamorphosis of simple tenses into compound ones, the emergence of tentacle-like clauses reaching in every direction. With differences, however, stemming from the specificity of the writer's imagination: amorphous, distended, jelly-like sentences in Burroughs, crisper and more frantic in Heller, more haunted and flamboyant in the later Purdy. The diction reveals here a voice, an obsession, easily identified, magnified and reverberating as in a nightmare, as opposed to the blank anonymity of the paratactic fragments where the reader would be hard put to ascribe an isolated sentence either to Brautigan, or Barthelme, or Michaels, or West for that matter.

Representation: the paranoid fluidity. When one comes to consider the representational characteristics of the conjunctive mode, what impresses is the vanishing of the geometrical patterns so prominent in the schizoid vision. The spectatorial quality, in which sight is the privileged medium, gives way to more diffuse sensation verging on synesthesia. Contours and obstacles seem to dissolve in a viscous fluidity; the details are fused into the all-pervading flux and eddies of a unifying ambience. The differences between the inner and the outer are abolished: what was seen from the outside is now experienced from within. Colors have a tendency to blur the outlines, as in impressionist paintings. Smells and other organic perceptions, physical pain in particular, give a premium to subjective sensations over objective reality. This could be felt in the quotation from Pynchon where smells obliterate the actuality of the moment and bring the past into the present. Another striking instance is in the following passage from *Naked Lunch,* the power of the stinking green haze which destroys all traces of external representations: "His flesh turns to viscid, transparent jelly that drifts away in green mist unveiling a black centipede. Waves of unknown stench fill the room, searing the lungs, grabbing the stomach. . . ."[32]

Such modalities are to be observed in many texts. Let us mention briefly the scatological odyssey of Slothrop in the toilets and sewers of the Roseland Ballroom in *Gravity's Rainbow,* the nocturnal scenes of John Gardner's *Grendel,* the pornographic daydreams in *The Sot-Weed Factor.* But here again the fact must be stressed that these representations are rarely maintained throughout a book. Like the hypotactic style which seems to be their favorite vehicle, they rather appear as a kind of climactic reaction against the constraints of both paratactic style and schizoid forms. As in the cases of Djuna Barnes and William Faulkner, the conjunctive mode is often used in correlation and contrast with the disjunctive. This may be explained by the fact that the schizoid forms, more pointed and emphatic in their function of code, which make one immediately aware of their message, should, in the literary text, either precede the paranoid forms or be associated with them according to the degree of obsessional intensity attributed to such and such a character. Examples of those dialectical interactions and mutations are to be found in Burroughs, Mailer, Heller, Gaddis, Hawkes, when, following a feeling of isolation in a character's consciousness, the irrational certainty takes shape in his mind that he is the object of a universal conjuration, that an inexorable fatality is responsible for his predicament. In short, to oversimplify a complex situation, let us suggest that in that case we can observe the shifting from one type of external, disconnected but objective perceptions to an opposite type of organic, phantasmic, and subjective ones.

One of the essential features of the conjunctive mode is the emphasis on the interiorization and the imaginative manipulation of external data. It generally implies the presence of a deeply involved narrator, highly sensitized, no longer the detached narrator-from-behind-the-window, but on the contrary an overactive consciousness which selects, interprets, distorts, unifies, and magnifies those of the events which can feed the fire of his obsessional compulsions. Mailer's narrators in *An American Dream* or *Why Are We in Vietnam?* provide convincing instances of this passionate, hallucinated subjectivity which, through the pressure of a torrential language, jumbles and dissolves the clear-cut, jagged disjunctive outlines. We might define such paranoid writers with the general comment applied by. Susan Sontag to Jean Genêt: "a baroque and insolent writer whose ego effaces all objective narration."[33]

Narration: resurrection of the novel. On the level of the narrative proper, the dialectical relations between schizoid and paranoid forms produce by far the most interesting resolutions. On the one hand, an initial vision of the universe which tends to emphasize the forces of entropy, the shattering and crumbling down of forms, accumulation, coldness, stasis. And on the other hand the opposite tendency, which discerns and exposes a malevolent intention, a generalized plot behind those manifestations. Two great categories of fictions can be distinguished according to the role of the main character, who is most of the time the narrator as well, as we have seen. Those categories depend on whether he is the victim or the tormentor, dominated or dominator, manipulated or manipulator.

In the first case, a dynamic principle is introduced. The narrative is unlocked and gropes toward an objective, even if the end of the quest remains out of reach forever. The character then appears in the role of a solver of riddles, a decipherer of codes. A meaning, however occult it may be, is ascribed to the world which surrounds him. His existence is assumed to be shaped and threatened by obscure forces. It therefore has a sense, follows a direction. It is the search for that direction, for that sense which is the subject matter of the action. There of course we recognize the organizing principle of Kafka's novels, whose contemporary American versions can be found in *The Lime Twig, Catch 22, Grendel, Gravity's Rainbow.* In giving those examples, I mention only those in which war, its apparatus and its sequels, as well as the mental attitudes it fosters, constitutes both a generalized metaphor for a mysterious, arbitrary, powerful force shaping individual destinies and also the very generator of the fiction. For conjunctive fiction is essentially dependent upon a conflict triggered by a will power attempting to assert itself.

In the second case, by far the most fascinating, the tables are turned. The purpose is no longer to show the inefficacy or impotence of the isolated individual threatened and destroyed by an inexplicable order, but to invest the center of the web, the origin of the plot, the radiating fountainhead where the signals are concocted and codified. The will to power, which is the other face of paranoia, is then apprehended from the inside, heard and visualized in its attempts to impose a mad design upon the world. As if the narrator of *Moby Dick* had been Ahab, telling us about his schemes against the social order, the crew, the white whale. That inversion of novelistic functions makes it possible for the writer to go beyond the existential anguishes of schizophrenia and ignore the obstacles it puts in the way of the narrative, blocking every attempt to proceed. The word can then burst and expand into a paragraph, the paragraph swell into a chapter, chapter after chapter grow into that resurrected genre, the novel. That is what John Gardner is about in his *Grendel,* all the more significant in that its android narrator is first a victim before turning into an aggressor, and that he remains a victim so far as he partly identifies with the society he wants to annihilate, in that way belonging to the two antithetic modes.

Hawkes's case is interestingly revealing of the duality, the ambiguity attached to the conjunctive strategy. In *The Owl* he gives a ruthless and terrifying picture of the paranoid imagination, and also, although in a more subdued way, in *The Blood Oranges,* where the totalitarian designs of the narrator, focused on his sexual activities, are lengthily, lyrically justified, all the objections and obstacles carried away by the flow of his eloquence, with, as a result, the destruction of the self-contained erotic utopia he had managed to erect. Whereas in his last novel, *Death, Sleep and the Traveler,* the mode is definitely schizoid and disjunctive. As opposed to Nathanael West, who experimented with the first person singular in his magazine version of *Miss Lonelyhearts* and then reverted to the third person in his book version so as to preserve the distance and irony,[34] Hawkes conceived and wrote his first novels in the third person,[35] essentially bearing witness to the misery of a shattered universe. Then, a posteriori, he felt in each case the necessity to superimpose a narrator whose obsessions introduce the conjunctive mode in a kind of contrapuntal structure, Zizendorf, the neo-Nazi leader in the first and last part of *The Cannibal,* the sadistic sheriff in the prologue of *The Beetle Leg,* and Hencher, a victim and a transmitter of his own phantasm in the first third of *The Lime Twig.* Through those additions, which create a voice for the expression of the paranoid imagination, a tension, singularly absent in the monotone disjunctive mode, is created between representation and narration, between narration and diction, a tension which generates contrasting effects and gives Hawkes's fiction its unique and particularly subtle and complex resonances.

The various categories of new American writing being, I hope, clearly defined and the various ways in which it does—or does not—function as fully analyzed as could be done within the limits of this essay, it remains to be seen what is the situation of the New Fiction in the mainstream of the American novel. As interesting as its productions may be, there is no point ignoring the fact that they are not the offsprings of spontaneous generation. The writers I mentioned, and many others could have been considered, often exploit—whether consciously or not is irrelevant—the researches and findings of other pioneers who were also working outside the main tradition. I took as a starting point the novels of West and Barnes, but the immense influence of Nabokov upon this generation must not be neglected, nor, in a more diffuse fashion, that of Joyce and Borges, or Roussel, or Beckett, and also, beyond modernism, that of Rabelais, Cervantes, or Sterne. Without the French Nouveau Roman, without the theater of the absurd, American literature today would not be what it is. Although we may affix the adjective "new" to the fiction written now, it is not so much its newness in itself which is impressive as the convergence, among the most gifted writers of their time, of a general questioning of the relevance of the modernist techniques and assumptions to their present problems.

If I had the choice of only one name by which to locate the true ancestor of the New Fiction, I would unhesitatingly mention Edgar Allan Poe, who seems to crystallize in his own work most of the virtualities developed these last few years. These virtualities were bypassed by the more popular form of the traditional novel which became the instrument of social protest and political reform during the major crises of the past century. In a more permanent way it was overshadowed by the central theme of the novel, the American Dream, with its train of illusions and nostalgias. With Poe and the Wastelanders, on the contrary, fiction is not propelled forward in an ever-ending flight or an equally disappointing quest. Neither is it turned backward to the lost paradise of a mythic America. As in the romance, it rather tends to go up or down the paradigmatic, metaphorical axis, with a strong attraction toward the fantastic. Or to occupy the motionless center of its own essence and ponder about its origin, its nature, and its powers.

In 1830 as in 1960 the possibilities of a new literature, which speaks of the present for the present, seem stifled by the authority of existing models. On one side gothic or romantic British fiction, and on the other side the modernist novel. In the two historical situations the same sensation of "exhausted possibilities" experienced by the young writer with such discomfort whenever he tries to write, this obsession also with the *déjà vu,* the *déjà fait,* strikingly rendered by William Gaddis in his novel *The Recognitions,* dealing with the problems of the bogus, the imitated, the counterfeited work of art, an obsession that Poe expressed over and over again in his critical writings. And, together with it, the necessity of a tabula rasa, of a new start, which is satisfied in two ways:

1) Through the subversion of existing forms, the burlesquing of clichés by means of pastiche and parody, as in Poe's *Tales of the In-Folio* or Barth's *Sot-Weed Factor.* Also by means of "denudation," a wink to the critical sense of the reader when the literary device is underlined and ridiculed within the text itself. There we have critical and self-critical fictions that imply a new type of relationship between writer and reader, the latter no longer a passive consumer, but a participant, an accomplice.

2) By the elaboration, within the fiction itself, and not a posteriori as in James's prefaces, of an implicit theory of fiction which gives the writer the means to do away with imitation and give rise to new types of discourses no longer based on the reproduction of reality but on the production of nonrealistic patterns which invert the order of priority between writing and plot, the former no longer considered as the support or vehicle of the latter, but vice versa.

Even if we consider the predominance of themes over the concern with words, structures, ideas, one cannot help noticing that even in the turbulent midst of the mainstream novel the accent is more often set on a questioning of the *being* than on the process of the *becoming,* on the problematic nature of the character rather than on his existential reality; that the obsession with space is another way of denying the action of time, a way of breaking away from the definitions imposed by society, of refusing to grant the character any depth, any roundness, both qualities claimed by the traditional novel. As if the American novelist had been writing novels in spite of himself and had wanted to rescue his hero from the cramping definitions demanded by the rules. As if he had wanted to protect him from some irreversible incarnation, to preserve some precious quality, some miraculous virtualities which no actual possibility could adequately fulfill. As if he had also wanted to delay indefinitely a resolution which could only be disappointing and mutilating. The same characteristics, the same reluctance that we find fully exemplified in the disjunctive writings today.

Most fiction rests on the art of postponing an issue inscribed in its premises. This art has found in the United States its most successful achievement in the very quality of incompleteness that characterizes it. Let us ponder the "interrupted" quality of the endings in some of the most significantly "engaged" masterpeices, from *Sister Carrie* to *Invisible Man,* not to mention the open-ended, unresolved final pages of *The Scarlet Letter, Moby Dick, Huckleberry Finn* . . . American fictions rarely conclude, they merely pause.

Those profound and lasting tendencies are to be found in the New Fiction, which recognizes them, assumes them, exploits them, and carries them to the utmost limits of their virtualities, to the absurd logical consequences of having almost totally "arrested" fictions, disjointed narratives, unhinged sentences, paralytic nouns. The New Fiction has disencumbered those national propensities from the carapaces of pre-texts and con-texts which had so far, with a few exceptions, hidden the real nature of its specificity. Revealed now, retrospectively, through the magnifying glass of the disjunctive and the conjunctive modes.

Régis Durand

7. THE EXEMPLARY FICTIONS OF ROBERT COOVER

> *Moi, je parle, je parle, dit Marco, mais celui qui m'écoute ne retient que les paroles qu'il attend . . . ce qui commande au récit, ce n'est pas la voix: c'est l'oreille.*
>
> Italo Calvino

POSITIONS 1: DISCURSIVE MACHINES

I am disappearing. You have no doubt noticed. Yes, and by some no doubt calculable formula of event and pagination. But before we drift apart to a distance beyond the reach of confessions (though I warn you: like Zeno's turtle, I am with you always), listen . . .[1]

How are we to read Coover (or for that matter a good deal of the fiction of today), and worse still, to write about him? As he is about to embark on yet another parasitic discourse on literature, no critic can help feeling faintly giddy in front of the virtually unlimited combinations offered by the critical machinery. Unless of course he is already committed to a particular kind of discourse, his predicament must be not unlike that of the writer himself as he is confronted with the infinite possibilities of fiction.

Committing oneself blindly to one kind of discourse, be it fictional or critical, appears more and more as an untenable position if one does not first of all question its underlying assumptions and its place in the overall production of discourse. The particular appeal and relevance of contemporary fiction and contemporary criticism lie in the fact that they make certain questions inevitable, certain realizations unavoidable. For the novelist, it is the realization that what fiction is about is not so much "life" as *fiction* itself. Hence the name of "metafiction," which in the words of Stanley Fogel "entails exploration of the theory of fiction through fiction itself."[2]

For the critic it is also—among other things—the fact that fiction is a kind of machine or matrix that produces endless variations on the same basic archetypes.

The result is that a new kind of attention to language is called into play: language is considered, as Roland Barthes puts it, "intransitively." And it becomes clear that in order to be subversive, it is not necessary for a writer or a critic to profess revolutionary convictions: it is enough to talk about language, instead of merely *using* it.[3]

All the same, many questions remain pendent, one of the most disturbing being the problem of the objective complicity that has long existed between fiction and a certain kind of criticism, a complicity to which some Marxist critics like Fredric Jameson or Charles Grivel are beginning to draw attention. What would seem to be called for, then, is a criticism focusing on the production and the situation of discourse (both fictional and critical) devised to expose rather than conceal its mechanisms, to annul rather than make believe, to be quite literally *exorbitant* rather than to purr smoothly in the orbit of the novel. The least one can say is that it is far from being the most widespread type of criticism at the present time, and the reasons for this are of a technical but also largely ideological nature. I do not propose, however, to go into them here, and if I mention briefly some of the dominant critical discourses it is not with a polemical intention, but rather to try to assess their relevance to contemporary fiction, and in particular to the writer we are here concerned with.

There is always, of course, "cosmetic criticism,"[4] that is, the kind of critical discourse which spreads over the text, coating and outlining every accident, curve, and cranny of the expressive contents, designed like makeup, to give a fresh, "natural" look, to enhance. We owe to this type of discourse some elegant, sensitive commentaries. But it will be easily seen that the mask of fiction continues to leer behind the paint. One of Coover's stories, "Scene for Winter," can serve as a kind of inbuilt refutation of such readings, by showing that there is no such thing as continuity, or rather that continuity is an effect (a mirage?) achieved under certain circumstances (angle of vision, lens, focus, etc.). If we step back, change the lens, or rub our fictional eyes, the scene shifts, shuffles, and rearranges itself into something quite different—a different story, which in turn . . .

> Slowly, *quickly,* we swoop backwards from the man and the sound, leave him there coiled in the snow, helpless like a beetle on its back, slide away from the vast and blinding pain, returning gratefully to the comforting shadows of the forest, the great weighted forest with its low-slung canopy of snow-laden boughs. *For a brief stunning moment, we suddenly see the man's hysterical face again, as though in a memory, a sudden terrorizing recollection that drives a cold and unwanted terror through us*—but we gradually perceive that it is not the man at all, no, it is only the face of the white rabbit, nothing more, its wide-nostrilled nose quivering, its rodent eyes cloudy, its mouth split in a sardonic grin. As we slip back, we discover that it is between the jaw of the lean-bodied dog. . . .[5]

Several of Coover's stories contain such fables or allegories of fiction and of the misfortunes of a particular kind of critical eye.

As for structural criticism, it is invaluable when it comes to laying bare the wheels and cogs of the literary machinery. Indeed, there would appear to be a natural affinity between a fiction that turns back on itself and a critical approach designed to point out the structures which generate the text. Coover's stories often make clear their awareness of a structural process:

> Yet, for all that, there is in fact a milkmaid approaching, on her head a tall gently curving pitcher filled with fresh milk for the market. It is almost as though there has been some sort of unspoken but well understood prologue, *no mere epitaph of random design, but a precise structure of predetermined images, both basic and prior to us, that describe her to us before our senses have created her in the present combination of shapes and colors.*[6]

But because structural criticism has become inlaid within, and a constituent of, the fictional apparatus, it finds itself invalidated, in danger of becoming a mere tautology, perhaps another work of fiction.

Confronted with a fiction that subtly undermines the critical task and forces it to reexamine itself, one may be tempted to yield to what Charles Grivel calls "the hysterical desire to be unsatisfied,"[7] an attitude widespread enough which denies all relevance and significance to criticism, especially when it comes to contemporary literature: "What is there to say about a work of literature that isn't already said in a much better way in the work itself?" Or, in a somewhat more sophisticated form: "Literature speaks precisely of what it (*It?*) alone can speak about."

It seems to us, on the contrary, that the role of criticism is precisely to articulate what literature cannot articulate about itself. How, where, and under what circumstances the task can best be done is another matter. The first step would perhaps be to stop treating literature as a teeming wilderness of words upon which some sort of order, some sort of sense, has to be imposed, and to accept a dialogue instead of seeking refuge behind armored, terrorist pieces of criticism. One could hope then for a criticism which would be sympathetic and close yet detached, grounded simultaneously in continuity and fragmentation, attentive to disruptions, shifts, but ranging freely over the text;[8] a criticism that would take into account strategy, displacement, transference of energy and impulses.[9] No such thing, unfortunately, will be found in the notes that follow, merely a prologue to a reading which, by lending Robert Coover an attentive ear, would add its own invisible helix to the intricate pattern of his fictions.

POSITIONS 2: THE RETURN OF THE VANISHING DESIGN

> The return to Being has returned us to Design, to microcosmic images of the macrocosm, to the creating of Beauty within the confines of cosmic or human necessity, to the use of the fabulous to probe beyond the phenomenological, beyond appearances, beyond randomly perceived events, beyond mere history. But these probes are above all, like your knight's sallies—challenges to the assumptions of a dying age, exemplary adventures of the Poetic Imagination, high-minded journeys towards the New World. . . .[10]

"Novelas ejemplares," "ficciones": the father of classical narrative, to whom Coover pays a half-serious, half-whimsical homage, joins hands here with Borges, the precise surveyor of the arcana of fiction. And Coover's prologue to his "Seven Exemplary Fictions" may serve as an indication of the strategy he assigns to his fictions. Just as Cervantes took the conventions of the romance and turned them inside out, Coover proposes to start from the narrative form as we have inherited it from Cervantes and to turn it against itself. Not only the reference to Cervantes but also the strictures against our "literature of exhaustion" would seem to indicate in Coover a "reactionary" bent. In fact, the return to design is quite the opposite, a carefully thought-out strategy to free fiction from the ideological morass that persistently clings to it.

The task of modern fiction, if it is to break away from the degraded form of writing that has become subservient to the tastes and needs of a particular class of readers, will be twofold. First, it must attempt to free itself from what Coover calls the "unconscious mythic residue in human life,"[11] the archetypes by which it is governed. It has now become clear that, no matter what aesthetic satisfactions it affords, the novel in particular is primarily an attempt—conscious or unconscious —to recapture some original archetype, a reiteration with a purpose.

Second—and the task is complementary to the first—it must bring forward, into active play, all that has been expelled, censured, or repressed: negativity, organic life, history, madness, death, what Coover calls "literal history" (as opposed to "poetic analogy"): "In fact, your creation of a synthesis between poetic analogy and literal history (not to mention reality and illusion, sanity and madness, the erotic and the ludicrous, the visionary and the scatological) gave birth to the novel."[12]

Coover believes that the literature of recent years has succumbed to the appeal of pseudomodernity, to the facilities of the inchoate, the unfocused, thereby becoming a doubly pernicious form of mystification. The best way to expose it is probably to lay bare the very process and mechanics of it, and in order to do so, it is necessary to revert to narrative, to point out ironically its power and its perversions while retaining control over it. Narrative appears first and foremost as a necessary polarization, a means of focusing, of absorbing the "peripheral vision" of the reader.[13] Hence the character of Coover's fictions, which are first and foremost studies in narrative and design. Most of them are written in sequences of short paragraphs which are sometimes numbered, the tale is stripped of its "natural" flow, of its semblance of reality, and its real nature is revealed: that of an aleatory and unstable construct. Hence also Coover's predilection for subjects and vehicles which turn out to be already structured like a narration: fairytales, tall tales, legends, biblical episodes . . . A double exposure is thus given to the tales that pattern our unconscious (fictional) memory as well as our social being, erasing the reassuring lifelike gloss, revealing the props and mechanisms, but also the void, the horror. "Little Red Riding Hood," "The Tale of the Milkmaid," become explorations in lust and illusion, a panel game, a vertiginous race toward death, a magic act a mangling of bodies. The smooth surface of fiction reveals a series of deliberate choices, masks, mystifications. This does not mean of course that Coover does away altogether with the discreet charm of narrative. One simply never does: "Every telling has a taling." But something else is at work in the telling, which plays with the codes, disorients, produces a text which escapes the logic of causation, of origin, continuation, and closure, of the reiteration and celebration of archetypes; something which negates, opens the safe reservation of past narrative to the thrust and threat of the present.

ORIGINS

> No sound, it gets going with utter silence, no sound except perhaps an inappreciable crackle now and then, not unlike static, but our ear readily compensates for it, hears not that sound but the absence of sound, stretches itself, reaches out past any staticky imperfections there might be and finds: only the silence. And that's how it starts.[14]

What distinguishes the new fiction from the old is that it can no longer be innocent, no longer take for granted certain devices or loci: narrators, beginnings, and ends—"the beginning always comes after" (Philippe Sollers). The subject of several of Coover's fictions is precisely their relation to established codes of fictional narrative, "norms." But there is no such thing as simply overturning a norm; one can only play a close game with it, undermine its foundations. Thus with origin: in Coover's fictions, origin never goes without saying, never simply eases the way for the narrative. Instead, a strategy is put forward, tested, which in turn generates a certain type of fictional disposition:

> At first, in an instant half-real half-remembered the leper is at rest; then he begins his approach, urgent across the—no, no! impossible! he has always been beginning, always approaching, it was the glare, just the glare caused the illusion: sun at its zenith and this leper coming on.[15]

The security of past narrative is dropped and a disturbing present reintroduced; the act of writing becomes implosive, shatters the relations between writer and story, writer and reader. The linguistic code itself is questioned, for it appears that it plays a determinant role not only as an instrument but as a fabricator of fiction:

> Klee, Wilbur Klee, dies. Is dead, rather. I know, I know: too soon. It should come, after a package of hopefully ingenious preparations, at the end. In some languages, it is possible to say: *to die oneself*, as in: I die myself, you will die yourself, he would have died himself, and so on, cunningly planting the idea that one's own hand was perhaps involved.[16]

No past is called upon to shore up the fragments of Coover's present, except occasionally the freakish demonic survivor of an earlier age, a dirty, lecherous, and lyrical figure who lets out in bursts a solitary flow of words. Morris the shepherd hunted down by the armies of technology, the caretaker's son on an abandoned island, a wayfarer on the side of a highway: singers of pricksongs all, keepers of the Magic Poker, old lechers with a past. They are the closest one comes to origins in Coover's fiction, a fiction which most of the time invents, as it hurtles down the spiral of design, its several mock-beginnings.

THE ENERGY OF WORDS

> But name a man and you make him what he is. Of course he can develop. And in ways you don't expect. Or something can go wrong. . . . But the basic stuff is already there. In the name. Or rather in the naming.[17]

In the novel the names of protagonists have always been powerful generators of fiction. With Flaubert, Proust, and the modern novel, they become systematically productive. The mastermind of the Universal Baseball Association, sole proprietor of an entirely fictional universe—a perfect image of the writer—knows that names contain whole dramas, whole universes. The task of the writer is therefore to allow them to release their potential, their fictional energy. Hence the pattern of many of Coover's stories: a name, or a mere word, serves as a starting point, and the text grows out of it, as an exploration of the possibilities it contains. Hence also the many associations, distortions, the gusto and comic spirit of Coover's writings. "Rational" language holds a precarious grip on our life and our unconscious: let its hold slip, and a wild energy is unleashed: words, names, associate freely and whirl faster and faster; against the cold rationality of the many forms of order, power, censorship, another language begins to flow, carrying with it all that had been repressed or forgotten. But the tempo increases, the pitch becomes frenzied. Insanity, terror, hysteria set in as the speaker realizes that he is swept away, hurled into an abyss and toward death. And in this mad, doomed scramble for an answer, for THE ultimate answer, Death, we see a perfect allegory of the origin and end of all fiction:

> So think, stickleback. Freshwater fish. Freshwater fish: green seaman? seaman: semen. Yes, but green: raw? Spoiled? Vigorous? Stickle: stubble. Or maybe scruple. Back: Bach: Bacchus: baccate: berry. Raw berry? Strawberry? Maybe. Sticky berry in the raw? In the raw: bare. Bare berry: beriberi. Also bearberry, the dog rose, dogberry. Dogberry: the constable in . . . what? *Comedy of Errors!* Yes! No.[18]

GAMES WRITERS PLAY

In *The Universal Baseball Association,* one of the most powerful contemporary fables of fiction, Henry Waugh creates his fictional world by rolling dice and referring each throw to elaborate strategy charts. "The Baby Sitter," perhaps Coover's best story, is another example of the same strategy. A story begins: a babysitter arrives as the parents are about to leave to go to a party. From then on the story proceeds in a series of "throws," each one of them offering several choices according to what level, what angle of the story it is referred to, but also creating binding sequences. Thus, we find in the same story a mixture of rigorous dramatic progression and of nonsequential, overlapping levels of narrative. As an emblem for this intricate process, baseball, in addition to its mythic value as the All-American game, appears best suited. It is even better than chess, which often appears in contemporary fiction as a symbol for, or a device in, the production of fiction (Nabokov, Sollers):

> To be good, a chess player, too, had to convert his field to the entire universe, himself to the ruler of that private enclosure—though from a pawn's eye view, of course, it wasn't an enclosure at all, but, infinitely, all there was. Henry enjoyed chess, but found it finally too Euclidian, too militant, ultimately irrational, and in spite of its precision, formless really—nameless motion.[19]

Fiction, in its modern form, free of sequential compounding, is the ultimate game for which all other games are only metaphors.

THE NARRATIVE EAR

The act of writing always presupposes not only a narrator but also a "narratee."[20] In contemporary fiction the presence of the reader becomes an integral part of the process of writing. In the case of Coover, the narrative "voice" is often not unlike the "impersonal" voice or eye of Robbe-Grillet's novels, focusing on objects, setting up a geometry of space. Here, the narrative voice implicates the reader ("we") and tends to appear in the guise of ringmaster, master of ceremonies, or stage director (Coover's stories often have a theatrical quality about them). Often, too, the "we" figure watches from a distance and records the scene with mounting horror. It is then that the implication of the reader is strongest: the safe distance between reader and writer is abolished, an act as socially accepted as reading is shown to conceal, like other seemingly innocent activities, dangerous fantasies and threats. The traditional implication of the reader ("lector amantisimo," "hypocrite lecteur . . .") is no longer playful rhetoric but the words that seal the inevitable: "Under the desert sun. We wait, as he waited for us, for you. Desperate in need, yet with terror. What terrible game will *you* play with us? me."[21]

VOICES OF FANTASY

Sometimes a voice is heard, dredging up a spate of words from areas of speech and self long buried and suppressed by the totalitarian discourses of society, the voice of the frustrated but unyielding individual, the lone survivor:

> And then he spoke. He spoke rapidly, desperately, with neither punctuation nor sentence structure. Just a ceaseless eruption of obtuse language. He spoke of constellations, bone structures, mythologies and love. He spoke of belief and lymph nodes, of excavations, categories and prophecies. Faster and faster he spoke. His eyes gleamed. Harmonies! Foliations! Etymology! Impulses! Suffering! His voice rose to a shriek. Immateriality patricide ideations heat-stroke virtue predication—I grew annoyed and shot him in the head. At last, with this, he fell.[22]

But the suspicion, the censure that bears on discourse, is not only that of institutions, police, ideology. It is also that of the individual toward his own discourse. For discourse is treacherous, it is liable to undergo the most radical shifts, to grow into the most unspeakable fantasies. In "The Elevator" Martin arrives early for work one morning, and instead of going up to the fourteenth floor where he works, goes down to the basement. This simple change in his routine is enough to trigger a rebellion against the humiliations he suffers, and wild fantasies of sexual power, violence, death. Martin's fantasies, however, are explored "from the inside," they remain an expression of an individual psyche. On the contrary, in "The Baby Sitter" the voice heard is no longer that of the protagonist; it exceeds the limitations of individual vision and becomes multiple. It is the mechanism itself of fiction which becomes deranged and produces confused and conflicting incidents. The "incidents" do not really add up to a "story," they chart out the multiplicity of narrative possibilities; the outcome remains undecided and makes no attempt at being "plausible." Is the babysitter assaulted by two boys, one of whom may or may not be her own boyfriend? Or by Mr. Tucker? Has this, or part of this, been happening on TV? The logic of traditional narration is deconstructed and parodied, and there appears in its place a fiction that "invents itself" at every stage of its development.[23]

GLISSEMENTS PROGRESSIFS

Where does this illusion come from, this sensation of "hardness" in a blue tea-kettle or on an iron poker, golden haunches or a green piano?[24]

Coover's fictions have a clear, hard-edged quality, a surface "legibility," an uncanny air of being about what they appear to be: a helix, a lens (sentient, to be sure!) a voice, a story, or the telling of a story. It is not, then, that subject or anecdote are lacking, but rather that they are no longer innocent, that they have lost their character of certainty, of being "natural." The center of vision shifts, different "takes" of the same scene, of the same sequence are made, from a slightly different angle, revealing unsuspected aspects. Through progressive slidings, a new narrative syntax emerges, a syntax of desire and fantasies. All syntaxes rely on a particular kind of erotics: the appeal of the traditional narrative is based on continuity and progression leading to a climax. With Coover, as with other contemporary novelists and film makers, we experience the text in terms of fragmentation, repetition, multiple exposures, and sudden violence. Fragmentation is in itself an index of the battle against unity and "good sense," a battle of an obviously ideological nature. Because of the subtlety and of the power of their strategy, Coover's fictions may rightly be said to be exemplary of the attempt to disrupt and subvert this semantic unity that our culture imposes on the works of fiction. There is in his pieces something hard and perfectly economical that will not easily be reduced to the pulp of "expressive" or "common sense" ideology.[25]

Pierre Gault

8. GENESIS AND FUNCTIONS OF HENCHER IN "THE LIME TWIG"

THE NECESSARY ORDEAL OF THE READER IN "THE LIME TWIG"

In the course of the first chapter of *The Lime Twig* and sometimes with the first pages, the reader has decided whether he should pursue his reading or not. Hawkes's difficult writing carries a sort of challenge which does not necessarily stimulate his taste or his courage.

This obstacle, though, has been deliberately placed at the beginning of the novel as a postulate, and it is only after having adapted himself to the author's exactions that the reader assents to the more conventional reading of the pages that follow them.

The present article will thus be devoted to the reader's necessary sufferings on his way to the pleasures of Hawkes's fiction. If we superficially examine the structure of the book, we are baffled by a disturbing anomaly: Hencher, who appears throughout the early chapter as the major character of *The Lime Twig*, disappears prematurely by the first third of the novel. Hawkes will uncover the corpse only in the final assembling of elements. This sleight of hand leaves the reader frustrated: after becoming accustomed gradually and with difficulty to Hencher's disconcerting logic, he has the feeling that the author has fooled him.

Yet Hencher's disappearance is but the ultimate function of a manifold character through whom we are guided into a reflection on the novelistic genre. The primary function of this *mise en abyme*[1] is to disorient the reader.

That we shall try to explain, throughout the different stages of Hencher's genesis. The first sentence of the novel is a direct aggression upon the reader— the word "fiction" would be more adequate, and we shall regard "novel" as neutral synonym: "Have you ever let lodgings in the winter? Was there a bed kept waiting, a corner room kept for a gentleman?" (p. 4).

If we want to understand Hawkes's discourse, we must identify at once with a conventional lodger. The invitation is quite explicit. In the lines that come after, a few additional details focus the image of the lodger. They are sufficiently representative and generalizable to make the identification quite uncompromising. Indeed, we may admit that we once hung the sign and waited for "the gentleman." We may admit too that we did not answer the bell because there was something wrong about the eyes of the man seen through the windowpane.

After this introduction the reader is thus ready to assume the situation of a landlord behind a window, waiting for someone to ring the bell, and he is likely to feel the presence of the other as an intrusion. Still, Hawkes does not intend that the too easily convinced reader should slumber in the landlord's chair, satisfied with a comforting Manichaeism. The situation is suddenly reversed, compelling us to identify with "the other," more urgently than before.

"Or perhaps you yourself were once the lonely lodger" (p. 4). The process of identification here has quite a different quality; there is something more emotional about it, perhaps because of the aspect of loneliness evoked. The reader's participation will soon be organized around more compromising sequences: Hawkes, still faithful to his aggressive "you," is going to create situations of compounded intimacy, through an increasing precision of details. Conscious that the identification will be more difficult to accept, because more specifically intimate, the author makes the reader's immersion more attractive by allowing him choices of participation. Explicitly, Hawkes invites us to play a game according to several sets of conventions: "Perhaps the moon was behind the cathedral. You walked in the cathedral's shadow while the moon kept shining on three girls ahead." According to his taste, the reader may yield to the temptation of romance, or dream: "... and you followed the moonlit girls, ..." Or he may choose realism: "'... or followed a woman carrying a market bag. ...'" Or indulge in some obscure symbolism: "... or followed a slow bus high as a house with a saint's stone shadow on its side, and smoke coming out from between the tires." (p. 4)

If he has been able to follow the author to this point, the reader will be then confronted by a more disturbing choice. His participation now requires that he accept a kind of violation of his privacy. With this same aggressive "you," the reader is made personally concerned with certain intimate gestures or precise sensations. There is certainly something irritating in this deliberate intrusion of the author, forcing trivial or sordid assertions upon you: the following abusive generalization, for instance: "You must have eaten with your fingers" (p. 4), immediately taken for granted and inserted in the logic of the narration, thanks to additional details and a change of tense: "And you were careful not to lick your lips when you stepped out into the light once more ..." (p. 4).

We are far from that comfortable distancing which allows the reader, even in the so-called realistic novel, to keep his hands clean. Here there is no refuge to be found in sentimentalism or in an aesthetic participation. Unless he discards the book, the reader finds himself involved in the narration to the point of being in fact the first and major character of *The Lime Twig*. This dynamic situation which forces the reader to have a share in the "writing" of the book is presented from the first page as a difficult but necessary postulate: it is *necessary* to be both *one* and *the other,* to accept that one must be on both sides of the windowpane. Playing that game necessitates refusing to settle in any easy identification, It requires the effort of willing to be anyone, and this demands a complete dispensability.

Only such a postulate may justify the sudden emergence of "I" in the following piece of advice: "I wouldn't advise Violet Lane—there is no telling about the beds in Violet Lane—but perhaps in Dreary Station you have already found a lodging good as mine, if you were once the gentleman or if you ever took the tea kettle from a lady's hand" (p. 5).

Sure of his reader, the narrator hides no longer behind generalizations that have become unacceptable. Hawkes obviously intends to cast the "character-reader" in the fictional universe of the book by situating the narration in the imaginary space of a transposed London.

This passage into fiction will be naturally followed by a new mutation, since the narrator, now replacing the "character reader," explicitly invites the latter to identify with him. We must understand the ambiguous quality of that "I" alternating with "you"; we are not able safely to fix the respective whereabouts of reader and narrator. We might say that the latter will be born gradually from an "ego" nourished on the reader's substance. In other words, the narrator cannot speak in his own name before his existence has been established by the reader himself. The recognition of an "ego" is explicitly confirmed in the reference to the mother and the childhood, introducing a chain of intimate memories: "It was from Mother that I learned my cooking" (p. 6).

We notice that this is the second use of "I" in the book. The first appearance of "I" was termed "ambiguous." Now we understand that the narrator prepares his existence as *a character of fiction,* and that his "ego" must find its roots in a childhood, in a past, according to the conventions of the psychological novel. It is thus significant that in the introductory sentence the word "Mother" precedes "I" and that "my" comes next as a confirmation of a dawning identity. The existence of the two characters, mother and son, in reference to one another, now endowed with a kind of global independence, appears in the use of a common possessive adjective: "Our pots, our crockery, our undervests, these we kept in cardboard boxes, and from room to empty room we carried them until the string wore out and her garters and medicines came through the holes" (p. 6).

Indeed, the reader now witnesses the settlement of a character in his fictional universe, and Hawkes deliberately multiplies the signs of this installation. While the two newborn characters literally move into their new lodgings with their Penates, the narrator arranges his existence according to the dimensions of the novel. The realistic side of the narrator, or, let us say the illusion of realism, is but the pretext for a characterization the mechanism of which is patent.

If we want to define Hawkes's procedure, we may say that his narration develops through a succession of stages, and that each time he invades a space, he takes full possession of it. Here the relations that have just been established between mother and son achieve a high degree of intimacy which is immediately exploited by the author: the two characters have just moved into their new flat, and the narrator's "Here's home, Mother" confirms it; now the nightly ritual can take place, the mother undressing behind a screen. She gives the signal herself: "You may manipulate the screen now, William" (p. 6).

What does this invitation to pull down the curtain reveal? First, it confirms the growing intimacy in the relations between the two characters. The reader has the feeling of being an intruder, a voyeur. Hawkes increases this disturbing sensation through an accumulation of pathetic details, too sordid to make any identification easy but certainly emotional enough to provoke sympathy. The last gestures of the ritual justify our interpretation: ". . . I would set up the screen first thing and behind it Mother would finish stripping to the last scrap of girded rag—the obscene bits of makeshift garb poor old women carry next to their skin . . ." (p. 6).

Moreover, as consequence of this increasing intimacy, we learn the narrator's Christian name, the first step towards a conventional characterization. Still, Hawkes does not intend to yield to the temptation of the "realistic novel." Just as he was refused any convenient identification, the reader is defrauded of the pleasure of emotion. The seventh page takes us, through streets with symbolic names, back to Dreary Station and the fictitious space of the novel where anything can happen according to the author's whims.

It is difficult to identify willingly with a rather negative model, the process being generally seen as a promotion. The character named William has appeared in a rather repulsive context created by intimate and personal notations which allow the reader to withdraw from the scene to the safety of an aseptic distance.

Once more Hawkes will question this convention and oblige the reader to stoop before the character. The first step of this humiliation is a return to the preceding situation, through a substitution of pronouns: "If *you* live long enough with your mother, *you* will learn to cook . . ." (p. 7, italics added). Thanks to this "you," the intimate ritual of the installation of the two characters is generalized, its gruesome components become *ours,* part of common experience: "Your flesh will know the feel of cabbage leaves, your bare hands will hold everything she eats. Out of the evening paper you will prepare each night your small and tidy wad of cartilage, raw fat, cold and dusty peels, and the mouthful—still warm—which she leaves on her plate" (p. 7).

The identification is completed when Hawkes, in a puzzling statement, envelops reader and character in a common past: "Mother wipes her lips with your handkerchief" (p. 7). It is no longer *your mother,* but Mother, William's or anybody's. How should we interpret this confusion of roles? If we examine Hencher's evolution from the first page, we may explain this new address to the reader as an invitation to take his bearings. Hawkes makes sure that the reader has not yielded to the usual temptation of fiction, and at the same time he allows the one who has followed him to measure how far he has been deliberately misled. This will be the last explicit invitation. From the seventh page on, the narrator, now certain that he has been understood, will use the first person, and a generalizing "you," much more conventional and less compromising.

Another consequence we might have expected: the allusion to the *mother,* and to particularly intimate relations between mother and son, is going to precipitate the reader toward another temptation, that of the "psychoanalytic" novel. Hawkes immediately confirms this possible dimension: ". . . I remember a little boy who wore black stockings, a shirt ripped off the shoulder, a French sailor's hat with a red pompom. The whipping marks were always fresh on his legs and one cheekbone was blue . . ." (p. 8). Apparently he intends to conform to the rites of post-Freudian characterization. The incursion into the past provides the reader with a loose system of signs more or less related to the theme of death, all of them necessary elements of the structure of the book. It would be vain, though, to attempt to interpret these signs at first reading; the textual dynamics alone will justify them. Once more Hawkes has opened a door and suggested a possible interpretation, but he has immediately closed it, leaving the reader in a state of utter frustration. In researching the past of Hencher, he gives the illusion of endowing him with more authenticity, but at the same time, he discourages any attempt to interpret the elements he gives.

This might be justified by a desire to keep the character out of grasp, necessitating a permanent questioning of its existence. Hawkes, while he displays the whole scale of his talents, refuses the reader any reassuring vision, any comprehensible situation. With a purism that is at times exasperating, he uses the best resources of his art to lead his reader astray. The only explicit "message" of the whole passage is its conclusion. After he has illustrated the strange relations between the child and his dog, the narrator says: "Love is a long scrutiny like that. I loved Mother in the same way" (p. 9). This amazing message of love will permit the introduction of two important characters: Michael and Margaret who will take the place of William's dead mother. The young couple will become objects and victims of his cumbersome love. Their relations will give birth to the plot. But let us return to William. In the first pages we have been the witnesses of a confusing characterization, more reminiscent of the technique of the French Nouveau Roman than of traditional fiction. Before we may come to a more conventional type of reading, before the book becomes what we might call a fiction, the narrator will undergo another modification. After having used the notion of love to introduce Michael and Margaret, Hawkes will fix the character of William through the same notion. Since Michael and Margaret Banks are the first fully named characters of the book, say, the first properly fictitious ones, they will be entitled to install Hencher in his new function. We have already seen that this "installation" is both proper and figurative:

> . . . there is a room waiting if you can find it, there is a joke somewhere if you can bring it to your lips. And my landlord, Mr. Banks, is not the sort to evict a man for saying a kind word to his wife or staying in the parlor past ten o'clock. His wife, Margaret, says I was a devoted man. (p. 9)

Banks being the lodger, it is Margaret who will have the privilege of casting the first judgment upon the narrator, thus determined by a psychological criterion: his devotion to his mother. Nothing is left to chance in Hawkes's writing, and in the next lines the narrator confirms Margaret's judgment: "Margaret's estimation of my character is correct" (p. 9). We notice immediately the ambiguity of the word "character," William of course refering to his personality, and Hawkes meaning a fictional character. In other words, William recognizes Margaret as a character of the book, and in accepting her judgment he situates himself at the same level. We may then understand why the narrator, resuming his modification, adds the following statement: "Heavy men are most often affectionate. And I, William Hencher, was a large man even then" (p. 10). This quite explicit apposition concludes the transformation of the "I" into a full-size character already given a Christian name and now ready to receive a sur-name. The next stage will be Hencher's participation in the narration as a functional character. He is helped in this by the interference of the "Captain" who appears for the first time in the book. The latter acknowledges the narrator's new quality by mentioning him by name in the course of the narration: "Don't worry about it, Hencher" (p. 10). We understand now why Hawkes renounces a pseudoautobiographic style, and uses for Hencher, now a character of fiction, the conventional third person.

We still have to draw conclusions from this genesis, the rigorous mechanism of which we have defined as faithfully as possible. It seems that Hawkes, quite deliberately, has not named the first character of his book before ascertaining the dynamic participation of the reader. The notions of *reader* and *character* are thus mingled, their existences are dependent, as if the second could not exist without the first. The reader's engagement is such that there might be no possible reading without accepting that the character is part of himself, practically flesh of his flesh.

CREATION OF A FICTIONAL CHARACTER: HENCHER'S EMANCIPATION

It is only from the second chapter on that Hencher, whose painful genesis we have followed, will become a character of fiction: the third person will now be consistently used and he will play an active part in the development of the plot. Still, this fictional "installation" is delayed by a long transition during which Hencher, freshly endowed with a name, will undergo another modification. It is the mechanism of this new mutation that we are going to study now.

The orientation of our analysis is supplied by Hawkes himself, the last sentence of the second chapter being an invitation to take one's bearings. Hencher, commenting on his own evolution, says, "I can get along without you, Mother." As we can easily conclude, the character himself claims his independence, cuts the navel string, and invites us to proceed with our reading.

Before being born into his fictional existence, Hencher, then, will have to free himself and to undergo some new mutation. The different stages of his emancipation will be rhythmed by the last moments of his mother. We remember that during a bombing the boxes in which she has gathered all her ridiculous belongings have caught fire. While she tries to save what we might call "the story of her life," her night-gown itself catches fire.

On hands and knees she was trying to crawl back to me, hot sparks from the fire kept settling on her arms and on the thin silk of her gown. One strap was burned through suddenly, fell away, and then a handful of tissue in the bosom caught and, secured by the edging of charred lace, puffed at its luminous peak as if a small forced fire, stoked inside her flesh, had burst a hole through the tender dry surface of my mother's breast. (p. 15)

In a quite significant manner the mother's death is seen first as a destruction of the maternal breast. We shall not interpret that dream that continues in the next lines with the vision of mother and son both wrapped in Hencher's robe: "Mother and son in a single robe." Such Freudian stylizations are obviously for the reader invitations to play the psychoanalyst, but it is to the invitation itself and not to the game that we shall pay attention now. Hawkes's intention is probably to suggest the importance of Freudian symbols, but in no case does he wish to gather around the character of Hencher the elements of a psychoanalytic diagnosis.

If we want to understand the precise function of the invitation, we only have to follow the author. He has placed there one of the numerous lime twigs of the book, but shows the reader how not to get glued, as he comes back to the lodger of the first pages: "A lodger is forever going back to the pictures in black frames, back to the lost slipper . . ." (p. 16). This generalization, including the intimate detail of the pink slipper caught in the stairway the day his mother died, reduces Hencher to an archetype. We understand, then, that it is not in the meaning of each scene that we are going to search the particularities of Hencher but rather in their combination and in the way Hawkes will use them. From these scenes pregnant with meaning will remain a network of referential signs with which the author will play. Before watching this new game, we have to learn its rules. To the last moments of the mother correspond several "signs." First, it is rhythmed by Hencher striking the water pipes in order to signal the Captain. In his mind, his mother's death will be thus associated with the noise of water rushing. He will also remember the smell of burning clothes. In addition, several more punctual signs such as the already mentioned pink slipper will complete his global perception of the event, a whole system of references being finally formed. Of his whole history the character will keep this network of signs, thanks to which he will be able to determine his place in the space of the book.

Before he is able to play this part, Hencher must free himself, leaving behind him the cumbersome chrysalis of his past. One might interpret the metamorphosis as a grotesque version of the well-known myth, Hencher being born again from his mother's ashes, like some adipose Phoenix, the somewhat disgraceful appearance of the character underlining the parodic side of the scene.

An instant before the drama Hencher can smell the smoke: ". . . a faint live smell of worn carpet or paper or tissue being singed" (p. 13). This smell, associated a moment later with the fire that will cause his mother's death, is qualified as faint and live, as if she were slowly consuming her last energies. At first unaware of how tragic the situation is, Hencher seems to impregnate himself with the smell, Hawkes clearly insisting on the mechanism of an inhalation: "I held to the arms of my chair and slowly breathed into my lungs that smoke" (p. 13). The character, perfectly still on his chair, celebrates the absorption as if it were part of a cere-mony. As realistic as it might appear, the scene will only interest us in so far as it will justify that celebration. Let us notice first the composite character of the smoke: Hencher recognizes his belongings in it ... perhaps his past. "... the sleeve of a coat of mine was crumbling and smoking out of a black pasty hole" (p. 14), but it is chiefly the history of his mother's past that disappears in the flames: "The smoke was mostly hers and thick ..." (p. 14).

Mother and son face each other with an ultimate shout, each calling the other by name before the explosion of a flask of ammoniac puts an end to this strange combustion. Later, when Hencher remembers his past, all these smells will loom up, associated with the vision of his burnt mother. "And even today I smell them: smell the skin, smell the damp sheets I wrapped her in, smell the room turned in-firmary. I smell that house" (p. 16).

It is as if, when dying, his mother was bequeathing to him, with this smoke and these smells, her own history. A prisoner of her past, Hencher is going to free himself: the very night of her death, we find him in the courtyard: "I had left Mother comfortable and tonight, this night, I was going to stand bareheaded in the laundry court and breathe" (p. 18).

Again we find the same static air of a celebration, Hencher now bareheaded as for some sacred rite. In breathing the outer air, he prepares himself to receive the signs of a new existence.

For the last time Hawkes seems to yield to the temptation of a "psychoanalytic" novel and as a confirmation takes us back to the vision of the child and his dog. But now the image is fugitive, like Hencher's last glance at his childhood before the important episode that will confirm his liberation.

Let us recall the scene: Hencher standing in the courtyard, sees his contempla-tion interrupted by the approach of a plane that comes down as slowly as a "child's kite." The comparison, taken from children's iconography, should be understood as an ultimate transition from the world Hencher is about to leave. Indeed, the following vision of the plane is quite different and refers to a new character.

> ... beneath the pilot's window I saw the figure of a naked woman painted against the bomber's pebbly surface. Her face was snow, something back of her thigh had sprung a leak and the thigh was sunk in oil. But her hair, her long white head of hair was shrieking in the wind as if the inboard engine was sucking the strands of it. Her name was Reggie's Rose and she was sitting on the back of a parachute. (p. 19)

The reader now witnesses a succession of gestures, reminding us of the ritual of some coronation, the function of which will appear gradually. The first stage of the ceremonial is an ascension to the pilot's cockpit: "I climbed up poor Rose, the airman's dream, and big as one of the cherubim ..." (p. 21).

Once more it is a trying experience for the reader who must find the logic of the indication. Only the first part of the sentence shows an immediate coherence. We understand that Reggie's Rose may symbolize the erotic and sentimental phantasms of the pilot. On the contrary, the comparison with the cherubim is very puzzling. The only possible explanation requires elaborate efforts. We have noticed the obsessional importance of the cherubim on top of Dreary Station. We remember Hencher and his mother's peregrinations, all taking place around these "gilded cherubin big as horses. . . ." We understand then that the dimensional relation is only a pretext. In fact, it is the notion of dream that works as a pivot in the sentence, and for Hencher this notion is based on the vision of horses. We know that the materialization of this dream will give birth to the plot, and we must notice how, card after card, almost without our knowledge, Hawkes provides us with the elements of a game that leads us to the logic of the novel.

As he climbs up into the cabin, Hencher carries with him all the unexpressed dreams and phantasms that have failed to make him leave the morbid world of his childhood. . . . It is probably the need for a change, the desire of some modification, which may justify his last reticence, before the celebration of the ritual: "I should have had a visored cap, leather coat, gauntlets" (p. 21). Obviously, Hencher wishes he might look like the pilot, but the briefly sketched silhouette might be that of a knight. In fact, we should interpret this reticence as nostalgia of heroism. "My breath came free. The inhalation was pure and deep and sweet. I smelled tobacco and a cheap wine, was breathing out of the pilot's lungs" (p. 22).

With his first breath, as we can see, corresponds a notion of freedom that foretells Hencher's emancipation. The first step toward this emancipation is expressed in the surprising passage from a simple preterit to a progressive form, without the *subject* being repeated. Still, the one who, breathing through the mask, recognizes the smell of tobacco and that of wine, is different from that other one who has impregnated his lungs with the pilot's living substance. The omission of the second "I" is thus a sign of Hencher's mutation. With this breath, which is a rebirth, he is going to assimilate the logic and the dreams of the airman and think in a more concise and energetic language, italicized in the text. "Cold up here. Cold up here. Give a kiss to Rose" (p. 22). The modification is going to develop in the direction of this new energy. As Hencher is about to seize the helmet, a martial music rises from the abandoned earphones: ". . . the sounds of some strange brass anthem." It is of course a heroic anthem serving as a prelude to the climactic moment of the coronation. Hencher has only to raise the helmet over his head, ". . . a heavy wet leather helmet large enough for him. . . ," to crown himself the first character of the book. This fresh dignity expresses his liberation so well that he immediately asserts his rights before his dying mother: ". . . I turned my head as far to the right as I was able, so that she might see how I—William Hencher—looked with my bloody coronet in place at last" (p. 23). This apposition, used for the second time, consecrates Hencher as a character of fiction.

What has happened between the first acknowledgment of Hencher's evolution and the second? The composite being resulting from a first genesis has progressively transformed himself by freeing himself from his history. In other words, Hencher, who appeared as a common production of Hawkes and the reader, breaks with them in order to claim his fictional existence. The deliberate invitation to identify with the character could be an obstacle to fiction. From now on, we begin to overcome this difficulty. Hencher, now knighted, will have a share in the dynamism of the narration; freshly endowed with a heroic dimension, he will free himself from the tergiversations of a Nouveau Roman—like writing in which conventionally nothing happens. With his "bloody coronet in place at last," he will be able to assume his tragic destiny.

HENCHER'S RITUAL

When he moves in at the Banks's, in the flat he had once inhabited with his mother, Hencher has only kept from his past that network of references we have already mentioned. For him events have lost their obsessive presence, and that "live smoke" which had accompanied his mutation has now become "the old dead odor of smoke." The character's new "installation" will not be that slow accession to an identity which we witnessed during Hencher's first genesis. It will rather be a progressive and dynamic occupation of a space according to a ritual that we shall easily understand.

Let us remember that the night of the "coronation" has been presented as a transitory moment, ". . . that night, that tonight," the second part of the fragment mingling past and present into a curious intermediate time. Let us keep in mind, too, that Hencher's mother died that night between three and four. The ritual of installation, let us call it that, will then take place at night between three and four, between the third and the fourth day. The first night, Hencher says, "I dared not spend the night in the lavatory, but smoked my cigars in bed."

The first ritual gesture is then a symbolical absorption of that "live smoke." the first sign of his self-recognition. Out of some sense of decency, and in order to conform to the rhythm of four days, he will not dare to penetrate into the toilets during the second night, to listen to water rushing through the pipes: "And then, there was the second night, and I ventured into the hallway" (p. 24).

We have to wait until the third night, after the four strokes of four, to watch in the toilets the ultimate gestures of a strange commemoration, like some grotesque mass celebrating Hencher's resurrection. We shall not try to decipher the code of the ritual. We have already seen that Hawkes uses psychoanalytic schemes as the elements of a game, and we have to accept the sexual symbols of the novel as a simple iconography, in order to enter its logic.

On the other hand, it seems more adequate to wonder why Hawkes invites us to play that game. Hencher's grotesque gestures, as he attempts to assume his existence, are very different from the strange and disturbing refinements of his first lucubrations. The extreme schematization of the character has more to do with some behaviorist type of writing.

For the reader it is necessary to understand the relation that exists between these two aspects of the same character: Hencher's ritual allows him to conciliate his past and his present. However grotesque and schematic this ritual might be, it should not be taken merely as an entertainment for intellectuals, but as a game whose rigorous rules concern us more directly than we might think. Neither should we be lured by the consistent use of humor. We remember that we had felt some kind of irritation when Hawkes had forced us to identify with his character at the most sordid level.

We have to go beyond this irritation and recognize in each of us the existence of a ritual, probably as grotesque as Hencher's. Hawkes will help us in this, by provoking a confrontation that will illustrate the mechanisms and the function of such rituals. Let us get back to Hencher, sitting in the bathroom after he has just celebrated the anniversary of his metamorphosis: ". . . thinking now of comfort, tranquillity, and thinking also of their two clasped hands—I wondered what I might do for them. The bells were slow in counting, the water dripped. And suddenly it was quite clear what I could do for them, for Michael and his wife" (p. 24).

For the reader only one thing is clear: Hencher is going to prepare breakfast for Michael and Margaret, who are still in bed. If we take it literally, the whole scene will be justified by the simple desire of creating intimacy between himself and his new lodgers. However, Hawkes once more mystifies us, transforming a simple attempt to communicate into some kind of black magic, as Hencher with the comforter hooded round his head, like some evil monk, celebrates his mass after having ritually purified his hands and head. In fact, it is rather a birth that we are going to witness, for the teapot placed on the tray is curiously compared to a new-born child, ". . . a tea-pot small as an infant's head. . ."

Or perhaps, it will be a resurrection, for Michael and Margaret look much like two recumbent figures:

> They lay beneath a single sheet and a single sand-colored blanket, and I saw that on his icy cheeks, Banks had grown a beard in the night and that Margaret— the eyelids defined the eyes, her lips were dry and brown and puffy—had been dreaming of a nice picnic in narrow St. George's Park behind the station. (p. 26)

Hencher's function will appear plainly: he will have to animate these almost lifeless bodies, and transmit to these still undefined characters the sacred breath that will give them their fictional existence. Conscious of this mission, he prepares himself: "Could I not blow smiles onto their nameless lips, could I not force apart those lips with kissing?" (p. 26), and his words to describe the awakening of the couple are those of a father receiving twins, a boy and a girl: "Then both at once they opened their eyes and Banks's were opalescent, quick, the eyes of a boy, and Margaret's eyes were brown" (p. 26).

Obviously, this is another *mise en abyme*. Hawkes leaves it to Hencher to give life to these figures of clay. By transmitting his own dreams, Hencher allows Michael and Margaret to spring into fiction. Why does Hawkes chose to parody the creation of characters, replacing it by the magic of a grotesque ritual?

The first temptation is to believe in the artificiality of any fictional universe: as he refuses Michael and Margaret the seriousness of an elaborate novelistic creation, these characters will be necessarily limited. They will be the protagonists and eventually the victims of a very artificial plot, which is nothing but the projection of Hencher's dreams.

The creation of a world of fiction, then, would be for the author himself a sort of game, a sort of ritual, that he chooses to present as such, in *The Lime Twig*, Hencher being his mediator. Still, if we come back to the genesis of this mediator, we remark that the transition between the first Hencher, who reminds us of the personages of the French Nouveau Roman; and the fictional Hencher, has been almost imperceptible. His mutation from one genre to another reminds us of Escher's engravings, showing that amazing transition from fish to birds, from one world to another. The transition between the water and the air is permitted by the use of common genetic elements, fish and birds being contained in equal geometrical figures. In *The Lime Twig* the common element is the reader, who is once more explicitly invited to identify with Hencher. Hawkes generalizes the character's rituals, and they become ours. Let us recall the scene: Hencher has managed to send Michael and Margaret away, in order to be able to sleep in their bed and celebrate in his own way their strange rebirth: "But red circles, giving your landlord's bed a try, keeping his flat to yourself for a day—a man must take possession of a place, if it is to be a home for the waiting out of dreams" (p. 27).

A private ceremony is transformed into a general law that we are supposed to accept as ours, Hawkes involving readers and characters in a common personal pronoun: "So we lead our lives, keep our privacy in Dreary Station, spend our days grabbing at the rubber roots, pausing at each other's doors" (p. 27).

This will be the last invitation, Michael and Margaret being then precipitated into the plot thanks to Hencher's offices. Before the story begins indeed, and before Hencher is able to experience his freedom, as he declares, "I can get along without you Mother" (p. 28), the reader must understand that the following adventures will concern him directly; Hencher's solitude and his desperate quest for communication and love, his grotesque and pathetic attempts, have familiar vibrations.

THE DEATH OF HENCHER

After the preceding study, devoted to the genesis and function of Hencher in *The Lime Twig,* I felt the necessity to indicate more precisely the method I used in my analysis and to justify its different aspects. It should have appeared more logical to follow the reverse order, mentioning first the method, and then the results. But, if we except the first page of the book, which requires a totally innocent reading, any extract is necessarily polarized by the narration, inserted in a whole and indissociable from it. We shall now study the passage that precedes Hencher's death. The knowledge we have acquired about the character permits the elimination of certain narrative or thematic points. We know, for instance, what smoking a cigar may mean for Hencher, and the fact that he meets death with his unlighted cigar in his mouth does not surprise us. The page being thus freed from its anastomosis, we shall be able to devote ourselves exclusively to the textual development and understand its mechanisms. In our study we shall examine as closely as possible the measurable elements of its progression, yet without using a purely linguistic approach: why do specific words or fragments follow others? Why are they generated by such a vision or such an image apparently isolated, with no foreshadowing? We shall try to understand the explicit transitions, and to discover the reasons why the author has chosen implicit ones, before the text appears in its limpidity. We shall not intuitively say that we pass from reality to dream, from strange to fantastic; we shall try to measure this passage.

We should be able, then, to attempt conclusions with Hawkes's writing and suggest a possible reading.

> But in the cab Hencher already braces the steering wheel against his belly; the driver's open door swings to the movement of the van. Cowles and the jockey and stableboy walk in slow procession behind the van, which is not too wide for the overgrown passage between the row of stalls, the long dark space between the low stable buildings, but which is high so that now and again the roof of the van brushes then scrapes against the rotted eaves. The tires are wet from the dampness of tangled and prickly weeds. Once, the van stops and Hencher climbs down, drags a bale of molded hay from its path. Then they move— horse van, walking men—and exhaust fumes fill empty bins, water troughs, empty stalls. In darkness they pass a shovel in an iron wheel-barrow, a saddle pad covered with inert black flies, a whip leaning against a whited post. Round a corner they come upon a red lantern burning beside an open and freshly white-washed box stall. The hay rack has been mended, clean hard silken straw covers the floor, a red horse blanket lies folded on a weathered cane chair near the lantern.
>
> Lovely will fetch him down for you, Hencher, says Cowles.
>
> I will fetch him down myself, if you please.
>
> And Lovely the stableboy grins and walks into the stall; the jockey pushes the horse blanket off the chair, sits down heavily; Cowles takes one end of the chain while Hencher works with the other.
>
> They pry up the ends of the chain, allow it to fall link upon ringing link into bright iron pools at their feet until the raised and padded ramp swings loose, opens wider and wider from the top of the van as Cowles and Hencher lower it slowly down. The gray men stand with hands on hips and look up into the interior of the van. It is dark in there, steam of the horse drifts out; it appears that between the impacted bright silver flesh of the horse and padded walls no space exists for a man. . . . (pp. 59–60)

The characters who participated in the theft of the horse are reunited on the front seat of a black van. Between the quay and the stable, extremities of the journey, two incidents occurred; the original group was composed of five men: Hencher, who drives the van, Cowles, Lovely, the stable boy, and the jockey, the latter transported in the barge with the horse, and finally Michael. First incident on the way: Michael, too scared to be involved in the plot, has been allowed by Hencher to return home. Second interruption: the van stops before Larry, who pulls the strings of the plot. Larry reproaches Hencher for having yielded to Michael's request, thus altering the straightness of the designed journey. During this scene it appears plainly for the first time in the novel that Hencher is just a puppet in Larry's hands and that his dynamic participation in the plot has come to an end.

It was necessary to recall these events in order to introduce the following scene devoted to Hencher's death.

The word "but" provides the transition between Larry's departure and the return to Hencher. The reader's interest, first of all, is displaced; the projector has swung about, focusing on a new sequence in a different setting. From an open framework we are taken into a restricted one, the cab of the van.

The suddenness of the transition coupled with the limitation of the scene allows our interest to be concentrated on a single character. Moreover, in keeping with this spatial reduction, we find Hencher psychologically reduced, as he has just been involved in a humiliating situation. While that "but" implies the reasons why Hencher may feel diminished, it introduces at the same time the need for a counter-part. The character must counterbalance that negative emotion by something positive and even try to obliterate the memory of his recent mortification.

We must note we are not interested here in a psychological study of humiliation or mortification. What is important is their negative value insofar as it determines the logic of the textual development. One should not try to determine the profound motivations of "paper characters." Let us rather return to the necessity of a counterbalance, and let us try to understand Hencher's gestures when he finds himself alone in the cab. ". . . Hencher already braces the steering wheel against his belly." The need for compensation appears immediately as a necessary mechanism, thanks to the function of "already." Not only do we witness a total reduction of time to the instant, which would only mean a simple equilibrium between past and future, with the present as a fulcrum, but Hencher's gesture potentially overlaps the present. That "already" hastily obliterates the past and anticipates future events, as if the freshly reestablished balance was immediately upset in favor of Hencher. This haste to reestablish his importance appears in a quasivisceral invasion of space, which confirms the reflex of compensation we have already mentioned. Hencher wishes to control things again, and we must understand that his eagerness to brace the steering wheel literally compensates for the loss of his power in the fiction itself. Besides, Hawkes has multiplied the situations which illustrate Hencher's fascination with instrument boards, handles, knobs, dials; this fascination reveals his need to sublimate his own inertia by holding the strings that make other characters act.

In keeping with this inertia verging on impotence, we must point out the importance of the character's physical aspect: Hencher is corpulent, vaguely repulsive, and his gestures are always grotesque or excessive. His silhouette lends itself to expressionistic compositions which stylize the subtleties of a situation with more efficiency than any psychological commentary.

Let us return to that visceral and pathetic gesture through which Hencher attempts to find his identity again, by seeking with his very flesh the comforting and unquestionable contact of the steering wheel. We know that his endeavor will be the last one, as Hawkes, still hesitating between the grotesque and pathos, has placed Hencher on the front seat of his own hearse.

The next sequence suggests to the reader the vision of a burial procession; the three accomplices mentioned one by one, slowly follow the van in order of importance. The solemnity of their progression is marked by the repetition of "and" linking names and providing equal intervals between the three men. We may also explain the reasons for the qualitative aspects of the progression: starting with a named character, "Cowles," we proceed with the stock figure of the jockey, important enough to be preceded by a definite article "the" but too functional to be named, and we finish with the stableboy, whose more secondary function is expressed by the ellipsis of this article. We may interpret this progression from the particular to the general which is paradoxically expressed in a decrescent order, as the beginning of an arithmetical progression that may be prolonged to infinity.

Leaving the cab of the van, the reader abandons Hencher's logic and rejoins the course of the narration. The restricted space of the cab in now replaced by a more global vision of the scene. Once more we shall pay attention to the progression from one sequence to the other. One of the keys to Hawkes's reading is certainly to be found in the rigor of the transitions which guide us from reality to fantasy through the apparent incoherence of his fictitious universe: here the passage has been possible thanks to the cab door, left ajar, the double function of which we shall examine now.

First it appears as a kind of crack in the microcosm of the cab, where Hencher has sought refuge. The precarious character of Hencher's recovery is immediately underlined in the reader's mind by the global vision of the scene, which we have just studied.

Second, this door that beats against the side of the van will give to the description of the procession a binary rhythm, a swinging movement perceptible from the inside of the cab and from the outside as well. The reader will be thus allowed to watch the scene from two different points of view.

Let us accept the invitation to leave Hencher alone and return to the vision of the procession. The funeral cortege is described in an interminable sentence in which Hawkes has multiplied devices of *enlisement*,[2] two clauses apparently contradictory since they are linked by "but," the second incidentally provoking a new consequent clause; the author obviously suggests the possibility of other additions and arbitrarily closes the series.

This "eternization" is still increased by the "now and again" and the "then" of the last clause compounding the binary rhythm and its vacillating character. But the *enlisement* does not concern time only. By pressing the limits of space against the sides of the van, Hawkes determines a system of parallel lines which tend to prolong the way to infinity: long rows of stalls determine a dark corridor riveted to the dimensions of the van. The description is primarily functional: the vegetation that grows among the abandoned stalls measures the width of the van, while the eaves give the vertical limits of the corridor. It seems that the van literally cuts a channel through the night, or rather that it is wedged between four rails without any possible escape. The reader's ambiguous position is maintained by the proportions between elements in the description. Noises of brushing and scraping that belong to the register of contacts as well as that of sounds, create the perception of the van's dimensions. The three men as well as Hencher may be participating. The reader is still allowed to choose his position. He may decide to place himself within or without, or both. On the other hand, the next vision is definitely that of someone watching from outside. Hencher cannot see the tires of the vehicle he is driving. Only the walking men can see the wet tires and feel the prickly weeds. In order to compensate for this exclusively exterior vision, Hawkes decides to place a bale of hay in the way, thus interrupting the descriptive progression. Nothing is purely gratuitous. The bale of hay is primarily functional; so is the interruption. It will permit the last enumeration of the different elements of the cortege. The progression stops for an ultimate focusing, then resumes its ineluctable course.

Interruption ("Once"): During Hencher's momentary dissociation from the van, his dual role as both master and victim of its progression is stressed.

Van plus Hencher: Resumption of the movement ("Then"): The different elements of the cortege are gathered into a collective "they" immediately specified by an apposition: the van has become the HORSE VAN; it reminds us of the presence of the horse and implicitly joins horse plus van plus Hencher in a visualizable trilogy.

The global vision of the procession is also synthesized by the expression "walking men."

What precisely is the function of this apposition, since it only repeats, in a slightly different way, the preceding vision?

We have already viewed the constituents of the funeral procession. Let us recall its different elements: a very fleshy Hencher at the steering wheel; his three accomplices, named individually, follow the van; through an accumulation of realistic or expressionistic details, Hawkes has inserted the scene into the logic of the story.

But after Hencher's last appearance the cortege will be merely silhouetted. We have left a pseudorealistic description for another level of understanding. We might say that because of a process of abstraction the vision has become allegorical.

The author will immediately seize the opportunity and place the characters and the reader in a modified setting in which all realistic elements will gradually vanish. The transformation comes from the van itself. The exhaust gas invades all the hollows, transforming the already rotting and half-abandoned scene into a truly fantastic setting. Thanks to this emanation the progression of the van becomes almost immaterial, without any brushing or scraping; reality dissolves in a space where everything becomes possible.

Curiously, details will reappear, but in a strikingly stylized manner; a shovel in a wheelbarrow, black flies on a pad, a whip leaning against a white post. All these elements are described with the precision of etchings. Linear or punctual, they are silhouetted against the background, like the wheelbarrow and the shovel, or contrasted: black dots on a white background, black line of the whip against the whiteness of the post. They belong to the logic created by the new dimension of the cortege, and because of the evil emanations of the van that pervade the whole setting, this dimension may be easily qualified: the wheelbarrow and the shovel unmistakably remind us of the gravedigger's tools, the black flies wait for a corpse. (They will have lost their inertia when Michael, following word after word the same trip, will face Hencher's dead body, on p. 66.) These elements are therefore purely functional. They have been distributed along the path of the van to show its ultimate way. Their succession announces the end of the ride, the last stop in front of the stall prepared to receive Rock Castle, the stolen horse.

Before resuming the course of the narration, let us examine once more the transition. The first indication of a change appears in the enumeration of the three elements we have just mentioned. We have seen what they had in common; let us examine now what makes them different.

1	2		1	2		1	2
Shovel—Wheelbarrow			Pad—Black flies			Whip—White post	
Death	Horse		Death		Horse		
A	B		A		B		

This diagram illustrates the pairing of the elements and their grouping in two different series. Let us call the first DEATH, the second HORSE. We can see that the first pair belong to the logic of the preceding scene, which we may call the scene of the burial cortege. The third pair belongs to the next scene, devoted to the passage of the horse from the van to the stall. The central group shows an inversion of the two series, that permits a kind of hooking:

We understand plainly that the horse will be in a moment the instrument of Hencher's death. The author has only to "dress" this diagram to allow a smooth passage from one scene to the other; the straightness of the way is clearly altered by a curve, and the whitewashed post that was already announcing it . . . . The atmosphere of the preceding scene is still prolonged by the words "open and freshly," which might be followed by "dug" confounding "grave" and "stall" in the reader's subconsciousness.

With that red light, a new logic is created: Hawkes clearly means to immerse the scene of Hencher's death in a tragic chiaroscuro. Before the different members of the cortege can inhabit this new space, its dimensions must be delineated. The schematization in black and white of the preceding sequence is replaced by an enumeration of clearly defined elements. Once more no gratuitous details—only what we need to know to understand that everything has been carefully planned by the gangsters, and that the stall is ready to receive the horse. As before the celebration of a ritual, the instruments are waiting: the blanket is folded, the straw is still stiff. The red light softens the surfaces and reduces the contrasts. In the general dimness only geometrical lines appear clearly, such as the hay rack and cane chair.

The repetition of the word "lantern" closes the description, Hawkes explicitly showing that the setting is in place, ready to receive the actors. Still, before the setting may serve according to its function, before the horse can fill the empty space of the stall, we have to witness the last stage of Hencher's passion. But let the author guide us step by step . . .

Let us return to the series of objects that compose the setting. We remark that one of them, the last one, a chair, does not belong to the coherence of the others. In a moment one of the personages is going to remove the blanket intended for the horse, and sit on that chair, "heavily," the author says. This means that the jockey is going to act as a spectator, the action taking place out of the limits of the setting. The theatrical conventions are inverted: the audience, Lovely and the jockey, will sit on the lighted stage where nothing can happen yet, and the two actors, Cowles and especially Hencher, will perform in a half-darkness.

To stress this inversion and confirm the necessity for Hencher to be both actor and victim, a brief dialogue casts the different parts, so that the curtain can be raised.

A new angle is determined out of the red light, facing the back of the van. Let us recall the respective positions: the reader, like the two spectators, is going to watch the scene from behind, the intensity of the lighting decreasing from stall to van.

As the chain rings link after link, the curtain opens. Confirming the inversion we have already mentioned, the stage appears from top to bottom, Hencher and Cowles respecting the conventional solemnity and conscious of celebrating an important ritual. We shall not insist on Hawkes's skill as he plays with gleaming surfaces and sounds in this nightly scene. Let us rather watch the textual organization. The space is now sliced into three distinct zones clearly indicated by an apposition, inviting the reader to take his bearings. The scene is now constructed on two grounds which imply a third one, that of the spectator still sitting in the stall. The silhouettes of Hencher and Cowles determine a middleground, and it is of course purposely that Hawkes has drawn them hands on hips, as to orientate them toward the black rectangle that provides a new frame for the action. The intermediary situation of the two characters is underlined by that gray color halfway between the lighted zone and the darkness of the van.

How should we interpret this new sequence? Once more we have only to follow the author's indications as literally as possible. The actors of the preceding scene, Hencher and Cowles, have become spectators. Their parts consisted in revealing the most important personage of the book, that malevolent horse, the production of Hencher's fantasies.

Now the inversion can be fully comprehended: the fantastic horse, literally produced by darkness, will reach the place prepared for it, and in that tragic red light it will assure the dynamism of the book. On the contrary, the grayness of Hencher's silhouette is already a step toward his annihilation.

Maurice Couturier

9. NABOKOV'S PERFORMATIVE WRITING

There is always a moment of hesitation when one starts to write a short study like this: from the very first word one feels committed to a certain approach which seems to exclude all the others. I realize, for instance, that the outline I have adopted introduces a dangerous and somewhat erroneous division of the subject I am going to write about, since it claims to examine successively various aspects of Nabokov's *récit*[1] which cannot properly be isolated, under penalty of disfiguring the very object under examination: Nabokov's novels. But is it not constantly the critic's lot to introduce the principle of segmentation and division in his studies, in an attempt to force the literary object to surrender an additional modicum of meaning? We may as well accept it, provided we always keep in mind that the new object thereby evolved is no mere reflection of the first one, but a new text in its own right.

This process which consists in inserting an ever-widening gap between the first object and the successive ones which are based upon it, may well be the founding principle of Nabokov's writing. The first object in the writing of a novel often was, in the past, a historical event, a reminiscence, or a personal experience; when he wrote *The Turn of the Screw,* for instance, James had constantly in mind the narrative he had heard from the archbishop one Christmas night, and which he had summed up in his *Notebooks.* If we trace the genesis of the *récit* as we have it now, we realize that it went through a number of narrations: the story was told to the archbishop, the archbishop told it to James and his friends, James recorded it in his *Notebooks,* and he wrote the novel. But even in the novel he managed to introduce a triple narrative, his own, that of his friend who read the manuscript, and the manuscript itself. Even though we cannot discover, either from the novel or the *notebooks,* what actually happened in that English country house (if anything did happen!), we are constantly led to exert our power of perception and psychological insight, and to try to discover the real core of the story, because we feel that behind these successive narratives there hides a dreadful event. There is no better proof of what we are saying than the great number of often psychologically perceptive articles written about this novelette. Even though, as James claimed, this is "a fairy tale, mere and simple," we feel encouraged by the text to give more value to the reported events than to the telling of the story.

This is perhaps the most significant difference between representational writing, as exemplified by James, and the new "performative" writing exemplified in American literature by Nabokov. With James's writing, the reader is invited to riffle the text for the meaning the author seems to have deposited there; which does not mean, of course, that the text cannot yield a multiplicity of unintended meanings if examined under new angles with the assistance of new methods (e.g., linguistics or psychoanalysis), but that is quite a different matter. As Ricardou put it, when talking about the New versus the traditional novelists, it is the author's conception of his writing which is really involved here:

> Each period can be characterized by the importance it gives to the language in its overall conception of the text. With rhetoric, there is the blessing of harmony between the established meaning (the something to express) and the language. The latter, when skillfully handled according to time-honored rules, is capable not only of expressing something, but of expressing it gracefully. With the Expression-Representation there is the curse of a discrepancy between the established meaning and the language. . . . The classical age works *with* the language; the romantic age *in spite of* the language. With the production, the relation between the meaning and the language is reversed: the meaning no longer is a pre-established institution which must be revealed, it is the, now problematical, effect of the arrangement of a calculated language.[2]

The traditional novel pretended that reality was the model of its own construction and consequently worked "in spite of" the language, which was considered as a mere tool. In James's case the tool is so perfect that it constantly threatens to impose its own categories on the story it tells; nevertheless it does not take precedence over the story—which makes James both the last of the great traditional novelists and the herald of the new trend.

In the last part of Ricardou's text, a new type of writing is introduced, a writing which is not fettered by a preexisting reality or meaning to be represented or expressed but which creates its own realities and its own meanings. It is not dependent upon anything that came before, but is free at any moment to produce something new: it is what Benveniste (and Austin before him) calls a performative writing:

> A statement is performative when it *designates* the performed act, that is when Ego utters a formula containing the verb in the first person of the indicative present: "I *hereby declare* the session closed."—"I *swear* to tell the truth." Therefore a performative statement must designate both the speech performance and the speaker.[3]

He also wrote earlier that "a performative statement is genuine only if it is authenticated as an act."[4] Can the text of a novel be authenticated as an act? Not in the traditional novel which claims to report and represent, but it can in the New

Novel and in Nabokov's works where the writing designates no other reality than the novel itself. That is what was cleverly summarized by Ricardou when he said that a New Novel "is not the writing of an adventure but the adventure of a writing."[5]

I have no intention of comparing Nabokov's novels with those of Robbe-Grillet, Butor, Simon, and others (though it would make an interesting subject in itself), but rather of analyzing the performative nature of Nabokov's writing, which happens to have a lot in common with that of the French New Novelists (whom he cleverly parodied in some of his novels). We shall base this study on three of his latest novels, *Pale Fire* (1962), *Ada* (1969), and *Transparent Things* (1972). The *récit* evolved by the writing will be examined under the two aspects defined by Todorov, the *récit* as a story and the *récit* as a discourse. These two categories have been adopted in preference to those defined by Genette in *Figures 3*[6] because they are subordinated to the concept of *récit* and are admitted as having no objective existence of their own. In Nabokov's novels we never hear two voices, that of the story (or history) and that of the narrator, but only that of the *récit* which creates both the story and its narrator.

THE "RÉCIT" AS A STORY

The Elusive Referents. In his latest novels, pervaded with an ever-thickening atmosphere of unreality, Nabokov refuses to draw a line between dream and reality: "What are dreams?" Van asks in *Ada*. "A random sequence of scene, trivial or tragic, viatic or static, fantastic or familiar, featuring more or less plausible events patched up with grotesque details, and recasting dead people in new settings."[7] Or, as the narrator puts it in *Transparent Things:* "All dreams are anagrams of diurnal reality."[8] Nabokov has often described the process of waking up from a dream, of passing through successive layers or levels of reality, as in *Ada* for instance:

> For a few moments the brief dim dream was so closely fused with the real event that even when he recalled Bout's putting his finger on the rhomboid peninsula where the Allies had just landed (as proclaimed by the Ladore newspaper spread-eagled on the library table), he still clearly saw Blanche wiping Crimea clean with one of Ada's lost handkerchiefs. He swarmed up the cochlea to the nursery water-closet.... He also gave a minute's thought to the sad fact that (as he well knew from his studies) the confusion of two realities, one in single, the other in double, quotes, was a symptom of impending insanity. (p. 231)

Both the dreamer and the insane have a distorted vision of reality which deprives them of the power to apply the reality test. But then, Nabokov asks in *Transparent Things,* is it not the fate of all men?

> Men have learned to live with a black burden, a huge aching hump: the supposition that "reality" may be only a "dream." How much more dreadful it would be if the very awareness of your being aware of reality's dreamlike nature

were also a dream, a built-in hallucination! One should bear in mind, however, that there is no mirage without a vanishing point, just as there is no lake without a closed circle of reliable land. (p. 93)

We have here a perfect representation of the process mentioned in our introduction: each new *récit* takes us a step further from the "vanishing point" and makes it impossible to retrieve the actual object or even its psychological reality (Jakobson's referent); each new *récit* inserts a succession of receding images/mirages (there is only an *r* between them).

Only on very rare occasions are we faced with hard facts; even then we may be incapable of understanding their true nature. In *Transparent Things* there are two tragic dreams which, though they represent scenes which are verifiably untrue, contain a second layer of truth. Person, in his attempt to explain how he came to strangle his wife in his sleep, says that he was having one of his bad dreams: the house was on fire and he was trying to prevent a girl, Julia, from jumping out of the window. The dream, though hardly connected with reality, caused the actual death of Armande (in the novel). Person's own death happens in similar circumstances while he is dreaming he is proposing to Armande on the plane:

> Here comes the air hostess bringing bright drinks, and she is Armande who has just accepted his offer of marriage though he warned her that she overestimated a lot of things, the pleasure of parties in New York, the importance of his job, a future inheritance, his uncle's stationery business, the mountains of Vermont— and now the airplane explodes with a roar and a retching cough.
> Coughing, our Person sat up in asphyxiating darkness and groped for the light, but the click of the lamp was as ineffective as the attempt to move a paralyzed limb. (p. 103)

The hotel is "actually" on fire and he is about to die (in the novel). What, or where, is the referent? Presumably the sound of the explosion and reminiscences; but then we have never been told how or where he proposed to marry Armande, and we are led to believe it took place in Switzerland, under different circumstances. Then again, the fire reminds us of the scene where Armande forced him to rehearse an escape from the fire in the very same hotel, years before. When and where is Person going to wake up or to die? We do not know and hardly care to know; what matters is that the novel is coming to an end. In such a context, of course, the problem of the referent is quite irrelevant.

By one of those typically Nabokovian coincidences, the "hero" of the novel is a professional proofreader who not only corrects Mr. R.'s manuscripts but also tries to read through the text for the proofs that will reveal the realistic dimension of the novels: "... in what circumstances, the writer had begun to debauch Julia: had it been in her childhood—tickling her in her bath, kissing her wet shoulders, then one day carrying her wrapped in a big towel to his lair, as delectably described in the novel?" (p. 76). Mr. R., whose latest novel Person is proofreading, does not care, any more than Nabokov does, for such collating of clues; he is far more interested in the quirks of the fate he embodies, and which enrapture him so much. He likes to fool reality and the too gullible reader: with him art is artful, art is craft. Most of Nabokov's favorite (but fictitious) painters, for instance, are addicted to the *trompe l'oeil* and collage techniques; they will stick an actual piece of gold on the canvas instead of painting one. In *Ada* the film Vitry made from Van's *Letters on Terra* has a special attraction because of "a little scene that canny Vitry had not cut out: in a flashback to a revolution in former France, an unfortunate extra, who played one of the under-executioners, got accidentally decapitated while pulling the comedian Steller, who played a reluctant king, into a guillotinable position" (p. 581). The scene—which, to all appearances, is faked by the actors in the film—is the real thing: art also uses the quirks of the, for the artist, uncontrollable fate to achieve its ends through successive levels of deception.

Art is not always of the artist's own making but can also be achieved by nature which, for instance, modeled Lucette's beautiful body:

> In the guest bedroom, Lucette stood with her back to him, in the process of slipping on her pale green nightdress over her head. Her narrow haunches were bare, and our wretched rake could not help being moved by the ideal symmetry of the exquisite twin dimples that only very perfect young bodies have above the buttocks in the sacral belt of beauty. Oh, they were even more perfect than Ada's! (*Ada,* pp. 414–15)

Of course, this work of art would have passed unnoticed without Van's intervention, both as an observer and a writer. It is clear, however, that Van was an artist in life before he began to compose his first and only work of art, *Ada:* he could increase the amount of erotic pleasure by simultaneously caressing two girls (p. 414), or by picturing Ada while making love to a whore (p. 357).

For him, and for Nabokov, there is actually a constant interplay of art and life: Dan, Van's uncle, dies a Boschean death after collecting "the paintings, and faked paintings, associated with the name of Hieronymus Bosch" (*Ada,* p. 433). Van, while being fondled by Ada, suddenly views the whole scene in a pictorial perspective:

> Through it [Ada's hair] the student of art could see the summit of the *trompe l'oeil* school, monumental, multicolored, jutting out of a dark background, molded in profile by a concentration of caravagesque light. She fondled him; she entwined him: thus a tendril climber coils round a column, swathing it tighter and tighter, biting into its neck ever sweeter, then dissolving strength in deep crimson softness. There was a crescent eaten out of a vine leaf by a sphingid larva. . . . Whose brush was it now? A titillant Titian? . . .
>
> A moment later the Dutch took over: Girl stepping under the little cascade to wash her tresses . . . (p. 141)

Here there is an additional problem that will be examined later: is it Van the protagonist or Van the narrator who thought up this pictorial correlative? This does not alter the fact that, for certain people like him and Ada, life holds in store a treasure of quite exceptionally artistic occurrences and scenes, as if nature were ever ready to imitate art.

Earlier we have seen dream and reality dangerously flirting with each other; now it is art flirting with reality. It is of course the novelist who plays the trick (we shall see how in the second part) because it is *within* the novel that all these deceptive concepts of reality/dream/memory/art meet or rather combine to make the novel, according to the process illustrated in the following passage from *Transparent Things*. Person is trying to relive the past, years after his wife's death:

> Person, *this* person, was on the imagined brink of imagined bliss when Armande's footfalls approached—striking out both "imagined" in the proof's margin (never too wide for corrections and queries!). This is when the orgasm of art courses through the whole spine with incomparably more force than sexual ecstasy or metaphysical panic. (p. 102)

Reality, dream, memory, dissolve into art which, in its turn, becomes the only worthwhile reality: the novel has created a new reality by negating the old one; the referent has become a counter-referent, as it were, and only to that extent can we say that the novel has realistic grounds. However, the new reality so much transcends the old one that it appears to be utterly divorced from it, as a result of that "orgasm of art."

Time and Space. Despite the author's suggestions that the only reality that matters is the one invented by the novel, we may be tempted to apply what we called earlier the reality test, by assessing the actions of the novel according to the only reliable coordinates we claim to have: time and space. This is not an easy test to apply, since both the characters and the narrators constantly ridicule these two halfwits as if they had never existed.

One will remember that in many of Nabokov's novels the locus the characters are supposed to live in is completely made up or simply ignored; the obvious cases are *Invitation to a Beheading* (does it take place in Russia or in France?), *Bend Sinister* (where is Padugrad, in Germany or in Russia?), *Pale Fire* (what is that mythic Zembla, earlier mentioned by Pope?). Nabokov went a step further in *Ada:* he invented a new planet, Antiterra, with a completely fictitious geography which bears some very remote resemblances to our own: most countries have been given new names; France is now part of England; Crimea has taken the place of Vietnam ...[9] The distances are shorter or longer at Van's will, for he is an inveterate traveler and feels at home wherever he goes. The borders have apparently disappeared and passports are never requested. Even the physical laws are different: on Antiterra electricity has long been banished and people communicate over the dorophone, which uses the water pipe system.

Space has no objective reality in Nabokov's novels because it is never an obstacle: it becomes a psychological entity which everybody can play with. In *Pale Fire* the space represented by the novel can either be considered as a chessboard or a mythic universe. As Mary McCarthy and Janet K. Gezari have convincingly proved, this novel, which originated in an unfinished story called "Solus Rex," is like a protracted game of chess in which everything is fictitious, if gauged by our so-called realistic standards, but real or true if viewed as a creative game.[10] But perhaps too much emphasis has been put by these two critics on the allegorical dimension of the novel; Nabokov has always ridiculed the psychologists, artists, and critics who blindly exploit the idea of symbols and myths (his constant parody of Freud can probably be understood in this perspective) because they seem to believe in the objective existence of the reality which symbols and myths represent subjectively. A game of chess is nothing more than a game of chess; nothing happens outside of the chessboard. Therefore, we would certainly misread Nabokov if we were to consider his countless references to chess as so many clues to explain the central plot; I would personally rather consider them as one of the many devices used by Nabokov to immerse the reader in the referentless world of his novels, and the chessboard as a miniaturization not of our own world but of the word-evolved space of each novel.

Among the other devices used by either the characters or the narrators to fool space or negate its objective existence, we can mention shadowgames and mirrors. The first time Ada is alone with Van, she suggests they play a shadowgame:

> The shadows of leaves on the sand were variously interrupted by roundlets of live light. The player chose his roundlet—the best, the brightest he could find —and firmly outlined it with the point of his stick; whereupon the yellow round light would appear to grow convex like the brimming surface of some golden dye. Then the player delicately scooped out the earth with his stick or fingers within the roundlet. The level of that gleaming *infusion de tilleul* would magically sink in its goblet of earth and finally dwindle to one precious drop. That player won who made the most goblets in, say, twenty minutes. (*Ada*, pp. 51–52)

At this early stage of their relationship, Van fails to understand the purpose of the game; to him the shadows are intangible and therefore unreal, because he has always considered them as the shadows of something else (which is real), whereas Ada accepts them as real, regardless of what projected them.

Mirrors, likewise, are never a mere ornament or a clever technical device allowing us to see things, or ourselves, in a new perspective; they are treasure boxes containing unusual objects, a whole new world. Witness the king, in *Pale Fire*, drinking in a lake, Narcissus-like:

> In its limpid tintarron he saw his scarlet reflection but, oddly enough, owing to what seemed to be at first blush an optical illusion, this reflection was not at his feet but much further; moreover, it was accompanied by the ripple-warped reflection of a ledge that jutted high above his present position. And finally, the strain on the magic of the image caused it to snap as his red-sweatered, red-capped doubleganger turned and vanished, whereas he, the observer, remained immobile. He now advanced to the very lip of the water and was met there by a genuine reflection, much larger and clearer than the one that had deceived him.[11]

This is quite an exceptional situation; the king is fleeing from his palace which had recently become his prison, and when his supporters hear of his escape they dress up in the "carnivalesque" way the king is dressed and roam the country to divert the attention of the police. Here the king, who does not know anything of the plot, accidentally meets one of his impersonators, or rather his image. At first he thinks he is looking at his own image in the water but suddenly realizes how deceptive a mirror can be: one can enjoy the mirror image of the impersonator without ever meeting the impersonator himself. Here again the problem of the referent is irrelevant, since the image is just as real as the impersonator, or, for that matter, the king himself. This may be the reason why the only portrait of Person, in *Transparent Things,* is made from his mirror image in the elevator: ". . . the no less rapt mirror in the lift reflected, for a few lucid instants, the gentleman from Massachusetts, who had a long, lean, doleful face with a slightly undershot jaw . . ." (p. 4). The portrait of this strangely named character is as true as any one the narrator could have drawn: it does not depict a man made of flesh and blood but shows that Person is merely a figment of the author's writing.

All attempt to assess the spatial dimension of things and people in Nabokov's novels having proved unsuccessful, it will come as no surprise that the attempt to assess the temporal dimension meets with a similar failure since, as Van puts it in *Ada,* "we measure Time (a second hand trots, or a minute hand jerks, from one painted mark to another) in terms of Space (without knowing the nature of either)" (p. 542). The problem of time in the novel has recently been tackled by Genette in *Figures 3* in a way that may not be entirely relevant to the study of Nabokov's writing on the diegetic or referential time. Whenever a novel claims to be realistic (either historically or psychologically), the concept of diegetic versus "discursive" time[12] may be useful, but such is not the case in Nabokov's novels, where no trace can be found of a pre-story (or pre-text) being relayed by the novelist. Nabokov's writing imposes its own rhythm and therefore its own time, for, as Van writes in his notes for *The Texture of Time,* "maybe the only thing that hints at a sense of Time is rhythm; not the recurrent beats of the rhythm but the gap between two such beats, the gray gap between black beats: the Tender Interval. . . . The ample rhythm causes Time to dissolve, the rapid one crowds it out" (*Ada,* p. 538). Genette's categories tend to indicate that there is such a thing as an objective time after which the time of the novel can be measured. Proust (whose *Remembrance of Things Past* served, however, as a basis for Genette's study) has convincingly proved that it was not so, and Van echoes him in his notes on time where he speaks above all about the past:

> The Past, then, is a constant accumulation of images. It can be easily contemplated and listened to, tested and tasted at random, so that it ceases to mean the orderly alternation of linked events that it does in the large theoretical sense. . . . Such images tell us nothing about the texture of time into which they are woven except, perhaps, in one matter which happens to be hard to settle. Does the coloration of a recollected object (or anything else about its visual effect) differ from date to date? (*Ada,* p. 545)

Indeed, the texture of time is impalpable, but since the most palpable trace of passing time lies in the accumulated images, Nabokov's novels, which are crammed with thousands of unforgettable images (some of which will be examined later), can be said to create a new past for their readers and therefore to produce a span of time incommensurate with the few hours it takes to read any one of them. Once we have read *Lolita, Pale Fire,* or *Ada,* we have digested, as it were, a past which we have not actually lived and could not possibly have lived: with the author's help, we have fooled time!

The two greatest passions experienced by the characters in these novels happen to be the two major time-consuming and past-generating passions in man, art and love. In *Transparent Things* we follow the workings of art "manufacturing time." It all begins with a pencil accidentally found in a drawer, one of those commonplace objects one rarely notices but which the narrator views as one of those "transparent things" colored by the patina of time. We are told its ludicrous story from the beginning: "We recognize its presence in the log as we recognized the log in the tree and the tree in the forest and the forest in the world that Jack built" (p. 8). Are we not back where we started, since the ridiculous pencil belongs to "the world that Jack built"? Not quite, because the story of the pencil is going to stick in our mind and therefore be added to the gallery of images that constitute our past.

The same thing is true of love as celebrated in *Ada,* for instance; Van wonders:

> What, then, was it that raised the animal act to a level higher than even that of the most exact arts or the wildest flights of pure science? It would not be sufficient to say that in his love-making with Ada he discovered the pang, the *ogon',* the agony of supreme "reality." Reality, better say, lost the quotes it wore like claws—in a world where independent and original minds must cling to things or pull things apart in order to ward off madness or death (which is the master madness). For one spasm or two, he was safe. (pp. 219–20)

Love is not merely an escape from the here and now; it gives birth to a new reality which will be incorporated in our memory: Van or Humbert will always remember that they once lived in a death-free world. The former, who is painfully aware that death means, among other things, "the wrench of relinquishing forever all one's memories" (*Ada,* p. 585), fools time by writing his memoirs: he makes sure that his memories will never die and that he will continue to live in his book. Loving and writing therefore fulfill the same purpose, defeating time, as Van makes clear in the next passage:

> I wish to caress Time. . . . I delight sensually in Time, in its stuff and spread, in the fall of its folds, in the very impalpability of its grayish gauze, in the coolness of its continuum. I wish to do something about it; to indulge in a simulacrum of possession. (*Ada,* p. 537)

Such was his purpose in writing *The Texture of Time,* such also was Nabokov's in writing *Ada, or Ardor: A Family Chronicle.* A chronicle is supposed to retrieve a slice of lost time; this one goes a step further: it creates or invents a slice of time that was clearly never lived before, either by men or cherubs, but still takes its place in the past of mankind.

Puppets and Puppeteers.[13] Earlier in this study we raised a problem which we must now tackle: that of the two or three identities of Van in *Ada,* and, in general, of the fluctuating identities of both characters and narrators in Nabokov's novels. It is not possible, within the limits of this study, to give a full treatment of the subject; only the aspects which are relevant to our purpose will be examined.

In no other work can one find such an array of doubles as in Nabokov's. One of the greatest novels he wrote in Russian, *Despair,* is the case history of a man who thinks he has found his double. Pnin, the sensitive but absent-minded scholar, keeps taking one man for another; besides, one of his colleagues at Waindell College has reached quite a fame for impersonating him, which leads the narrator to remark at the end: "Finally the whole thing grew to be such a bore that I fell wondering if by some poetical vengeance this Pnin business had not become with Cockerell the kind of fatal obsession which substitutes its own victim for that of the initial ridicule."[14] The best cases are still to be found in *Lolita* and *Pale Fire.* Quilty, Humbert's shadow throughout the second part of the novel, has both the wit and scholarship of Lolita's stepfather; he is Humbert's Mr. Hyde, and that is why he gets killed at the end. In *Pale Fire* everybody looks like everybody else; a German lecturer once tells Kinbote that he resembles the "unfortunate monarch" of Zembla, but Kinbote protects his incognito as best he can: ". . . when I negligently observed that all bearded Zemblans resembled one another—and that, in fact, the name Zembla is a corruption not of the Russian *zemlya,* but of Semblerland, a land of reflections, of resemblers—my tormentor said: Ah, yes, but King Charles wore no beard . . ." (p. 265). He is also said to look like John Shade, who himself claims to look like Judge Goldsworth, Kinbote's landlord. All these resemblances have one clear effect in the novel: they deprive the characters of whatever real existence they themselves claim to have. They are not made of flesh and blood but of paper and ink: they are dummies, mannequins, which, not unfrequently, betoken an exceptional resemblance to human beings. There is not much difference between them and the clever robot Dreyer is having built in *King, Queen, Knave.* Nabokov proceeds the same way in creating and animating his characters as Ada does in inventing new species of butterflies by putting together various parts taken from actual butterflies. This process must not be confused, however, with the one advocated by Nathalie Sarraute in *L'Ère du soupçon:* with Nabokov the characters, though synthetic, as it were, hardly ever change within the span of the novel.

Sometimes, however, when they are about to leave the stage of the novel they tend to disintegrate completely as, for instance, at the end of *Invitation to a Beheading:* "Cincinnatus slowly descended from the platform and walked off through the shifting debris. He was overtaken by Roman, who was many times smaller and who was at the same time Rodrig: "What are you doing!" he croaked, jumping up and down."[15] Cincinnatus is supposed to have been beheaded in the preceding scene; however, the author allows him to descend from the platform as does an actor from the stage at the end of his performance. At the end of *Despair* the protagonist, in order to escape, pretends he is rehearsing a scene for a film.

Pale Fire is a clear landmark in that respect: here the narrator turns out to be the protagonist, though he may also be standing in for the clever author who masterminded the whole spoof of a variorum edition. In the notes, Kinbote does his utmost to prove that he is King Charles (though in his "actual life" he refused to acknowledge it, or so he says now!) but his only "reliable" witness is Gradus, alias Vinogradus, alias Jack Gray, who unfortunately dies some time after he has murdered John Shade:

> It is evil piffle to assert that he aimed not at me (whom he had just seen in the library—let us be consistent, gentlemen, ours is a rational world after all), but at the gray-locked gentleman behind me. Oh, he was aiming at me all right but missing me every time, the incorrigible bungler. . . . (*P. F.,* p. 294)

Here the narrator is trying to force one of his invented characters to testify to his true identity. At the end, of course, we realize that most of the book has been invented by a madman; but what about the poem? Who wrote it, a poet called Shade or an over-brilliant writer who then faked madness after writing the poem? We cannot be sure of the true identity of either the narrator or the characters; the whole novel is actually based on the constant shift of identities, and it is only a "pale fire" that remains at the end. All we know is that we have been walking around a hall of mirrors and that we have not met anyone . . . except perhaps the porter or the guide!

The status of both narrators and characters in *Ada* is somewhat reminiscent of that of Marcel and his characters in *Remembrance of Things Past.* Van and Ada are not dummies; they may be the only "true" people we have met in Nabokov's novels, if by "true" we mean truly present in our imagination. Still, we never know for sure which Van (and which Ada) is actually present in any given page of the novel: young Van who seduced, or was seduced by, Ada, or the old man who is writing his memoirs with the help of nonagenarian Ada, and embellishing the past in the process? It is like following two plays, performed on two adjacent stages at the same time, by two sets of actors standing in for Van and Ada at two different periods of their lives. The second plot is developed in the dozens of parentheses like the following one: "(It is not necessary, here or elsewhere, there was another similar passage, to blotch a reasonably pure style with vague anatomical terms that a psychiatrist remembers from his student days. In Ada's late hand)" (*Ada,* p. 118). In some cases, particularly in chapter 19, they even share the work of writing the memoirs, leaving it to Mr. Oranger, the editor, to correct the mistakes. It is not clear at all who wrote the last chapter in which they seem to be dying at approximately the same time; it is not even clear what is happening to whom in the next passage where Van is supposed to go for the doctor: "Van found him reading in the serene garden. The doctor followed Ada into the house. The Veens had believed for a whole summer of misery (or made each other believe) that it was a touch of neuralgia" (p. 587). The "anonymous" narrator of this last chapter gives the impression that there are not two persons (the former chief narrator and the former chief character) but only one:

Actually the question of mortal precedence has now hardly any importance. I mean, the hero and heroine should get so close to each other by the time the horror begins, so *organically* close, that they overlap, intergrade, interache, and even if Vaniada's end is described in the epilogue we, writers and readers, should be unable to make out (myopic, myopic) who exactly survives, Dava or Vada, Anda or Vanda. (p. 584)

It is not the problem of who is going first but of how to finish the book that is raised here: Van and Ada die *into the book* the same way as they had been born *with or in the book*. Though we fully realize that they have never existed outside of these six hundred pages, we still envy the beautiful idyll they lived in the Garden of Eden: we have been witnessing a new kind of creation.

The problem of authorship is again our main concern when we read *Transparent Things,* one of those rare Nabokovian novels without a homodiegetic narrator.[16] Among the many characters of this novel, we find an eccentric novelist, Mr. R., who somewhat reminds us of Nabokov himself. The chief protagonist, Person, who is also R.'s proofreader, has constantly in mind the characters and the plots of R.'s novels, and finds it very difficult to distinguish between his own reality and the reality invented by Mr. R.: he thinks he recognizes R.'s stepdaughter, with whom he once had an affair, in one of the novels he proofreads. Mr. R. also had an affair with his own stepdaughter when she was a nymphet. Besides, the novelist is so much interested in Person that we are tempted to think he is the narrator of the novel we are reading. In his last letter to his publisher, he writes: "Please tell all this [about Person] because Hugh was one of the nicest persons I knew and also because you can smuggle all kinds of secret information for this poor soul [R. himself whose mail is read by Tamworth] in your letter about him" (*T. T.,* p. 83). This is the key passage in the novel: Mr. R. wants to establish a code to communicate with his publisher (and his reader, we presume) by getting the assistance of his proofreader, who is also the main character of this novel he himself may have written (one's syntax gets badly tangled when one writes about Nabokov's plots!). After we have read this letter, we are told that Mr. R. died a few days later; how could he have written the novel since there are twenty pages after this letter? The well-constructed world of cross references collapses, and we are faced with the void. This is the last (or latest, rather) stage in the narrator's metamorphosis in Nabokov's novels: we are left only with an invisible puppeteer who hides behind the dark curtains, or rather between the black covers of *Transparent Things* (Nabokov's novels are usually bound in black cloth), and who constantly pops up as one of his own puppets. There is no need to worry about anybody's fate since it is merely a game!

THE "RÉCIT" AS A DISCOURSE

So far we have considered the relationship between Nabokov's novels and the world of referents, and we have reached the conclusion that these novels evolve their own reality and defy the laws of our everyday logic. We are now going to view the problem from a different angle, that of the writing. As Ricardou remarked in the passage quoted earlier, the classical rhetoric and the romantic theory of writing were both founded on the creed that the world of facts and the world of writing were completely divorced from each other, and only the methods of bridging the gap between the two worlds differed. With Nabokov this is no longer the case, as we have begun to find out in the first part, since reality, dream, and fiction cannot satisfactorily be isolated; but also because, as we are going to see in this second part, Nabokov's novels are made to appear as nothing but literal entities and therefore cannot suffer from any fundamental divorce between form and substance.

The Generators.[17] As we said earlier, Nabokov's novels are not based on any pre-(hi)story or pre-text, but invent their own plots and their own realities step by step; the narrator's main concern, as John Shade indicates in *Pale Fire,* is the "testing of performing words" (p. 64) which will eventually build up a lofty edifice.

The narrator must of course have some kind of pattern to work on if he does not want to write the rambling kind of works composed by the surrealists. In *Pale Fire* Nabokov used not only one but at least three patterns to write his novel: geometry, chess, and literary parallelisms. We will not examine the second one, chess, since it has already been studied before by Mary McCarthy and Janet K. Gezari. Few critics, on the other hand, have noticed the obsessive recurrence of the figure *8* in this novel: it appears as "a lemniscate left / Upon wet sand by nonchalantly deft / Bicycle tires" (p. 37), as "TV's huge paperclip" (p. 35). Sometimes it assumes slightly altered shapes: "an ampersand" (p. 53), "clover leaves" (p. 65), a Vanessa's wings (p. 69), or the sign of recognition the karlists are supposed to make and which corresponds to "the X (for Xavier) in the one-hand alphabet of deaf mutes" (p. 179). It also appears in a number of dates.[18]

If one investigates the matter further, it becomes clear that this figure *8* represents the deep structure of the novel as a *récit* (this is quite an exceptional case with Nabokov, but an ordinary one with the French New Novelists). *Pale Fire* can be represented as two circles which apparently never touch: one is Shade's autobiographical poem which is completely self-sufficient, and the other is the story of King Charles as it is reported in Kinbote's notes. Only through the editor and annotator of the poem, Kinbote (who also claims to be the king), do the two stories ultimately meet. In the first pages of the notes, it seems Shade is not involved in the second story, but it is gradually revealed that Shade gets killed because of his short acquaintance with Kinbote, which involves him for a short but fatal moment in the circle of the second story. The two circles now touch and form the figure ∞ or *8*. After the poet's death Kinbote, who has secured the cards containing the poem, decides to annotate Shade's work in the light of what has happened, attributing a new meaning to many "innocent" words: he feeds back into the poem the knowledge he has acquired since it was written, and also smuggles in the story of King Charles as he told it to the poet while he was writing "Pale Fire." The two stories are interconnected through Kinbote's writing, and the book, which was in danger of looking fragmented, acquires a new unity.

The literary parallelism upon which the novel is partly based operates in a similar way, but unknown to the narrator himself. Just before he lays down his pen, John Shade tries to find a title for his poem: "(But this transparent thingum does require / Some moondrop title. Help me, Will! *Pale Fire*)" (p. 68). But Kinbote fails to recognize the reference:

> Paraphrased, this evidently means: let me look in Shakespeare for something I might use for a title. And the find is "pale fire." But in which of the Bard's works did our poet cull it? My readers must make their own research. All I have with me is a tiny vest pocket edition of *Timon of Athens*–in Zemblan. It certainly contains nothing that could be regarded as an equivalent of "pale fire" (if it had, my luck would have been a statistical monster). (p. 285)

Earlier, in his note to lines 39-40, Kinbote "accidentally" gave the Zemblan version of the very passage of *Timon of Athens* from which the title is taken, but, unfortunately, "pale fire" was lost in the translation which reads: "The moon's a thief: / he steals his silvery light from the sun" (p. 80), whereas the original reads: "The moon's an arrant thief, / And her pale fire she snatches from the sun: . . ."[19] The parallelism is doubly relevant: Kinbote's writing shines with the glow borrowed from Shade's poetry (the figure *8* may therefore stand for the twin orbs); besides, Kinbote lives in a world apart, like Timon in his cave.[20] This does not mean, however, that *Pale Fire* is a mere allegory of *Timon of Athens;* it simply makes use of a theme and image present in the play; it builds upon them and eventually turns them into something new which has little in common with *Timon of Athens*. It is, as it were, a matter of out-Shakespearing Shakespeare.

In *Ada* Nabokov does not use a particular work but a whole genre, that of the traditional novel, which he constantly derides in sallies like the following one: "Then Van and Ada met in the passage and would have kissed at some earlier stage of the Novel's Evolution in the History of Literature" (*Ada,* p. 96). Or again:

> That library had provided a raised stage for the unforgettable scene of the Burning Barn; it had thrown open its glazed doors; it had promised a long idyll of bibliolatry; it might have become a chapter in one of the old novels on its own shelves; a touch of parody gave its theme the comic relief of life. (p. 137)

These recurrent sallies make it clear that this is not an ordinary novel with some realistic import, but rather a new type based on literary clichés, borrowed mainly from Tolstoy: the sententious statements, the psychological analyses, and the "going behind." The opening of the novel is actually a parody of the first line of *Anna Karenina:* "'All happy families are more or less dissimilar; but all unhappy ones are more or less alike,' says a great Russian writer in the beginning of a famous novel" (p. 3). But whereas Tolstoy pretended to base his chronicle on "facts," Nabokov deliberately emphasizes the elements of parody and artificiality, so that *Ada* turns out to be the reversed picture of *Anna Karenina*. However, there is no reminder at the end that it all started as a parody of Tolstoy's novel, for the simple reason that it has developed into something completely new which does not need that reference to be considered as a great novel in its own right.

The secret of Nabokov's achievement in this novel may be partly due to the fact that another generator, the title, operates throughout these six hundred pages. *Ada* is one of those rare cases mentioned by Mr. R. in *Transparent Things* where the title "was born with the book, the title to which the author had grown so accustomed during the years of accumulating the written pages that it had become part of each and all" (*T. T.*, p. 70). We are told, on two occasions, that "Ada" means "hell" in Russian (*Ada*, pp. 29, 332); it is made to rhyme with "arbors and ardors" (p. 54); it contains the Russian word meaning "yes" and the beginning of all continents "except you" (p. 345); it appears in "Scheherazade" (p. 217) and in the name of one of Ada's own friends, Vanda; at the end of the novel it combines with Van to form a new name, Vaniada. The author juggles so cleverly with these two syllables that we wonder, sometimes, if he is talking about the book being written or our beloved delphinet:

> ... he recalled his first railway journey to Ardis and tried—what he sometimes advised a patient doing in order to exercise the "muscles of consciousness"— namely putting oneself back not merely into the frame of mind that had preceded a radical change in one's life, but into a state of complete ignorance regarding that change. He knew it could not be done, that not the achievement, but the obstinate attempt was possible, because he would not have remembered the preface to Ada had not life turned the next page, causing now its radiant text to flash through all the tenses of the mind. (p. 470)

As we reach the end of the novel, with the characters imperceptibly disintegrating, we are left with nothing but a beautiful word, "Ada," a word which is not only the name of an unforgettable (though fictitious) delphinet, but also the title of a great poetic novel in which the author has explored the various resources of that one word, made of only three letters (actually two), impossible to anagrammatize. What came first, the delphinet, her name, or the book? We cannot tell because, for us, they are all happening at the same time: Ada was born with or out of (*iz* in Russian) *Ada* and vice versa.[21]

This circular type of composition in which the generator is born in and with the novel culminates in the many references, made in every single novel, to the previous ones. The plot of *Lolita* first appeared as an anecdote in *The Gift* almost twenty years earlier;[22] Lolita appears in *Pale Fire* as a major hurricane that took place in 1958 (the year when the novel was published in the United States), and in *Ada* as a little town in Texas or the main character in Osberg's (Borges) *La Gitanilla* (p. 77). Also in *Ada* we can read a short poem written by John Shade, the author of "Pale Fire" and one of the main characters in the novel which bears the same title. In *Transparent Things* Hugh and Armande share a *femme de ménage* "with a Belgian artist in the penthouse immediately above them" (*T. T.*, p. 72) as did Van in *Ada* (p. 390). Besides, Nabokov is mentioned in almost every single novel, either by name as in *The Gift*[23] or more discreetly as "the fellow whose novels you and John think so phony" in *Pale Fire* (p. 161). In *King, Queen, Knave* Nabokov turns up with his wife at a seaside resort to witness the denouement of the novel.[24] These personal notes can be interpreted as either the artist's signature in the corner of the canvas, a mild joke at the expense of the unwary reader, or a smile of approval for the lucky reader who recognized the author. Above all, these "metalepses"[25] underline the artificiality or the arbitrariness of the novel, or rather its *littérarité,* as Barthes puts it: they are the obvious signs or signals that what we are reading has only a literary existence and needs no other justification than the ones it contains. At the same time they bind Nabokov's novels into a huge book which stands loftily by itself without any need of props or crutches, somewhat like a living organism born by spontaneous generation.

The Logic of the *Récit*. Until the beginning of this century most novelists strove hard to give logic and unity to their novels in an attempt to copy the "real world," and also because they believed in the existence of some unifying principle in that world. James's emphasis on "composition," "unity," "harmony," "intensity of illusion,"[26] was but a new formulation of the old creed. Nabokov does not believe in the existence of such a unifying principle and consequently does not try to create a highly unified and logical *récit* but one that is confused and labyrinthine.

Earlier we saw how he used literary parallelisms to compose some of his novels; there are many cases, however, where these literary references do not play such a structural part, but rather give a peculiar texture to the *récit* as a whole. When, for instance, we read in *Pale Fire;* "This observer never could emulate in sheer luck the eavesdropping *Hero of Our Time* or the omnipresent one of *Time Lost*" (p. 87), we realize of course that the literary references are not meant to add a borrowed glow to the author's writing, as was often the case with Eliot's "objective correlative," but simply to emphasize the originality of the book we are reading. This may be a trick to mislead the "knowledgeable" reader and force him to play the sleuth, as Appel and Mary McCarthy did for *Lolita* and *Pale Fire.* But, obviously, the "knowledgeable" reader can as easily get caught in the quagmire of the novel as the ignoramus, since, after he has followed all the right and false tracks prepared by the author in these literary references, he is often too confused to find out what the game is really about. In fact, most of these references are meant to entangle the *récit,* to cover the tracks of both the characters and the narrators, as we realize in the following passage from *Ada:*

> The two girls were now kissing him alternately, then kissing each other, then getting busy upon him again—Ada in perilous silence, Lucette with soft squeals of delight. I do not remember what *Les Enfants Maudits* did or said in Monparnasse's novelette—they lived in Bryant's château, I think, and it began with bats flying one by one out of a turret's *oeil-de-boeuf* into the sunset, but *these* children (whom the novelettist did not really know—a delicious point) might also have been filmed rather entertainingly had snoopy Kim, the kitchen photofiend, possessed the necessary apparatus. One hates to write about those matters, it all comes out so improper, esthetically speaking, in written description. . . .
> (p. 205)

Monparnasse is both the pen name of Mademoiselle Larivière, the governess, and an oblique reference to Maupassant, whom she emulates in her novelettes; besides, there is a clear reference to Chateaubriand's own story. In this passage the *récit* goes through a number of transformations: an erotic scene becomes a passage in the novelette of a writer plagiarizing another, and then a sequence in a film, until it becomes what it has always been, an extract from *Ada* with which the narrator pretends not to be satisfied. These digressive references therefore emphasize the written nature of the scene, its *littérarité;* also, they constitute a shunted *récit* which threatens to disrupt the main one, and an elaborate metaphor that contributes to make the scene more vivid and, at the same time, more unreal or surreal.

We have just used a word borrowed from the old rhetoric and which seems to contradict the theory elaborated in this study. It is true that Nabokov, contrary to such modern writers as Robbe-Grillet, for instance, wallows in metaphors and protracted comparisons; but with him, metaphors and comparisons are not a mere ornament: they usually play a structural part in the *récit* as, for instance, in this description of Ada who has just refused to make love:

> ... uncontrollably and marvelously her dazed look melted into one of gentle glee, as if in sudden perception of new-found release. Thus a child may stare into space, with a dawning smile, upon realizing that the bad dream is over, or that a door has been left unlocked, and that one can paddle with impunity in thawed sky. (*Ada,* p. 286)

Though she is only fourteen, Van had not particularly insisted before on her childishness; but here, after he has noticed her change of expression, he compares her with a child until, by the end of the comparison, she becomes a child, which will account for her change of mind (they are going to make love after all). The comparison is not meant as an ornament but as a sequence or a link in the *récit.* It happens, of course, that such comparisons lead nowhere, as the next one for instance:

> Designing and re-designing various contingencies pertaining to that little duel might be compared to those helpful hobbies which polio patients, lunatics and convicts are taught by generous institutions, by enlightened administrators, by ingenious psychiatrists—such as bookbinding, or putting blue beads into the orbits of dolls made by other criminals, cripples and madmen. (*Ada,* p. 307)

This is a typically digressive comparison, in the best Gogolian tradition: words are strung like beads on a thin thread which finally snaps from its overload and spills its varicolored beads. We were expecting to get a necklace and we are left with a boxful of useless, punctured, tiny balls.

This type of extravagant comparisons is one of the many devices used by Nabokov to keep his *récit* hanging in midair. For him any *récit,* even though it may look like an exact picture of reality, is a pure invention or a "fairy tale"; he can draw, for instance, three different *récits* from one "innocent" family picture in which a complete stranger appears:

... a terribly tweedy gentleman with sightseeing strappings athwart one shoulder: actually (according to Ada), a tourist, who, having come all the way from England to see Bryant's Castle, had bicycled up the wrong road and was, in the picture, under the impression of accidentally being conjoined to a group of fellow tourists who were visiting some other old manor quite worth inspecting too. (*Ada*, p. 407)

In the parenthesis, Van discreetly suggests that the stranger may be one of the many anonymous lovers Ada kept around her in those days: this is his own personal *récit* on the picture. Ada's conjectural one is that the stranger was a stray tourist, who had his own interpretation of the scene (third *récit*). All these micro-*récits* hold their share of truth, but no single one can claim to be the real one, except perhaps the hypothetical *récit* that would combine all the imaginable micro-*récits*. There being no end to the process, we can safely conclude that the final *récit* will never be written and therefore does not exist; all we can do is to enjoy the fragmentary or fictitious one at our disposal: it is the only reliable fact in the here and now of the book.

It is a similar point that Nabokov seems to make at the end of *Transparent Things*, where he gives a series of telescoped *récits* which are either dreamt up or imagined by Person, just before he wakes up from one of his bad nightmares or dies in a fire, or which may have been invented by the narrator to get rid of his protagonist, before laying down his pen:

Rings of blurred colors circled around him, reminding him briefly of a childhood picture in a frightening book about triumphant vegetables whirling faster and faster around a nightshirted boy trying desperately to awake from the iridescent dizziness of dream life. Its ultimate vision was the incandescence of a book or a box grown completely transparent and hollow. (*T. T.*, p. 104)

Our ultimate vision is also "the incandescence of a book" which originated in an ambiguous word: "Here's the person I want. Hullo, person! Doesn't hear me" (p. 1). This noun, which can mean either anybody or nobody in French, was promoted to the rank of a family name in the second chapter and gave birth to the protagonist Hugh Person (pronounced "you" by *h*-dropping Armande, Hugh's wife), according to a process widespread in the New Novel; incidentally, Nabokov acknowledged his "debt" to the New Novel, especially in this parody of Butor's *La Modification*, which is written in the second person:

The chocolate proved unpalatable. You were served a cup of hot milk. You also got, separately, a little sugar and a dainty-looking envelope of sorts. You ripped open the upper margin of the envelope. You added the beige dust it contained to the ruthlessly homogenized milk in your cup. You took a sip. ... (*T. T.*, pp. 46–47)

Since the character does not even bear a name of his own and is nothing but a puppet, the narrator is completely free to manipulate him in any way he likes and make him perform incredible stunts; he is only limited by the size of the novel, or rather by two blanks. He plays a game somewhat reminiscent of the one described by Robbe-Grillet in *L'Année dernière à Marienbad* in which the outcome cannot be altered but the sequences can be reshuffled at will.

This reference to the Marienbad game brings us to another key technique, used both in the New Novel and in Nabokov's novels, and which Gide called *mise en abyme;* Hugo, in his *William Shakespeare,* had defined it before, without giving it a name, as "a subplot that runs through the play and reflects it in miniature."[27] Ricardou gives, as an illustration, Van Eyck's "Portrait of the Arnolfinis." This technique is thoroughly exploited in *Ada,* where we find the following evocation of an Italian painting in the chapter describing Ada and Van's boisterous love-making:

> Van could not recollect whose picture it was that he had in mind, but thought it might have been attributed to Michelangelo da Caravaggio in his youth. It was an oil on unframed canvas depicting two misbehaving nudes, boy and girl, in an ivied or vined grotto or near a small waterfall overhung with bronze-tinted and dark, emerald leaves, and great bunches of translucent grapes and limpid reflections of fruit and foliage blending magically with veined flesh. (p. 140)

There are a number of these quattrocento paintings hanging on the walls of the various houses and penthouses in *Ada;* it is a nude attributed to Parmigiano which marked the end of Demon's love affair with Marina, as Demon himself writes in a letter: "Now *that* is the sketch made by a young artist in Parma, in the sixteenth century, for the fresco of *our* destiny, in a prophetic trance" (p. 16). Similarly, the painting recollected by Van led to the actual staging of an erotic scene in the following page: "A moment later the Dutch took over: Girl stepping into a pool under the little cascade to wash her tresses" (p. 141). These echoes point at the workings of the *récit,* they are a sign of *littérarité;* also, like the extravagant comparisons mentioned earlier, they sometimes constitute a structural link in the *récit,* as is the case in the passage quoted above; and that is where Nabokov really innovates.

He even went a step further in *Transparent Things:* he repeatedly mentioned a novel written by Mr. R. which may be the one we are reading. Early in the novel we realize that there is much in common between the world of Mr. R.'s novels and that of *Transparent Things,* as, for instance in the following passage where Armande and Hugh are discussing *Figures in a Golden Window:*

> "Well, there's a rather dramatic scene in a Riviera villa, when the little girl, the narrator's daughter—"
> "June."
> "Yes. June sets her new dollhouse on fire and the whole villa burns down; but there's not much violence, I'm afraid; it is rather symbolic. . . ." (*T. T.,* p. 26)

This scene prefigures the concluding scene of *Transparent Things;* besides, June is obviously Mr. R.'s stepdaughter Julia, with whom Person had an affair once. It is this affair which is apparently recorded in another of Mr. R.'s novels, *Three*

Tenses (pp. 46ff.). It gradually dawns upon the reader that Person may well be Mr. R.'s own invention and the chief protagonist of his latest novel, *Tralatitions,* of which we know practically nothing except the title. The whole game of *mise en abyme* is here burlesqued and turned into the warp and woof of the novel we are reading, whose main theme seems to be the working of this technique.

Transparent Things marks one of the latest stages in Nabokov's attempt to liberate the *récit* from its old shackles and create a new type of *récit* which ignores our every-day logic. Which comes first, the liberating or the creating, is hard to tell, and no doubt the question is irrelevant as far as Nabokov is concerned. Unfortunately, it is not irrelevant to us, for we are compelled to emphasize the newness of the technique in our attempt to circumscribe the originality of the work we are ex-amining, if we do not want to flounder in the subjectiveness of aesthetic pronounce-ments. Here lies, perhaps, the most fundamental difference between the artist and the critic: the latter is forced to elaborate his *récit* (for that is what his criticism basically is) on a pre-text which is the writer's work.

The Pathways of Writing. From the beginning of this study we have had the feeling that our subject was always in danger of evading us. In our first part we found out that it was difficult to write about reality, time and space, characters and narrators, because these concepts had no objective or durable existence in Nabokov's novels. In the first two sections of this second part, the generators and the logic of the *récit* also eluded us because of the way Nabokov handled them, but also because they operate on reality/time/characters. We have been walking in a circle, under the spell cast by Nabokov, and we have caught but a fleeting glance of the magician and the techniques he has been using. There is only one thing that we can "safely" examine without running the risk of seeing it disintegrating under our pen, it is the writing or *écriture* itself.

In *The Rhetoric of Fiction* Wayne C. Booth has devoted many pages to the old, but misleading, distinction between "telling" and "showing," pertinently con-cluding that "the line between showing and telling is always to some degree an arbitrary one" and that "the author's judgment is always present, always evident to anyone who knows how to look for it."[28] Many American novelists today still believe in the old Jamesian creed and strive to make themselves heard but not seen. Nabokov, like Sterne before him, seems to enjoy being seen in the act of writing, and the same thing goes for his narrators. In *Pale Fire* Kinbote often mentions the circumstances under which he is writing his notes: "There is a very loud amusement park right in front of my present lodgings" (p. 13). He says that he cannot stand the noise. After quoting a variant to Shade's poem, he continues: "This describes rather well the 'chance inn,' a log cabin with a tiled bathroom, where I am trying to coordinate these notes" (p. 235). In *Ada,* also, there are many open references to the circumstances of the writing: "But impatient young passion (brimming like Van's overflowing bath while he is reworking this, a crotchety gray old wordman on the edge of a hotel bed) . . ." (p. 121). At the end of the novel the secretary who is typing the text under Van's dictation is introduced, along with the editor:

> Violet knocks at the library door and lets in plump, short, bow-tied Mr. Oranger, who stops on the threshold, clicks his heels, and (as the heavy hermit turns with an awkward sweep of frieze robe) darts forward almost at a trot not so much to stop with a masterful slap the avalanche of loose sheets which the great man's elbow has sent sliding down the lectern-slope, as to express the eagerness of his admiration. (p. 577)

This passage being written in the present tense, the scene seems to be described while being enacted; but it cannot be, since Violet is showing Oranger in and not typing. Even when she is actually typing, we still hear Van's voice as if it had been recorded: "E, p, i—why 'y,' my dear?" (p. 578). Presumably, Violet is not stupid enough to type such a remark; so the circumstances of the writing get muddled and all these extras, who might claim a part in the writing, are bodily removed from the novel and leave us face to face with Van (or is it Nabokov?) at work.

A similar effect is achieved by the many asides of the narrators on their writing, such as: "When lightning struck two days later (an old image that is meant to intimate a flash-back to an old barn) . . ." (*Ada*, p. 284). Or: "They took a great many precautions—all absolutely useless, for nothing can change the end (written and filed away) of the present chapter" (*Ada*, p. 432). Or again: *"Et trêve de mon style plafond peint"* (*Ada*, p. 536). Van even suggests adding a note which will never be written (p. 537). In *Transparent Things*, as in the novels of Sterne and Fielding, many chapters conclude with remarks like: "More in a moment" (p. 2), and "Let us now illustrate our difficulties" (p. 5). Chapter 17 begins with: "We shall now discuss love" (p. 62). Nabokov deliberately emphasizes the artificiality of his writing, whereas many novelists still try to conceal it; he constantly points at (or pretends to point at) the workings of his writing and at his problems as a narrator, condescending, as it were, to show himself as he really is. However, many of these notes are so unexpected and far-fetched that we sense a trick and lose our countenance: we thought we had caught a glimpse of the author and now we realize that it was only a mirage.

This ought to suggest that the author is no more real than the narrator, and that we should stop listening to his "small voice" and start considering the text without looking for the signs, sprinkled by the author, that would confirm our interpretation. But we are still laboring under the curse of the old rhetoric and are unable to consider the writing independently from the writer, perhaps because we still believe in the Saussurian dogma about the oral essence of language. Nabokov, along with the New Novelists, tries hard to divorce his writing from our everyday speech, to emphasize its literal essence, as, for instance, in the following passage from *Transparent Things* in which he seems to be reporting a conversation:

> An adjacent customer, comically resembling Person's late Aunt Melissa whom we like very much, was reading l'*Erald Tribune*. Armande believed (in the vulgar connotation of the word) that Julia Moore had met Percy. Julia believed she had. So did Hugh, indeed, yes. Did his aunt's double permit him to borrow her spare chair? He was welcome to it. She was a dear soul, with five cats, living in a toy house, at the end of a birch avenue, in the quietest part of— (p. 45)

This is an extreme example of what Ann Banfield in a recent article called "free indirect style."[29] The reader is completely at a loss when it comes to deciding what was actually said, if anything at all was ever said, and by whom. The reference to Person's late Aunt Melissa may have been simply borrowed from Person's thoughts by an omniscient narrator, unless it is the narrator's rendering of Person's speech; "l'*Erald Tribune*" betrays a French accent, therefore an utterance by a French-speaking person (or perhaps an English-speaking one who is trying to imitate the French accent). The parenthesis can probably be attributed to the narrator, unless Julia, Armande, and Person are acting out a scene from Mr. R.'s *Three Tenses.* If Person actually asked the "adjacent customer" to "borrow her spare chair," he certainly did not address her as "his aunt's double." Finally, the lady with five cats is presumably the aunt, and not the customer, but we cannot be sure, for the simple reason that this sentence can either have been uttered by Person or written by the narrator. The confusion keeps growing as we read, and we must accept the fact that all these questions have no answer because there is no one (narrator or author) to provide it. We are forced to admit that everything in the novel, whether it be a reported speech, an interior monologue, a dialogue, a description, or an authorial note, is on the same level of writing, and that the question of authority, of spoken versus written scenes, of showing versus telling, of *haplé diégésis* versus mimesis, is irrelevant in the context of Nabokov's novels.

We must therefore concentrate our attention on the idiosyncrasies of Nabokov's writing as we would on the techniques of a chess maestro. First, they do not rely on one code only, that of the English language, but use a number of ciphers like those invented by Ada and Van to communicate epistolarily (*Ada,* p. 157). The Shadows use similar codes in *Pale Fire.* Sometimes less drastic means are used: words are twisted: "powder"/"red wop" (*P. F.,* p. 45); "van/ouissements" (*Ada,* p. 375), or foreign words are given a fancy transcription (the English twins, in *Transparent Things,* "called gullies Cool Wars and ridges Ah Rates" (p. 89). Well-known names become hardly recognizable: Dr. Froid of Signy-Mondieu-Mondieu is Freud, Lowden is both Lowell and Auden (*Ada,* p. 245). Finally anagrams crop up on almost every other page, especially in *Ada:* "horsecart" (for "orchestra"), "as you insist, sinister insister," "Eros, the rose and the sore" (pp. 72, 193, 367). In these novels the language is constantly shifting; the words cannot be trusted since they can easily be twisted, turned inside out, or given a number of far-fetched connotations. Sometimes they even get so overloaded that they turn out to be empty shells by the time we reach the end of the novel. Incidentally, the extravagant metaphors analyzed earlier achieve a similar purpose at times, that of sterilizing words or images.

This process of sterilizing, or better perhaps of neutralizing, the "standard" language, leads up, eventually, to the creation of a new written language, and, through it, of a new world. This process is briefly analyzed in the next passage from *Pale Fire:*

Line 819: Playing a game of worlds
My illustrious friend showed a childish predilection for all sorts of word games and especially for so-called word golf. He would interrupt the flow of a prismatic conversation to indulge in this particular pastime, and naturally it would have been boorish of me to refuse playing with him. Some of my records are: hate-love in three, lass-male in four, and live-dead in five (with "lend" in the middle). (p. 262)

These games of words are indeed games of worlds. Manipulating words is never as artificial or gratuitous as it may seem; it is bound to generate meaning even if it was not intended to do so. For instance, Lucette's loss at a game of Flavita (a word game invented by the children in *Ada*) indirectly leads to her being driven away from Van and Ada. Despite her charms which, as we saw earlier, even surpass Ada's, she has no place in their Garden of Eden because she is not a very good word handler. Ada, on the other hand, has a very special talent: she can play with shadows, she can invent new species of butterflies, and, above all, she can raise word games to the level of an art: "She suggested to Van that verbal circuses, 'performing words,' 'poodle-doodles,' and so forth, might be redeemable by the quality of the brain work required for the creation of a great logograph or inspired pun and should not preclude the help of a dictionary, gruff or complacent" (p. 222). One is reminded here of Nabokov's "complacent" but weary old *Webster's* which appears in some photographic portraits of the novelist. Ada actually gives us a clue as to what Nabokov's writing is really about: it is about "the brain work required for the creation of a great logograph or inspired pun." This is a new version of Ricardou's "adventure of a writing."

At the beginning of this second part, we came across the same phrase used by Ada in the passage just quoted, "performing words," that time in connection with John Shade's methods of composition. Despite their being written, the words of a poet assume the directness of the words spoken by an actor on the stage, whereas most of our ordinary words sound dead once they are written; such seems to be Ada's opinion: "I see now that it is just as dreadfully hard to put my heart and honor in script—even more so because in speaking one can use a stutter or a shutter, and plead a chance slurring of words" (*Ada,* p. 332). The written word is irrevocable and can be used as evidence against its author, especially if, as was often the case in the nineteenth-century novel, the author fails to cover his tracks. That is the main reason why Ada, who once tried to become an actress, considers a play to be greater than a novel:

"In 'real' life we are creatures of chance in an absolute void—unless we be artists ourselves, naturally; but in a good play I feel authored, I feel passed by the board of censors, I feel secure, with only a breathing blackness before me (instead of our Fourth-Wall Time), I feel cuddled in the embrace of puzzled Will. . . ." (p. 426)

In a play the actor does not have to account for his origins, his psychological features, to be real: he is there on the stage, and, even though he may fake the erratic gestures of a robot or a puppet, he is still a man and we must take his words on trust. His words do not have to be connected with our reality to sound "real"; it is enough that they make sense for him. He is superior to the characters in a novel because he is not simply the product of a writing; he is what his speech makes him in the here and now of the performance, regardless of a would-be playwright hiding in the wings. This is a perfect example of what Benveniste calls a "performative speech": "The telling *is* the act; the one who utters it accomplishes the act by enunciating it."[30] As Beneveniste points out, this is the speech of the master, not of the slave; it is the speech of God creating the world in Genesis.

Nabokov's writing, especially in the three novels we have been examining, is truly performative: since it does not claim to create a world connected with, or similar to, our own "real" one, but rather a completely imaginary world which exists only in the novel, the process of writing is the same one that produces the imaginary world, and the writing itself is the very flesh and blood of the fictitious characters. Shade, in his discussion of the various methods of writing poetry, shows exactly how the process goes, while trying to explain why "method A is agony":

> Is it, perhaps, because
> In penless work there is no pen-poised pause
> And one must use three hands at the same time,
> Having to choose the necessary rhyme,
> Hold the completed line before one's eyes,
> And keep in mind all the preceding tries?
> Or is the process deeper with no desk
> To prop the false and hoist the poetesque?
> For there are those mysterious moments when
> Too weary to delete, I drop my pen;
> I ambulate—and by some mute command
> The right word flutes and perches on my hand.
>
> (*P. F.*, p. 65)

This is a highly poetic passage where the "poetesque" looms bigger than the theme, but where also this apparent discrepancy between form and substance does not really matter since the whole passage *is* about the "poetesque" and how it is achieved. Not only is it a perfect example of performative writing, but it is also a miniature of the whole novel which is about writing as a performance. Here Nabokov got closer to writing a play than in any other of his novels: from beginning to end there is a heated argument between Shade and Kinbote who both want to impose their writings and eliminate each other from the stage of the novel.

In the final analysis, it is of course the novelist who succeeds in imposing his writing: he is the master, and his characters and his narrators are his slaves despite the extensive freedom they seem to enjoy. Only his name and the title will appear on the cover of the book, and even if that title has been borrowed from the great bard, it becomes his property and his invention by right of the few hundred pages he has written. The high quality of his performance erases the reference and the referents, and plunges us into the self-activating and self-referential world of his writing.

It has been claimed for some time now, especially in France, that the novel is moribund. It is true that many new sciences, particularly psychoanalysis, linguistics, and sociology, have dealt the traditional novel an almost fatal blow, by confiscating many of the subjects which were the favorite hunting grounds of the novelists until the beginning of this century; it is true, also, that other forms of art, like the cinema, tend to cater more and more to the public's need for fiction. James had already become aware that, if the novel were to be rescued, it had to be promoted to the rank of a noble art, like poetry, and be granted a charter in the form of a "rhetoric of fiction" which, if well applied, could dissimulate the artful or artificial element, boost the natural and the realistic, and achieve an "intensity of illusion."

Nabokov also is well aware that the novel is a besieged genre, but he refuses to come to its rescue, as we saw in our study of *Ada,* if it means fighting a rearguard battle. The novel was born in an optimistic age when man believed he could one day comprehend and master the world, and therefore grasp the full significance of his daily reality; the sciences which we mentioned earlier have exploded this myth and threatened, therefore, the very existence of the novel. Unless, of course, it takes a new turn, which it did with Nabokov, and capitalizes on this discovery that reality has no objective existence. It will still strive to achieve "intensity of illusion" but not in the sense James understood it—that is, as an illusion of reality—but rather as an illusion of another illusion. . . . Since the world is "a variegated void," as Nabokov put it in "The Leonardo,"[31] the novelist can, if he chooses, play a game of words and worlds which will invent its own rules as it goes, and abolish the void of the blank pages; by and while creating a novel almost completely divorced from our everyday reality, he ignores the void for a moment, and builds up an object whose reality cannot be questioned. The success of his enterprise will depend upon the cleverness or skill of his moves (or performance), it will depend on the quality of his art. However, his art is not an objective, preestablished entity, no more than our so-called reality: it creates itself in the process of inventing or playing the game. Van, like Marcel in *Remembrance of Things Past,* truly becomes an artist by or while creating a work of art: he is as much the cause as the result of his art. That is probably why, in Nabokov's novels, the main theme is art, as both a skill and a performance; since the novel is a self-sufficient, self-sustaining entity, it tells about nothing except its own making—that is, except the author's art.

What, one will object, is the purpose or the relevance of the game? Are we not back to the old business of "art for art's sake"? Certainly not, since art itself has no actual existence outside of the work. Art does not have to be functional or practical, as Nabokov's novels exemplify, but it usually has a strong impact (usually unintended on the part of the artist, and unrecognized at first by the critics) on society's behavior or way of thinking. The novels we have just analyzed, despite being far removed from reality, may eventually teach us new ways to look at it and multiply the angles from which we can view it; consequently, they tell us that our knowledge of "reality" depends largely on the angle from which we look at it. Besides, they enrich our experience and provide us with a wide array of images which will take their place in our imagination and in our memory: therefore, they help us fool time to which we are enslaved in our everyday life. And, of course, they afford us much pleasure, not only by proxy—that is, by allowing us to live other lives—but above all by direct participation as readers in the making or activating of the work of art.

Though we cannot possibly list all the "uses" that can be made of Nabokov's novels (we are aware of only a few), we must finally mention what they teach us about the very nature of poetic writing as a special form of language, completely divorced from our everyday speech. Too often we tend to consider speech as a vehicle, as a means of conveying a piece of information to another person, and therefore we take it for granted that the test of its relevance lies in the piece of information it is meant to convey. In his novels Nabokov no longer uses the writing as a means but as an end: he is not interested in how the writing can express an idea or represent a situation, but in how it can produce an unprecedented *récit* which creates its own relevance. With Nabokov the novel forsakes its traditional mission but assumes a new one, which it shares more and more with drama and poetry.

Jacques Favier

10. SPACE AND SETTOR IN SHORT SCIENCE FICTION

The literature grouped under the label of science fiction confounds all classification and definition. The part of it which is published under the form of the short story appears almost too rich to be enclosed within the boundaries of a set genre. Most critics of the field have noticed that, paradoxically with this form of popular fiction, few formulas have a chance of ever satisfying the least sophisticated of readers for very long.[1] This applies particularly to the "SF" of the last decade: the genre has burst out of its transitory shell like some impatient, nightmarish insect.

Yet the science fiction short stories of the fifties and sixties have some common characteristics, and the most relevant among these define the specificity of "SF-and-fantasy" as opposed to the "Mainstream" (conventional fiction).

It is our intention to try to trace some of the most noticeable among those specific trends, which will concern here two elements of the setting: one is space in the space opera, and the other, less obvious, will appear as a sort of frontier between the setting and the actors, which we will call "settor."

THE SPACE OF SCIENCE FICTION

Preamble. In this exploration of SF space the greatest care will be taken to highlight the variety of its characteristics, not so much in order to isolate themes, a comprehensive catalog of which would fail to unveil the specificity of SF, but rather, through a description of the recurring trends in this imaginary space, to expose the technical means used in the creation of a new mythological literature.

To take an example, the noxious or hostile character of space will not be studied in connection with its role in the illustration of eternal themes, such as man's smallness or helplessness before nature; the inquiry will rather look into the diversity of forms that this hostility is given by SF authors.

Indeed, both ways of exploring the field may seem to have much in common at first sight; but this investigation of the conditions of literary creation seems to lend itself more to a descriptive approach than to an exaggeratedly thematic concern in this literary (or sociological) phenomenon that is SF. This latter approach always tends to channel criticism into an overstructured ideological viewpoint, in which the diversity of individual expression has to disappear, or blend itself with the univocal, universal character of the species's expressed fears and hopes. In other words, the emphasis is usually too heavily laid by most critics upon the "voice" of SF, and not on its "voices," or on how, why, or in what they differ.

Space and Spaces. It is necessary for the reader of the following description to keep in mind that there is not really *one* SF space, but a multitude of spaces, very alike indeed, corresponding to a multitude of writers, and even narratives; it would be absurd, then, to try to work out an "average space" in order to find some impossible common denominator, absurd to try to elaborate anything but a typology, whose value would lie more in the points of divergence than in those of convergence.

Space has ceased to be the exclusive field of the SF of space opera, considering that space has been conquered as far as the moon's orbit, and probed further with unmanned machines. Indeed, it is essential not to confuse SF stories with narratives having for a setting the space explored by "likely" astronauts: SF contains an extra element of the "unattainable" (always linked to the limitations of science and techniques) which distinguishes it from any other popular literature of adventure of a "scientific" inspiration. In SF science is used by literature and imagination. In "likely" stories the literary is subordinated to scientific information.

Consequently, contemporary SF space usually starts from the moon. However, when set between the earth and the moon, it occupies a high position in the hierarchy of major interests in the narrative *only* when it shows abnormal characteristics (new phenomena, mysterious properties). Otherwise, the story is relegated into the non-SF category mentioned above.

In most of the stories of the corpus (1950–70), space is principally considered as the high seas of the sky, the infinitely empty and infinitely rich milieu where human and alien ships travel between the stations, asteroids, or planets. It is surprising how unanimous and coherent SF creators are in their descriptions of interstellar space. The accepted data, as well as the hypotheses they make, have a broad common basis. But where the relationship between man, the traveler, and space is concerned, their points of view diverge, for science is more reticent, because of lack of experience.

Still, all respect the image that "space navigation" has imposed on the mind and vocabulary: space is (nearly always) a limitless ocean, the rockets are ships, the planets are islands or continents. The sea of the cosmos is not devoid of incidents (reefs, storms, pirates), and many an island is terra incognita, inhabited by strange natives with whom communication is a basic problem. The great majority of space opera plots use this transposed marine world as a background. The immediate problems related to survival or conquest constitute the mainspring for the functions of entertainment and intellectual stimulation.[2]

The literary treatment of space participates in the creation of the myth of space as the latest frontier, a mysterious domain, with extremely powerful forces of attraction and repulsion converging on man.

Space and the Traveler's Soma. The writers' imagination is relatively cramped by the data from real American and Soviet space trips. The phenomena brought about by acceleration, deceleration, zero gravity, and other classical contingencies are already sufficiently well known to constitute for SF creators nothing more than an opportunity to invent original gadgetry. Usually they prefer to delve into more purely fictional subjects like hyperspace (permitting speeds faster than light), or less often the growth of mass toward "absolute mass" when getting close to a star (cf. "To the Dark Star" by R. Silverberg). Or else the stories deal with the reactions of human (or alien) organisms to space cold (cf. "Jay Score" by E. F. Russell), or space heat (cf. "The Perihelion Man" by Christopher Priest).

This medium, whose effects on man (even purely physiological) are still mostly uncharted, already constitutes, for this very reason, a highly specific setting, inasmuch as its mystery stimulates the wildest speculations. Apparently equivalent settings in mainstream fiction rarely leave any comparable freedom to the imagination: the underwater world, the closed-in worlds of caves, or the immense voids of deserts, the teeming jungles, the mountaintops or frozen poles are all hostile, unfamiliar places for man, but their dimensions, mysteriousness, and possibilities compare weakly with space.

The mark left by space on the physical person of the traveler is seldom as beneficial as T. L. Thomas seems to think in "The Far Look": all the cosmonauts on their return from the moon seem to radiate warmth, wisdom, and beauty; their faces are particularly fascinating and handsome:

> And the eyes were different. A network of deep tiny creases laced out from the corners of each eye. The crinkled appearance of the eyes made each man appear older than he actually was. And there was a look in those eyes of things seen from deep inside. It was a far look, a compelling look, a powerful look set in the eyes of normal men. (p. 212)

In fact, man's contact with space is usually harmful for the traveler. The choice of terms most frequently used in the description of interstellar space is revealing in this respect: "evil," "menacing," "lurking," etc. Pitilessly hostile, space annihilates man when he is deprived of the matrix-like protection of the spaceship.[3]

Often the simple fact of leaving his mother planet traumatizes man like a second birth. On his return from Mars the first explorer of that planet realizes that he has undergone a strange transformation: his body still lives in our time sphere, but his brain is 3.30077 minutes in advance of our time ("Man in His Time" by Brian Aldiss).

The tragedy of man forsaken in space has been often presented by space opera short stories, for obvious dramatic reasons, but also because here the hostility of the world toward man appears with its greatest intensity.[4] In a very rich story by Ray Bradbury, "Kaleidoscope," a spaceship explodes between the earth and the moon, after part of the crew have already put on their spacesuits; the bodies of the dead and survivors have been scattered in all directions of space, with the debris of the rocket; their helmet radios, when working, permit a last conversation to take place between the few doomed men; as the title indicates, the story presents us with a palette of human reactions, from stark madness to serenity, as the spacemen find themselves suddenly confronted with death, whether near or remote, swift or slow, but horribly diversified: instant death in the explosion, or soon after, fall on the surface of the moon, endless drift toward the stars, death by asphyxia, through perforation of the suit or lack of air supply, burning and disintegration in the stratosphere, etc.

> It was a second later that he discovered his right foot was cut sheer away. It almost made him laugh. The air was gone from his suit again. He bent, and there was blood, and the meteor had taken flesh and suit away to the ankle. Oh, death in space was most humorous. It cut you away, piece by piece, like a black and invisible butcher. (p. 25)

But the danger most often selected for the purposes of dramatization is the myth of space pollution, the dread of contamination by an unknown organism, the origins of which can be multiple, but whose effects are almost always horrible: mutations, mutilations (cf. "The Hands" by John Baxter), cachexias of all kinds, and, less spectacular but worse still, mental disorders.

Innumerable germs or spores haunt interstellar space, it seems; the void teems with a microscopic fauna; and although the lesson is often that man is his own worst enemy, and that he can find the remedy to his troubles within himself (both theses are often finely developed), those epidemics, those aggressions from alien microbes, have generally no other aim than to disquiet and horrify, to enhance a suspense which would otherwise lack vigor.

It is to be noted that the device of the contamination of human or alien organisms traveling in space is one (latterday) aspect of the larger device of invasion: the idea here is to create the tense atmosphere proper to the "problem story." Very often the lives of the whole crew of a ship, of a whole planetary colony, of the whole earth, possibly of the whole galactic empire, have to be threatened with destruction by this contamination, before sufficient interest is generated for the least sophisticated readers . . .

Certain writers, confronted with the seriousness of the perils they have created, are forced to destroy the germ-bearing ship or planet in heroic suicides or opportune accidents. Usually the point is to preserve established values, the status quo of the human condition, with its joys and sorrows, for no one knows whether there is more to be gained than lost by a disruption of the existing ecological balance. Generative of reactionary clichés, this protectionist attitude as a solution to the problems of coexistence between living species is cleverly presented by some authors in space opera narratives. A prime example is Isaac Asimov's "Misbegotten Missionary": in this space colony where all beings, united by telepathy, merge into one immense personality, order reigns; "terran" visitors encounter it, and flee from this society where there is no place for the individual. One little alien, sent by the common brain to bring the word of love and union to humanity, manages to infiltrate the ship; in order to escape notice, the stowaway, a protean amoeboid, disguises itself as an electric wire in the circuit of one of the outer doors; alas! it perishes, carbonized, at the very moment when the door opens after landing on earth. Individualism triumphs, but so do anarchy, war, and want. Other authors take the opposite view of things with a militant optimism often coupled with naivety.

Space and the Traveler's Genes. The American Ray Bradbury (in "The Rocket Man," for instance) and the British John Wyndham (in "Mars, A. D. 2094") have repeatedly insisted on the century-old myth according to which certain beings are born with space "in their blood," just as certain seamen or aviators have the sea or the sky in their blood. It is questionable whether one can be a pioneer or an adventurer in the steps of one's father (as E. R. Burroughs would have it, in his novelette "Pirate Blood," for instance), but it is a fairly common opinion that the conquest of space must be seen as a projection of the old frontier dream. The space of SF is opened to all known ethnic groups (in theory) . . . and to a good number of imaginary races, from the "almost human" humanoid to the alien of so alien a nature that the (not unfriendly) contact between representatives of both species (human and alien) is very painful and potentially damaging to their mental and physical healths (as in "Stranger Station" by Damon Knight).

SF space has its part to play in the mutations and/or the evolution of the human race, in gradually producing generations which are better suited to the specific environments where they are forced to live. The rhythm of these transformations accelerates with special difficulties encountered during exceptional trips in space (or time—with telepathic mutants particularly).[5] Many writers (cf. S. Delany's ("Aye, and Gomorrah") even imagine the birth of a new human subspecies, as it were; these beings, who are all professional spacemen, have been created androgenic and sterile, so as better to resist space radiations which destroy the gonads.

Space and the Traveler's Psyche. The influence of space upon the psyche and the behavior of the traveler varies a lot but is never negligible. Space fascinates. It does so by its beauty most often: the harmony and majesty of space have inspired some of the most lyrical descriptions in SF. It also fascinates by its immensity, the impression of freedom it gives the beholder. The spaceman's choice of directions to take is almost unlimited. For man it is an opportunity of pure escape comparable to the intoxication of speed:

> All the gaps and spaces. And that's how I got to thinking about the stars. I thought how I'd like to be in a rocket ship in space, in nothing, nothing, going on into nothing, with just a thin something, a thin eggshell of metal holding me, going on away from all the somethings with gaps in them that couldn't prove themselves. I knew then that the only happiness for me was in space.

The story from which this passage is taken, Ray Bradbury's "No Particular Night or Morning" (p. 111), insists also on another aspect of the exhilarating contact with space: space permits a liberation from the constraints of our human dimensions; the difficulty the spaceman has to judge in terms of relative size generates a feeling of wonder which, when too strong, can cause a very nauseating anxiety, or another kind of fascination, that of horror.

The horror of the spatial void is often shown as a conflict of attracting and repelling forces which climaxes in hysteria. Bradbury's leitmotif in his treatment of man in space, the "child afraid of the dark," is not only a device but the subject itself of "The Wilderness." A young woman feels the upsurge of an overwhelming panic at the thought of taking the rocket for Mars where her husband works. This agoraphobia originates in a traumatic experience as a child: she fell down a dark staircase into a cellar.

Horror of space can be represented, in certain borderline cases, as a psycho-pathological trance. In "No Particular Night or Morning" Bradbury invents another disastrous influence of space upon the human psyche: a hypertrophied sense of one's ego as opposed to the emptiness of space, which constitutes a devastating, contagious space disease. The patient systematically questions the reality of his fellow travelers and their environment:

"There isn't any season here; winter and summer are gone. So is spring, and autumn. It isn't any particular night or morning; it's space and space. The only thing right now is you and me and this rocket ship. And the only thing I'm positive of is me. That's all of it." (p. 107)

Such a fascination is so destructive that it must be avoided at all costs. On a long journey, the traveler retires within himself; the crew and passengers, confined to restricted quarters in their section of the spaceship, contract strange psychoses, going sometimes as far as suicidal dementia:

Hitchcock was alone. He climbed into a space suit. He opened an air-lock. Then he walked out into space—alone. (p. 113)

The doomed man talks to himself:

"No more spaceship now. Never was any. No people. . . . No hands. I haven't any hands any more. No feet. Never had any. No face. No head. Nothing. Only space. Only space. Only the gap." (p. 114)

Bradbury of course is not the only SF writer to have dealt at length with the subject of space madness. P. F. Woods in "The Countenance" uses it as the mainspring of his plot, without giving any more precise information on its origin. On board an intergalactic liner one passenger, of a more curious frame of mind than the others, is puzzled by the complete lack of portholes in the hull of the ship; exploring a maze of corridors, he finds his way into a small watchtower at the end of a secret passage; his mind recoils with fear as he looks in the direction of our galaxy, but when he turns the other way . . .

He saw at last what had so long been the subject of his search: limitless emptiness. As he gazed, all his attention was swept into the vacuum of the awful view. From that moment, he was doomed. His whole being was drawn into the empty vastness by forced attention raised to the nth degree. The first stage was catatonia; even that was brief. His personality was being sucked into galactic space. Within a minute, his body died. (p. 96)

Such dramatization of man's contact with space gives free rein to the elaboration of the myth, which itself feeds back further fantasy. This myth is reinforced with connotations belonging to the Judeo-Christian code of reference: "The face of God is like unto a countenance vast and terrible" (p. 97). The mystery giving its strength to the myth is deepened further by the failure of the ship's captain to give any satisfactory scientific explanation:

> "Space does it," he said. "There's too much of it out there. It would swallow us all, swallow any number, without making any difference. It's the worst possibly way to die." He turned away. His voice dropped. "But you know, I don't think it's worth dying any other way." (p. 99)

Raised to the level of an aesthetic, even ethic necessity, the myth is thus made extremely powerful.

But space, whether "animated" (in "The Wilderness" the metaphor was "a black panther"), personalized ("It would swallow us all"), even almost deified ("the face of God"), space is not the only guilty party: man makes mistakes in his fight against the limitless foe. The promoters of space technology are prepared to run risks, especially since they would not be the first victims in case of accident. In "The Wreck of the Ship John B," Frank M. Robinson stresses one danger of life on board a spaceship which, when dramatized, becomes a space disease: excessive automatization. Idle, freed of demanding responsibilities, the spaceman is forced back upon himself, lets himself be lulled into indifference by routine:

> The crew had faded into long-voyage apathy, remote to one another, remote even to themselves. The ship was now a jungle of shadow screens preserving Privacy. Crew members went out of their way to avoid one another, and when they did meet, it was with hostile noncuriosity. (p. 116)

Some of the crew end up by losing their sanity and threaten to leave the ship. The captain must use force with some, and persuasion with others. The contrast between the cramped quarters of the ship and the immensity of space constitutes a constant negation of the spacemen's human physical and psychic dimensions. But the author goes one step further than Bradbury in the use of this dramatic device: life in the spatial setting of a rocket gives birth to dehumanizing situations that can hardly be transposed into mainstream fiction: one can think of other "craft" (plane, ship, submarine, railway carriage, truck, lift) or of a caravan in the desert, an autonomous expedition to a remote land, or of other enclosed places (prison cell, island, etc.), but isolation on one hand, character behavior on the other, would still belong to our standard earthly scale, with its well-known physical and psychological laws. These do not apply in the alien environment that is space. At the level of Robinson's story life in the traveling spaceship is to be learnt the way town planning has been learnt, through trial and error, toward the creation of the adequate environment:

"We didn't need one another—and the horrible thing was that it had all been planned that way. The Colonization Board was afraid we might kill one another during the long voyage, so they provided shadow screens, taught us to respect privacy above all, and arranged routine so we could avoid one another. And no weapons of course. Which made us even more helpless in the face of the unknown. And like the city dwellers, the final result was loss of identity. We became remote from one another, from ourselves, from our own feelings." (p. 132)

The message is clear, and so is the technique for its deliverance: the process begins by restating a problem which society has not been able to solve by intelligent town planning, and had to learn to live with as best it could; then the author heightens our awareness of the problem by transferring it into a microcosm, where it takes on a highly dramatic dimension; in the last stage, the only one which is specific of SF, the problem finds its solution (or rather the question finds its answer) thanks to the originality of the setting itself. Everything happens as if the problems of the earth found their solutions when transposed into the developing-bath of a spatial environment.

Among other space diseases of a psychic nature that threaten men, one must note the highly recurrent, pathological hypertrophy of certain instincts, particularly those of reproduction and the preservation of the species; we have seen that the individual is often to be found in predicaments the mainstream equivalent of which is difficult to imagine. Life in a restricted environment, the progressive loss of "terran" ways, of the memory of the earth, even, in voyages that can last over several generations, can cause peculiar situations; these have sometimes been provided for before the start of the journey, as we have seen with J. Merril's "Survival Ship," where the crew is almost entirely feminine, a few stallions being allotted in rotation. But when things go wrong, pathological behaviors permit the writer to build particularly convincing conflicts between instinct and intelligence. In "Period of Gestation" by Thorn Keyes, a ship has been isolated from the rest of mankind during seven years, on some scientific mission; one of the (entirely male) crew fancies himself pregnant. One by one the other spacemen come to believe in this gestation, in spite of their efforts to ward off insanity. After nine months, as the impatiently expected baby does not show up, the crew operate a ghastly Caesarean on the supposed parturient. In "Survival" by the British writer John Wyndham, a frail pregnant woman on board a marooned spaceship steals a gun and kills the rest of the passengers and the whole crew, in order to feed her offspring.

Another recurring motif in the treatment of the man/space intercourse is what has been called a "deep dissociation" from whatever concerns our planet. It is a milder but seemingly inevitable form of the space neuroses described above. Accustomed to interplanetary, interstellar, or intergalactic trips, the spaceman becomes an outsider, a mythical character, with fast and safe reflexes, superhuman self-control, and a distant look in his eyes. The estrangement which becomes the lot of the spaceman does not originate in the perilous mysteries of space any more, but rather in the attitude of his fellow men toward him, down on earth. His romantic prestige is enhanced by an inner conflict: he is torn, in the same way of course as the seaman, between the two worlds to which he belongs—the earth and the cosmos. In "The Rocket Man" Bradbury presents the character of an inexperienced captain who has become a sort of demigod for his younger son. The spaceman has reached the retiring age of forty, and finds himself a prisoner of his own myth: he cannot spend the last years of his life in a peaceful but prosaic retirement with his body in a suburban back garden and his mind among the stars; he leaves for a last trip and meets his end as the myth demanded: his ship sinks into the sun.

Yet this aloofness from earthly matters is, with many writers, but a transitory phenomenon that is felt only during the first contact with space:

"Everyone has a little touch of space the first time out. I've had it. Yet get wildly philosophical, then frightened. You break into a sweat, then you doubt your parentage, you don't believe in Earth, you get drunk, wake up with a hangover, and that's it." ("No Particular Night or Morning," p. 109)

Other writers, such as Mack Reynolds in "Earthlings, Go Home," do not even have such a "dedramatizing" attitude, for their spacemen remain impervious to the void:

"So, okay, in a spaceship you have butterflies in the tummy during count-down and blast-off, and then you sit around doing nothing and with nothing to see except space, of which there is a lot, until you get to your destination. So it's boring." (p. 279)

But usually, without necessarily bringing about the states of crisis depicted above, the contact with space does not leave the spaceman as indifferent as M. Reynolds would have it. There is no question of total inurement. Those stories which would show a human character totally indifferent to space would make a gross misjudgment: the reader himself demands that the myth of this setting be protected, that its mystery remain intact; because, here again, it is inseparable from the common notion of the infiniteness of space. This setting transcends man; the former will never let itself be entirely known, understood, subdued by the latter. In a majority of space opera short stories, a passage such as the following one comes up inevitably. It is representative of the modus vivendi established between fictional cosmonaut and cosmos:

As he watched the outer door of the entry port closing ponderously in the silence of airless space behind him, he felt the usual inner coldness that came over him at times like this. He had a mild but very definite phobia about space, with its myriads of unchanging stars. He knew what caused it—several psychiatrists had told him it was nothing to worry about, but he could not quite accept their unconcern. He knew he was a very lonely individual, underneath it all; and subconsciously he guessed he equated space with the final extinction in which he expected one day to disappear and be forgotten forever. He could not really believe it was possible for someone like him to make a dent in such a universe.

And yet, in this passage from "Hilifter" by Gordon Dickson (p. 26), we have here one of those SF James Bonds, a hero whose prestige ranks somewhere between the mere detective and the demigod (superman and its by-products), a hero endowed with almost superhuman gifts, aptitudes, and attributes. Thus, the transcendental character of space is even further enhanced.

Other Space Incidents. Besides the dangers or fascinations with which space travel is fraught, the imagination of SF writers makes use of a constantly renewed repertoire of devices to satisfy the reader's inexhaustible "curiosity." One of these is the artifact of human construction (space stations in orbit, wrecks and derelict ships of all sorts); another is the strange natural phenomenon, such as those space barnacles in "Barnacle Bull" by Winston P. Sanders: they cling in a thick coating, putting the controls out of order, but miraculously protecting the ship from a cloud of meteorites which would have destroyed it otherwise.

In space opera stories can be found all the surprises of "hyperspace," such as "space-warps." Space, too, is one of the settings for the encounters with alien civilizations, which it would take another article to examine. Nothing is apparently easier than to people the interstellar void with fantasies. Nevertheless, a balance has been found in recent years between relevant space objects and redundant ones, between space such as the present state of scientific knowledge reasonably allows the writer to imagine it, and space such as prewar SF dreamt it. Few monstrous cephalopods, few gigantic, hairy arachnidae still cavort in the ether of contemporary space opera. With sophistication the field has acquired sobriety, and demoted its dragons to the realm of heroic fantasy. SF space purified itself as it became less populated.

But its pollution level, nevertheless, is still high: wrecks, armaments, artificial satellites, spies and mechanical sentries left over by aliens, or man himself (as with Fred Saberhagen's "berserkers"). Among recurring preoccupations in stories presenting such objects, one must note a desire of the authors to stimulate wonder and even bewilderment in the reader's mind, by constant reference to immense periods and astronomical distances. This insistence must be ranked with the techniques which prompt a comparison between the inhuman (limitless space and time) and the human (actors, if human, narrator-author, reader). A good instance of this technique appears in "Night Watch" by James Inglis. The only actor in the story is a sort of highly sophisticated robot probe, unmanned, with a virtually eternal lifespan; its role is to wander from star to star, from galaxy to galaxy, in search of other forms of life. Its systematic quest enables it to compile extremely detailed information about the worlds it passes, stocking it in its quasi-illimited memory blocks. It is not alone in its duty; every billion years or so it comes across one of its innumerable colleagues, bent on the same task; they too were launched by technically advanced societies, desirous of contact with hypothetic, alien counterparts. An exchange of information takes place between them, and they part, each enriched with the other's mass of knowledge. But this immense aim recedes as the limits of the universe recede, that is to infinity. Who then can ever use the enormous sum of science acquired by the "terran" probe, when the human species, after

a few thousand years, becomes extinct? Symbols of the absurdity that is characteristic of a certain trustful attitude toward science, the robots carry on their
futile, inane quest.

Conclusion. The space of space opera, with its rarely neutral role, its often disquieting or horrific, always inhuman, character, is, among other SF settings, richest
in elements that enable a dramatic treatment of the plot. In opposition to the
mother planet or the spaceship, whose role is on the whole that of security, the
void brings much to the function of tension in the narrative, inasmuch as space
remains the Great Unknown. It has for man all the negative characteristics (aggressivity, inexorability), and all the positive ones (novelty, mystery) of an "animated setting" or "settor," in the sense we will give to the phrase further on. In
this sense also, space is one of the most specific of SF settings.

ANIMATED SETTINGS

The Settor. Science fiction, whose settings are, because of their nature and dimensions, usually less rigid than those of mainstream fiction, presents us with many
stories in which elements of the traditional setting have been promoted to the rank
of actors, thus modifying the course of the plot and interfering with the relationship between the actors proper.

The elements chosen by the writer to compose the setting of his short story can
thus combine and organize themselves so as to shape a distinct "entity," endowed
with a role similar to that of a traditional actor—that is, a character, or a group of
characters playing the same part.

We have chosen to call "settors" those ambiguous elements, combinations of
settings and actors.

Pseudosettors. The distinction between pseudosettors and real settors is rendered
necessary by the great number of stories in which a turn of the plot introduces an
apparently animate setting in the early stages of the tale; in these stories, usually,
more information is delivered in the course of the action, leading us (and the other
actors) to consider that this setting is not really animate. By "animate" we mean
(rather restrictedly): endowed, either naturally, or artificially (through possession,
in the manner of demons, for instance) with faculties similar or comparable to
those possessed by human beings (intelligence, sensitivity, will power, purpose);
an inanimate object then only becomes animate insofar as it reveals a more or less
anthropomorphic psychology. Actually, the reader of SF does not need any other
indication to make up his mind about this.

Among those pseudosettors which pretend to be real during part of the plot
(or through the whole plot, if the story is based upon a hesitation indicative of pure
fantasy),[6] the planet in "Getaway from Getawehi" by Colin Kapp could be given
as a good example. We have here a globe with a very puzzling behavior: along with
other inexplicable phenomena it shows a variable gravity pull in a direction which
does not remain perpendicular to the ground, but keeps rocking in a manner so

unpredictable that the explorers come to consider the planet as a gigantic, living organism (not an uncommon motif in space opera, such as in the classic "Meatball" by James White). The phenomenon is elucidated, near the end of the story, by the Unorthodox Engineers, a highly intuitive brain trust of specialists in technical feats and cosmic puzzles, the Sherlock Holmeses of the future: in the core of the globe nuclei of very dense matter revolve, as so many interior satellites, whose complex pulls cause the planet's center of gravity to wander in a way which defies human calculation, but which a good computer can cope with.

The parallel with the Holmes–Conan Doyle method is not gratuitous: the classic formula used in many mystery stories is applied freely to SF plots. As everyone knows, it consists in starting from some inexplicable fact (or one which can be accounted for only by a belief in the supernatural); then, with the use of deduction and the exploration of all possibilities ("however improbable"), discovering the positive, "natural" solution. Frequently found in the SF of the fifties and sixties, rather outdated in recent SF of the traditional vein, this formula often uses the pseudosettor, which belongs to the "positive" world, whereas the genuine settor belongs to the supernatural.

At the border between real and pseudosettors can be found a number of settings of an ambiguous, unexplained nature (often thus willed by the authors), which give a fantastic turn (in Todorov's sense) to the stories in which they appear. Some critics have blamed Ray Bradbury for using this device a little too often. In "The Veldt" by that author we find such a settor: pseudo or real, we shall never know. In an affluent world of the near future, two children have been given a wonderful toy by their parents: a room whose blank walls disappear at will, revealing a programmed, three-dimensional illusive environment of striking fidelity; the children's favorite program is the hostile South African bush. The explanation of the mechanism is (perforce) very evasive:

> "Crystal walls, that's all they are. Oh, they look real, I must admit—Africa in your parlor—but it's all dimensional superractionary, supersensitive color film and mental tape film behind glass screens. It's all odorophonics and sonics...."
> (p. 9)

This mechanism, or robot, was conceived originally to obey the orders given mentally by the imaginative children. It is just a sophisticated toy. But when a conflict arises between children and parents, the setting reflects the hostility and aggressiveness of the children, a fact the family psychiatrist realizes:

> "You've let this room and this house replace you and your wife in your children's affections. This room is their father and mother, far more important in their lives than their real parents. And now you come along and want to shut it off. No wonder there's hatred here. You can feel it coming out of the sky. Feel that sun!" (p. 16)

We have here already an implicit autonomy of the setting, an ability to choose its side, which turns the machine into something much superior to a mere robot;

it seems to have chosen the children's side of its own free will. To what extent is this choice guided, what kind of freedom does this robot enjoy? Such points have not been elucidated by Bradbury. On one hand, since the children are only half-conscious of the violence of their hatred, the machine can be considered as "animated" only by the subconscious part of the children's minds; in a complex way indeed, but one still conceivable in a "positive" light, with the help of a great number of electronic memory cells. On the other hand, it is tempting to believe in the presence of another force, alien to the actors: this power, unknown, threatening, pervades so many stories of promethean robots in revolt against their creator, a power that transcends their dependent, mechanical nature; a demonic (or less often, godly) power, likely to cause the birth not only of the instinct of revolt, but of the entire psychological setup specific of animate beings.

Whichever interpretation is given to this settor, the phenomenon which accounts for the destruction of the parents by the setting/settor (the lions from the veldt devour them, while the children have their tea in truly Freudian fashion) remains inexplicable and unexplained. The setting has indeed outgrown its own nature, as the latter has been defined at the beginning of the story: a mere glass case, whose elements (the lions) have no reality of their own (and consequently should by no means erupt from the screen into the parents' "reality"; H. B. Breitsek's movie adaptation in 1969 shows the same flaw).

Indeed, it seems to be difficult to "animate" a setting without making, at the same time, the choice of most animated elements extremely delicate. The greatest circumspection in the selection of those elements is imperative, if the writer does not want either to clog his narrative with uneasy rational justifications, or disappoint his reader with the arbitrariness of the purely wonderful.

Real Settors. In the first stage the settor is felt by the other actors and the reader (either through them or directly) as an entity having reached a grade superior to that to which it belongs in common life: a house that thinks, an automobile that starts talking. This perception (entirely subjective, then), is still free from any attempt at rationalization, indeed; but the important point here is that the other actors apprehend the settor as an element of the same natural order as themselves, or of a neighboring order. This perception of a sudden, radical change in the way of their world defines the fantastic aspect of real settors in SF: there is indeed a climactic, usually dramatic hesitation, uncertainty, on the part of the actors *and* reader confronted with individual perceptions that no habit has rendered acceptable.

In later stages, when the other actors pass from the plain, subjective level of perception to that of an attempt at reasoning out the phenomenon where the settor is concerned, then (and no sooner) it is possible to consider the "objectified" settor as specific of SF. (In the wonderful tale, or folktale, the surprise may last, but no attempt at finding the logical or even magical reasons and processes for the creation of the settor is ever made. The animated setting remains disconnected from any organized, explanatory cosmology.)

In the chronology of the narrative, then, the settor belongs to fantasy at first, then becomes specific of SF, not through any idiosyncratic character but merely through the treatment it is given in relation to the other actors' minds (be they human or alien).

A further proof of the specificity of the settor can spring from the comparison of a SF short story where a settor appears, with a corresponding mainstream story. *Bucolic* by Van Vogt, for example, presents us with a complete reversion of the parts played by the settor and the other actors; the human beings who visit this faraway, apparently uninhabited planet are only secondary characters, for the hero here is a classical element of the planetary setting, usually considered as totally inanimate: a primeval forest, covering the whole surface of the globe. Gifted (somehow) with a specific form of intelligence, able to create a high-level coordination between its innumerable components (the trees), conscious of its growth, extension, and might, this forest thinks in its own terms, builds logical processes, *plans;* among other feats, it manages to rout and expel all invaders, including technologically superior earthmen. It seems difficult to find any satisfactory equivalent of this SF device: to keep the reader interested, the story of the growth of a conventional forest, or even of a tree, must deviate from the form of fiction, and shift toward natural history for children, the inspired bucolic poem, or the ponderous moral allegory. With Van Vogt's narrative, the political fable develops harmoniously and naturally, with the help of this device of the intelligent settor.

The elements of the setting which are liable to turn into settors can have two origins. Either they belong to the traditional settings of mainstream fiction, whose nature is not usually oriented toward animation: trees, houses, books, water, or even electric power. These are more or less familiar "objects." (It is to be noted that in recent years SF has undergone a change and sophistication, one aspect of which is precisely the search for original, convincing settor material, with the result that, because of competition, this material has become more and more unexpected.) Or else the material support of the settor is an artifact, or more precisely, a mechanism designed to perform certain services, and whose activities resemble those of animate and intelligent beings; to this extent, the material support is already considered almost as a full-fledged actor: machines, computers, all sorts of robots theoretically bound by Isaac Asimov's iron Laws of Robotics. The table at the end of the present article lists a number of settors whose material supports have various origins; the "animating spirits" which combine with these objects have also various origins, mainly human and alien.

In fact, this phenomenon of "animation" is no more than another rational "lifejacket," or security, provided by the author, often tongue-in-cheek. Few explanations are given, for very obvious reasons. Actually, pseudoscientific explanations are not any more convincing for a twentieth-century reader than those presented by theologians of earlier times to account for witchcraft and other demonic possessions.

Fluid Settors. Their nature is that of more or less familiar objects suddenly considered as organized and animate entities. The choice of the supporting material for these settors depends on two main factors. The first is the impact, the degree of surprise felt by the reader. Folktales had trees, toys, or household objects became animate all of a sudden. SF must find something more subtle.[7] Besides, the more the animated object belongs to the familiar environment of the reader, the more this reader feels concerned by the phenomenon; reason alone helps overcome the instinctive fear which the uneasy reader feels and perversely seeks; hence the primitive delight and thrill of the fearsome tale, as H. P. Lovecraft noted it.[8] The second factor is the symbolic potential of the animated object, which must help the author in the exposition and illustration of his thesis. Whether the story is written with pure entertainment in view, or with a desire to stimulate serious reflection, the first or the second of these factors is privileged.

The first factor has certainly been foremost in the mind of a number of SF writers whose endeavors rely mostly on the originality of their settors. One of the most amazing and representative stories of this type is "Mr. Waterman" by Peter Redgrove. It takes the form of a confession in the psychiatrist's cabinet, and the patient's problem concerns his wife's affair with—the garden pond. The latter is immediately presented to the psychiatrist as an element of the neuropath's familiar setting, endowed with rather peculiar powers:

> "We never really liked that pond in the garden. At times it was choked with a sort of weed, which, if you pulled one thread, gleefully unravelled until you had an empty basin before you and the whole of the pond in a soaking heap at your side. Then at other times it was as clear as gin, and lay in the grass staring upwards. If you came anywhere near, the gaze shifted sideways, and it was you that was being stared at, not the empty sky. If you were so bold as to come right up to the edge, swaggering and talking loudly to show you were not afraid, it presented you with so perfect a reflection that you stayed there spellbound and nearly missed dinner getting to know yourself. It had hypnotic powers." (p. 47)

The pond's aggressivity is tinged with humor (a highly superior, though not specifically human, characteristic). It plays practical jokes on its owner; an important point is that it is capable of deliberate motion: this autonomy suggests an amoeboid protoplasm, but this is not the case, or at least not explicitly, for then the settor would belong to the category of pure aliens, come under this form from another world. The author is careful to avoid such a facile presentation: "'I dipped a finger into the pond and tasted it: it was brackish'" (p. 48). The hypothesis of a convincing, run-of-the-mill alien must be dropped:

> "It had accidentally included a goldfish in its body, and when the goggling dolt swam up the neck into the crystal-clear head, it dipped its hand in and fumbled about with many ripples and grimaces, plucked it out, and offered the fish to my wife. She was about to prepare dinner, but I explained quickly that goldfish had a bitter taste, and he put it back where he had picked it." (p. 49)

Note the relevant passage from "it" (the pond) to "he" (Mr. Waterman). The absence of wonder at, or questioning of, these unnatural phenomena by the narrator should not surprise us: the confession takes place in the psychiatrist's cabinet, and we take it for granted that the patient is mentally deranged. As the story progresses, the settor passes from a child's behavior to an adult's attitude. And after playing with his shape in a highly creative manner (he has discovered art), he culminates in his evolution by borrowing from man not only his appearance and his intelligence, but also his basic instincts:

"I dread the time (for it will come) when I shall arrive home unexpectedly early, and hear a sudden scuffle away in the waste pipes, and find my wife ('Just out of the shower, dear') with that moist look in her eyes, drying her hair; and then to hear him swaggering in from the garden drains, talking loudly about his day's excursion, as if nothing at all had been going on." (p. 49)

In the ultimate stage, his human-like psyche is complete, with its perversions and neuroses. The final twist of the short story is finely achieved: the psychiatrist shows his client out with a few encouraging words and says:

"The next patient, nurse. Ah, Mr. Waterman. Sit down, please. Does the gas fire trouble you? No? Well, now, we're quite private in here. You can tell me your troubles. A married, air-breathing woman, I think you said . . ." (p. 50)

From man's powers to man's weaknesses, the settor has acquired everything. Traditional fantasy has also often succeeded in giving a personality or a voice to oceans, lakes, rivers or springs; but the symbolic function is dominant, sometimes stifling, and the animating imagination is much more timid than in SF. It seems pointless to turn back to the problems of appurtenance to one or the other genre, or to argue that "Mr. Waterman" does not belong to SF but wholly to another genre (fantasy or the folktale). It is more interesting to note that the irreplaceable character of this settor excludes this story from the mainstream; and that it was published in an anthology of SF short stories (spontaneous, if intuitive, judgment by the editor); besides, this choice can be justified by the persistence, throughout the whole story, of a preoccupation with coherence, paralogics, and pseudoscience; everything appears perfectly coherent once the first step has been taken (and not questionable at any moment, as is the case with nonsense fiction). Actually, this step is hardly as big as one might think, nor as bewildering as certain leaps or plunges of the traditional wonderful tale: the abrupt metamorphosis of a pumpkin into a carriage hardly raises an eyebrow, for the magic of the fairytale need not justify its own existence. Mr. Waterman's transformations are more easily rationalized. because the fluidity of water, and the memory the reader has of having observed amoebae under the microscope (even if Mr. Waterman is not amoeboid), are part of our common experience.

In "High Eight" by David Stringer another natural element serves as a material support for the settor: electric power, which flows in the wires and transformers of a power station. The animating entity might very well be of extraterrestrial origin, but the narrator does not elucidate this point, and says nothing about the shape this alien might have had in its original environment, that is, if it had any shape at all.

Although the concept of materialized electricity, endorsed by the vernacular, springs from a rather puerile imagination and impairs the credibility of the settor, at least in this story it highlights the dramatic effect through the growth and behavior of the electrical being, which soon represents a lethal threat to the other actors. The electrical entity lives and goes wherever electricity can flow, particularly in household circuitry, water pipes, etc. It even has hypnotic powers similar to those displayed by Mr. Waterman. But whereas the latter is simply bent upon a peaceful imitation of man, the electrical settor uses its powers to subdue and then destroy man with the utmost violence. The aim behind the first murders (by a combination of hypnosis and electrocution) is fundamentally to exert a sort of blackmail which will enable it to get more energy from the engineers in charge of the power plant. This is the first stage, that of the animal struggling for its survival; then, with the almost limitless powers soon acquired, the settor destroys human beings systematically, while mankind remains unaware of the nature of the peril almost to the end. At this second stage the gratuitousness of its destructive frenzy gives to the fable its moral dimension, with the exposition of a pathology proper to our species.

Indeed, the intention of the author to create a symbol is clear both in Redgrove's story and in Stringer's. These settors are but a distanciated, alienated image of man himself, the psychopathic destructor, the disgraceful summit of of evolution. And yet in both stories the effect is more important than the meaning in the writer's eye; the possibilities opened by the choice of such settors are exploited diversely, with a good measure of humor by Redgrove, and horror by Stringer; but these antithetic treatments constitute an end in themselves—if not the only one, at least the major one. The vigor of these stories does not spring so much from the surprise elements (which generate terror here, humor there) as from their great fertility in potential new combinations, a fertility due to the choice of the settors.

It is not irrelevant to compare a story by Fritz Leiber, "The Man Who Made Friends with Electricity," to Stringer's tale. Electric power is presented here as a being which communicates with one of the actors (a Mr. Leverett), using for this purpose a high-voltage pylon whose vibrations have matured into a language for Mr. Leverett; he explains that electricity is an entity which travels everywhere and thus knows everything:

".. our every last secret. Only it wouldn't think of telling most people what it knows, because they believe electricity is a cold mechanical force. It isn't, it's warm and pulsing and sensitive and friendly underneath, like any other live thing." (p. 94)

Leiber's electrical being shows the same basic features as Stringer's, but here no object has been "possessed" by an external entity; on the contrary, it appears that electricity has always been an animate being, or rather a family of beings:

"Electricity doesn't mind working for us. It's generous-hearted and it loves its job. But it would be grateful for a little more consideration, a little more recognition of its special problems. It's got its savage brothers to contend with, you see—the wild electricity that rages in storms and haunts the mountaintops and comes down to hunt and kill. Not civilized like the electricity in the wires, though it will be some day." (p. 97)

Once again we find the same ascension toward the human level; at first the being is similar to man, with its nobler qualities (sensitivity, generosity); then it becomes superior to man:

"Civilized electricity's a great teacher. Shows us how to live clean and in unity and brother-love." (p. 97)

In a last stage, it becomes a god:

Mr. Scott thought of what a neat little electricity cult Mr. Leverett could set up. He could imagine the patio full of earnest seekers while Krishna Leverett— or maybe High Electro Leverett—dispensed wisdom from his rocker, interpreting the words of the humming wires. Better not suggest it, though—in Southern California such things sometimes have a way of coming true. (p. 98)

In Stringer's tale electricity was definitely "possessed" by an alien.[9] In Leiber's story the absence of any exterior animator for the settor corresponds to a desire not to provide any rational justification to a phenomenon which undermines the reader's most deeply rooted certitudes. The loud buzz[10] which first prompted the creation of the settor is its only tangible manifestation. In a sense, this story is also a good tale of fantasy: the end does not reveal the true identity of the electrical god; Leverett's death by electrocution leaves room for two interpretations. It can be taken for an accident fraught with bizarre circumstances (the police report of course sustains only this point of view). Or else it can be seen as the outcome of an argument between man and god: Mr. Leverett, a staunch anticommunist, cannot bear the thought that electricity should indiscriminately "lend itself" to all countries, even beyond the Iron Curtain. The author does not seem to favor either interpretation, thus creating a hesitating effect specific of fantasy.

Established Settors. It has become very frequent in SF that the writer refuses to show the animating process, and consequently takes for granted the animate nature of an object or a usually inert element of the setting. We have seen that such a procedure was the only one used in the fairytale. Actually, it has become so common in recent SF that such a question hardly ever constitutes the central subject matter of a story; it is merely used as a point of entry: the reader readily accepts the idea of an object which talks, of a crystal which thinks, of a vain flower that sings and loves (as in "Prima Belladonna" by J. G. Ballard), especially if those settors inhabit or come from a faraway planet. The interest of the reader is promptly focused upon the generally conflicting relationship between the settor and the other actors (or else, as we have noted, upon the symbols presiding in the choice of such or such a settor).

John T. Sladek's choice of books as settors whose animating process is of secondary importance constitutes a good example. *A Report on the Migration of Educational Materials* supposes that one day our world is at last relieved of the burden of its culture and other myths (red tape, money, etc.) It is a naive fable with an elegant treatment: the books of the whole world, the oldest ones in the lead, suddenly take to the sky like birds, flapping their covers, soon followed by official files, banknotes, income tax returns, checkbooks, etc. In great formations of migrating books they fly to a distant zone of Amazonia. Of course, the progression in the explanations provided by the scientists for this phenomenon cleverly orients the tone of the tale toward humor, so that the reader soon perceives the author's satirical and utopian purpose, ill-concealed behind the serious facade of the narrator's earnestly "scientific" report. The notable point is of course the unquestioned acceptance of the animate, almost anthropomorphic nature of the migrants (they act like birds, but they think like free men): this is also, as we know, a prerequisite, or at least a constant, in all philosophical fables, from Voltaire to Kafka.

Conclusion. The study of settors is most revealing about the specific elements of the technique used by SF. It seems that the tendency toward animism, on the one hand, and on the other, a bias toward anthropomorphism, are both highly developed in the writer and the reader of SF. The brevity of the short story form lends itself well to the presentation of original animated settings; their very originality ensures a strong impact on the reader, but the writer would probably find their interest short-lived were he to use them as characters in a novel. In no literary field other than SF can be found a similarly extensive use of the animating procedures which create settors, except perhaps in the folktale. In this sense, SF could be termed today's folktale or fairytale, if the rationalist demands of twentieth-century readers did not compel most authors to veil their wonderful fantasies behind the thin mist of pseudoscientific gibberish.

This animating process has been often overused and misused by SF. Indeed, severe criticism is often justified in a minority of cases. But a greater number of notably successful tales remain unparalleled in illustrative potential by mainstream fiction.

REAL SETTORS AND THEIR COMPONENTS

1. The animating spirit is of alien origin(?).
   The animated object is originally:
   a. *Inert, nonartifact*
      water: "Mr. Waterman" (Peter Redgrove)
      electricity: "High Eight" (David Stringer)
      mountain: *The Mountain without a Name* (Robert Sheckley)
   b. *Alive, nonartifact*
      vine: "The Vine" (Kit Reed)
      forest: *Bucolic* (Van Vogt)
      flower: "Prima Belladonna" (J. G. Ballard)
      various animals
   c. *Inert, artifact, nonoriented toward animation*
      books: *A Report . . .* (J. T. Sladek)
      house: *The 1000 Dreams of Stellavista* (J. G. Ballard)
      cities: "The Lost City of Mars" and "The City" (Ray Bradbury)
   d. *Inert, artifact, oriented toward animation*
      all sorts of mechanisms "possessed" by alien entities; innumerable examples
         in pulp SF

2. The animating spirit is of human origin.
   The animated object is originally:
   a. *Inert, nonartifact*
      wonderful metamorphoses of the fairytale, classical mythology, or gen-
         erally speaking the popular or folktale
   b. *Alive, nonartifact*
      same remark as above
   c. *Inert, artifact, nonoriented toward animation*
      slot machine: "Pretty Maggie Moneyeyes" (Harlan Ellison)
      statues: *237 Talking Statues* (Fritz Leiber)
   d. *Inert, artifact, oriented toward animation*
      computer controlled by bodiless brain: "The Fiend" (F. Pohl)
      electronic "prostitute" and its human lover "fused" by love: "Mistress
         of the Mind" (Lee Harding)
      computer "integrating" little girl's personality: "Sweet Dreams, Melissa"
         (Stephen Golding)

Robert Silhol

11. PORTRAIT OF AN IDEAL CRITIC

Since one never speaks of anything but oneself, and since the use of a method, no matter how prudent it may be, never quite manages to eliminate the subject's unconscious wishes—sublimating or deviating them, unless it simply disguises them —I will start with my own experience and lay down that literature, and art in general, have pleasure as their function.

That this is not their primary function can be submitted to discussion later, and it is certain that one cannot limit the scope of the question to the narrow dimension of the individual subject; it is in this fashion, however, that literature touches me, and it is with the problem of pleasure that it seems fit to begin. But the formulation remains too vague; one must be more specific. To speak of function may mean two things, and it is necessary to know whether the observation bears on the origin of the phenomenon or on its result. In fact, it amounts to considering the literary work either as an object which has a task to fulfil or as an ensemble whose activity can be observed. In the second case, however, one must be careful not to envisage the text as an autonomous whole, an organic body which, in an animist perspective, would possess a life of its own or even a soul which would be free from the determinisms to which men are submitted. Function is to be understood here as "the effect literature has on the reader—on me." This particular use of the word "function" amounts to the hypothesis that the observation of the phenomenon may help to formulate a theory as to one of its determinations. Art gives me pleasure; this deserves analysis.

But of course there are motives for my arguing thus, and to one aware of ideology it becomes obvious that my reasoning belongs to a period in history where the problem of pleasure and of the individual subject have become one of the most important preoccupations; thus, the manner in which I apprehend my relationship to literature appears as produced by determinants which are to be sought for elsewhere than in the work or in the reader. Already one may begin to understand why sociology will have to be brought up as a possible method of investigating the literary fact.

But what is literary pleasure? And how can words on a page be a source of emotion? Fascinating power of our imagination, no doubt, but the explanation is not sufficient, since not all texts move the reader in the same manner.[1] Beyond the mere pleasure of the imagination, which by the way can be seen at work in many nonartistic activities, we must come to postulate the existence of a specific textual pleasure (and if the word "textual" pleases you, it is perhaps because it is so near "sexual," the notion being taken in its most general sense) whose characteristic is that it is produced by language, written language in the present case. This is not saying that the problem can be easily solved now, and it will be seen that much research is yet to be done in the two related—though distinct—fields of literary response and literary production. But already, to begin with an interrogation on pleasure is to formulate the problem differently, in a way that may soon prove rich in consequence.

And to follow the same inspiration, it seems worth while wondering why aesthetics rarely if ever begin with this interrogation, and what may be the signification of a practice which evades the subject of pleasure, consistently concealing it where it precisely appears as one of the fundamental factors.

The answer is no doubt to be found in an analysis of the social function of literary criticism. Criticism deals with values—beauty, truth, ideals, that may elevate man's spirit—and is not primarily interested in pleasure; at most, critics will deign to consider it as a by-product of art, and if they concede that literature can afford some gratification, it will always be a pleasure of a higher, finer nature, a pleasure, besides, that is to be found only in works that are morally acceptable. One may find this portrait unfair and unnecessarily scathing, and it is true that some critics, at least, refuse to be concerned with values only. But then they should refuse the name of critics[2] and insist, as I do, upon the danger inherent in a study of literature that makes one look for aesthetic values, unaware of what the concept "aesthetic" may amount to, and forgetful of its etymology: "Of or pertaining to αἰσθητά, things perceptible by the senses, things material (as opposed to νοητά, things thinkable or immaterial) also 'perceptive, sharp in the senses'" (OED). It is an ideological danger that cannot be denounced enough. Even the critic who claims he is only interested in a description of the literary object and of its functions often falls a victim to it. Unable to resist pronouncing value judgments on the work he studies, he strays from his original purpose (or perhaps the unavowed design of his elaborate description was merely an excuse for trying to account for the "beauty" of the literary work). For indeed there is no privileged "objective" standpoint, and thematicians, structuralists, and even semiologists, at times, are deluding themselves when they think they can ward off the pitfalls of ideology in prudently limiting their task to a description of the work of art. It is an illusion to believe that axiologically neutral approaches can also manage to be ideologically neutral. The first thing a "scientist" must do is to question his own tools and remain aware of their ideological meaning. Any descriptive operation whatever commits a theory, entails a choice which must be clearly known and if possible analyzed. Even the very choice of this or that work as an object for analysis also amounts to a judgment of value; simply, it is not explicit.

How can we then avoid making such judgments? We cannot, and this need not worry us too much. If one is to remain interested in literary analysis, it has to be realized one cannot escape making value judgments. Indeed, it is now being recognized that *taste* is a socioeconomic product, that is to say, determined by the socioeconomic structure and, in the last analysis, by history. And as there is no enjoyment of art—any form of art—without taste, a taste pertaining to a relevant culture or subculture, this means that even our literary pleasures are in the end socioeconomically determined. What matters is that we should know this, accept the (historical) relativity of "good" taste. In fact, the literary critic who considers it his duty to distinguish between "good" and "bad" literature does so according to rules which are never revealed and which the critic himself does not know. It is true that there are standards: of style—but what is style?—of propriety or novelty —depending on the ciritc—but they vary with the times, and it should be deemed significant that critics cannot choose but borrow their standards from the works of art themselves.[3] Some critics, it must be admitted, often belonging to literary movements, are eager to discover new art forms, and generously welcome innovations; but they are a minority. Besides, as has been remarked, schools are rarely founded by the author whose works are at the origin of the new "style," but by disciples of lesser "talent"[4] and often at a time when the school has no longer anything new or of consequence to produce.

Because there is no objective basis[5] to the critic's judgment, we shall therefore refuse him the right to prescribe what we should read. We shall accept his judgment for what it is: the expression of his own subjectivity and, above all, the expression of the taste of the social group or class to which he belongs or which he represents. It may be that his kind of subjectivity agrees with mine, or it may be—and this seems a far more comprehensive explanation—that I belong to the same social group as he does, therefore having the same taste, but this is not a sufficient argument for me to make of my standards universal, absolute points of reference. What way have I, in truth, to prove that my reading pleasure is superior in nature to that of the member of another cultural group who reads, say, a "poor" detective novel? And what does "superior in nature" mean? Here again we see how reasoning and terminology are fraught with ideology, and sociologically induced. Taste varies from one sociological group to another, and what we agree to call good taste in literature is nothing but the taste of the dominant class. Perhaps it is because this class reads more than others and was for centuries the only class to read[6]—but already this is a two-edged argument; perhaps it is because as a dominant class it *naturally* came to impose its standards and values on the rest of society; it emphasizes at any rate the relativity of taste.

But Shakespeare and the metaphysical poets? But Milton? But Coleridge and Wordsworth and Byron and Keats and Shelley? We like these poets, we read them, at times; they are part of our literary heritage. Relative the value of *Hamlet* and *King Lear*? Relative *Paradise Lost* and *Samson Agonistes*? And "Kubla Khan" and the "Odes"? Yes, relative, but our values all the same, *my* values. There is no reading and enjoying literature without them, it is true, but this does not make *universal* values of them, for "universal" means of all times and of all places, which applies to all people, everywhere . . . and clearly this is not the case.

What this points to, in fact, is that literary pleasure, the enjoyment of art, is only possible through the possession of a particular code. To be in a position to enjoy a book, the prime requisite is obviously that one should be able to read. For centuries it has been the task of critics and teachers—and they are often the same person—to facilitate the access to this code. The critic is therefore the indispensable guide to literary pleasure, the person who teaches us to read precisely, the person who has read the book—many books—before us, and whose function it is to lead us[7] into the obscure labyrinth of the work. Provided he keeps to this role of familiarizing the reader with the code, he will help the beginner save time.

But there may be readers who will ask questions: Why this book or poem and not that one? What determined the critic's choice? Can he account for it? Such questions amount to a questioning of the critic's mission. If he can answer them, or if he says he is unable to do so but quite realizes it, this will set the reader's mind at rest. But if he fails to see the point of the question, adding, even, that such things are beyond discussion or explanation, that the beautiful is "The Beautiful," that it can be felt and that this is a matter of (good) taste, I fear the apprentice reader will not be satisfied. Of course, we all agree[8] as to what good taste is, and it is true that we apply its standards to the books we read and to the films we see; but what it simply means is that at the moment there is no other taste, no other taste than that of the dominant class. But it is not because, in our culture and until today, we have been unable to do without the teacher-critic that we must refrain from analyzing his role. A knowledge of the code is necessary to our appreciation of art, but this must not deter us from critically looking at it. Whatever our love of literature—of "good" literature—we must come to admit its evident cultural, and that is to say ideological, nature. This cannot be escaped: while promoting and defending (good) taste, while giving access to the code of appreciation, criticism reproduces the code, reproduces the dominant culture, our only culture. After all, until recently, bourgeois and revolutionaries always found it easy to agree upon this one point: the merits of the "great" art of past centuries. Because this is part of our history, and also because one cannot get rid of one's history, one may continue, for the time being, to accept this code from the hands of the critics, but one should not be blind as to its origin and functioning, and one should remain aware of its "subjective" meaning.

Denouncing the ideological function of criticism naturally implies that research which has the literary work as its object will have to forgo thinking in terms of traditional values,[9] and that value assessing, at any rate, will no longer constitute the critic's main task. He may even refuse to call himself a critic, and I suggest a new title for him (but why should a title be needed at all?), that of "literary anthropologist."

No longer interested in values, can it be assumed that our literary anthropologist will be concerned with meaning? One cannot begin the discussion without first defining the term. For what is "meaning"? The information strictly contained in the linguistic message, an information which could easily be summarized by way of simple graphic illustrations, for instance? But this is only the surface meaning, and there are shades or ambiguities which cannot be rendered thus. Is it, then, the message below the surface? But how do we go about it? By intuition alone? And what is the precise relationship between the surface and what is assumed to lie in the depth of the text? Or is there no relationship, and how are we to proceed? In what way is this different from a vague affirmation that literature is mostly concerned with symbolism? Is it, finally, the objective meaning of the text, as some Marxists understand it, that is to say, its historical and socioeconomic signification, irrespective of its contents?

But again, what signs of this objective meaning are there in the text? Many of these questions are serious ones, and some have already been given partial answers, as we shall see below. But first, there are a few methodological precautions which we should take. As far as "meaning" is concerned, for instance, I shall bluntly begin by saying that there is no meaning. By this is to be understood, as was hinted at earlier on, that the text cannot be considered as an entity which generates a particular message. Linguistics and psychoanalysis—as well as modern physics—have taught us there is no privileged *objective* observer: what is said by the transmitter—the author, if you wish—is always reconstructed by the receiver. And the reconstruction is always done along the lines of the receiver's *subjectivity* (which, by the way, also includes his knowledge of a specific language). In that way, and without any exaggeration, we can say that the meaning of a book or poem is always the reader's own. In that way, literature does not communicate; there may be some form of communication involved, and there is one on the level of the linguistic message, on the level of the "manifest," but it does not take place as we used to think. Whereas when the information sent is univocal—it never is, but we shall suppose it can be—as in "Pass me the salt, please," the message is decoded with relative precision, as soon as we deal with literature, things become far more complicated, if only because literature does not aim at informing.

And yet isn't there something the author wanted to say, a piece of information even, which he has entrusted to paper and which is here for the reader to learn? We saw that the reader always reshapes the text, receiving only certain parts of it, perceiving this and concealing that according to his own subjectivity; we are now going to find out that, at the other end of the process, something else also precludes literature from being communication in the usual sense of the word, inasmuch as one always says more than one wishes, more than one knows, for language is never information alone. The text had a particular meaning for its author—and also meanings he was unaware of; it has a particular meaning for each reader, a different meaning for each class, a meaning for each different historical period, but not one single, specific meaning to be observed throughout the centuries, eternal and immutable. Indeed, there is no meaning.

This is not of course to say that there are no limits to the construction of meanings by the various readers; there *probably* exist senses which cannot be read into a given text, but this is difficult to prove. The only reasonable approach to the problem—if one is concerned with establishing the "limits" of the text, and I fail to understand why one should worry about this, after all—is statistical, and it in no way suffices to define the text with precision. As there is no sense, and partly because of this, so there is no text. At any rate, the text is not the words on the page—not only the words, to put it more dialectically—and this will become clear when it is understood that reading and writing are processes.

To put it plainly, a text is either being written or being read and has no existence beyond those two operations; the words on the page have no value in themselves, but only in relation to an author or a reader. This is no mere phenomenological trick, and should it be, it would not deserve much interest. What is implied is more matter of fact, and perhaps obvious to many: we must stop considering the literary work as an achieved object, closed and finite. If it is such an achieved whole, it is from a marketing point of view only or, to be more specific, from the point of view of its material manufacture: paper, ink, and book. But one must not confuse the text with its material support, falling thus a prey to commodity fetishism. The connection between the dearly bought, leather-bound book embossed with gold and proudly placed on a bookshelf in my library and the text it harbors is a very remote one: I may never open the book, the text may never be read, thus confining it to its economic status of commodity. Should a visitor, however, borrow the book in order to read "it," then it becomes something else than a mere piece of merchandise. Simply, it so happens in our society that everything has its price and has been turned into a commodity, art and literature alike. Not a finite object, and something other than a piece of merchandise, neither should the text be considered as the mysterious depository of a secret to be unearthed by readers or scholars. As we saw above, there is no final meaning, the book is not a self-contained object. *In fact, what constitutes the text is nothing but two sets of relationships: the relationship between an author and the material produced by him thanks to language, and the relationship between readers and such material—words on the page as left by the author.*

But what makes matters rather difficult is that you can never be a writer and a reader at the same time, the producer of a text and the producer of a particular meaning (reading). It may be argued that the author who reads his own text is at once a writer and a reader; but two different processes are at work here which very likely mobilize two different levels of activity in the subject. It might also be observed that writing is in fact an elaborate form of reading, since one always starts writing from a model, as if the sum of all literary productions throughout the centuries were one long continuous book (whether the writer sets out to imitate or to go against the tradition is immaterial). But it confines the problem to the sociological, or even historical, ground, and in this case it is irrelevant since the present inquiry is precisely concerned with the nature of literary production—more concerned, that is, for this part of my analysis at any rate, with differences than with similarities.

Since one cannot, then, be at the same time the writer of a text and its reader, since "the text" is nothing but two sets of *processes,* we must no longer speak of it as a simple unambiguous object, and it will be necessary to specify what kind of object we are dealing with. The literary work will therefore be *one* of the two relationships described above: writing process or reading process (construction of one particular meaning). It is of course possible that the two processes slightly overlap or coincide, and research will have to be carried out according to this hypothesis. At present, however, it seems more methodologically urgent to insist on differences and to analyze writing and reading as two distinct activities. Once the notion that the text is two sets of relationships is firmly established and has led to constructive hypotheses and demonstrations, then will it be possible to devote some time to those coincidental areas, but only then.

It is now clear that "the text" is an abstraction which has little operative value, a fleeting object indeed, liable to change at every new reading. If, to sum up, we want a mental representation of what the literary work is, we can say that it is, on one hand, the writing of it—that is to say, the various processes that led to its emergence—and, on the other hand, the various interpretations on several levels, from that of simple information to that of the most personal and secret gratification (such as psychoanalysis can discover): in a word, *all the various readings of it which have so far taken place*. And tomorrow, or next year, the text will have been modified by further readings.

But what of the critic, and what of research on literature? The critic is a reader —a more cultured reader, one with more experience possibly—and sometimes a gifted rhetorician who can write well on writing, but on nothing else. I shall therefore read his critique as I read any other text, for pleasure, knowing full well that I will inevitably reconstruct his text according to my own fancy. If we happen to agree, I shall find him a good critic, and if we disagree, this will not show too much, as I take it there will now and then be enough in his text to build a reading of it that suits me. Which means, of course, that I will now and then use his text to boost my ego, even at his expense, finding pleasure in disagreeing with him.

But one may also decide to refuse reading the critics, inasmuch as they aim only at imparting to the reader a meaning. Yes, if the critic insists on being first and foremost a privileged reader—that is, the discoverer of a sense which he claims to be The Sense of the work under scrutiny—then perhaps he should not be read. We saw there is no Sense; we can now stress what methodological weakness it is to confuse reading and analysis. The reading process is a highly subjective activity; in it subject and object are one, for the simple reason that reading amounts to constructing one's own sense according to one's own unconscious desire; what takes place in reading concerns only the subject, even though what triggers off the (dialectical) process could be found on the page. This is doubtless what is meant when a reader says he identifies with the elements of the text. That there are books where this "identification," this forgetting of one's conscious self, does not occur, so that one comes to consider the literary page as an object and exercises some critical activity toward it, does not disprove my argument but rather adds to its strength. It is only when one can stand at a certain objective distance from the literary work that analysis can take place; and it is only right, therefore, to ask of the critic that he place himself at such a distance, distinguishing, in the event, his reading from his analysis. This amounts to repeating that "scientific" knowledge cannot be founded on value judgments; as to what kind of analysis the critic can engage in when he is not busily trying to justify his personal construction of a sense, this is another matter that will be discussed presently.

It must not be thought that there are no longer any tasks for the amateur who is not a producer of literature himself.[10] Thousands of people have written and will write, millions read and will probably continue doing so: writing and reading— and one can now include viewing—are important human activities; they deserve study and analysis. It might be the work of literary anthropology to deal with these activities. As the only possible objects of study are the two sets of relationships alluded to above, the literary anthropologist will be concerned with the conditions of production of the text and then with responses to it. Not a historian nor a linguist, he will however need some knowledge of history and linguistics, and will at times have to collaborate with researchers in these fields. What is meant by "conditions of production of the text" is that activity which involved the author and language—taken here in its widest sense and including literary forms and genres— that relationship between a producer, or subject, and its raw material which resulted in the text.

That there is no text, as I wrote, should not bother us here. Let us be very clear about this: there is no text as such, only processes, and these processes have left their traces in what the writer has bequeathed us. Or rather, and more specifically, we are now in a (historical) position to deduce the conditions of production of the work from the traces left in it by those who produced it. Once again, what will be analyzed, unearthed, yes, will not be the meaning, but only a temporary explanation of what happened between writer and book.

Some may object that this is of scanty interest and strongly relishes of psychobiography or even of the antiquated "life and works" method. But it is not psychobiography that I am advocating—even though there were some notable pioneers in this field. Between literary anthropology and psychobiography there may be some remote connection, but this is only because both apply psychoanalytical methods to their object. It will soon be obvious that it is quite a different application of psychoanalysis that is advised here, and it is not primarily the author who is the object of inquiry but a precise relationship between someone—whoever he or she may be—and language, a process, once again, which it may be of interest to analyze. Not a study of The Sense, not a detailed study of the author's life, literary anthropology aims at being a reflection upon the nature of literature. Nature being understood here not as an essence, but as the temporary limits of the object, an object which will take on another nature as history develops and new tools come to be used. Literature is what writers produce, and then, in turn, what their readers produce: it can be studied from the point of view of the psychical conditions of production and from the point of view of the sociological conditions of production. The methods which we have at our disposal—psychoanalysis and Marxist sociology—throw quite a considerable light upon the nature of such parts of the text as the relationship between author and final material; the research devoted to "literary response" is likely to progress thanks to the same tools, even though the difficulties seem greater here, as the object of analysis is either an abstraction—the sum total of all individual readings of a given book or poem— or of a highly diversified form since it may vary with each individual.

One may object to psychoanalysis and its application to literature, saying that analysis is what happens between the analyst and a person free-associating on a couch, and this only, and add, as a final demurrer, that dead authors can in no way be psychoanalyzed! Quite. But Freud's discovery and the findings of his disciples cannot be restricted to the soliloquy on the couch. More fundamental than a therapeutic technique whose operating conditions may change with time,. psychoanalysis is a theory of the unconscious in man, in us. Literature is a work of language and, among other things, the unconscious manifests itself in language. For not only can we no longer see in the literary work the equivalent of the reality it portrays—the "empirical illusion" of the critics of ages past—but we must realize that language has a reality of its own. And because the notion of language may not be precise enough and too much of an abstraction, I shall say that literature is written speech, the speech of a particular subject.

The nature of speech is twofold at least: it informs and it represents. By information is meant the relative *univocity* of language—linguists sometimes speak of *dénotation* or of "competence"—the minimal agreement on signification without which there would be no communication, no reading or readings. This first function implies the existence of a code—transindividual, of necessity, and homogeneous in nature, even though it can never be more than an abstraction (cf. language as opposed to speech). And it is because it is an abstraction that the second characteristic of speech must be called in: its function of representation. Speech represents, that is to say replaces, comes in the place of, this reality it is pointing at. And when I write, or speak for that matter, I represent, using, for a purpose that is not of description only, elements given by the code. Language—this abstraction before it comes to be used (speech)—helps me to fill a void. The sign of an absence, the word on the page also occupies the empty space left.

The realm of literature is comprised between those two extremes: the telephone book, which is pure information from the point of view of production, and the surrealist poem, which is almost pure representation and contains almost no information. What it is essential to bear in mind is that speech is always information *and* representation at the same time. But the information is the surface of the text, its facade, and is not generally a source of great difficulty. (I am not here suggesting that what is on the surface is not what the author is saying; it may be what he wanted to say, but we all know, and much more so since Freud, that we do not always say what we want.) It of course happens that books are found difficult because one is not sure what the author wants to say. And yet no extra indication of coherence is to be discovered by a further harassing of the information imparted. One knows and understands all the words and even the separate sentences, but when all is put together it does not make sense! For there is sense enough, but not on the surface; and if this surface is sometimes strangely organized it is simply because the organizational motive is not here but elsewhere to be found, in the writer's psyche for instance. As in a dream, in a way, the coherence of the object does not lie in the manifest part and will be sought in vain there. In literature the information, which has or may have a function of its own, is primarily a sign of something else than itself, or rather, it is here as itself and not as a sign: it upholds *and* masks at the same time, giving a material shape—the manifest—to what is only latent in the writer's psyche.

To operate satisfactorily, this function of representation must of course remain veiled, concealed behind appearances, short of which the absence will not be properly filled and the representation fail. Indeed, literature is a mask which must never be felt as such, for to point to the mask amounts to a refusal to see it replace what it is its function to replace. No wonder then that psychoanalysis finds it so difficult to be accepted by teachers of literature and critics: literature is a make-believe, and psychoanalysis insists on the reader's blindness; literature is a source of pleasure because it helps us to resist—in the Freudian sense—and psychoanalysis points to the resistance! If research on literature is to go on, it will be at this price.

But the lover of literature need have no fear; his apprehensions are unfounded, and this must be stressed. For reading and analysis are two very different activities, and this is one of the reasons why I have carefully distinguished the one from the other, as I will do again in a moment. The analyst does enjoy books and films just as much as anyone else, letting himself resist thanks to the book or film, and constructing whatever fantasies he will—his unconscious, that is—out of the material he is reading or viewing. It is precisely because analysis—since Freud at least—does not work in that way that it can be defined as radically distinct from reading.

As in any practice aiming at some scientific consistency, analysis naturally requires that object should be held apart from the experimenting subject. But with the advent of psychoanalysis, the notion of subject was to be fundamentally revised. Freud's discovery was the unconscious; what he mostly tried to bring home to us was that the "real," "true" subject in us is not what we think it is, where we think it is, not to be observed on the surface at any rate. Because we are thus divided, it is easy to see how the difficulty is increased when we choose ourselves as an object of observation—and this includes what happens when we read or write—since the subject and object of the experiment are almost inextricably entangled. It is the aim of psychoanalysis to disentangle "true" self from "false" self, and in this sense it can be called a positive "scientific" approach. Reading, on the other hand, appears as a noncriticial activity, when subject and object are one. And they are one in two ways at least: when the reader makes sense of the object as his unconscious wishes, and when subject and object in him (true and false subject) coincide. It is the true subject which reads the text, but of this the false subject is never aware. Thus, reading, it will be clear by now, can never be used as a basis for an analysis of the text.

But what about analysis? How can it be different? Does not the psychoanalyst of literature, like anyone else, begin with a reading of the text? Of course he does, but what makes an analyst of him instead of a reader is that he has learnt to consider his first interpretation in a critical fashion. The precaution may be more methodological than actually effective, and it is true that this does not always work ideally. But the principle remains, which has started an entirely new practice. The analyst knows of his unconscious wish—even though he may not always know its very nature—and by integrating this conviction in his practice he is able to step aside from the text in what we must agree to call a more objective way. Aware of the existence of the unconscious, furthermore, like a scientist he will agree to go on correcting his views.

Perhaps it is because the psychoanalytical attitude is so long and difficult to attain that there are so few psychoanalysts of literature. For it is not sufficient to admit the fundamental ambiguity of speech or the fantasmatic nature of literature to qualify. A smattering of Freudianism and some jargon—à la mode—will not do, and there is not much psychoanalysis in the writings of critics which construe the author's fantasies as proof of the excellence of his work, thus raising to the status of "absolute depth" what is simply hidden below the surface and common, in fact, to all literature. Those critics are only interested in making value judgments; their attitude, without their knowing it, is ideological. Others, actually not different from traditional critics, will use the text mostly as a pretext to vent their own fantasies; the representations they construct owe as much—if not more—to the critic's psyche as to the object under analysis. Some of them may be writers and can be read as such, but in no way do they qualify as students of literature. Talent— whatever this means, but we know its appreciation is almost entirely cultural—is their touchstone, and this is something that cannot be transmitted except as values. No method, theory, or body of thought can seriously be founded on such a practice, and its only possible result is the emergence of talkative disciples.

Psychobiography is of more interest. But then, the psychobiographer's analyses are very much like the case studies of the psychoanalyst, with the difference that no free-associating on the couch is possible, and no cure, the only result being some further knowledge of the workings of man, a corroboration of Freud's theories. Such a school may be considered as a junior branch of psychoanalysis, and indeed many psychoanalysts, including Freud himself, have given us a "clinical" view of literature;[11] but this does not deal with literature per se. Too often treating the work under scrutiny as oneiric material only, and analyzing it as they would a dream, these "critics" forget to see it as a work of language. Their procedure is of course perfectly correct, and this is how one should begin. Speech, however, should be brought into the picture and given due analysis in its turn. For literature, after all, though a product of the writer's imagination, appears in the end as primarily made of words; once the purely pictorial aspect of the text has been examined, attention must be paid to speech. But possibly I am at fault here, not capable yet of imagining a real interdisciplinary system, where old feudalities would be broken and no field the privileged and exclusive object of any discipline, school, or scholar.

Necessary to the constitution of a text, the words on the page, however, only very temporarily belong to the writer; he received them from society and passes them on to others. The determinants of speech are to be found in the speaker's psyche, but also and primarily in the social structure. As "man is the product of his social relationships" (Marx), so is language man's most signifying activity. Starting from the two notions that man is a social being and that ideas and concepts have their material origin in man's practical activity—an activity which eventually appears as economic, in the widest sense of the word—one comes to envisage literature as a social product also. Man's concrete existence and his ideological productions are closely linked. Once again, the text is nothing but its conditions of production, but this time we are dealing with sociological conditions. Thus is the text fraught with ideology in more ways than one. We have ideology of conscious content, which amounts to the surface message the author "wishes" to deliver, and this mostly consists of values he supports. We have, far more important, what I shall call latent ideology which, this time, consists of values upheld by the text without the writer's knowledge, clearly demonstrating that literature is not the simple product of an individual subject only[12] and can be ascribed to a social group or class.

But we must go further and leave the relatively smooth ground of articulate meaning to give consideration to structure. In the same way that psychoanalysis started from the now verified assumption that man's words and gestures have an objective significance, a raison d'être outside themselves, so it is possible to assume that man's behavior has a social significance. This objective sociological signification organizes the literary work, gives it a particular structure, or architecture, if you wish, which in fact constitutes part[13] of its originality. Thus is Shakespeare's *Richard III* structured by values such as individual ambition, violence, and the virtues of economic exchange; thus is Camus's *L'Étranger* constituted by the relationships between three economico-political groups; thus is Erich Segal's *Love Story* a discourse upon the war in Vietnam if only because it was unconsciously devised to function as a defensive screen to be placed between a nation's consciousness and reality. That the examples above are not simply random hypotheses quickly becomes obvious once one agrees to view literature as a social product; provided the adequate questions are put to the text, the demonstrations which validate them are not too difficult. By studying the values on which a text rests, by studying the social classes or economic entities represented—at a latest level, by analyzing the tensions that underlay the literary work, we become capable of understanding why it was thus produced and acquire a further knowledge into one of our most fundamental artistic activities.

Finally, beyond ideology consciously and nonconsciously transmitted, and beyond structure, there are yet *forms* to be accounted for. By forms is meant "literary genres," but also, and very simply, language and the way it is used. Forms also have an objective signification, and this calls for analysis. The occurrence of the five-act tragedy in alexandrines is no chance happening; neither is that of the eighteenth-century English novel or of surrealist poetry. Here are particular forms which should be explained, for they have a sociological meaning. Lukacs has done much to throw some light on the origin of the bourgeois novel, but one finds his demonstrations a bit general nowadays; personally, I find him still too much of a Hegelian and not enough of a materialist; we must try to improve the tools he has left us. Last but not least, language also is a form which depends on the times: the transformations it undergoes at the hands of schools or individual authors has some significance. In the same fashion as each of us uses language to represent, so does society in its own way.

What the sociology of literature—in its Marxist sense— teaches us is that the ultimate producer of the work of art is not the individual but society. The author only serves as the mediator of the socioeconomic forces which shape history and which are to be seen at work in the text. But let me correct this, lest it should seem too grim a view of artistic production. What I am saying here is only what I am able to say now, in 1977. To the socioeconomic theory of history, which I take to be the best methodological tool we have at our disposal for understanding what is happening to us in the world today, may be in time added, say, a biological theory of man which will offer a still more comprehensive view. So far, no such theory is available, and we can only remain wisely at a stage of our knowledge where society —production relationships and productive forces— is concretely seen to determine our lives. A dialectical view of man shows him as included in two overlapping totalities: one that is biological and one that is socioeconomic and historical, and it is on the latter set of determinants that we seem capable of having some influence. For the time being, the one advance in knowledge we can make is therefore to define the text as lying at the intersection of two sets of determinants: the psychical ones and the sociological ones. That the psychic determinants will eventually be shown to be part of social ones, I have little doubt; but this will not do away with the individual subject, as he is the necessary mediator. It must then be understood that the possibility exists of a materialistic theory of literature which does not exclude the individual psyche as partial producer of the text. Simply, it will have to consider the individual subject as part of a dialectical unit, and Marxist theory of literature will have no further use for such inoperative notions as the mystery of literary creation, inspiration, or genius.

Those specifications made, we can now turn to society as a producer of literature and see how it acts. Lucien Goldmann has shown the way in this field, and several of his hypotheses are highly valuable, even though I feel I cannot accept the whole of his theory. But it is true that history—whose characteristic is that it is always in the making—also shapes art. And shape is the important word in this context, for Goldmann has clearly explained how literature is not a mere reflection of socioeconomcic tensions. Expressing themselves thanks to literature, classes and social groups thus formulate, at a latent level,[14] an adequate interpretation[15] of its historical future. Between the mental structure of the social group and those constitutive of the text, a homology can be found by which the literary work appears as part of the total "consciousness" of the group. Texts can therefore be ascribed to specific social groups which have a socioeconomic entity. For "class" is obviously not to be taken in its functionalist acceptation (cf. status) and should be understood in relation to the position occupied in the production process, that is to say, in fact, in relation with class struggle or with contradictions in the social structure.

It can then be seen how the text is the result of its conditions of production, inquiry being able to trace back its particular elements at the same time to socioeconomic forces and to the writer's psyche, therefore making of each of these two factors the necessary but not sufficient condition.

It is possibly because he refused to consider the literary work as such a joint product—a joint product, let me repeat, as far as social sciences go to this day—that Goldmann left so many questions unanswered and remains so open to criticism. His theory of coherence (of the "great" literary work) is unclear and almost impossible to apply; his aesthetics make no room for a sense of relativity and are in fact little different from traditional standards.

But the central hypothesis of genetic structuralism, according to which society and social forces are the ultimate producers of the book, must be preserved, for it can prove extremely fruitful. Secretly inhabited by the vague intuition that the "beautiful" is in fact nothing but the "sociological," it may lead to a new and compelling research which could yet bring astonishing results.

NOTES

INTRODUCTION: CHRISTIANE AND IRA JOHNSON

1.   Alexis de Tocqueville, *Democracy in America* (New York: Vintage Books, 1945), vol. 2, pp. 58, 59.
2.   Cyrille Arnavon, *Les Lettres américaines devant la critique française: 1887-1917* (Annales de l'Université de Lyon, 1951).
3.   Thelma M. Smith and Ward L. Miner, *Transatlantic Migration: The Contemporary American Novel in France* (Durham, N. C.: Duke University Press, 1955).
4.   Jean Simon, *Le Roman américain au XXᵉ siècle* (Paris: Boivin, 1950).
5.   William Faulkner, *Sanctuaire* (Paris: Gallimard, 1933), R. N. Raimbault et Henri Delglove, préf. André Malraux.
6.   André Gide, "Interview imaginaire." *Fontaine* 27-28 (août 1943, Algers): 7-11. Reprinted Paris, 1945.
7.   Readers interested in learning more about structuralism cannot do better than to consult Robert Scholes, *Structuralism in Literature* (New Haven, Conn.: Yale University Press, 1974).

1: JEAN-PIERRE VERNIER

1.   Saul Bellow, *Mr. Sammler's Planet* (New York, 1971). All page references are to this edition of the Fawcett Crest reprint.
2.   Robert B. Dutton, *Saul Bellow*, p. 13.
3.   Saul Bellow, "Distractions of a Fiction Writer," *The Living Novel: A Symposium*, ed. Granville Hicks, p. 6.
4.   K. M. Opdahl, *The Novels of Saul Bellow: An Introduction*, pp. 7-8.
5.   "He had only one good eye. The left distinguished only light and shade." *Mr. Sammler's Planet*, p. 8.
6.   Bellow, review of Sholem Aleichem's *The Adventures of Motel the Cantor's Son* (*Saturday Review*, May 30, 1953). Quoted by Irving Malin, *Jews and Americans*, p. 8.
7.   Dutton, p. 160.
8.   The scene may also be an oblique parody of Revelation 16:15: "Behold, I come as a thief. Blessed is he that watcheth, and keepeth his garments, lest he walk naked, and they see his shame." The rhetoric linking Genesis to Revelation need hardly be stressed.
9.   Bellow, "Distractions," p. 20.
10.   *Dialogues of Alfred North Whitehead*, as recorded by Lucien Price (London, 1954), p. 22.
11.   Ibid., p. 366.
12.   Bellow, "Where Do We Go from Here: The Future of Fiction," *Saul Bellow and the Critics*, ed. Irving Malin, p. 220.
13.   Bellow, *Recent American Fiction*, p. 12.

A Short Bibliography of Secondary Material

Bellow, Saul. *Recent American Fiction*. Washington, D. C.: Library of Congress, 1963.

Clayton, John J. *Saul Bellow: In Defense of Man*. Bloomington and London: Indiana University Press, 1968.

Critique: Studies in Modern Fiction 7:3 (spring-summer 1965).

Dommergues, Pierre. *Saul Bellow*. Paris: Grasset, 1967.

Dutton, Robert. B. *Saul Bellow*. New York: Twayne, 1971.

Eisinger, Chester E. *Fiction of the Forties*. Chicago: The University of Chicago Press, 1963.

Galloway, David. *The Absurd Hero in American Fiction*. Austin and London: University of Texas Press, 1966.

Hicks, Granville, ed. *The Living Novel: A Symposium*. New York: Macmillan, 1957.

Malin, Irving. *Jews and Americans*. Carbondale and Edwardsville: Southern Illinois University Press, 1965.

– – –, ed. *Saul Bellow and the Critics*. New York: New York University Press, 1967.

– – –. *Saul Bellow's Fiction*. Carbondale and Edwardsville: Southern Illinois University Press, 1969.

Opdhal, K. M. *The Novels of Saul Bellow: An Introduction*. Philadelphia: Pennsylvania State University Press, 1967.

2: DANIEL ROYOT

1.   Leslie Fiedler, *The Return of the Vanishing American* (London: Paladin, 1972), p. 162.

2.   Jay Gurian, "Style in the Literary Desert: *Little Big Man*," *Western American Literature* 3 (winter 1969): 296.

3.   M. Molho, *Romans picaresques espagnols* (Paris: Gallimard, 1968), pp. 53–755.

4.   Thomas Berger, *Little Big Man* (New York: Dial Press, 1964); all quotations refer to the paperbound edition (Greenwich, Conn.: Fawcett Publications, n.d.).

5.   Mark Twain, *Huckleberry Finn* (New York: Norton, 1961), p. 7.

6.   Lesage (1668–1747), *Gil Blas* (1715–24–35; complete edition 1747).

7.   Fiedler, p. 52.

8.   Mark Twain used the same derogatory term to describe Pap Finn in *Huckleberry Finn*, p. 20.

9.   George Lukacs, *La Théorie du roman* (Paris: Gonthier, 1971), pp. 91–108.

10.   *The Writings of Mark Twain* (New York: Gabriel Wells, 1932), vol. 22, p. 62.

11.   Leo E. Oliva, "Thomas Berger's *Little Big Man* as History," *Western American Literature* 8 (spring and summer 1973): 33–54.

12.   William T. Pilkington, "Aspects of the Western Comic Novel," *Western American Literature* 1 (fall 1966): 217.

13.   Frederick W. Turner, III, "Melville and Thomas Berger: The Novelist as Cultural Anthropologist," *Centennial Review* 13 (winter 1969): 105.

14.   George P. Elliot, "Heap Forked Tongue," *Book Week* 2 (Oct. 11, 1964): 24.

15.   Gerald Walker, "Pecos-Picaresque," *New York Times Book Review* (Oct. 11, 1964), p. 42.

16.   See France Vernier, "Les Disfonctionnements des normes du conte dans *Candide*," *Littérature* (February 1971), pp. 15–29.

3: ANDRÉ BLEIKASTEN

1.   Quoted by John Hawkes, in "Flannery O'Connor's Devil," *Sewanee Review* 70 (summer 1962): 400.

2.   On the theme of the child-parent conflict, see the stimulating essay by Claire Katz, "Flannery O'Connor's Rage of Vision," *American Literature* 46 (March 1974): 54–67.

3.   "My own feeling is that writers who see by the light of their Christian faith will have, in these times, the sharpest eye for the grotesque, for the perverse, and for the unacceptable." In "The Fiction Writer and His Country," *Mystery and Manners* (New York: Farrar, Straus & Giroux, 1969), p. 33. Subsequent quotations from O'Connor's essays will be identified with the abbreviation *MM* and a page number in parentheses.

4.   See "A Good Man Is Hard to Find," in *Flannery O'Connor: The Complete Stories* (New York: Farrar, Straus & Giroux, 1971), p. 117. Subsequent quotations from the stories are from this edition. References will be parenthetically indicated in the text.

5.   *Wise Blood* (New York: Farrar, Straus & Cudahy, 1962), p. 39. Subsequent quotations are from this edition; they will be identified with the abbreviation *WB* and a page number in parentheses.

6.   See "Flannery O'Connor's Devil," pp. 395–407.

7.   "L'Univers de Flannery O'Connor," *Nouvelle Revue Française* 13 (September 1965): 488. My translation.

8.   "I am more and more impressed with the amount of Catholicism that fundamentalist Protestants have been able to retain. Theologically our differences with them are on the nature of the Church, not on the nature of God or our obligations to Him." Letter to Sister Mariella Gable, May 4, 1963, as quoted by Carter W. Martin, in *The True Country: Themes in the Fiction of Flannery O'Connor* (Vanderbilt University Press, 1968), p. 20.

9.   See, for example, O'Connor's statement on old Tarwater: "[He] is the hero of *The Violent Bear It Away*, and I'm right behind him 100 per cent," as quoted by Granville Hicks in "A Writer at Home with Her Heritage," *Saturday Review* (May 12, 1962), p. 22.

10.   *The Violent Bear It Away* (New York: Farrar, Straus & Cudahy, 1960), p. 39. Subsequent quotations are from this edition; they will be identified with the abbreviation *TVBIA* and a page number in parentheses.

11.   *The World of Flannery O'Connor* (Bloomington: Indiana University Press, 1970), p. 43.

12.   On this point, see my essay "Aveugles et voyants: Le Thème du regard dans *Wise Blood*," *Bulletin de la Faculté des Lettres de Strasbourg* 40 (January 1969): 291–301.

13.   It is interesting to note that the two women with whom Motes has sexual intercourse are both perverse and parodic mother figures: "Momma" Watts, the prostitute, treats Motes like a child; Sabbath Lily becomes a travesty of the Virgin Mary in the mummy scene. It is remarkable too that most female characters in the novel are associated with castration symbols: Motes's mother appears with a stick (p. 63); Mrs. Watts uses a "large pair of scissors" (p. 33), her grin is "as curved and sharp as the blade of a sickle" (p. 60), and her teeth are pointed like those of the woman with the cadaverous face Motes sees in the swimming pool (cf. pp. 33 and 84).

14.   On the schizophrenic's sense of engulfment, see, for example, R. D. Laing, *The Divided Self* (London: Tavistock Publications, 1959).

15.   Joseph Conrad, preface to *The Nigger of the Narcissus* [1897] (London: J. M. Dent & Sons, 1945), p. 3.

16.   "The Role of the Catholic Novelist," *Greyfriar*, Siena Studies in Literature 7 (1964): 9.

17.   The theme of Christ recrucified is developed in "The Displaced Person," and, even more ambiguously, in *Wise Blood*.

4: SIMONE VAUTHIER

1.   The quotation is from "Rotation and Repetition: Walker Percy," in John Carr, *Kiteflying and Other Irrational Acts: Conversations with Twelve Southern Writers* (Baton Rouge, 1972), p. 40. This is an expanded version of "An Interview with Walker Percy," which was published in the *Georgia Review* (fall 1971). See also Carlton Cremeens, "Walker Percy, the Man and the Novelist: An Interview," *Southern Review* (spring 1968); Ashley Brown, "An Interview with Walker Percy," *Shenandoah* 18 (spring 1967); Zoltán Abádi-Nagy, "A Talk with Walker Percy," *Southern Literary Journal* (fall 1973); William F. Buckley, "The Southern Imagination: An Interview with Eudora Welty and Walker Percy," *Mississippi Quarterly* (fall 1973).

2.   Carr, 1972, pp. 42–43.

3.   Ibid., p. 46.

4.   Walker Percy, "From Facts to Fiction," *Washington Post Book News* (Dec. 25, 1966), repr. *Writer* (Oct. 1967), p. 46.

5.   The quotation is from Lewis A. Lawson, "Walker Percy's Indirect Communications," *Texas Studies in Literature and Language* (spring 1969), pp. 881–82. The only book-length study of Percy's work (Martin Luschei, *The Sovereign Wayfarer: Walker Percy's Diagnosis of the Malaise*, (Baton Rouge, 1972) pays little attention to the technique.

6.   The effect was not originally intended since Percy's title, *The Confessions of a Movie-goer*, was changed by the editor (Percy's letter to S. Vauthier, July 14, 1974). This, however, does not detract from its efficacy.

7.   The terms are Franz Stanzel's (*Narrative Situations in the Novel*, Bloomington, Ind., 1971). Since the narrator-hero is so conveniently provided with two names, I will call the narrating self Binx and the experiencing self Jack.

8.   References are to the Alfred A. Knopf 1962 edition. Lack of space unfortunately compelled me to make a few deletions in the transcriptions. They have of course been acknowledged.

9.   William Dowie, "Walker Percy: Sensualist-Thinker," *Novel* (fall 1972), p. 59.

10.   See the difference between "I am a model tenant . . ." and "I am a stock and bond broker" (p. 9); the former can be a self-oriented sentence, a way of patting oneself on the back; the latter is other-oriented.

11.   The diegesis being defined as the space-time world of the story, diegetic is what belongs or refers to this world, extradiegetic what does not. See Gérard Genette, *Figures 3* (Paris, 1972): 72, 238, 241.

12.   Scott Byrd, "Mysteries and Movies: Walker Percy's College Articles and *The Movie-goer*," *Mississippi Quarterly* 25 (spring 1972): 176.

13.   Binx "is a spiritual voyeur," says Alfred Kazin, "The Pilgrimage of Walker Percy," *Harper's* (June 1971); "Here also the commuter is a kind of voyeur," says Richard Lehan, commenting on rotation ("The Way Back: Redemption in the Novels of Walker Percy," *Southern Review* [spring 1968], p. 312.)

14.   Binx's medical lexis may reflect that of Walker Percy, M. D. Or it might be an indication that the locutor is Jack, the medical student of the epilogue.

15.   The use of "screen characters" has been studied by Byrd, loc. cit., and Mary Thale, "The Moviegoer of the 1950s," *Twentieth Century Literature* (July 1968).

16.   Byrd, 177.

17.   "Metaphor as Mistake," *Sewanee Review* (winter 1958); "Symbol, Consciousness and Intersubjectivity," *Journal of Philosophy* (July 17, 1958); Walker Percy, "The Symbolic Structure of Interpersonal Process," *Psychiatry* (Feb. 19, 1961).

18.   "The Man on the Train: Three Existential Modes," *Partisan Review* (fall 1956).

19.   Gabriel Marcel, as quoted by Carr, 1972, p. 44. See too Percy's remarks on the stare and "its unique and indispensable role in the sustaining and validating of my consciousness" in "Symbol as Hermeneutic in Existentialism," *Philosophy and Phenomenological Research* (June 1956), p. 528.

20.   Émile Benveniste, *Problèmes de linguistique générale* (Paris, 1966), ch. "L'Homme dans la langue."

21.   Genette, 266.

22.   See John Carr's avowal in his excellent interview with Percy: "Binx always kind of disturbed me," p. 50.

23.   Jim Van Cleave, "Versions of Percy," *Southern Review* (autumn 1970), p. 998. As explained later, I cannot agree with the rest of Van Cleave's comment.

24.   See Frederick Hoffman: "The Epilogue cheats a bit. He and Kate are married, he is to start medical school in the fall, [incidentally he *has* started medical school] and his aunt is fond of him again. But *this is not really a part of the novel* . . ." (emphasis added), *The Art of Southern Fiction* (Carbondale, Ill., 1968), p. 133.

25.   The poem begins: "It was my thirtieth year to heaven/Woke to my hearing the morning. . . ." Dylan Thomas, *Collected Poems, 1934-1952* (London, 1952), pp. 102–4. The symbolic importance of the thirtieth year was also stressed by Camus:

Un jour vient pourtant et l'homme constate ou dit qu'il a trente ans. Il affirme ainsi sa jeunesse. Mais du même coup il se situe par rapport au temps. Il y prend sa place. Il reconnaît qu'il est à un certain moment d'une courbe qu'il confesse devoir parcourir. Il appartient au temps, et, à cette horreur qui le saisit, il y reconnaît son pire ennemi (*Le Mythe de Sisyphe* [Gallimard, Paris, n.d.], p. 28).

Again I cannot examine here the relevance of such ideas to *The Moviegoer*, but I cannot resist pointing out an echo of them in the transformation that has Binx say, "Thus *ended* my thirtieth year . . . ," whereas Thomas "marvel[ing] [his] birthday away," yet faces the future in the opening and concluding lines.

26. We have no way of evaluating the time lag between the narrative moment and the diege-tic moment, because the point of reference of the dating is still Jack's thirtieth birthday: in June . . . on Mardi Gras morning of the next year . . . the following May.

27. Carr, 1972, p. 49. The passage contains another such hint at Jack's conversion, since Kierkegaard remarked that the religious man could still go to Dyrehaven, the Luna Park of Copenhagen (*Post-Scriptum* [Paris, 1946], p. 230), and Jack takes the children for a train ride in Audubon Park.

28. George Wright, "The Lyric Present: Simple Present Verbs in English Poems," *PMLA* (May 1974), p. 567.

29. Percy says: "Most people will deny that it's there. They stand me down." "That's not true. You don't baptize Binx in that book" (Carr, 1972, p. 51).

30. The device can sometimes be seen as simply a "historic present" (see p. 123). But to call it so is not really illuminating.

31. Genette calls *"prolepse* toute manoeuvre narrative consistant à raconter ou evoquer d'avance un événement ultérieur et . . . *analepse* toute évocation après coup d'un événement antérieur au point de l'histoire où l'on se trouve" (82).

32. It would be interesting to study how analepses and prolepses are inserted into the narration. Here the evocation of the departure is linked to the so-called present by an implicit association. Sharon is shown behaving as a girl friend, and we are offered an inner reflection of Binx: "By some schedule of proprieties known to her, she did not become my date until she left her rooming house" (p. 123). A flashback then describes their setting forth in the present tense. The return to the diegetic present is even less obtrusive: "Sharon comes piling into the car and up against me. Now she can touch me, 'Where is Joyce from?'" The sentence "Now she can touch me" splices two time units, that of the flashback and that of the supposed present of diegesis and enunciation. The narration blurs the seams of such insertions so that we are deluded into ignoring the time dimension in the belief that we are carried on by an ongoing present.

33. Cremeens, p. 271.

34. Roy Pascal, "Tense and Novel," *Modern Language Review* (Jan. 1962), p. 10. Pascal thinks the present misapplied in the case of a character with a sense of reflection, which is disproved by *The Moviegoer*.

35. William Alexander Percy, *Lanterns on the Levee: Recollections of a Planter's Son* (Baton Rouge, 1973), p. 23; emphasis added.

36. This is only a subjective impression, but a statistical study of the frequency of simple and progressive forms would, I think, bear out my contention. In order to restore some of the aspects of the progressive and keep those of the simple present, Percy makes frequent use of a compromise: birds "go sculling up," "come twittering," so-and-so "goes humping," "stands blinking," "stands gaping," "goes huffing," "comes howling," "comes ransacking," "comes nosing," "sits shivering," others "lie embracing," "lie drowsing," "sit holding hands," etc.

37. A. A. Mendilow, "The Position of the Present in Fiction," in P. Stevick, *Theory of the Novel* (New York, 1967), p. 272, repr. from *Time and the Novel* (London, 1952).

38. This is a possibility with which John Barth's *The Floating Opera* keeps teasing us.

39. Charles Grivel, *Production de l'intérêt romanesque* (The Hague, 1973), p. 101.

40. Walker Percy, "The Man on the Train," p. 483.

41. Mendilow, p. 272. Mendilow discounts the fact that the present may be a convention. Of course, *The Moviegoer* is not exclusively written in the present since *some* reminiscences are told in the preterit. In a study of the manipulation of time in *The Moviegoer*, it would be necessary to investigate the relative frequency of all verbal forms.

42. Pascal, p. 7.

43. *"The tense of subjectivity,"* as Suzanne K. Langer has shown *"is the 'timeless' present,"* hence its appropriateness to lyric poetry:

> Lyric writing is a specialized technique that constructs an impression or an idea as some-thing experienced, in a sort of eternal present. . . . The lyric poet creates a sense of con-crete reality from which the time element has been canceled out, leaving a Platonic sense of "eternity." (*Feeling and Form: A Theory of Art* [New York, 1953], p. 268).

Justifying my application of her concepts to *The Moviegoer*, Langer gives as "the most perfect example of *virtual subjectivity"* Portrait of the Artist as a Young Man," (though in prose form) because "it is a complete poetic transformation" (p. 257).

44. Wright, p. 565.
45. Thale, p. 88.
46. Ibid.
47. Bruce Morrissette, "The Alienated 'I' in Fiction," *Southern Review* (spring 1974), p. 19.
48. Genette, 93.
49. These delayed avowals both throw light on the psychology of the hero and function thematically to tell us something of the nature of self-knowledge.
50. Carr, 1972, p. 48.
51. The dialogue in *The Moviegoer* is internalized, going on between parts of the self that have rejected the aunt's *Weltanschauung,* though not all "romantic" aspirations.
52. See "Naming and Being," *Personalist* (spring 1960), p. 153.
53. Lawson, p. 887.
54. Van Cleave, p. 996.
55. Abádi-Nagy, p. 6.
56. "The Man on the Train," p. 487; emphasis added.
57. Ibid., p. 478.
58. Cremeens, p. 286; Carr, 1972, pp. 40, 45; Abádi-Nagy, p. 5. Incidentally, Percy declares that Roquentin "would not find anything remarkable about a Jew" (A.-N., p. 8), but a Jewish composer and a black singer figure very much in the thoughts of Roquentin at the end when he envisages the possibility of accepting himself: "That makes two people who are saved; the Jew and the Negress." "I should like to know something about that fellow. I should be interested to find what sort of troubles he had, whether he had a woman or whether he lived alone . . .," *Nausea* (London, n.d.), trans. Robert Baldick, p. 249–52.
59. Lawson, p. 876.

5: YVES LE PELLEC

1. "Ce que je suis," *Le Nouvel Observateur* (June 23, 1975).
2. Pierre Macherey, *Pour une théorie de la production littéraire* (Paris, 1971).
3. "The Art of Fiction," *Paris Review* 45 (winter 1968): 100. Among the most interesting essays on *Rabbit, Run,* David Galloway (*The Absurd Hero in American Fiction,* University of Texas, Austin, 1966) concentrates on the "yes" and studies Harry Angstrom as an existentialist saint, unlike the majority of critics who underline the "but" from a Christian standpoint.
4. *Paris Review* interview, p. 101.
5. *Rabbit Redux,* p. 159. From now on page references will appear after quotations with the abbreviations *RRu (Rabbit, Run), RRe (Rabbit Redux), C* (Couples), plus the page number in the Penguin edition.
6. Both books open with a domestic crisis and the separation of a couple, misleadingly suggesting the narrative will follow the ups and downs of their relation. In actual fact, it soon becomes obvious that this plot is secondary, husband and wife being from the start incapable of change. The focus is on Harry's adventures during his sentimental vacation: he shares the life of a woman (Ruth/Jill), flirts with another one (Lucy Eccles/Peggy Fosnacht), makes friends with a man and has with him long conversations seemingly inconclusive (Eccles/Skeeter), is indirectly the cause of a death (Becky's/Jill's) but escapes the "net of law." He eventually finds himself no further than where he started, exposed to the critical judgment of his family (parents, sister, son), neither a true moral anarchist nor a person who fits.
7. For example, "With this Ruth, Rabbit enters the street" (*RRu,* p. 60)/"With this Jill, then, Rabbit enters the street" (*RRe,* p. 119); "Sunshine, the old clown, rims the room" (*RRu,* p. 167/*RRe,* p. 259); "Globes of ether, pure nervousness, slide down his legs" (*RRu,* p. 248/*RRe,* p. 342).
8. An approach suggested by the impression that the way Harry moves is on the whole more eloquent than the words he utters, as well as by the following sentence in which Updike evokes the pleasure he experienced when writing the last pages of *Couples:* "Going from character to character, I had myself the sensation of flying, of conquering space" (*Paris Review* interview, p. 111).

9. Jack Kerouac, *Visions of Cody* (New York, 1973), p. 98; John Updike, *Paris Review* interview, p. 93. A comparison of Updike's and Kerouac's first novels—both written at about the age of twenty-five—will suffice to show the discrepancy between their respective conceptions of literary creation. Updike dramatizes an inner moral debate between social idealism and Christian humility in the form of a psychological conflict opposing a poorhouse prefect and a ninety-four-year-old inmate. Kerouac's *The Town and the City,* though one of his only two attempts at "fiction" as opposed to what he called "picaresque narratives," remains, in spite of the multiple persona into which the author casts himself, a piece of thinly disguised autobiography. Before *The Poorhouse Fair* Updike had retraced the steps of his adolescence in a book called "Home." It is significant that he thought it wise to withhold it from publication.

10. *Vanity of Duluoz* (André Deutsch, London, 1969), p. 279.

11. *The Same Door* (Crest Book, 1964), p. 175.

12. "Minority Report," *Midpoint and Other Poems* (Crest Book, 1970), p. 76.

13. *Bech: A Book* (Alfred A. Knopf, New York, 1970), p. 3.

14. Ibid., p. 54.

15. This might perhaps be on the part of Updike a kind of indirect homage to a writer usually much abused by the American literary establishment. Actually, he seems to consider Kerouac as a significant author, going as far as to suggest that his "spontaneous prose" is not as different from his own technique as it may appear. See the *Paris Review* interview.

16. "Flight," in *Pigeon Feathers* (Crest Book, 1973), pp. 41, 42.

17. Ibid., p. 42.

18. This message, which Rabbit ponders for the rest of his trip, has rightly been considered by most critics as a comment on the mistakes Harry makes throughout the book. It is still relevant as far as his erratic moves in *Rabbit Redux* are concerned.

19. Prenez le cas de Harry Angstrom dans *Rabbit, Run:* on y trouve tous les arguments qui peuvent justifier l'abandon d'une épouse par son mari. Dans les années 50, les beatniks recommandaient les voyages intercontinentaux comme remède à l'inquiétude de l'homme; et moi j'essayais simplement de dire: "Oui, il y a sûrement du vrai, mais il y a aussi tous ces gens qui paraissent atteints par une blessure." Cette distinction est, dans mon esprit, un dilemme moral. ("Réalisme et mélodrame dans le roman: Un entretien avec John Updike," *Dialogue* 3, no. 2 (1972): 109.)

20. A feeling shared by many a prodigal son in Updike's stories, for instance Robert in "Home":

> Ever since he could remember, he had been planning to escape. The air, the people, had seemed too thick, too apt to choke him. He had made that escape. It had seemed necessary. But it had left him feeling hollow, fragile, transparent—a vial waiting to be filled with tears by the next Doris Day movie. Coming home filled him with strength, a thicker liquid. (*Pigeon Feathers,* p. 110)

21. *Olinger Stories* (New York, 1964), foreword, v.

22. See n. 12 above. Symbolically, the brambles that rake the sides of Harry's car on the "road of horror" (*RRu,* p. 31).

23. In the light of Alice and Kenneth Hamilton's analysis of the religious connotations of northward movement in Updike's fiction, this dream could be considered as a figment of a repressed desire to resume the spiritual quest of *Rabbit, Run.* See *The Elements of John Updike* (New York, 1970), pp. 99-101.

24. See Gerry Brenner, "*Rabbit, Run:* John Updike's Criticism of the 'Return to Nature,'" *Twentieth Century Literature* 12, no. 1 (April 1966), and Larry E. Taylor, *Pastoral and Anti-Pastoral Patterns in John Updike's Fiction* (Southern Illinois University Press, 1971).

25. To use Piet Hanema's phrase in *Couples,* p. 224.

26. Hamilton, pp. 99-100.

27. "Eros Rampant," *Museums and Women* (Penguin, 1975), p. 214.

28. For many of Updike's characters—Piet Hanema, for instance—it is neither uncommon nor blasphemous to experience at the same time religious feelings and erotic sensations: "Prayer and masturbation had so long been mingled in Piet's habits that in hearing the benediction he pictured his mistress naked . . ." (*Couples,* p. 29).

29. The razor blades Chinese women reportedly placed in their vaginas in order not to be raped by the Japanese.

30. This "other guy" is perhaps Stavros, but only in part. He is more generally speaking the outsider in every sense of the term.

6: ANDRÉ LE VOT

1.   John Barth, *Lost in the Funhouse* (New York, Bantam Books, 1969), p. 116.
2.   Ibid., p. 88.
3.   Ibid., p. 115.
4.   *Atlantic Monthly* (August 1967, repr. in *The American Novel since World War II,* ed. Marcus Klein (Greenwich, Conn., Fawcett Publications, 1969), p. 267.
5.   Robert Coover, *Pricksongs and Descants* (New York, New American Library, 1970), p. 78.
6.   Nathanael West, *The Day of the Locust,* in *Complete Works of Nathanael West* (New York, Farrar, Straus & Cudahy, 1957), p. 299.
7.   West, "Some Notes on *Miss Lonelyhearts,*" *Contempo* 3 (May 15, 1933), repr. in *Nathanael West,* ed. Jay Martin (Englewood Cliffs, N. J., Prentice Hall, 1971), p. 66.
8.   John Graham, "John Hawkes on His Novels," *Massachusetts Review* 7 (summer 1966): 457.
9.   Richard Brautigan, *The Hawkline Monster: A Gothic Western* (New York, Simon and Schuster), p. 27.
10.   Coover, p. 240.
11.   Gilbert Durand, *Les Structures anthropologiques de l'imaginaire* (Paris, Presses Universitaires de France), pp. 187-99.
12.   John Hawkes, *The Cannibal* (New York, New Directions, 1949), pp. 10, 13.
13.   Barth, p. 115.
14.   Coover, *The Water Pourer* (Columbia, S. C., Bruccoli-Clark's Collector's Edition, 1972), first page of author's preface.
15.   Donald Barthelme, *City Life* (New York, Bantam Books, 1971), p. 69.
16.   Barth, p. 92.
17.   Kurt Vonnegut, Jr., *Slaughterhouse-Five* (St. Albans, Herts, U. K., Panther Books, 1972), pp. 62–63.
18.   Roman Jakobson, *Essais de linguistique générale* (Paris, Les Editions de Minuit, 1963), p. 179.
19.   Barthelme, pp. 65, 68.
20.   Ibid., p. 92.
21.   Ibid., p. 000.
22.   West, *Miss Lonelyhearts,* ed. cit., p. 104.
23.   Barthelme, p. 93.
24.   Ibid., p. 113.
25.   Richard Brautigan, *Trout Fishing in America* (New York, Dell, 1967), p. 13.
26.   Barthelme, p. 159.
27.   Djuna Barnes, *Nightwood* (London, Faber & Faber, 1936), p. 17.
28.   Thomas Pynchon, *Gravity's Rainbow* (New York, Viking, Compass Book, 1973), p. 703.
29.   Ibid., p. 434.
30.   Ibid., p. 25.
31.   Ibid., p. 3.
32.   William Burroughs, *Naked Lunch* (New York, Grove Press, Evergreen Black Cat Edition, 1966), p. 104.
33.   Susan Sontag, *Against Interpretation* (New York, Dell, Laurel Edition, 1969), p. 87.
34.   See Carter A. Daniel, "West's Revisions of *Miss Lonelyhearts*" in West, ed. cit., p. 53.
35.   "John Hawkes: An Interview," in *Wisconsin Studies in Contemporary Literature* (summer 1965), p. 150.

Bibliography

Barnes, Djuna. *Nightwood,* London, 1936.
Barth, John. *The Sot-Weed Factor.* New York, 1960.
–––. *Lost in the Funhouse.* New York, 1968.
Barthelme, Donald. *City Life.* New York, 1970.
Brautigan, Richard. *Trout Fishing in America.* New York, 1967.
–––. *The Hawkline Monster: A Gothic Western.* New York, 1974.
Burroughs, William. *Naked Lunch.* New York, 1959.
Coover, Robert. *Pricksongs and Descants.* New York, 1969.
Gardner, John. *Grendel.* New York, 1971.

Hawkes, John. *The Cannibal.* New York, 1949.
―――. *The Beetle Leg.* New York, 1951.
―――. *The Lime Twig.* New York, 1961.
―――. *The Blood Oranges.* New York, 1971.
―――. *Death, Sleep and the Traveler.* New York, 1974.
Heller, Joseph. *Catch 22.* New York, 1961.
Mailer, Norman. *An American Dream.* New York, 1965.
―――. *Why Are We in Vietnam?* New York, 1967.
Pynchon, Thomas. *Gravity's Rainbow.* New York, 1973.
Vonnegut, Kurt, Jr. *Slaughterhouse-Five.* New York, 1969.
West, Nathanael. *Miss Lonelyhearts.* New York, 1933.
―――. *The Day of the Locust.* New York, 1939.

7: RÉGIS DURAND

1.   Robert Coover, "The Magic Poker," *Pricksongs and Descants* (1969), p. 30. Most references will be to *Pricksongs and Descants* (designated below as *Pricksongs*). Other works by Robert Coover include: *Origin of the Brunists* (New York, Putnam, 1966); *The Universal Baseball Association, J. Henry Waugh, Prop.* (New York, Random House, 1968); *A Theological Position* (New York, Dutton, 1972), 4 plays.

2.   Stanley Fogel, "'And All the Little Typtopies': Notes on Language Theory in the Contemporary Experimental Novel," *Modern Fiction Studies* 20, no. 3 (autumn 1974): 328. Fogel notes: "Novelists and literary critics alike have come to realize that fictional language is not a transparent medium through which one passes into an inhabitable realm. Rather language, itself, is the essential property out of which the novelist makes his construct."

3.   Roland Barthes, "To Write: Intransitive Verb?" *The Structuralist Controversy* (Baltimore, The Johns Hopkins Press, 1970).

4.   The term is actually Roland Barthes's. Quoted in Stephen Heath, *Vertige du déplacement: Lecture de R. Barthes* (Paris, Fayard, 1974).

5.   *Pricksongs*, p. 138.

6.   Ibid., p. 139. Italics mine.

7.   Charles Grivel, *Production de l'intérêt romanesque* (The Hague, Mouton, 1973).

8.   A plea for and an example of such a criticism can be found in Roland Barthes's article on Philippe Sollers: "Par-dessus l'épaule," *Critique* 318 (Nov. 1973): 966-76. See also J. F. Lyotard's concept of "critical apathy" as a defense against "theoretical terrorism." The concept of "passionate apathy" is borrowed from Sade. J. F. Lyotard, "De l'Apathie théorique," *Critique* 333: 254-65.

9.   As does Roland Barthes's in *Le Plaisir du texte* (Le Seuil, 1973).

10.   "Dedicatoria y prólogo a Don Miguel de Cervantes Saavedra," *Pricksongs*, p. 60.

11.   *Pricksongs*, p. 61. Cf. the following observation, also addressed to Cervantes:

> You teach us, *Maestro*, by example, that great narratives remain meaningful through time as a language-medium between generations, as a weapon against the fringe-areas of our consciousness, and as a mythic reinforcement of our tenuous grip on reality. The novelist uses familiar mythic or historical forms to combat the content of those forms and to conduct the reader *(lector amantisimo!)* to the real, away from mystification to clarification, away from magic to maturity, away from mystery to revelation. (*Pricksongs*, p. 62)

12.   *Pricksongs*, p. 61.

13.   See preface to "The Water Pourer," unpublished chapter from *The Origin of the Brunists* (Columbia, S. C., Bruccoli-Clark, 1972).

14.   "Scene for Winter," *Pricksongs*, p. 134.

15.   "The Leper's Helix," *Pricksongs*, p. 143.

16.   "Klee Dead," *Pricksongs*, p. 83.

17.   *The Universal Baseball Association*, p. 48.

18.   "Panel game," *Pricksongs*, p. 63. For this relation of fiction to death, see a recent striking formulation by Jean Ricardou, novelist and critic: "Ainsi, au centre du dispositif, se trouve une nouvelle auto-représentation verticale productrice. La fiction se dispose comme une métaphore de l'activité qui la constitue: l'écriture, la lecture. La lecture qui touche au-dedans, à la parole; l'écriture, qui touche au-dehors, au silence. Et l'ensemble à la mort" (*Poétique* 22, 1975: 226).

19.   *The Universal Baseball Association,* p. 105.
20.   Gerald Prince, "Notes Towards a Categorization of Fictional 'Narratees,'" *Genre* 4 (March 1971).
21.   "The Leper's Helix," *Pricksongs,* p. 145.
22.   "The Wayfarer," *Pricksongs,* p. 99.
23.   The phrase is Robbe-Grillet's, in *For a New Novel: Essays on Fiction,* (New York, Grove Press), p. 127.
24.   "The Magic Poker," *Pricksongs,* p. 25.
25.   This is to be followed by a study of the process of fragmentation in the fiction of Coover (and Barthelme). For a precise formulation of the ideological impact of "metafiction," see for instance a recent article by Jean Ricardou, "La Population des miroirs," *Poétique* 22 (1975): 196–226.

Bibliography

A useful Coover checklist has been published by Larry McCaffery in *Bulletin of Bibliography* 31, no. 3 (July-September 1974).

Articles about Coover are few. In fact, only two are of more than passing interest:

Cope, Jackson I. "Robert Coover's Fictions," *Iowa Review* 2, no. 4 (fall 1971): 94–110.
Hertzel, Leo. "What's Wrong with Christians?" *Critique* 11, no. 3 (1969): 11–24.

References to Coover can be found here and there in articles dealing with contemporary American fiction: in Robert Scholes, "Metafiction," *Iowa Review* 1 (1970): 100–15; in two issues of *Modern Fiction Studies* devoted to the new fiction: 19, no. 1 (spring 1973), and 20, no. 3 (autumn 1974).

The present writer hopes to have a short book on Coover ready by the end of 1978.

8: PIERRE GAULT

1.   There is no equivalent for this convenient word, frequently used by modern critics since Gide defined it in 1893. Originally the *abyme* is a term of heraldry and means the center of an escutcheon. The *mise en abyme* consists in inserting the concentrated pattern of the escutcheons at the heart of that same escutcheon. The term is now used for a reflection of the writer on his fiction, included in the fiction itself. The intrusion may be direct, but it may also develop into elaborate compositions *en abyme;* for instance, the writer may introduce a character as his spokesman (which is the case for Edouard in Gide's *Les Faux Monnayeurs*). Another possible device consists in including the parody of a genre within the genre itself— in Robert Pinget's play *Architruc,* the actors comment on their own acting, and they make of the drama a play within a play.
2.   This term literally means the process of being sucked down, as in quicksand. It is used by modern critics, especially Jean Ricardou, to account for any device that has the effect of interrupting the course of the narration. A description, for instance, can be seen as a "procédé d'enlisement."

9: MAURICE COUTURIER

1.   Since there is no single word in English to express at once the narrative, the "succession of events" related in the narrative, and the act of telling, we have preferred to keep the word which is commonly used in modern French criticism. See *Communications* 8 (Paris, 1966).
2.   *Nouveau Roman: hier, aujourd'hui* (Paris, 1972), vol. 1, p. 23. My translation.
3.   *Problème de linguistique générale* (Paris, 1966), p. 274. My translation.
4.   Ibid., p. 273.
5.   *Pour une théorie du Nouveau Roman* (Paris, 1971), p. 32.
6.   *Figures 3* (Paris, 1972).

Je propose, sans insister sur les raisons d'ailleurs evidentes du choix des termes, de nommer *histoire* le signifié ou contenu narratif (même si ce contenu se trouve être, en l'occurence, d'une faible intensité dramatique ou teneur événementielle), *récit* proprement dit le significant, énoncé, discours ou texte narratif lui-même, et *narration* l'acte narratif producteur et, par extension, l'ensemble de la situation réelle ou fictive dans laquelle il prend place. p. 72

7. *Ada* (London, 1969), p. 359.
8. *Transparent Things* (New York, 1972), p. 80. *T. T.* from now on.
9. Percy died in Yalta during the Crimean war. *Ada*, p. 319.
10. Mary McCarthy, "A Bolt from the Blue," *New Republic* 146 (June 4, 1962): 21ff. Janet K. Gezari, "Roman et problème chez Nabokov," *Poétique* 17 (Paris, 1974): 96ff.
11. *Pale Fire* (London, 1962), p. 143. *P. F.* from now on.
12. In *Figures 3* Genette distinguished between "discours" (the telling) and "diégèse" (the story told). The latter was borrowed from Plato by the film critics.
13. "Nabokov's Puppet Show" was the title of Alfred Appel's review of *Speak, Memory,* in *New Republic* 156 (Jan. 14, 1967): 27ff.
14. *Pnin* (London, 1957), p. 189.
15. *Invitation to a Beheading* (New York, 1965), pp. 222-23.
16. A homodiegetic narrator, in Genette's terminology, is a narrator who is present as a character in the story he is telling. *Figures 3:* 252.
17. Ricardou calls "générateurs" the various patterns, objects, references, words, from which the *récit* builds itself up in the New Novel. *Pour une théorie du Nouveau Roman,* pp. 118-58, 211-33.
18. Iris Acht died in 1888; 1958 marks the end of King Charles's reign. *P. F.,* pp. 122-23.
19. *Timon of Athens* 4.3.
20. Kinbote has everybody against him: the late John Shade who refused to believe his story, Shade's wife and friends who now think he is mad. His persecution complex makes him a lonely man, the "Solus Rex" of the story published in *A Russian Beauty and Other Stories* (London, 1973).
21. Aqua, Demon's wife, signs her farewell note, "My sister's sister who *temper' iz ada* ("Now is out of hell")," p. 29.
22. *The Gift* (New York, 1970), pp. 198-99.
23. It is his grandfather, "The Minister of Justice, Nabokov," who is actually mentioned. Ibid., p. 304.
24. *King, Queen, Knave* (Greenwich, Conn., 1969), p. 209. This passage was added by Nabokov when the novel was translated into English.
25. Genette's term for "the shift from one narrative level to the other." The best examples are to be found in *Tristram Shandy*. *Figures 3:* 243-45.
26. *The Rhetoric of Fiction* (Chicago, 1961), pp. 45-55.
27. Quoted from Ricardou, *Le Nouveau Roman* (Paris, 1973), p. 49. My translation.
28. *The Rhetoric of Fiction,* p. 20.
29. "Le Style narratif et la grammaire du discours direct et indirect," *Change* 16-17 (Paris, 1973): 188ff.
30. *Problèmes de linguistique générale,* p. 274.
31. *A Russian Beauty and Other Stories,* p. 24.

10: JACQUES FAVIER

1. The considerable extension, in recent years, of American SF on the French market (in translations of uneven quality), has prompted several critical approaches. See a selective list of the most recent ones in the bibliography.
2. "Space is a source of endless knowledge, which may transform our civilization in the same way that the voyages of the Renaissance transformed the Dark Ages," says Jeremy Bernstein in *The Making of Kubrick's 2001* (New York, 1970), p. 26.
3. More or less felicitous Freudian symbols have not escaped the notice of psychoanalytically minded critics. The spaceship is alternatively a phallus and a womb; space either emasculates or enhances manliness. *The Making of Kubrick's 2001* presents an interpretation of A. C. Clarke's famous novel in Freudian terms. A few convincing analyses can be found in best-selling SF anthologies; but much of the others seem to be pseudoscientific nonsense, unpardonable as nonfiction, especially when devoid of humor.
4. Bernard Bergonzi perceives the short story as the form of fiction that best expresses the relationship of hostility between man and his environment. Cf. "An Appendix on the Short Story."
5. In Judith Merril's *"Survival Ship"* twenty women have to share four men, the trip being programmed to last several generations.

6.   Tzvetan Todorov defines fantasy *(fantastique)* as a form of fiction presenting uncommon facts and events which the reader can choose to account for either in terms of the natural or in terms of the supernatural. The sustained hesitation in this choice constitutes the specificity of the genre. This point of view has been much questioned in recent years. *Introduction à la littérature fantastique.*

7.   Yet the temptation of anthropomorphism seems to be particularly strong in a certain form of naive contemporary symbology, which one can find traces of in the language adults use when addressing children (even in school textbooks), as well as in the language of advertising: tartar, dirt, are represented as cartoon villains, often reduced to the main features of a peeved face; cars, bottles, products of all sorts are given a rudimentary face with a limited range of expressions. Comparisons between SF and the medium of the comic strip are seldom uninteresting. There are strong affinities in the techniques of those two contemporary popular art forms. On the levels of theme and market, the connections between the two "literatures" are well known.

8.   See H. P. Lovecraft, *Supernatural Horror in Literature.*

9.   This choice of electricity rather than water in both stories reveals a deliberate shift toward the artifact; electricity is not, any more than water, a creation of man's, but its production, conquest, and control are more recent and less familiar. At the level of symbols, it would be tempting to see in the electrical alien another classic image, that of the elements raging around the wizard's apprentice (man here).

10.   This continuous, peaceful humming gave Bradbury the idea for one of his vaguely mystical stories: "Powerhouse." A runaway couple (Joseph and Mary obviously) are in search of a shelter. They spend the night in an unmanned power station, and find some sort of comfort in the loud humming of the transformers. Although this element has more portent here than a mere physical phenomenon should, its role remains that of a strangely reassuring sound (pseudosettor?) and does not become the voice of a true settor.

Bibliography

Short Stories

Adliss, Brian. "Man in His Time." In *Nebula Award Stories.* London: V. Gollancz, 1967.

Asimov, Isaac. "Misbegotten Missionary." In *Tomorrow, the Stars.* New York: Doubleday, 1952.

Ballard, J. G. "Prima Belladonna." In *Billenium.* New York: Scott-Meredith, 1962.

———. *The 1000 Dreams of Stellavista.* New York: Ziff-Davis, 1962.

Baxter, J. "The Hands." In *New Writings in SF III.* London: Dobson, 1964.

Bradbury, Ray. "The City." In *The Illustrated Man.* New York: Doubleday, 1951.

———. "Kaleidoscope." In *The Illustrated Man.*

———. "The Lost City of Mars." In *I Sing the Body Electric.* New York: Knopf, 1969.

———. "No Particular Night or Morning." In *The Illustrated Man.*

———. "The Rocket Man." In *The Illustrated Man.*

———. "The Veldt." In *The Illustrated Man.*

———. "The Wilderness." In *The Golden Apples of the Sun.* New York: Doubleday, 1952.

Burroughs, E. R. "Pirate Blood." In *The Wizard of Venus.* New York: Ace, 1970. Written 1932; manuscript signed John Tyler McCullouch; printed with *The Wizard of Venus* by Ace Books only in August 1970.

Delany, Samuel. "Aye, and Gomorrah." In *Nebula Award Stories III.* London: V. Gollancz, 1968.

Ellison, Harlan. "Pretty Maggie Moneyeyes." In *The Year's Best SF I.* New York: Sphere, 1968.

Golding, Stephen. "Sweet Dreams, Melissa." In *The Year's Best SF II.* New York: Sphere, 1969.

Harding, Lee. "Mistress of the Mind." In *New Writings in SF XVIII.* London: Dobson, 1970.

Inglis, James. "Night Watch." In *New Writings in SF IV.* London: 1965.

Kapp, Colin. "Getaway from Getawehi." In *New Writings in SF XVI.* London: 1970.

Keyes, Thorn. "Period of Gestation." In *The Best of SF IV.* New York: Mayflower-Dell, 1963.

Knight, Damon. "Stranger Station." In *In Deep.* London: V. Gollancz, 1964.

Leiber, Fritz. "The Man Who Made Friends with Electricity." In *The Best of SF IV.* New York: 1963.

———. *237 Talking Statues*. New York: Mercury Press, 1963.
Merril, Judith. "Survival Ship." In *Tomorrow, the Stars*. New York: 1952.
Pohl, Frederic. "The Fiend." In *New Writings in SF III*. London: 1964.
Priest, Christopher. "The Perihelion Man." In *New Writings in SF XVI*. London: 1970.
Redgrove, Peter. "Mr. Waterman." In *The Best of SF IX*. New York, 1967.
Reed, Kit. "The Vine." In *The Year's Best SF I*. New York: 1968.
Reynolds, Mack. "Earthlings, Go Home." In *The Best of SF IV*. New York: 1963.
Robinson, Frank M. "The Wreck of the Ship John B." In *The Year's Best SF I*. New York: 1968.
Russell, Eric Frank. "Jay Score." In *Tomorrow, the Stars*. New York: 1952.
Sanders, William P. "Barnacle Bull." In *Analog I*. New York: Street & Smith, 1960.
Sheckley, Robert. *The Mountain without a Name*. New York: 1955.
Silverberg, Robert. "To the Dark Star." In *The Year's Best SF I*. New York: 1962.
Sladek, J. T. *A Report on the Migration of Educational Materials*. New York: Mercury Press, 1968.
Stringer, David. "High Eight." In *New Writings in SF IV*. London: Dobson, 1965.
Thomas, L. T. "The Far Look." In *Spectrum 5*. London: 1966.
Van Vogt, A. E. *Bucolic*. New York: Mercury Press, 1966.
White, John. "Meatball." In *New Writings in SF XVI*. London: 1970.
Woods, P. F. "The Countenance." In *Best SF Stories from New Worlds II*. New York: 1969.
Wyndham, John. "Mars, A. D. 2094." In *The Outward Urge*. London: M. Joseph, 1959.
———. "Survival." In *The Seeds of Time*. London, 1956.

SECONDARY SOURCES

Baudin, Henri. *La Science-fiction*. Paris: Bordas, 1971.
Bergonzi, Bernard. "An Appendix on the Short Story." In *The Situation of the Novel*. London: Macmillan, 1970.
Du fantastique à la science-fiction américaine, a collective work of Association Francaise d'Études Américaines. Paris: Didier Études Anglaises, 1973.
Gattegno, Jean. *La Science-fiction*. Paris: P. U. F., 1971.
Lovecraft, H. P. *Supernatural Horror in Literature*. Ed. August Derleth. New York: Ben Abramson, 1945.
The Making of Kubrick's 2001. Ed. J. Agel. New York: Signet, New American Library, 1970.
Sadoul, Jacques. *Histoire de la science-fiction moderne*. Paris: Albin Michel, 1973.
Stover, Leon E. *La Science-fiction américaine*. Paris: Aubier, 1972.
Todorov, Tzvetan. *Introduction à la littérature fantastique*. Paris: Seuil, 1970.
Van Herp, Jacques. *Panorama de la science-fiction*. Verviers (Belgium): Gérard, 1973.
Versins, Pierre. *Encyclopédie de l'utopie et de la science-fiction*. Lausanne: L'Age d'Homme, 1972.

11: ROBERT SILHOL

1. This can mean many things, and among others that the determinations which go to fashion our receptivity are to be sought in the area of ideology and sociology.
2. In its current meaning. Some do, but not many.
3. There are many exceptions, of course: Poe, Baudelaire, Valéry, T. S. Eliot, Sartre, and others; but these were writers *before* being critics.
4. "Style," "Talent," these words (they are not elaborate enough to be called concepts) have more reality from the point of view of sociology than from the point of view of aesthetics; I use them here in their current, vague sense, and wish to point out that they carry no value on my part.
5. There is one, but it is in no way concerned with aesthetics.
6. It will be noticed that I speak of class here—as a whole—and not of individuals; it is the (dominant) *class* which reads, and this includes the children, the college students in it, and those members of it not directly engaged in business, irrespective of the reading habits of corporate managers and of the "aristocracy of company men."
7. And already these notions of "leading" and "leader" invite analysis.
8. "We," the intellectuals, the literate.

9.   I have added "traditional" to my text because one cannot help using values and value judgments, and I wanted this to be very clear. But what is primarily meant here is that values will cease to constitute the main interest of the scholar.

10.   I have not mentioned the historian of literature, because when he defines himself as such he specifies his domain, which is not criticism. But it is of course essential that he should not mix history and criticism. If he does, he then becomes a critic and what was said about criticism also applies to him. As for what the "proper" historical attitude is, it cannot be discussed within the limits of this essay.

11.   Cf. Ernest Jones, Marie Bonaparte, Phyllis Greenacre, Marthe Robert, Octave Mannoni, and others.

12.   I quite realize that concepts such as "ideology"—and earlier on "science," "scientific," and the like—call for a clarification and some theoretical discussion. The subject of ideology and that of the possible ideological nature of scientific knowledge cannot be discussed in such a short paper. Briefly, let us say that the word "ideology" as I use it here refers to the beliefs, ideas, and doctrines—not necessarily conscious—of a particular social group, class, or society in a given historical time. (The opposition between science and ideology, which can lead to an interesting debate, has not been taken into consideration.) As for the concept of "science," which is at present under considerable criticial examination, it is to be hoped that I have given relativity enough importance to make my position clear.

13.   Only partly, because I claim that the individual writer's psyche also provides a constitutive element of the "final" structure as we can see it today.

14.   This is Lucien Goldmann's *vision du monde,* a phrase far too vague to deserve the name of concept, and which should have been specified. It nevertheless provides us with a very helpful hypothesis.

15.   Adequate to Marxist theory, of course; and whereas I see no immediate methodological fault here, dogmatism must always be kept in mind as a possible danger.

Bibliography

Barthes, Roland. *Essais critiques.* Paris: Seuil, 1964.

———. *S/Z.* Paris: Seuil, 1970.

Bion, W. R. *Transformations.* London: Heinemann, 1965.

Goldmann, Lucien. *Le Dieu caché.* Paris: Gallimard, 1955.

———. *Pour une sociologie du roman.* Paris: Gallimard, 1964.

———. *Marxisme et sciences humaines.* Paris: Gallimard, 1970.

Holland, Norman. *The Dynamics of Literary Response.* New York: Oxford University Press, 1968.

———. *Poems in Persons.* New York: W. W. Norton, 1973.

Lacan, Jacques. *Écrits.* Paris: Seuil, 1966.

Laing, R. D. *Self and Others.* London: Tavistock Publications, 1961.

Macherey, Pierre. *Pour une théorie de la production littéraire.* Paris: Maspéro, 1966.

Sartre, Jean-Paul. *L'Idiot de la famille.* Paris: Gallimard, 1971.

INDEX

CONTRIBUTORS

André Bleikasten is a native of Strasbourg and has been on the faculty of the English department at the Université de Strasbourg since 1964. Awarded an ACLS fellowship for 1969-70, he spent a year at the University of Virginia doing research on Faulkner. His publications include *The Most Splendid Failure: Faulkner's the Sound and the Fury* (Indiana University Press, 1976) and *Faulkner's As I Lay Dying* (Indiana University Press, 1973). In addition he has published articles on Faulkner, Flannery O'Connor, James Dickey, and Ambrose Bierce. For *Littérature de notre temps: Écrivains américains*, recueil 1 (Casterman, 1972) he has written essays on O'Connor and William Styron; he has also contributed reviews to *Modern Fiction Studies, The Mississippi Quarterly*, and *Études Anglaises*. Most of his articles have appeared in *RANAM (Recherches Anglaises et Nord-Américaines)* published at Strasbourg, of which he has been coeditor since 1970.

Maurice Couturier, a native of western France, attended the universities of Angers and Paris, taught for a year in a British grammar school, then for four years at the Catholic University of Angers. He later taught for three years in the United States at Loras College and the University of Notre Dame. In 1972 he defended his *doctorat de 3ème cycle* on symbol and myth in Zona Gale. He has just completed his *doctorat d'État* dissertation on the formal aspect of Nabokov's novels while teaching at the Université de Paris IV. He comments that he was first influenced by Todorov, Genette, and the Russian formalists, and in the last few years mostly by Barthes, Julia Kristeva, and the *Groupe Change*.

Régis Durand obtained his *doctorat d'État* last year from the Université de Paris III. He has published mainly on language and narrative in fiction in various reviews including *Modern Language Notes, Études Anglaises, Langues Modernes, RANAM*, and *Caliban*. He is editor of *Myth and Ideology in American Culture* and *Études Canadiennes* and is *Maître de Conférences* at the Université de Lille III. He counts Northrop Frye, Jean-Pierre Richard, and Roland Barthes as those most important in his background, and is interested in the semiotic and psychoanalytic approaches to literature.

Jacques Favier obtained his *doctorat de 3ème cycle* from the Université de Paris VIII with a dissertation on the short story in contemporary English and American science fiction, and is now working on a study of Mervyn Peake for his *doctorat d'État*. A member of the English department at the Centre Universitaire de Valenciennes, he has appeared in *Littérature,* and is co-editor of *Cahiers de l'U.E.R. Froissart.* He considers that those important in his background reading are Barthes, Claude Brémond, Mark Schorer, and others, including Gilbert Durand, but he favors an "unbiased, esthetic approach, rather than an overscientific one."

Pierre Gault, who teaches at the Université de Tours, spent his junior year on a Fulbright at Haverford College and received the rest of his university training at the Université de Caen. Since then he has been working on his dissertation, which is concerned with John Hawkes and his place as a novelist in antirealist fiction; he has also written on Kosinski's *Painted Bird.* He favors "roughly" the structuralist school of criticism and their precursors, "Freud/Bachelard/Barthes/Todorov/ Ricardou/Genette/Greimas/Lacan," and "studies based on textual development rather than thematic."

Christiane Johnson (née Ducros) teaches American literature at the Université de Paris VII. Originally from southwest France, she spent a year in England and three years in Germany as a teacher of French, acquired her Master's in English at the Université de Bordeaux, and in 1961 went on a Fulbright to the University of Northern Iowa, staying on another five years to teach at Brooklyn College and at the SUNY campus at Cortland. She earned her *doctorat de 3ème cycle* at the Université de Paris IV with a dissertation on *La Réalité americaine dans l'oeuvre de F. Scott Fitzgerald.* In *Études Anglaises* she has published reviews, an interview with Scottie Fitzgerald, and a critique of Sherwood Anderson; she also appears in the 1976 *Fitzgerald-Hemingway Annual.*

Ira Johnson, an American, earned his B.A. at Drake University, his M. F. A. in the University of Iowa Writer's Workshop, and his Ph.D. at Cornell. He wrote *Glenway Wescott: The Paradox of Voice* (Kennikat Press, 1971); his short stories and criticism appeared in *Perspective, Folio, English Record, College English,* and *Tradition et Innovation: Littérature et Paralittérature* (Paris: Didier, 1974). He served on the faculties of Iowa State University, the University of Northern Iowa, and Louisiana State University, among others, and in France at the universities of Clermont-Ferrand, Paris IV, and Reims. Just prior to his untimely death he was *Maître de Conférences* at the Centre Universitaire de Valenciennes and coeditor of *Cahiers de l'U. E. R. Froissart.*

Yves Le Pellec is a member of the foreign language and literature department at the Université de Toulouse. Articles by him on Saul Bellow and Jack Kerouac have appeared in *Caliban,* and he is editor of the 300-page *Beat Generation,* a special issue of *Entretiens,* which appeared in 1975.

André Le Vot is professor of American literature at the Université de Paris III, where he founded in 1973 the Research Center for Contemporary American Literature. Before coming to Paris, he taught at the universities of Caen, Rouen, and Vincennes, and he has conducted summer courses at New York University and SUNY at Buffalo. An F. Scott Fitzgerald specialist, his *doctorat d'État* is a long study of Fitzgerald's imagination. He has also written an analysis of *The Great Gatsby*, and edited a bilingual edition of some of Fitzgerald's stories. His publications include articles on Melville, James, Dreiser, Farrell, and West, and he is now concentrating on contemporary fiction, contributing articles on Hawkes, Purdy, Updike, Pynchon, and other to *Études Anglaises, Les Langues Modernes, RANAM, Le Monde,* and *La Quinzaine Littéraire.* He prefers a "plurality of methods," in criticism and likes "any approach that will not rape a text and make it conform to a preestablished pattern."

Daniel Royot, who teaches at the Université de Clermont-Ferrand, pursued his studies at the Université de Dijon and then at the Sorbonne. He was a Fulbright Research Scholar at Bowdoin College in 1970 and visiting professor in American literature at San Diego State University in 1973. He is coeditor (with Pierre Deflaux) of *American Trails,* an anthology, and of *Histoire et Civilisation des États-Unis* (Nathan, 1974). He has appeared in *Langues Modernes,* is coauthor of *American Humor in France,* and is finishing his dissertation on "Yankee Humor." He considers Daniel Hoffman, Leslie Fiedler, and the trio Greimas, Durand, and Jolles as influences, fears the rebirth in criticism of another form of *la scolastique,* as indicated by the abuse of critical nomenclature, and favors the use of any method according to its relative validity. He has a special interest in contemporary mythologies, but remembers that "Hamlet will still be read when Lévi-Strauss is forgotten."

Robert Silhol, professor of American literature and civilization at the Université de Paris VII, has been an ACLS scholar in the United States and has taught at Swarthmore and SUNY at Buffalo. He has written articles and prefaces on Donne, Shakespeare, Melville, and Faulkner, among others. His book on Sinclair Lewis is entitled *Les Tyrans tragique* (Paris, P. U. F., 1969). For several years he has been engaged in research on Freud and Marx.

Simone Vauthier is coeditor with André Bleikasten of *RANAM,* and teaches American literature at the Université de Strasbourg. She has published articles in the *Journal de la Société des Américanistes, TILAS, Jahrbuch für Amerika Studien, The Southern Literary Journal, The Mississippi Quarterly,* and *RANAM.* Most of her criticism has been on southern fiction, from Calvin Henderson Wiley and William Gilmore Simms through James Weldon Johnson to Robert Penn Warren, Walker Percy, Shelby Foote, Madison Jones, and Reynolds Price. Presently she is writing a dissertation on the image of the black American in antebellum American fiction.

Jean-Pierre Vernier, Professor of English and chairman of the department of English at the Université de Rouen, associate editor of *Études Anglaises,* and editor of *The Wellsian,* is the author of *H. G. Wells et son temps* (Rouen et Paris, 1971). He has published in *Du fantastique à la science-fiction américaine* (Paris, 1973), *Science-Fiction Studies, Littérature universelle,* and the recent *H. G. Wells and Modern Science Fiction.* Currently his main field of interest in the modern and contemporary American and British novel.